Peter L. Simmonds

The Animal Food Resources of Different Nations

with mention of some of the special dainties of various people derived from the

animal kingdom

Peter L. Simmonds

The Animal Food Resources of Different Nations
*with mention of some of the special dainties of various people derived from the animal
kingdom*

ISBN/EAN: 9783337247911

Printed in Europe, USA, Canada, Australia, Japan

Cover: Foto ©Andreas Hilbeck / pixelio.de

More available books at **www.hansebooks.com**

Animal Food Resources of Different Nations.

THE

Animal Food Resources of Different Nations,

WITH MENTION OF SOME OF THE

SPECIAL DAINTIES OF VARIOUS PEOPLE DERIVED FROM

THE ANIMAL KINGDOM.

BY

P. L. SIMMONDS,

Author of " A Dictionary of Useful Animals," " The Commercial Products of the Sea," etc.

————◦◇◦————

" There's no want of meat, Sir ;
Portly and curious viands are prepared
To please all kinds of appetite."
MASSINGER.

" A very fantastical banquet,
Just so many strange dishes."
SHAKESPEARE.

LONDON:

E. & F. N. SPON. 125, STRAND.

NEW YORK: 35, MURRAY STREET.

1885.

LONDON :
PRINTED BY WERTHEIMER, LEA AND CO.,
CIRCUS PLACE, LONDON WALL.

PREFACE.

A QUARTER of a century ago I published a work on " The Curiosities of Animal Food," based chiefly on a Lecture I had delivered at a Literary Institution. Although the volume merely dealt cursorily with the wide subject in a popular point of view, it was favourably received and much quoted by various eminent scientific authors, writing on the Food question. That book has, like many of my other works, long been out of print.

The subject, however, of the Animal Food supply has since then risen into great importance. Having given much attention to this matter, I have endeavoured to condense into the present volume a large amount of practical and useful information not generally accessible, combined at the same time with some pleasant reading.

P. L. SIMMONDS.

85, FINBOROUGH ROAD,
  SOUTH KENSINGTON.
 February, 1885.

CONTENTS.

CHAPTER I.

INTRODUCTORY AND GENERAL.

CHAPTER II.

A Few Words on Cannibalism.

CHAPTER III.

Flesh Food from Mammals.

CHAPTER IV.

Flesh Food from Mammals.—Continued.

sumption of Horseflesh in Europe*—Asses and Mules
also Eaten—Quagga and Zebra—The Ruminants—
Statistics of Horned Cattle over the World—Con-
sumption in the United Kingdom—Average Weights
in Different Countries—Beef Imported into England
—Quantity Sold in the London Markets—Average
Prices—Buffaloes—Statistics of Sheep in Various
Countries—Large Imports of Carcases from New
Zealand—Imports of Sheep to the London Markets
and Comparative Prices—Average Weight of Dif-
ferent Kinds of Sheep—Goats' Flesh—Flesh of the
Camel Tribe—Alpaca—Giraffe—Venison—Reindeer
—Moose or Elk—Antelopes—Eland—Bison—Marine
Mammals—Whales—Seals—Sea Lion—Sea Elephant
—Walrus—Dugongs—Dolphins—Porpoises   .   .   82

FLESH FOOD FURNISHED BY THE FEATHERED TRIBES.

Buzzard, Kite, and other Birds of Prey Eaten—Beccafico
—Guacharo—Larks — Thrushes—Blackbirds—Bunt-
ings—Fried Canaries—Starlings—Rooks—Ortolans—
Edible Birds' Nests—Statistics of Supply—Parrots—
Toucans—Domestic Poultry—Fowls in Egypt and
Morocco—Weight of Different Fowls—Statistics of
Poultry in the United Kingdom—in France—in
Austria—in the United States—Value of the Poultry
Imported from Abroad—Turkeys—Christmas Sup-
plies—Statistics of Turkeys in France—Wild Tur-
keys of America—Peacocks—Formerly Served at
Royal Banquets—Bustards—Partridges—Game Birds
Consumed in Great Britain—Snipes—Woodcocks—
Grouse— Pheasants — Capercailzie — Game Birds of
Sweden—Prairie Hens—Ruffs, Reeves, and Godwits
—Quails—Game Pies of France—Pâtés de Foies
Gras—Tragopans—Pigeons, Domestic and Wild—

---

* While this work was passing through the Press (but too late for
notice in its proper place), an important article has appeared in the
"Bulletin of the Société d'Acclimation," Paris, for August, 1884,
p, 617, by M. Decroix. giving a *résumé* of the consumption of horses,
asses and mules in France from 1876 to 1883, accompanied also by
numerous recipes for cooking horseflesh in various ways.

CHAPTER VIII.

FOOD PRODUCTS OF THE SEA—SOME FISH DELICACIES.

CHAPTER IX.

FOOD PRODUCTS OF THE SEA—FISHES—*Continued.*

CHAPTER X.

VARIOUS INSECTS EATEN AS FOOD.

CHAPTER XI.

ANIMAL FOOD FURNISHED BY THE CRUSTACEANS AND MOLLUSCA.

CHAPTER XII.

ANIMAL FOOD FURNISHED BY THE MOLLUSCA AND RADIATA.

THE
Animal Food Resources of Different Nations.

CHAPTER I.

INTRODUCTORY AND GENERAL.

Man an Omnivorous Animal—Some Eastern Nations eschew
Animal Food—Varieties of Food of Different People—Man
the only Cooking Animal—Variable Food in Different Ages
and Climates—Less Animal Food Eaten in Tropical Regions
than in Temperate and Arctic Regions—Various Food Delicacies—A Chinese Dinner—Wild American Animals as Food
—Marrow—Tinned or Preserved Meats—Statistics of Imports
of Animal Food from America — Charqui — Dried and
Jerked Meats of Different Countries — Pastoormah —
Dendeng—Frozen Carcases—Choice Morsels held in Special
Estimation—Value of our Imports of Animals and Animal
Products for Food in 1883—Advance in Prices—Meat Con-
sumption in France—Meat Production and Consumption in
Russia — United States Consumption — Mutton Despised in
many Countries — Large Consumption in Great Britain —
Slaughter of Sheep in Buenos Ayres—Goats' Flesh very little
Eaten—Our Foreign Supplies of Animal Food—Average In-
dividual Consumption—Value of Cheese as Food—Imports of
Butter and Cheese from Abroad—Diseased Meat as Food—
Not considered to be Injurious — German Legislation
thereon—Extensive Use of Animals which have Died by a
large Low-Caste Population in India — M. Delcroix's Per-
sonal Experience of a Quarter of a Century Feeding on the
Flesh of Diseased Animals—Medical Evidence taken on this
Subject before the Irish Cattle Trade Defence Association—
Diseased Lung of a Bullock Cooked and Eaten—Opinion of
the *Lancet* on Diseased Meat.

PROFESSOR OWEN has well observed that—" Whatever
the animal kingdom can afford for our food or clothing,
for our tools, weapons, or ornaments—whatever the lower

creation can contribute to our wants, our comforts, our passions, or our pride, that we sternly exact and take at all cost to the producers. No creature is too bulky or formidable for man's destructive energies; none too minute and insignificant for his keen detection and skill of capture. It was ordained from the beginning that we should be the masters and subduers of all inferior animals."

Our range of food already is specially wide and varied. All the world is laid under tribute to supply our tables, and we are learning to imitate or improve on the culinary processes of every nation and every age. In Europe and in America—aye, and we may also add in the far East—men have hunted high and low, on land, in the air, and in the sea, to obtain a variety of food, and this not only in times of war and famine, but when peace and plenty reigned. Not only will men have variety, but they will have it at every meal. There are not, perhaps, ten people in a thousand who eat a single meal consisting of only one article, provided they can get variety. Science has taught us that as in nature clay produces one plant and sand another, so man also requires a variety of food to provide for all the elements of which he is made. Other creatures are generally restricted to one sort of provender at most. They are carnivorous, piscivorous, or something-ivorous, but man is the universal eater.

He pounces with the tiger upon the kid, with the hawk upon the dove, and upon the herring with the cormorant. He goes halves with the bee in the honey-cell, but turns upon his partner and cheats him out of his share of the produce. He grubs up the root with the sow, devours the fruit with the earwig, and demolishes the leaves with the caterpillar; for all these several parts of the members of the vegetable kingdom furnish him with food. Life itself will not hinder his appetite, nor decay nauseate his palate; for he will as soon devour a lively young oyster as demolish the fungous produce of a humid field. This propensity is, indeed, easily abused; viands of such incongruous nature and heterogeneous substances are sometimes collected as to make an outrageous amalgamation, so that an alderman at a City feast might make one shudder; but this is too curious an investigation—it is the abuse of abundance too, and we know that abuse is the origin of all evil. This fact should lead us to another point, the appreciation of goodness and beneficence. The adaptation of external nature has often been insisted on— the adaptation of men to all circumstances, states, and conditions is carrying out the idea. The inferior animals are tied down, even by the narrowness of their animal necessities, to a small range of existence; but man can seldom be placed in any circumstances in which his universal appetite cannot be appeased. From the naked savage snatching a berry from the thorn, to the well-clad, highly-civilised denizen of the town, surrounded by every comfort, every luxury; from the tired traveller who opens his wallet and produces his oaten cake beside the welling lymph which is to slake his thirst, to the pursy justice, "in fair round belly with good capon lined," who spreads the damask napkin on his knees, tucks his toes under the table, and revels in calipee and calipash,—what an infinite diversity of circumstances!

The Word of God tells us: "Every moving thing that liveth shall be meat for you; even as the green herb have I given you *all* things." Still Animal food is even now but sparingly used in Eastern countries, and by some nations held in utter abhorrence. All great legislators of the Orient have, moreover, forbidden the use of certain animals which they call unclean. Moses, Manu, and Mahomet proscribed them alike. Buddhism makes the killing of a living animal sinful. Nor does any nation on earth yet subsist on Animal food only; even the lowest in the scale of civilisation, those who live as fishermen and hunters, mix some vegetables with their diet.

That which characterises especially meat and fish, is the abundance of nitrogenous matter which can be assimilated into our tissues, and which conduces to healthy nourishment, and it is these foods the reproduction of which has to be encouraged, for the supply is at present insufficient, and hence the want is calculated to injure the health of the people, especially the labouring classes, whose daily work demands a nutrition more reparative.

The diversity of substances which we find in the catalogue of articles of Food is as great as the variety with which the art or the science of cookery prepares them; the notions of the ancients on this most important subject are worthy of remark. Their taste regarding meat was various. But they considered it, as we still do, the most substantial food, hence it constituted the chief nourishment of their athletes. Camels' and dromedaries flesh was much esteemed, their heels more especially. Donkey flesh was in high repute. Mæcenas, according to Pliny, delighted in it, and the wild ass brought from Africa was compared to venison. In more modern times we find Chancellor Dupret having asses fattened for his table.

The Romans seem to have indulged in as great a variety of Animal food as the epicures of the present day. A passage from Macrobius, quoted in Soyer's " Panthropheon " furnishes the following *menu* of a supper given by the Pontiff Lentulus on the day of his reception :—" The first course was composed of sea hedgehogs (*Echinus*), raw oysters in abundance, all sorts of shellfish and asparagus. The second service comprised a fine fatted pullet, a fresh dish of oysters and other shell-fish, different kinds of dates, univalve shell-fish (as whelks, conchs, etc.), more oysters, but of different kinds, sea nettles, beccaficoes, chines of wild boar, fowls covered with a perfumed paste; a second dish of shell-fish and purples (? lobsters), a very costly kind of crustacea. The third and last course presented several *hors d'œuvre*, a wild boar's head, fish, a second set of *hors d'œuvre*, ducks, potted river fish, leverets, roast fowls, and capitones (a large kind of eel) from the marshes of Ancona."

An eminent French economist justly observes :—" A

population which does not consume meat is not in a healthy condition; they have in themselves a deplorable cause of inferiority in works of strength and of mortality by diseases." *

Man is the only animal that cooks, and, indeed, humanity may be said to be divided into two epochs, that preceding and that following the discovery of cookery. Pre-historic man resembled savages of the present day, whether on the Continent of America, in Australia, or Polynesia, where fish, animals, and loathsome insects are eaten raw, as a kind of change from fruits. Man was not, as some savants allege, originally a vegetarian; the latter is perhaps an artificial kind of alimentation. Brahmins only became frugiferous where agriculture put within their reach that kind of food. Vegetables are easily consumed by birds and cattle, because they have gizzards and paunches—appropriate organs, but wanting to man; hence the necessity of the culinary art, to make rice and millet digestible. But to cook, it was essential to have fire, and for a long time humanity had not discovered this element. Indeed, it was even a marketable commodity, and some tribes still carry living embers as they camp.

Dr. W. Roberts tells us that the changes impressed on food by cooking form an integral part of the work of digestion—a part which we of the human race get done for us by the agency of fire-heat, but a part which the lower animals are compelled to perform by the labour of their own digestive organs.

The late Mr. John Crawfurd, in the "Ethnological Transactions," remarks :—" By his anatomical structure man is an omnivorous animal, and all the races, when attainable, will equally consume animal and vegetable food. A very few, the result of dire necessity, live on animal food only, such as the Esquimaux, who could not exist amid ice and snows if they did not. No race lives exclusively on a vegetable diet, for their position has

---

* Chevalier, " Des forces alimentaires des Etats," p. 47.

never rendered a restriction to it indispensable; the nearest approach to it is probably among the higher classes of Hindoos, but these are greater consumers of milk and butter, of vegetable oils and pulses, which contain the same chemical elements as animal food. Some tropical races, such as the Malays, have been supposed to be almost exclusively consumers of fruits and vegetables, which is not true, for they are large consumers of fish and of vegetable oils, or of substances containing these oils, as the cocoanut and ground pea or earth nut."

A recent writer, speaking of human diet, observes: "It is a remarkable circumstance that man alone is provided with a case of instruments adapted to the mastication of all substances—teeth to cut and pierce and champ and grind; a gastric solvent too, capable of contending with anything and everything, raw substances and cooked, ripe and rotten, nothing comes amiss to him."

If animals could speak, as Æsop and other fabulists make them seem to do, they would declare man the most voracious animal in existence. There is scarcely any living thing that flies in the air, swims in the sea, or moves on the land, that is not made to minister to his appetite. The daily food, however, varies in different ages and different climates. Queen Elizabeth and her ladies breakfasted on meat, bread and strong ale. Our modern ladies take tea and coffee and thin slices of toast or bread. The Esquimaux drink train oil, and the Cossacks koumiss, an ardent spirit made from mare's milk. The inhabitants of France and Germany eat much more largely than we do of vegetable diet, and drink at all times of the day thin acid wines.

In Devonshire and Herefordshire an acid cider is the common beverage, and in the Highlands of Scotland oatmeal porridge is in a great measure the food and whisky the drink of the inhabitants. The Irish peasant lives chiefly on potatoes, and the Hindoo on rice. Yet all this variety and much more is digested, yields nutriment, and promotes growth; affording undeniable evidence that man is really omnivorous, that he can be supported by great varieties of food.

In warm climates meat is often poor, dry, insipid and hard stuff, because perhaps it cannot be kept to render it in general fit for any man who has not the teeth of a shark, or the snout of a saw-fish.

In tropical countries Animal food ought to be indulged in as sparingly as is consistent with the digestive powers; for, on the whole, animal food is more easy of digestion than vegetable; and it may be added (*en parenthèse*) that the flesh of the mature animal is more easily absorbed into the human system than that of the young of the same kind. Thus, five-year old mutton is more wholesome than lamb; beef than veal; goat than kid. This may seem strange to those who have never studied the subject, but the physiologist assures us that such is the fact. This being so, there was perhaps something of an unconscious wisdom in that party of sailors who once drank a bowl of punch on the summit of Pompey's Pillar in Egypt, on Christmas Day, in choosing for their dinner a tough billy-goat, in preference to a younger animal, for the all-sufficient reason that it took more " chawing," and that, consequently, the flavour would linger on the palate much longer than if it had been less mature.

Still, while conceding that Animal food is necessary for the sustentation of human strength and health, it cannot be denied that an abundant supply of vegetables is highly beneficial to the great omnivore—Man, and particularly so in tropical climates. There can be no doubt that a bountiful Providence has adapted the food of man to his necessities in all climates, so that the product of any particular country is best suited to the people inhabiting it.

Habit, as is well known, will do much in accustoming the stomach to particular descriptions of food. Many persons live exclusively, or almost so, on vegetables, others on animal substances, and particular kinds of diet are forced on the inhabitants of many regions of the globe;

but as far as Englishmen are concerned, a due mixture of vegetable and animal matter is not only most palatable, but most conducive to health.

Let us briefly take a preliminary glance at some of the various articles which different people relish. Besides the local peculiarities of the vegetable and animal foods which are most abundant and attainable, we have the influence of those instinctive appetites for particular articles of food, which certainly exist, however difficult of explanation they may be. Religious or superstitious usages are also most important factors in the result in many instances, although they will not always serve to explain the abstention from certain perfectly wholesome and nutritious foods, or the consumption of absolutely noxious or useless materials like clay. — Professor Church's " Food."

Sir George Grey, in his " Travels in Australia," gives a graphic account of the food of the Australians, and particularly tells us of the feast of a whole tribe on a stranded whale. " It was a sorry sight (he says) to see a pretty young woman entering the belly of the whale, then gorging herself with blubber, and issuing forth anointed from head to foot, and bearing in each hand a trophy of the delicacy in question."

A young lady of the Sandwich Islands, even now, will swallow half a dozen raw mackerel for breakfast, without the smallest inconvenience to herself.

Sir E. Belcher, in a visit to some Esquimaux at Icy Cape, found the winter store room under the floor of their yourt or den, pretty well supplied with a mixture of reindeer, whale, walrus, seal, swans, ducks, etc., but *none fresh*. It was frozen into a solid mass beneath, but loose from those on the surface, and seemed to be incorporated by some unexplained process into a *gelatinous snow*, which they scraped up easily with the hand, and ate with satisfaction, fish and oil predominating. It was not offensive or putrid. How many years the frozen mass may have remained there he could not determine.

In North America, fish eyes, the roes of salmon, and

other small scraps, are buried in the earth by the natives until putrid, and then eaten cooked or raw. These substances produce a horrible stench when exposed to the air. The Chippewa Indians are said to indulge in this diet.

The Sioux prepare a favourite dish, used at great feasts, called " washen-ena," consisting of dried meat pulverised and mixed with marrow, and a preparation of cherries, pounded and sun-dried. This mixture, when eaten raw or cooked, has an agreeable vinous taste.

The Emperor Napoleon once partook of an African dinner, with tortoise broth for turtle soup, porcupine, gazelle, and loin of the wild boar for *pièces de resistance*, salmis of Carthaginian hens, antelope cutlets, and bustards for *entrées*, an ostrich for a roast, and for side dishes ostrich eggs in the shell, pomegranate jelly, and all manner of sweetmeats with unpronounceable names like " scerakboracs." Ostrich, by way of roast chicken, is however rather tough eating; and we wonder the Governor, who was his host, did not add a slice or two of lion to the *entrées*, and pickled rhinoceros' foot to the side dishes. They certainly would digest much better than Arab sweetmeats, which, with the exception of " hulwah " are abominable.

The late Marquis of Compiegne, writing on the tribes of Equatorial Africa, states that some of them will eat any substance, however putrid, and he relates that they took from the river the floating body of a kind of flying squirrel (*Anoma larus*), which had evidently been dead ten or twelve days and was green and horribly swollen, and the skin gone. And yet they roasted and ate this disgusting viand, without even disembowelling it, and considered it an exquisite repast.

Arabs often eat raw sheep's liver or kidney, seasoned only with salt ; some tribes of Bedouins consume other parts of the sheep in an uncooked state. Others eat gazelles and horseflesh, but this latter is never an article of diet of the northern Bedouins.

In Sweden roast reindeer steaks and game are dressed

in a manner preferable to that which prevails with us. The flesh is first perforated and little bits of lard inserted, and after being baked in an oven, it is served in a quantity of white sauce. Some of the purely national dishes, such as lut-fisk on Christmas-eve, are most extraordinary things.

A writer in "Temple Bar," giving an account of a grand Chinese dinner of which he partook, says:—"Some of the intermediate dishes were shark's fin; birds' nests brought from Borneo (costing nearly a guinea a mouthful); fricassee of poodle, a little dog rather like a pig, except for its head; the fish of the *konk* shell, an elastic substance like paxwax or india-rubber, which you might masticate but could not possibly mash; peacock's liver, very fine and *recherché;* putrid eggs, nevertheless very good; rice, of course; salted 'shrimps; baked almonds; cabbage in a variety of forms; green ginger; stewed fungi; fresh fish of a dozen kinds; onions *ad libitum;* salt duck cured like ham, and *pig* in every form, roast, boiled, fried: Foúchow ham, which seemed to be equal to Wiltshire. In fact, the Chinese excel in pork, but Europeans will rarely touch it, under the superstition that pigs are fed on babies. Of course a pig will eat a baby if it finds one, as it will devour a rattlesnake, but that does not prevent us eating American bacon, where the pigs run wild in the wood, and feed, from choice, upon any vermin they can find and are fattened with garbage. When in the Southern States I got two magnificent rattlesnakes, and my pigs ate them both. That did not prevent the pigs being eaten in their turn; and I think I would as soon eat transmutation of baby-flesh as of rattlesnake, especially the rattle. But I believe the whole to be a libel. The Chinese are most particular about their swine, and keep them penned up in the utmost cleanliness and comfort, rivalling the Dutch in their scrubbing and washing. They grow whole fields of *taro* and herbs for their pigs, and I do not believe that one porker in a million ever tastes a baby. The whole was cooked without salt, and tasted very insipid to me. The birds' nests seemed like glue or isin-glass; but the cocks'-combs were palatable. The dog meat was like very delicate gizzard well stewed—a short close fibre and very tender. The dish which I fancied the most turned out to be *rat;* for upon taking a second help after the first taste, I got the head, and I certainly felt rather sick upon this discovery. But I consoled myself by the remembrance that in California we used often to eat ground-squirrels, which are first cousins to the flat-tailed rats; and travellers who would know the world must go in boldly for manners and customs. We had tortoise and frogs; a curry of the latter was superior to chicken. We had fowls' hearts, and brains of some bird—snipe I think. And the soup which terminated the repast was surely boiled tripe, or some interior ar-rangement, and I wished I had halted a little time ago."

Dr. Macgowan, of Shanghai, tells us that in China little distinction is made between materia medica, and materia alimentaria, therapeutic properties being as-cribed to all articles that are used as food. Nearly all portions of animals, the human frame included, are supposed to be efficacious in the treatment of disease. Some animal substances are macerated in fermented or distilled liquors, and are termed wines—thus, there are mutton wine, dog wine, deer wine, deer-horn wine, tiger-bone wine, snake wine, and tortoise wine.

In the shops of Hong Kong fat pork chops dried and varnished to the colour of mahogany are seen suspended with dry pickled ducks' gizzards, and strings of sausages cured by exposure to the sun.

The diet of the Cochin Chinese is, to European ideas, often gross and disgusting in a high degree. Dogs' and alligators' flesh, rats, mice, worms, frogs and other rep-tiles, maggots, entrails, and putrid meats are among their favourite dishes. Ducks are boiled, and eggs are not valued until they are rotten or nearly hatched.

Fish pickle is their favourite condiment, into which nearly every morsel they eat is plunged: elephants' flesh is eaten only by the sovereign and nobility.

In Java the dried inner skin of the buffalo, as well as that of the gourami (*Osphromenus olfax*) and other fish, are parboiled, and fried or made into a stew.

In Chili the universal dish is the "casuelo," which consists of boiled chicken, potatoes, onions, carrots, tomatoes, and eggs, the whole being well seasoned with grease, aji (a species of capsicum), and a little garlic. The grease and aji are "browned" in an "olla" and poured over the dish just at the moment it is served up. In spite of its incongruous materials, to a hungry stomach this mixture is far from being despicable.

Horace Greeley, in his "Letters from the American Plains," thus relates the general opinion as to the wild animals used for food :—" Buffalo meat I found to be a general favourite, though my own experience of it makes it a tough, dry, wooden fibre, only to be eaten under great provocation. I infer that it is poorer in spring than at other seasons, and that I have not been fortunate in cooks. Bear, I was surprised to learn, is not generally liked by the mountaineers—my companions had eaten every species, and were not pleased with any. The black-tailed deer of the mountains is a general favourite ; so is the mountain-hen, or grouse : so is the antelope, of course; the elk and mountain-sheep less decidedly so. None of our party liked horse, or knew any way of cooking it that would make it really palatable, though, of course, it has to be eaten occasionally, for necessity hath no law—or rather, is its own law. Our conductor had eaten broiled wolf, under compulsion, but could not recommend it; but he certified that a slice of cold boiled dog—*well* boiled, so as to free it from rankness, and then suffered to cool thoroughly—is tender, sweet, and delicate as lamb. I ought to have ascertained the species and age of the dog in whose behalf this testimony was borne— for a young Newfoundland or King Charles might justify praise, while it would be utterly unwarranted in the case of an old cur or mastiff—but the opportunity was lost, and I can only give the testimony as I received it."

M. Bojir, writing in "Hooker's Botanical Miscellany," III., p. 253, remarks:—"The principal food delicacy in Madagascar is the flesh of an unborn and but half-formed calf, to obtain which they destroy the cows, an inhuman practice, which, since our visit to Emerina, has been forbidden by Government."

Marrow.—The marrow of bones is a dainty at European dinners, and is esteemed as a luxury even among savages. The Indians of North America hold it in high estimation, particularly that of the bones of the buffalo, the elk, the moose, and the deer. The round bones of these animals are roasted in the coals or before the fire, then split with a stone hatchet, and in some cases with a wedge driven in between the condyles, when the bone has these terminations. The marrow is then scooped out with a piece of wood in the form of a spoon, and eaten on the instant by the members of the party seated around the camp fire.

A feast of this kind can only be fully enjoyed after a successful hunt, when the marrow is collected in quantity for storing during the hunting season, which occurs usually twice a year; the bones of the larger animals are broken into small fragments and boiled in water, until all the marrow which they contain, and the grease which adheres to them are separated and rise to the surface, when they are skimmed off and packed in bladders, or in the muscular coat of the stomach and in the larger intestines, which have been previously prepared for this use. Not only is the marrow of the large bones of the limbs preserved in this manner, but also that of the vertebral column. The bones of this are comminuted by pounding them with a stone hammer similar to those which are occasionally ploughed up in the Eastern States.

The marrow still warm from the natural heat of the animal is considered among the Laplanders and the Greenlanders the greatest delicacy, and a dish of honour which they offer to strangers and to the employés of the Government.

Various additions have been made from time to time
to the supply of Animal food for Europe, for which there
are incessant demands.   The preserved mutton and
beef which have been largely supplied from Australia,
although consumed by the public as makeshifts, have
not been generally popular from their insipidity and
the difficulty of recooking them, or giving them gist and
flavour.   The trade has, however, grown, for in 1877
200,420 cases of preserved meats were received from
Australia.   In 1879 the imports had reached 566,758
cwt., valued at nearly £1,700,000.   In 1883 the quantity of preserved meat imported had risen to 609,335
cwt., the value of which was £1,751,584, but more than
half of this came from the United States, the relative
supplies being, from—

						Cwt.
Australia ...	...	...	...	...	...	226,059
United States	...	...	...	...	...	308,303
Other countries ...	...	...	...	...	74,973
						609,335

Let us glance at the statistics of our imports of animals and animal products from the United States, taking
first the live stock.   In 1880, we imported as many as
156,490 head of horned cattle.   In 1883, the number
had decreased to 154,928.   Of sheep we received 118,000
in 1879, and only 89,083 in 1883.   A few years ago we
imported from America 16,000 live pigs, and now we
receive none.   If we pass next to animal products, we
find the import trade is large, although scarcely so large
and important as formerly.   Some five years ago we
received from the States 4,500,000 to 5,000,000 cwt. of
bacon and hams, now this quantity has dropped to
3,000,000 cwt.   In 1882 we received 1,731,000 cwt. of
fresh beef, which is about the average received in
the three previous years.   The imports of salted beef
keep pretty steady at about 280,000 cwts. a year.
Butter and butterine have dropped from 301,000 cwt.
in 1879 to 120,163 cwt. in 1883.   The imports of
American cheese have also declined from 1,345,744 cwt.

in 1878 to 991,000 cwt. in 1883. Lard has declined from 901,214 cwt. in 1878 to 751,128 cwt. in 1883. Fresh and salted mutton is about the same—42,841 cwt. in 1878, and 41,000 cwt. in 1883. Preserved meat (other than salted) was as high as 472,086 cwt. in 1880, and only 309,579 cwt. in 1883. Of salted pork, 322,148 cwt. was imported in 1878, and but 247,667 cwt. in 1883. At a recent meeting of the National Wool Growers' Association at Chicago, it was stated that sheep-farming in the States yields £30,000,000 sterling in wool and mutton, there being 1,020,000 sheep farmers pursuing the industry, with £100,000,000 capital invested in it. Further details of our foreign supplies of animal food will be given in subsequent pages.

Jerked Meats.—Among the dried and smoked foods eaten by various people are jerked bear's meat, jerked seal and walrus, and porpoise meat, used by the American Indians; jerked and smoked buffalo meat, dried and smoked beef, dried and smoked venison, hams of various kinds, jerked squirrels, and other small mammals, desiccated meat, and meat extract.

The dried meat so largely prepared in South America and shipped to Brazil and the West Indies, as animal food for the negroes, has been tried for Europe, but met with no approval. It is known as "charqui," "tasago," or jerked meat. From 650,000 to 900,000 cwt. of this is shipped annually from Buenos Ayres and Montevideo, about half as much from the Southern provinces of Brazil, and some from Chili.

Beef jerking is confined to the hot and dry summer months, the jerking season in Chili being looked forward to like harvest time in England. In well regulated establishments the labour is divided; the jerkers having nothing to do with the killing, skinning, etc. So expert are they as to excite the astonishment of novices at the rapidity with which they slice the animal up, in slices so thin as to admit of a quick sun-drying on hurdles well elevated above the ground.

The climate of Chili, from its extreme dryness, is

better adapted for the curing of meat than Buenos Ayres, where there is a certain degree of humidity. The meat of Chili is of richer flavour and more approaching that of venison. In preparing it in Chili the bones and fat are removed from the flesh, which is cut into strips, a quarter or three-eighths of an inch thick, and hung up in the full rays of the sun, and in about eight hours it is dried almost as hard as a piece of glue. The slices are made into long bundles and packed in raw hides, which shrink upon it, and keep it very tight. Meat dried in this way does not putrefy, but after a time mites are found in it. In Buenos Ayres, where it is partially salted and afterwards dried, the fat is used, and the meat becomes rancid, but with the negro population it is a great treat to get some fat. In using the shreds of meat, they are roasted thoroughly brown over the embers of a fire, and pounded in very small pieces on a flat stone. For all purposes of soup or stew it is a valuable food.

In Wallachia and Moldavia beef is much consumed by the people under the name of " pastourma " or " pastoor-mah." The meat is salted and sun-dried, and seasoned with spices and garlic when cooked.

The tongues, sinews, etc., are sold to the sausage-makers, who generally season them highly. The marrow, carefully extracted from the bones, is preserved in goat-skins, and other vessels, and under the name of " cerviche " is much employed for culinary purposes in Constantinople.

The flesh of the beasts fattened on distillery refuse has a disagreeable odour. There is a large trade in pre-served meat in Moldavia. One house, Messrs. Powell & Co., employ 240 workpeople, and turn out 5,000 boxes daily, containing about 33,000 lbs. of meat.

In Siam elephants' flesh is dried and stored up for food. Goats' flesh is also thus prepared.

Dendeng is the Malay name for the jerked meat of commerce, that is of animal muscular fibre, preserved by drying in the sun, nearly the only mode of curing flesh in the Eastern Archipelago. Dendeng is made of the flesh of deer, oxen and buffalo, and by the Chinese of that of the wild hog. It is a considerable article of native trade in the East.

In India pieces of mutton are dried in the sun and cured with spices and a little salt. It is exported to Burmah and used locally. It is said to be very good when roasted and pounded.

This custom of drying meat in the sun is also practised in Africa. It is thus described by Captain Burton in his " Lake Regions of Central Africa." " The African preserves his meat by placing large lumps upon a little platform of green reeds erected upon uprights, about eighteen inches high, and by smoking it over a slow fire. Thus prepared, and with the addition of a little salt, the provision will last for several days, and the porters will not object to increase their loads by three or four pounds of the article, disposed upon a long stick like gigantic kabobs. They also jerk their stores by exposing the meat upon a rope, or spread upon a flat stone, for two or three days in the sun ; it loses a considerable portion of nutriment, but it packs into a conveniently small compass. This jerked meat when dried, broken into small pieces and stored in gourds or in pots full of clarified and melted butter, forms the celebrated travelling provision in the East, called kavurmek ; it is eaten as a relish with rice and other boiled grains."

The *charqui* of South America, salted, is a product of sun-drying ; and the desiccation of carcases, without decomposition, on the plains has been a matter of common observation.

It is stated in Turner's " Embassy to Thibet " (4to, London, 1806, p. 301), that the flesh of animals is preserved frost-dried—not frozen—and it keeps without salt. He says, " I had supplies of this prepared meat during all the time I remained at Teshoo Loomboo, which had been cured in the preceding winter. It was perfectly sweet, and I was accustomed to eat heartily of it, without any further dressing, and at length grew

C

fond of it. It had not the appearance of being raw, but resembled in colour that which has been well boiled. It had been deprived of all ruddiness by the intense cold."

Frozen meat, unless losing greatly in weight by evaporation, owing to the dryness of circumambient air, will, like frozen fish, decompose on exposure to warmth.

The decomposition is activated by atmospheric impurity; and it is easy to understand how, in the mountains of Thibet, the rarefied air, of great dryness, mobility and freedom from putrefactive germs, would satisfy the conditions for abstracting sufficient moisture, even from frozen meat, whilst effectually preventing decay. Pure dry air, either hot or cold, being an admirable desiccant, is under suitable conditions an excellent preservative.

Frozen meat has kept for ages, and during the Russian and North American winters, the people are compelled to put up with it. Freezing is, however, prejudicial to the meat, and commercially somewhat expensive, since it necessitates the construction not only of ordinary ice-houses, but of freezing chambers at the ports of shipment and landing, and there are innumerable impediments in the way of getting the frozen produce delivered untainted to the customer. Experimentally the process is simple and quite successful, but not as a means of supplying the nation's food. It has, however, of late years been brought more successfully into practice in the importation of carcases from Australia and America.

It is curious to notice the various parts of animals that are eaten, or selected as choice morsels by different persons or classes. Sheep's head, pig's head, calf's head and brains, ox head, the heads of ducks and geese, ox tongue, horse tongue, reindeer tongue, walrus tongue, cranes' tongues, cods' tongues, etc. Fowls' and ducks' tongues are esteemed an exquisite Chinese dainty. The pettitoes of the sucking pig, or the mature feet and hocks of the elder hog, sheep's trotters, calf's feet, cow heel, bears' paws, elephants' feet, the feet of ducks and geese and their giblets; ox tail, pig's tail, fat sheep's tail, kangaroo tail, beaver's tail. And the entrails again are not despised, whether it be bullock's heart or sheep's heart, liver and lights, lamb's fry or pig's fry, tripe and chitterlings, goose liver and gizzard, the cleaned gut for our sausages, the fish maws, cod sound, cod liver, and so on. The moufle, or loose covering of the nose, of the great moose deer or elk is considered by New Brunswick epicures a great dainty. The hump of the buffalo, and the trunk of the elephant, are other delicacies. Deer's sinews, and the muscle of the ox, the buffalo, and the wild hog, jerked or dried in the sun, and then termed "dendeng," are delicacies of the Chinese, imported at a high price from Siam and the eastern islands.

Under the name of sweetbread there is a delicate food, which should be the thyroid and sublingual glands of the ox, but the pancreas goes under the same name. That of the calf is most esteemed, but the sweetbread of the lamb is not unfrequently substituted for it.

The eggs of different animals, again, form choice articles of food, whether they be those of the ordinary domestic poultry, the eggs of sea-fowl, of the plover, and of game birds, of the ostrich and emu, of the tortoises and other reptilia, or the eggs of insects, and of fishes.

A remarkable instance of the increase in the sale of imported ox tongues is afforded by the trade done at Paysandu, a little town in Uruguay, from whence about 150 tons are packed in hermetically sealed tins and shipped annually to Great Britain.

The Russian tongues received are believed to be principally horse tongues dried and smoked. Reindeer tongues are another Northern delicacy, of which many are imported, and we also eat in this country sheep's and pigs' tongues. The tongues which are imported dried, require long soaking in cold water before being cooked.

Besides the dead meat brought into London, there are received at the Metropolitan and Foreign Cattle Markets an average of 320,000 head of cattle, 50 per cent.

being foreign; 1,400,000 sheep, of which 60 per cent. are foreign, and 12,000 pigs, nearly all of which are from abroad.

In 1870 it was officially estimated that the meat consumption in the United Kingdom was about 96 lbs. per head per annum. Later estimates gave it, in 1872, at 108 lbs. per head. We paid for the food substances of animal origin which we imported into this country, in 1883, the sum of nearly fifty-one and a-half millions sterling, made up as follows :—

Living Animals—cattle, sheep, and swine ...	£11,978,996
Bacon	8,178,123
Beef	2,878,264
Butter and butterine	11,755,419
Cheese	4,882,502
Eggs	2,728,396
Fish, cured	1,773,027
Hams	1,823,352
Lard	2,243,956
Beef and mutton, fresh or preserved ...	1,863,539
Pork	759,651
Poultry and game	591,367
	£51,456,662

This is a pretty good round sum for foreign imports, exclusive of our home meat supply, dairy produce, game, and fresh fish.

The prices of meat are, generally speaking, advancing year by year, as the following wholesale prices of butchers' meat (per stone of 8 lbs.) in the Metropolitan Cattle Market shows :—

	1870.	1880.	1882.
	s. d.	s. d.	s. d.
Large prime beasts ...	4 11½ ...	4 11¾ ...	4 9¾
Southdown sheep ...	5 7¼ ...	6 9½ ...	7 0¾
Lambs	6 10 ...	8 1¼ ...	7 10
Small prime calves ...	5 5 ...	5 11¾ ...	6 0¾
Small neat porkers ...	5 8¼ ...	4 11¼ ...	4 10½

In 1862 the consumption of butchers' meat in Paris (exclusive of pork) was said to be as high as 108 lbs. per head.

Adding together the alimentary products derived from the bovine, ovine, and porcine races, to those obtained from fowls, game, fish, eggs, and cheese, it was officially stated that the population of the eighty-nine departments of France consumed in 1862 only 57 grammes of nitrogenous food, while the average daily ration of animal food of the Parisian was 273 grammes.

In 1864, with a population of 1,696,141, the following amounts were returned as consumed in Paris :—

	lbs.
Butchers' meat	260,205,970
Pork of all kinds	15,908,418
Charcuterie, cooked ham, sausages, &c. ...	3,600,548
Meat pâtés, &c.	225,858

In 1865 the value of the import and export commerce of France in animal food amounted to over seven and a-quarter millions sterling, of which three-fourths was imports.

In France, as with us, there has been an almost general advance in the price of meat in the last ten years, as shown by the following comparison of prices per kilo. in the market of Villette, Paris :—

	1872. Francs.	1880. Francs.
Ox beef	1·53	1·59
Cow beef	1·40	1·36
Mutton	1·60	1·82
Pork	1·55	1·73

A calf weighs ordinarily at its birth 90 lbs. It consumes on an average about 3½ quarts of milk per day. At about three months it will weigh 360 lbs., and is sold to the butcher for about 6d. per lb. in France, where large veal is held in great esteem, being one of the most popular and general articles of food.

From official returns we find that the consumption of fresh meat for Paris in the year 1872* was as follows :—

---

* " Enquête de la Chambre de Commerce de Paris."

At the five slaughter-houses there were killed for food :—

Oxen	159,916
Cows	47,517
Calves	160,184
Sheep	1,343,852
Goats	298
Pigs	154,477
Horses	4,041
Asses and mules	612

The meat sent out for consumption yielded by these animals was—

	Kilos.
Beef, veal, and mutton	101,116,269
Pork	12,312,745
Horseflesh	1,010,250
	114,439,264

Of this quantity all but 5,500,000 kilos., sent to the suburbs, was consumed in Paris.

The population of the city in 1872 was 1,851,792, and in 1881 it was 2,269,023.

A peculiar feature of the business in the French slaughter-houses is that of blowing up the carcass as soon as the head and legs are cut off, which is done as follows: The body being placed on the dressing frame, an incision is made in the breast near the neck, and the nozzle of a bellows inserted. A man then works the bellows for about fifteen minutes, until the whole carcass is swollen out like a small balloon. The reasons given for this are that it makes the meat look better, more plump than it otherwise would, and that it enables the person who skins the carcass to get the hide off quicker and easier, without injuring it. All bullocks, calves, sheep, etc., slaughtered in these establishments are blown up in this manner.

The imports of meat into France were in—

	Beef. Kilos.		Salted and cured Pork. Kilos.
1879	5,850,000	......	35,675,000
1880	7,519,000	......	38,713,000
1881	5,741,000	......	19,710,000

The other salted meat imported in 1881 amounted to 4,146,000 kilos. The imports of pork were sensibly reduced by the stringent measures against American bacon, in consequence of the trichinosis.

The total quantity of butchers' meat consumed in Paris in 1883 was about 167,000 tons.

In Russia the production of meat may be roughly estimated from the animals slaughtered annually. This number cannot be very accurately determined, but may be approximately given. Not less than 3,500,000 head of large cattle are sent to the butchers, of which 2,200,000 are oxen, and 1,300,000 cows. The number of calves killed is on the average 4 millions, and of sheep 12 millions. We may assume, according to official data, for each head of cattle, 450 lbs. of meat and 60 lbs. of suet (an ox will give 550 lbs. of flesh and 100 lbs. of tallow, a cow 200 lbs. to 300 lbs. of meat and 150 lbs. of tallow); and hence we get a total produce of 700,000 tons of beef, irrespective of tallow. The 4 millions of calves at 80 lbs. give 140,000 tons of veal. Reckoning the sheep killed at 30 or 40 lbs. of meat each, exclusive of 10 lbs. of tallow, we have 170,000 tons of mutton; and 6 million pigs killed will yield 200,000 tons of pork.*

In the United States pork is the principal flesh food, constituting fully half the meat consumption. .In France pork forms 30 per cent., and beef 55 per cent. of the meat production, and mutton $13\frac{1}{2}$. In Great Britain mutton and beef share more equally in the food supply, swine flesh occupying nearly the place that mutton does in France.

About 130 lbs. per head would seem to be the average annual meat consumption in the United States.

In the town of Bremen the consumption of animal food per head in the five years 1872-76, averaged as follows, in kilogrammes of $2\frac{1}{5}$ lbs. :—

---

* Buschen, " Aperçu statistique des Forces productives de la Russe," 1867.

							Kilos.
Beef ...	...	...	...	...	...	...	33·56
Mutton	...	...	...	...	...	...	3·29
Pork...	...	...	...	...	...	...	18·72
Game and poultry ...		...	...	...	...	...	2·58
	Flesh generally ...		...	...	...	...	58·15

or about 128 lbs.

A remark may here be made of the general objection to mutton as food in Germany, Holland, and other parts of the Continent. I remember offending a learned Dutch professor by providing at dinner when he visited me, as a choice dainty, a quarter of lamb, not knowing the Dutch objection to the flesh of the sheep. The best of it is, a great deal of cow beef is used in Holland, a meat which we do not hold in estimation.

In other foreign countries mutton is disliked, or at least rarely eaten. The Calmucks and Cossacks seldom touch it, and the Mongols make a wine of it. In some parts of America and in Spain, mutton is scarcely considered fit for food. The dried flesh of the wild sheep, however, forms an article of commerce in Kamtschatka.

A sheep to be in high order for the palate of an epicure, should never be killed earlier than when five years old; at which age the mutton will be found firm and succulent, of a dark colour, and full of the richest gravy; whereas if only two years old, it is flabby, pale, and savourless. Wether mutton is always considered far superior to that of the ewe.

Harrison, who died in 1593, described our sheep as "very excellent, and for sweetness of flesh they pass all others." The last three centuries have added greatly to the improvement of the breed and the quality of their flesh. Southdown mutton in point of flavour and delicacy is thought equal to any that is killed. The older the mutton, the finer the flavour.

In highly fattened sheep the quantity of meat obtainable may reach as high as 65 per cent. of the carcase, but this figure will not be obtained from ordinary sheep.

In well-fed sheep a yield of 55 to 60 per cent. can be reckoned on, and 45 to 55 per cent. may be considered a fair average.

Mutton is seldom or never salted in England; in France *le gigot présalé* is a popular dish, but this is only mutton grazed near the sea coasts.

The annual consumption of home-grown sheep and lambs in this country, according to a reliable estimate, is more than 14,000,000, out of a total of 28,000,000. This was supplemented in 1883 by the importation of over one million live sheep. There has been an estimated loss of five and a quarter millions of sheep and lambs of late years by the rot, hence the foreign imports have to be largely supplemented to meet the food supply of the nation.

The value of the flesh of 14 million sheep which are now annually slaughtered for food in the United Kingdom may be taken to be worth over £20,000,000.

Each year in the province of Buenos Ayres, 10 million sheep are boiled down solely for their tallow and skins, hence a great waste of serviceable food occurs. The boiling down of sheep in Australia has been in a great measure abandoned.

Goats' Flesh.—The flesh of the goat is harder, tougher, and stronger food than mutton; it is very commonly eaten in Switzerland and other mountainous regions of the world. The haunches are frequently salted and dried. The flesh of the kid is generally esteemed, and has a flavour not very unlike that of venison. The Malabar goat, that browses on the rocks in Ceylon, is said to be a delicate animal. Of the consumption of goats' flesh for food it is difficult to form any accurate estimate, but in those countries where the animal abounds it is no doubt eaten in the young state. In England, however, the goat is not legally held to be a food animal.

Morocco, Spain, and India are the countries where the largest number of goats are found, but it is scarcely necessary to particularise the numbers, as they are kept more for their milk, hair, and skins than for their flesh.

We imported in 1880 into the United Kingdom the following quantities of Animal food supplies;—

	Quantity.	Value £.
Live animals for food (except pigs) ...	1,330,845 head	10,060,396
Bacon and hams ...	5,334,648 cwts.	10,985,642
Beef, salted and fresh	1,017,956 ,, ...	2,424,943
Butter	2,326,305 ,, ...	12,141,034
Cheese	1,775,997 ,, ...	5,091,514
Eggs	747,408,600 No.	2,235,451
Fish, cured or salted...	1,343,434 cwts.	1,666,710
Lard	927,512 ,, ...	1,852,160
Meat, salted or fresh...	149,010 ,, ...	429,073
,, preserved ...	655,800 ,, ...	1,905,717
Pork, salted or fresh...	409,267 ,, ...	684,192
Poultry and game ...	— ,, ...	421,645

£49,898,477

The proportionate quantity we consumed per head of foreign provisions of Animal origin is officially given as follows :—

	1879. lbs.	1882. lbs.
Bacon and hams	14·84	8·85
Butter...	6·57	6·72
Cheese... ... ...,	5·74	5·20
	No.	No.
Eggs	22·44	23·04

Cheese scarcely receives its proper place as a food material with us. Some systems do not take to it kindly, and such persons should not press it upon their digestive economy. Much cheese, too, because it is poorly made, is indigestible. These facts should be borne in mind. And yet as a food possessing great strengthening power and adapted to those who have hard physical labour to perform, there are few substances so satisfactory as rich and well cured cheese. We may give some authorities on this point. Dr. Austin Flint says : " Old cheese taken in small quantity towards the close of a repast, undoubtedly facilitates digestion by stimulating the secretion of the fluids, particularly the gastric juice. Here its effect is attributed to a different principle than that of its fermenting quality, but an active ferment may also increase the effect of the gastric juice." Dr. Flint adds: " New cheese is a highly nutritious article, as is evident from its composition." The long experience of English, Scotch, and Irish labourers proves cheese to be a wholesome as well as nutritious food. A small quantity of cheese, with them, takes the place of a larger quantity of meat, and enables them to endure such hard labour as the American thinks he can only perform upon a generous meat diet. In Germany farm labourers depend largely upon the curd of milk after being skimmed for butter. This curd is frequently used in a fresh state, and makes an important part of the labourer's diet. It is related of a certain Dane that he could carry a stone so heavy that it required ten men to lift it on his shoulders: that he performed such wonderful feats of strength upon a diet consisting of large quantities of thick sour milk, tea, and coffee. His enormous strength must have been sustained by the curd of the milk. This case refutes the common error, that milk does not furnish a diet for vigorous manhood. There are numerous cases in which a milk diet has sustained the system under the most exacting labour. The American Encyclopædia says : " The peasants of some parts of Switzerland, who seldom or never taste anything but bread, cheese, and butter, are a vigorous people. Our American women are not such flesh-eaters as men, and with their love of sweetmeats the nervous system becomes ill nourished. They may almost be said to be made of starch and sugar. If they would make cheese a more constant article of diet, and use more unbolted flour, with more open air exercise, they would soon become the most healthful and robust, women in the world." Cheese is less liable to putrefactive change than flesh, and thus much less likely to develop in the human system those scrofulous diseases attributed to animal food.

It is believed that we produce in the United Kingdom about 126,000 tons of ripe cheese, and 29,285 tons of butter per annum. From America and Canada we import about 60,000 tons of cheese per annum, and from other sources 30,000 tons, which together amount to about four-fifths of our home production.

IMPORTS OF BUTTER AND CHEESE INTO THE UNITED KINGDOM.

	Butter. Quantity. cwts.		Cheese. Quantity. cwts.
1861	992,772	......	706,395
1871	1,334,783	......	1,216,400
1881	2,047,341	......	1,840,090
1883	2,334,473	......	1,799,704

The value of the butter and cheese imported in the last named year was £16,664,333.

Diseased Meat as Food.—As their religion forbids their killing animals for food, the Burmese generally eat those that have died of disease.

The flesh of all animals that have died is not, as generally assumed, necessarily unfit for food. It is an old and widespread popular error that the unfitness of such flesh for human food is due to its not having been drained of blood; an error that seems to have come down to us from ancient times, when it was held that all diseases originated and were centred in the blood, and that as this contained the *materia peccans*, the flesh of a diseased animal would be perfectly wholesome if only all its blood were abstracted. Or this general belief may be partly owing to the methods of slaughtering commonly employed. Bleeding is, however, no essential part of proper slaughtering; indeed, for a time the system of killing without much loss of blood was strongly advocated and widely practised, more especially in England, on the ground that the blood itself is quite as nutritious as the meat, and that the latter is far tenderer and better flavoured when a portion of the blood is retained in it. The system of slaughtering with abstraction of blood holds its own chiefly because meat thus killed keeps longer and is supposed to look better.

That people should be deterred from eating meat that is good, simply because it has not been bled is of comparatively little importance ; the real danger of the error lies in the assumption that the flesh of diseased animals is harmless if only their blood be abstracted in the death-struggle.

In Germany diseased animals are often killed and their flesh eaten. In certain localities these are killed and their meat served up in the household, or for the domestics and work-people. In other cases the flesh of diseased animals is openly sold as meat of a reduced value. In country districts there are no lack of purchasers, who while knowing that the animals were not thoroughly healthy before they were killed, believe that the use of the meat will have no fatal effect.

According to the Prussian law relating to diseased animals, those suffering from pulmonary complaints may be slaughtered, and the flesh after it is properly cooked may be sold ; but the slaughter must be effected under the surveillance of a veterinary surgeon.

In a great number of cases where the animals are attacked with disease, they are secretly killed, and the purchasers do not know they are buying diseased meat. There are many butchers whose business it is to kill animals in bad health. In many diseases to which animals are subject, the flesh does not undergo any change which renders it dangerous to human health, or reduces its value as food. Frequently the slaughter of the animal is due to the impossibility of a cure, such for instance as the fracture of a limb, severe wounds, &c. In certain internal diseases, which would ordinarily terminate fatally, it is found best to kill the animal, and the flesh does not show, at least in the first stages, any considerable change.

The flesh of sheep attacked by the staggers, that of ruminants suffering in the lungs without having had the fever, and of animals showing symptoms of fractures, &c., can generally be used as food without danger. But occasionally in these and other diseases, the flesh may undergo a transformation which will render it dangerous, when the disease has attained any height, and especially when it has changed the blood.

The usage of the flesh of animals which have died of gangrenous diseases, is often the cause of great danger to man. It has been found that the meat of one diseased animal has affected more than 100 persons, terminating in the death of many.

Allusion may here be made to some recent cases, well known. Many hundreds of persons at Nordhausen, 206 at Wurzen, and 197 persons at Zeitz, were more or less seriously attacked, of whom many died. The great intensity of the poison shows that it cannot be checked by the ordinary preparation of food and insufficient cooking.

In many of the diseases from which animals suffer, the poisonous property is not always in the flesh, but changes are brought about, so that the meat decomposes rapidly after it is killed, and it becomes extremely dangerous as human food. This is especially noticeable in those which have had severe fever, and where whatever may have been the disease, they have been killed just before they would have died naturally.

According to an official report for the year 1873, there were killed from necessity (Nothschachten) 4,189 ruminants and 6,002 pigs. In other States where this necessitous slaughter is not controlled, it is probable that this is often done. The meat is generally sold for food, and it is frequently the case that animals, in the last death struggle from disease, are killed to dispose of the meat.

The following is a summary of Animal food that is injurious, according to the German laws :—

1. The flesh of animals that have died a natural death.

2. That of rabid animals, those suffering from glanders, bloody spleen, gangrenous affections, whether of the internal or external organs.

3. That of animals killed during the disease, after

having shown typhoid symptoms, and a falling away in flesh.

4. That of beasts which have been poisoned, or which shortly before being killed have taken poisonous substances, in considerable quantity.

5. Measly or trichinous meat; also that of scrofulous and tuberculous animals.

6. Meat visibly tainted or decomposed.

The value of meat is diminished, without its being injurious, in the following instances:—

1. In all febrile affections, as well as intermittent fevers, in which a wasting of the animal takes place.

2. The flesh of calves killed before they are eight or ten days old has little or no nutritive value.

3. The nutritive value of polonies, or hárd sausages, is diminished by the addition of flour and water.

4. Horseflesh is often sold as beef, and at the same price.

The following is an extract from a letter written to a friend in this country from Northern India, by the Rev. Dr. Marcus N. Carleton, a missionary twenty-five years resident in that country. The statements made are certainly very remarkable, but doubtless truthful. The matter is one which cannot fail to attract attention among physicians and the guardians of health everywhere:—

"In India, for at least twenty-five hundred years, we have had a class of village 'Kamius' (low caste), called *Chumars*. I seldom, if ever, saw a village so small as not to have at least one family of Chumars in it, and some towns have three hundred families. These people are tanners and shoemakers. Under ancient, as well as modern, Hindoo rule, and under English rule, they have a *legal status* and a legal right to all dead cattle.

"These people, the Chumars, are a large and thriving class, and eat all dead cattle, dying from whatever disease. The Hissar district is nearly as large as one half the State of Massachusetts. It is a great cattle-growing district, and a very large Chumar population is

found in it. About twenty-two years ago, Dr. Adam
Taylor, a distinguished English surgeon, was in charge
of the district, and from his lips I heard the following
statement :—

"A fatal epidemic broke out in the district among
the cattle. Dr. Taylor, by repeated post-mortem exami-
nations, declared that the disease, as far as he could discover, was like a form of typhus often called putrid
fever in the human subject. The epidemic raged for
months, till forty thousand head of cattle perished ; and
all these dead bodies were eaten by law, by legal right,
by the Chumar population. After the epidemic was
over, and these forty thousand head of cattle had all
been eaten, Dr. Taylor made a careful examination of
the Chumar population, and he could find no traces of
any disease among them caused by eating the dead
cattle, but on the whole they were more healthy than
any other class of villagers.

"During the last twenty-five years I have examined
nearly fifty such cases. I will mention one. In the
Hindoo village of Kamius there were twenty-two hundred head of cattle. An epidemic broke out among
them, and in five months about six hundred of them
died. In this village there are twenty-two families of
Chumars, of about eight persons to a family. These
families ate in five months about six hundred head of
cattle, all dying of a very fatal disease. I visited these
Chumars, saw their baskets of meat, saw in every house
large earthen pots, filled with meat, on the fire. I saw
little children, eighteen months old, sucking small bones
of this meat, as little New England children would suck
the leg of a roast turkey on Thanksgiving Day. I
visited these families after their generous meat diet, and
found them all in as good health as any of the people.
I have now lived twenty-five years among the Hindoos,
I have been in medical attendance on every class (there
are some thirty-six classes), and I do not think that
even among the Brahmins, the strictest vegetarians in
the world, there is better health than among the

Chumars, who for twenty-five hundred years have by law eaten all the cattle of India, dying by whatever disease."

M. Decroix (a confirmed hippophagist in France for twenty years), argues strongly that diseased animals are not unwholesome, and enters somewhat generally into the argument. M. Decroix made it a practice to eat the cooked flesh of horses killed in his service, which had had glanders or farcy, and, whether thoroughly or partially cooked, he found no evil results to his health. He has even gone further than this in his inquisitorial experiments as to whether the flesh of animals which have died was unwholesome. Ever since 1861 he has eaten the flesh cooked of all animals that have died within his reach, no matter from whatever disease. Desirous of ascertaining whether the flesh of cattle, sheep, and calves, seized by the inspectors of meat in Paris was really unwholesome, for six months he received from M. Chevreul, Director of the Jardin des Plantes, parts of the flesh thus seized, and given to the beasts of the menagerie. Several times a week during this period, he ate of this flesh, without any inconvenience to his health, except certain timid apprehensions and the natural repugnance resulting from prejudice. After a personal experience of fifteen or twenty years, and a number of observations collected from others, he affirms that one may eat with impunity the flesh cooked (not putrid) of any of the domestic animals, no matter what they had died of—glanders, typhus, hydrophobia, etc. Instead of the flesh of animals which have died naturally having a more repugnant appearance or a particular flavour, he states that he has placed the two kinds side by side in the same stew-pan, and with the same sauce, and in serving to different persons, many of them connoisseurs, the meat of the animals that have died has invariably been found superior to that of meat from the slaughter-houses. If the flesh of animals which have died, or were diseased, is unwholesome, he and those to whom he has given it, would have been

D

victims long since. The "Veterinarian," and other publications have discussed this subject from time to time.

We can never realise to its full extent the effect of the process of cooking in destroying organic poisons, which in their natural state might exert a deadly influence on our organism.

Take game, winged or other, say a partridge ; before cooking it appears almost in a state of decomposition. On the table, after proper cooking, it is splendid. Who would like to eat venison fresh ? Unless kept until in a high condition it is uneatable.

Certainly the flesh of animals which have died of anthracoid diseases, has proved actively poisonous when eaten in the raw state, but when sufficiently cooked has been perfectly innocuous. ·Of the fact that there is a large consumption of diseased meat, viz., the flesh of animals affected with pleuro-pneumonia, foot-and-mouth disease, and various febrile affections, no doubt can be entertained by rational people, and it is readily admitted that no obvious mischief results from eating such food ; the evidence, in fact, of the unwholesomeness of the flesh of diseased animals is absolutely *nil.* It is quite true that the idea of eating diseased meat is distasteful— to a sensitive stomach it may be nauseating—but. the fact remains, that, with few exceptions, there is no proof that the meat is really deleterious after it has been submitted to the action of fire.

The Irish Cattle Trade Defence Association, was at great pains lately to obtain professional testimony to prove that the flesh of animals affected with pleuro-pneumonia may, under certain conditions, be used with impunity as human food.

That we habitually eat the flesh of diseased animals, there can be no reasonable doubt. Whether we suffer by it, and if so, to what extent, are questions which have not been satisfactorily answered. Our knowledge of this subject is very imperfect, and we have but little trustworthy data to guide us. There are, however, some well-authenticated facts. It has been proved that the flesh of animals which have been suffering from malignant fevers has caused sickness, diarrhœa, febrile symptoms, and death; and it has also been proved that the flesh of such animals may sometimes be eaten with apparent impunity. Trichinised meat has produced the most disastrous results, and the flesh of animals containing tuberculous deposits is capable of transmitting the disease to carnivorous animals. There is no doubt at all about this; but, at the same time, abundant testimony has been adduced to show that this kind of diseased meat has often been used as food without any perceptible evil resulting.

Our immunity from evil consequences when we consume diseased meat appears to rest solely on culinary operations. We must suppose that by boiling our milk and thoroughly cooking our meat, we destroy these germs as we destroy parasites like Trichinæ, which, according to Cobbold, succumb to a temperature of 170 to 180 degrees Fahr.

No one can prove that our health is not impaired and our lives shortened by the systematic consumption of diseased meat, and that many of the ills to which the human race is heir may not be found indirectly to arise from that cause. But as we cannot yet prove that these evils are so produced, and as we cannot afford to throw away anything which appears to be fit for human food, we have no alternative but to get rid of our cattle-diseases in the interests of sanitary science, as well as in those pertaining to agriculture.

The medical men who reported for the Defence Association were Drs. R. Macnamara, Alex Macalister, and J. E. Reynolds. They state : There is no case on record wherein the flesh of cattle slaughtered while suffering from pleuro-pneumonia in any stage has ever been proved to give rise to disease in man. Reynal states that the flesh of animals who have suffered from this disease has been in daily use in Paris for the past twenty years without any appreciable results. Loiset asserts that for

nineteen years the flesh of 18,000 diseased animals has
been used as food in Lille, and that during that time
there were no appreciable alterations in the death-rate,
nor any unusual accessions of disease.

Dr. Fleming, in his work on " Veterinary Sanitary
Science," says, in speaking of pleuro-pneumonia :—"Since
the malady has been recognised it may safely be asserted
that the flesh of millions of diseased animals has been
consumed as food in every part of the world, and yet
there is not to my knowledge a single instance of any
accident attending or following its use."

From these considerations it is warrantable to con-
clude that the consumption of the flesh of cattle slaughtered in the early stages of pleuro-pneumonia is perfectly
harmless, and the destruction of such meat is a wasteful
expenditure of a material which is capable of supplying
a perfectly wholesome animal food. We have proved
that meat of the kind referred to has been largely used
in this and other countries, and the fact that not in any
one case has disease been traced to the consumption of
the flesh of a pleuro-pneumonia animal is a point of the
most significant and conclusive value as evidence, more
especially as we have precise and positive information
relating to the deleterious effects attending the consumption of the flesh of animals affected with anthrax, milz-
brand, etc., and also the decomposed flesh of healthy
cattle. The above remarks apply to the fresh and unchanged meat of animals which have been slaughtered
in the earlier period of the second stage of the disease,
but we are not prepared to advocate the use of the flesh
of animals markedly reduced in condition. It is certain
that the use of the seriously tainted or putrescent meat
of healthy and diseased animals alike is attended with
danger, and there can be little doubt that effects attributed to the virus of one or other of the diseases to
which cattle are liable have frequently been due to a
state of incipient decomposition of the food consumed.

It is true that there are some who prefer tainted to
fresh and wholesome meat, and who seem to be pro-

tected from the consequences of eating it partly by habit, partly by the culinary art, and in part by a species of dietetic disinfection almost unconsciously practised by persons of epicurean tastes. But these cases notwithstanding, there is no doubt that the general statement just made is true.

It follows, then, from the foregoing that the fresh and unchanged meat of animals slaughtered during an attack of pleuro-pneumonia may be safely consumed ; and that such meat is not sensibly less in nutritive value than that of other animals unaffected by any disease, but that it is of lower quality, owing to its greater tendency to undergo change.

I may here publish an anecdote which is given in an Australian paper, the *Geelong Advertiser* :—

" Mr. ——, we shall call him Mr. Vellum, of Melbourne, is blessed with the friendship of Mr. ——, we shall call him Mr. Stockwhip—whose cattle-station is not a hundred miles from Echuca. Stockwhip is in the habit of sending down tongues, potted butter, rolled beef, and fifty other little up-country niceties to his town friend as presents. On Tuesday last arrived at Vellum's office a good-sized keg, the address card in the usual well-known handwriting. It was late in the afternoon, just about time to start for Paradise Villa, South Yarra ; the gift was safely stored in the buggy, and off Vellum started with the treasure ; while tea was getting ready the keg must be opened. 'How heavy it is,' says one. ' What on earth can he have sent this time,' says another. Speculation was not allayed when the lid was prized open, and only dry salt presented to view. ' Dive deeper,' was the order of Paterfamilias, ' there must be something else in it.' The salt was carefully removed, and with considerable difficulty something bulky was dragged out, of indefinite shape and texture. ' Perhaps it's a Murray cod,' said one of the juveniles. ' Seems to be some preparation of pork,' remarked Vellum ; ' however, let's have some fried for tea, and see how it eats.' Fried a slice or two of it ; everybody tasted, but nobody liked it; it was horribly tough. Perhaps we don't know how to cook it properly, suppose we try it to-morrow for breakfast; stewed it was, and certainly it tasted a little more savoury, but still tough. The proper mode of cooking it had evidently not yet been hit upon; a piece was ordered to be boiled for dinner, and Vellum started for the day's business in Chancery Lane. There was the usual pile of letters to open, but one in Stockwhip's handwriting had the preference, and here it is—'Dear ——, The scourge has reached us at last. Two of my finest bullocks were found dead in the paddock yesterday morning, and on being opened the indications of pleuro-pneumonia were unmistakeable. The left lung of one of them Dr. —— here says is the most perfect specimen of diseased structure he ever saw. I want Dr. Macadam and Mr. Miscamble to see it, and therefore I send it——to——you——packed——in——salt.' Vellum's eyes began to swim. He did not dine at home that day."

The following remarks from the *Lancet* on the quality of meat deserve consideration :—

" Those who perpetuate the old English custom of living on food which is so far honestly cooked for the table that the eater may know what he is eating—who do not in fact use made dishes which may be made of anything—must have noticed of late a considerable depreciation in the quality of meat. It is either soft and flabby, or stringy, tough, and poor in flavour. This is a serious matter, and may be taken as a foretaste of what is to come, unless something can be done to stay the plague of reckless importation. It may be safe,. though we doubt the conclusion—to eat the flesh of unhealthy animals, some suffering from the loathsome febrile and wasting diseases, and killed to prevent their dying naturally; but it is not nice or prudent to do so; better diminish the proportion of animal food in our ordinary diet than eat measly pork, the flesh of sheep affected with liver disease, induced by the fluke parasite; and the wasted, or, which is quite as revolting, the artificially fattened, carcasses of unhealthy bullocks and cows. Poultry loaded with fat by a process initiated from the phenomena of disease, are appreciated by the palate. It does not, however, follow that these things ' are really good for food.' We believe that those who would be healthy should use healthy nutriments. It is impossible to provide this luxury in sufficient quantities. Let the public pursue a sensible course, and resort to articles of diet which supply an equally serviceable material, less costly, and more under control. We have no sympathy with the vegetarian craze, but unless Animal food can be furnished at a fair price, and in healthy condition, it will soon become necessary to prefer vegetable diet. The slaughterers of cattle and those who prepare their flesh for food are able to recognise many hideous diseases, and have terms of their own with which to designate them. For example, they know tuberculous disease when they see it, and yet they are content to remove the sickening mass and send the residue for human consumption, as though the whole animal were not poisoned."

CHAPTER II.

A FEW WORDS ON CANNIBALISM.*

Flesh of Whites not esteemed—Statements of Old Chroniclers on
the Practice of Cannibalism in Europe, Asia, and America—
Assertions of Modern Travellers—Evidences of Shipwrecked
Sailors and Others — Cannibalism Common in the Pacific
Islands and Australia, especially in the Fiji Islands—Evi-
dence of many Writers — Practised also in Islands of the
Eastern Archipelago, Celebes, Sumatra, Malacca — Many
African Tribes Anthropophagi—Statements of Sir S. Baker,
Bruce, Capt. Cameron, P. Du Chaillu, Thomson, and Lay-
land.

IT is sad for the honour of mankind that we must still
include man himself in the list of Animal food, but there
is comfort in the sure hope that the rapidly fading horror
will soon vanish entirely as civilisation and Christianity
extend unto the dark pagan districts of the globe.

In the anthropological section of a literary congress
held at Lille, one of the subjects discussed at some length
was the practice of anthropophagy. M. Broca thereat
made some remarks on the different nature of the flesh
of various nations. He said that the cannibals, perhaps
fortunately for us, do not like the flesh of whites; they
find it bitter and salt, whilst, notwithstanding the latter
quality, it does not keep well. Their special dainty is
the flesh of the negro, of which they like the flavour,

---

* In my former work on "Curiosities of Food," I was taken to
task by some critics for having overlooked or not alluded to the
practice of Cannibalism. The subject is a revolting one to deal
with, and I should have preferred to pass it over without notice,
but that it has been brought prominently before the public this
year by one or two uncontrovertible instances where necessity
has compelled persons to feed on the bodies of their fellow men.

and which becomes dry by keeping rather than decomposes by the natural process.

Locke, in his Essay on Government (sec. 57), quotes the following paper from Garcilasso de Vegas' " History of the Incas of Peru":—" In some provinces they were so liquorish after man's flesh that they would not have the patience to stay till the breath was out of the body, but would suck the blood as it ran from the wounds of the dying man ; they had public shambles of man's flesh, and their madness herein was to that degree, that they spared not their own children which they had begot on strangers taken in war, for they made their captives their mistresses, and choicely nourished the children they had by them till about thirteen years old ; they butchered and eat them, and they served their mothers after the same fashion when they grew past child-bearing and ceased to bring them any more children."

Gibbon, in the twenty-third chapter of his history, states that " a valiant tribe of Caledonia, the Attacotti, the enemies and afterwards the soldiers of Valentinian, are accused by an eye-witness (Jerom., vol. ii., p. 75) of delighting in the taste of human flesh. When they hunted the woods for prey, it is said that they attacked the shepherd rather than his flock, and that they curiously selected the most delicate and brawny parts, both of males and females *(pastorum nates et feminarum papillas)*, which they prepared for their horrid repasts."

Strabo (IV., v., sect. 35) says that the inhabitants of Jerne are more savage than those of Britain, and deem it honorable to devour their deceased fathers.

In reference to the last passage, Aubrey, in his " Remains of Gentilism," mentions *a holy maul* preserved in Wiltshire to his day, and previously used for braining the incurably sick and old.

According to Herodotus, the Massagetæ (i., 216) and the Padai (iii., 99) ate their relations.

There is, therefore, credible evidence that cannibalism existed in Europe, Asia and America. It might, therefore, be reasonably expected to be found in Africa. Thus

Schweinfurth states that cannibalism is practised to some degree among the Niam-niam, and to a still greater extent among the Monbouttons between the 3rd and 4th degrees of N. lat.

Cannibalism has existed almost universally among races living in a savage state, sometimes as a means of subsistence, as among the Monbouttons and some other African tribes, where shambles for human flesh are openly kept; sometimes with the idea of appropriating to themselves the qualities of the deceased.*

Wallace states the Cobeus of South America are cannibals.

In a history of French Guiana, published by M. Mousie, an account is given of acts of cannibalism committed by a band of escaped convicts in January, 1856, who murdered and ate two of their comrades on the River Lacomte. One, who escaped and reached the fortress, informed upon the criminals, who were pursued. Of the band of fourteen, two had been eaten and two had disappeared. Three of the principal culprits were hanged, and their accomplices were condemned to various punishments. When they were recaptured, the band were in the midst of their hideous feast, having broiled the tongue, the liver, the legs, and flesh of one of the slain.

It is not necessary here to enumerate the instances of those who, from shipwreck and starvation, have been driven to feed on their fellow creatures. Of this we have a lamentable instance in the details which have leaked out in America of the survivors of the Greeley Expedition. Although attempts have been made to throw doubts on the statements, the facts and evidence of the exhumed bodies of the dead corroborate the sad story.

It is unfortunately true that shipwrecked mariners and men in long sieges have been driven to an extremity which even the once cannibal Maoris did not reach, and

---

* Topinard's "Anthropology."

have supported life on the bodies of their own dead. The famous wreck from which Byron drew his passage about "two boobies and a noddy" is a case in point; the survivors of the yacht Mignonette, killing and eating the boy Parker in 1884 is another; and the horrors of the siege of Jerusalem naturally recur to the imagination.

Where the ghastly habit has survived into nascent civilisation, it has been through some connection with religion, as in Mexico, or (as in a recent case in the Soudan) with the purpose of sating revenge, or for some magical reason, that the eaters may acquire the strength and wisdom of the victim. In such cases, allowing for the wildness of the people who retain the practice, we feel much less horror than in face of the naked fact of cannibalism practised by civilised men for the sake of dear life. I merely here cite cases where the practice is indulged in for no such necessity.

A benevolent whaling captain, who undertook to do something towards civilising Easter Island in the Pacific, took a young man home with him, and gave him an education and the habits of civilised life, and returned him to the island. No sooner did he set foot on shore than his affectionate friends, finding him fat and in good condition, took him to a convenient place, butchered, cooked, and ate him in the shortest possible time.

Dr. Dunmore Lang, in his interesting account of the aborigines of Australia, mentions the following curious fact:—"The dead body of an enemy slain in battle is never eaten by his enemies, but by his own tribe and friends." In another part of his work, he says:—"The fights of the aborigines are frequent, and occasionally bloody; and on such occasions the dead of both parties of the combatants are carried off, skinned, roasted, and eaten by *their respective friends!* Davies had seen as many as ten or twelve dead brought off by one of the parties engaged, after one of their fights, all of which were skinned, roasted, and eaten by the survivors. There were so many assembled on such occasions, that the bodies of the dead were cut up and eaten in a

twinkling, there being scarcely a morsel for each."
This description of the Rev. Dr. Lang will remind the
classical reader of Juvenal's picture of the abominations
of the ancient Egyptians :—

> "—— Ast illum in plurima sectum
> Frusta ac particulas, ut multis mortuus unus
> Sufficeret, totum corrosis ossibus edit
> Victrix turba.
> . . . . Ultimus autem
> Qui stetit absumpto jam toto corpore, ductis
> Per terram digitis, aliquid de sanguine gustat."

Oceania had always been the land of cannibalism
until civilisation shed its humanizing influence. All the
Polynesians from the Sandwich Isles and the Marquesas
to New Zealand, have been more or less given to anthropophagy.

New Guinea, the Fijis, the Louisiades, certain parts
of the Phillipine group, notwithstanding the vicinity
of the Spanish colonists, killed men to eat them. The
Kanatis of the French colony of Nouka Keva with
difficulty renounced the practice.

"Why do you eat your enemies?" demanded M. Gar-
nier, an engineer, of one of these men. "Because," he replied, "they are good eating, as excellent as pork or veal."
A little deformed infant having been born, was washed in
the sea and cooked with the yams, and eaten by, among
others, the mother.

Cannibalism is altogether unknown in the Banks
Islands, but is more or less practised nearly everywhere
else in Melanesia.

The Tongans are not cannibals. Some of the Tongan
warriors who visited Fiji and fought in the wars there,
became man-eaters, but they were looked upon with
horror by their countrymen. This statement finds con-
firmation in the fact that there are no cannibal words
in the Tongan language. The Fijian, on the contrary, is
full of them.*

---

* "Transactions of the Royal Society of Victoria," vol. xvi.
p. 134.

Captain Erskine in his "Journal of a Cruise among the Islands of the Western Pacific," says:—"Although direct and authoritative proof may be necessary to convince some humane sceptics of the existence of this abominable practice, a visitor to the Feejee Islands need at once feel all doubt dispelled, which he may have entertained upon the subject; as the necessary details of every-day life abound with examples, which, if not spoken of by the white residents without disgust, exhibit at least no surprise. So habitual has the sight of the dead body for food become, that the missionaries assert that the Feejeean language contains no word for a simple corpse, but the word used 'bakola' conveys the idea of eating the body, and a term which, when translated, we at first considered a jest, 'paka balava' or long pig, is employed in serious parlance, to express the difference between the human body and that of a hog, to which the epithet 'dina' or true, is in distinction applied.

"The supply of human flesh was formerly, in all parts of Feejee, and is still in the districts to which the influence of the missionaries has not extended, furnished from different sources, the luxury being in general denied to women and slaves, although they are supposed sometimes to satisfy their curiosity or inclination in secret. All enemies killed in battle are, as a matter of course, eaten by the victors, the bodies being previously presented to the spirit. This source of supply, to which it is now believed all the negro races of the Pacific have recourse, as well as to the bodies of shipwrecked persons, in whose disfavour a strange superstition seems to have existed, even in countries now civilised, is by no means sufficient for the Feejeean demand, whose customs require that on occasions of ceremony, when strangers of consequence are entertained, the magnificence of the chief shall be exhibited by a feast of human victims. The method of furnishing these, by kidnapping neighbours, generally females, has been shown on the occasion of the Butoni visit to Bau; and sometimes much diplomacy is exerted to calm the excited feelings of the tribe whose women have thus been carried off. The chief of the fishermen whose duty it is to procure the supply, is, when a remonstrance is made, subjected to a public reproof, until he apparently conciliates, after a feigned disgrace, by an apology and present of whales' teeth, the favour of the reigning chief, whose object of entertaining his visitors properly is thus gained without the sacrifice of his popularity with his neighbours. It has been even asserted, that the Feejeeans do not object to banquet on the flesh of their dearest friends, and also that, in times of scarcity, families will make an exchange of children for this horrid purpose. This assertion I have heard contradicted, but it admits of no denial that children have been offered by the people of their own tribe to propitiate a powerful chief, and more than one white man has seen the canoe of Tanoa, after a condescending visit to Ovula, returning to Bau with the bodies of infants, offerings from the people of Levuka, ostentatiously hanging at the yard-arms."

Dr. Harvey, in a letter to Mr. N. B. Ward, says that "a large number of the inhabitants of the Feejee Islands are savages of the worst character. They are cannibals to a fearful extent; habitually feeding on human flesh, not from revenge or from necessity, but because they prefer it to other food. They eat their enemies or prisoners when they can; but if unsuccessful in catching these, their lawful prey, they will cook their own wives or children.

"Not long ago, a case occurred at Feejee, when a wretch ordered his wife to heat the oven, and when she had heated it, she asked him, 'Where is the food?' 'You are the food!' was the savage reply, as he instantly clubbed her, and then cooked her for himself and party!

"The captain of our vessel tells me that when he was in Feejee, in 1847, he saw a hundred human bodies laid out at one time ready for cooking at a great feast. Sometimes they cook a man whole (which they call a "long pig"), then put him in a sitting posture, with a fan in his hand, and ornamented as if alive, and thus they carry him in state, as a grand head-dish for a feast.

Others chew little bits of raw human flesh (as sailors chew tobacco), and put them into their children's mouths."

The natives of the Marquesas Islands are in the habit of wooing the fairest damsels they can find, wedding them and then eating them up. In New Caledonia cannibalism still prevails. The inhabitants of Formosa were accused by the Chinese of being cannibals.

Cannibalism was the universal practice of the races in the Pacific Islands. Cook had been specially instructed to institute inquiries on this point. There were many persons at home who were sceptical on the existence of cannibalism among any people. The result of his daily observations was to leave no doubt of its existence, and to establish the fact that it was not merely an occasional excess to which those who practised it were impelled by fury and the spirit of revenge against an enemy, but that human flesh was their almost daily and habitual food. A provision basket was seldom seen without having in it a human head, or other evidence of the fact. It is true that they told him that they ate only their enemies; but so incessant were their invasions of each other, that enemies were never wanting, or if the supply failed, slaves taken in former raids were substitutes at hand, and constantly killed in cold blood for the purpose.

The native religion of the blacks of Hayti, called "Vandouism," has its stated feasts, at some of which human victims must be sacrificed. These great feasts are held at midnight, in the depths of primeval forests, and all intrusion is carefully guarded against.

The eating of human flesh, it has been suggested, is of religious origin, though it is not always confined to religious occasions. The taste for such food is said to be easily acquired among certain people of peculiar temperament. It is not always renounced on professing Christianity, and the absolving Minister knows well what is meant when the convert discloses at the confessional that he has eaten a black pig without hair.*

---

* Major R. Stuart, " Embassy Reports for 1877," part ii., p. 110.

The mountains of the interior of the island of Celebes were inhabited, according to Crawfurd, by savages, who, like the wild races of Borneo, were professed head-hunters, and some of them alleged to be cannibals.

The Bataks, natives of part of Sumatra, he also tells us, undoubtedly practised cannibalism. The victims were enemies, criminals, and now and then a slave. The skulls were preserved as trophies, or sold at a handsome price to the friends of the victimised. Mr. Anderson, who visited there in 1822, writes :—" I am fully justified, not only from what I saw, and the proofs in my possession, but from the concurring testimony of the most respectable and intelligent natives whom I met, in asserting that cannibalism prevails, even to a greater extent on the east side of Sumatra, than, according to the accounts received, it does on the west. For the sake of humanity, however, be it mentioned that it is rapidly decreasing as civilisation and commerce are advancing. It is not for the sake of food that the natives devour human flesh, but to gratify their malignant demon-like feelings of animosity against their enemies."

More recent Dutch writers, in like manner, testify to the cannibalism of the Bataks, stating at the same time, that those subjected to the Dutch authority are readily dissuaded from it. The cannibalism of these people seems early to have been known to the Portuguese, for De Barros, speaking of the natives of the interior of Sumatra says :—" This was the race called Bataks, who eat human flesh, the most fierce and warlike people of all the land." (Decade 3, Book V.)

The Bataks inflicted the penalty of being eaten alive on criminals who infringed their laws. Sir Stamford Raffles, who was a spectator at one of these executions in the commencement of the century, states that the victim, who was one convicted of adultery, was lashed to a post, and the executioner, who was one of the principal chiefs, demanded of the husband what part of the crimi-nal he wished to eat. The ear being selected, it was cut off with a stroke of the sword and handed to him, and after dipping it in a sauce which had been prepared, he ate it before the assembled multitude. Then the various assistants cut and ate from the criminal such parts of the body as they considered the most appetising. Out of respect to the foreigner present the death was hastened by piercing the heart. Formerly their aged and infirm parents were slaughtered and eaten by these people.

The population of parts of the interior of Malacca are said still to be cannibals.

Some of the more savage tribes, both on the east and west coast of Africa, have from time to time acquired the ill renown of cannibalism—whether with justice or not is still matter of dispute ; but at least it cannot be denied that the charge is of very ancient date, and has often been repeated. It must have been a current belief in Shakespeare's time, for he notes among the wonders told by Othello to Desdemona, in running through the story of his life, " the cannibals that each other eat, the anthropophagi and men whose heads do grow beneath their shoulders." These must refer to Africa, as their birthplace. The only place in the Old World in which an African Prince could be supposed to meet with such adventures was his own, his native land.*

The old accounts of Arab navigators are full of deplorable statements of the negro men-eaters, who inhabited the coasts from Babel Mandeb to Sofala.

Sir Samuel Baker relates a scene of which he was witness :—" One of the female slaves having endeavoured to escape, her owner fired at her, and she fell wounded. She was very fat, and from her wound there dropped a quantity of yellow fat. The Makkaukas no sooner saw this than they tore out handfuls of this fat, and disputed for this horrible prey. They then despatched the woman with lances, and cut up and divided the body among them for eating. The other female slaves and children, horrified, fled and hid themselves among the

---

* " Food Journal," vol. ii., p. 232.

trees, where they were pursued, and many of the children were killed and eaten, and a horrible feast ensued.

Bruce relates that in his time there was still alive a man of the name of Matthews, who was present at a banquet of human flesh on the west coast of Africa, to the north of Senegal. Snelgrave fixes the stigma on the kingdom of Dahomey, and says that although he did not actually see it, his not doing so was solely due to his having been so thoroughly sickened by the previous atrocities of the horrible customs of which the banquet was to be the appropriate wind-up, that he could stand it no longer, and was glad to escape from the dreadful scene.

Norris corroborates him, but still not from personal observation, and Stedman, in his narrative of Surinam, quotes with an almost suspicious profusion of circumstantial details, the reports of the Africans :—

" I should not forget," he observes, " to mention that the Gango negroes are supposed to be anthropophagi or cannibals, like the Caribbee Indians, instigated by habitual and implacable revenge. Among the rebels of this tribe, after the taking of Boucou, some pots were found on the fire with human flesh, which one of the officers had the curiosity to taste, and declared it not inferior to some kinds of beef or pork. I have since been assured by a Mr. Vangills, an American, that having travelled for a great number of miles inland in Africa, he at length came to a place where human legs, arms, and thighs hung upon wooden shambles, and were exposed for sale like butchers' meat in Leadenhall Market."

Cameron, in his work " Across Africa," speaking of the inhabitants of the district of Manyuema, states that they are filthy cannibals.

" Not only do they eat the bodies of enemies killed in battle, but also of people who die of disease. They prepare the corpses by leaving them in running water until they are nearly putrid, and then devour them without any further cooking. They also eat all sorts of carrion, and their odour is very foul and revolting. I was entertained with a song setting forth the delights of cannibalism, in which the flesh of men was said to be good, but that of women was bad, and only to be eaten in time of scarcity; nevertheless, it was not to be despised when man meat was unobtainable."

Du Chaillu asserts the following with a precision of detail derived only from personal observation and inquiry :—

" The next morning we moved off for the Fan village, and now I had the opportunity to satisfy myself on a matter on which I had cherished some doubt before, viz., the cannibal practices of these people. I was satisfied but too soon. As we entered the town I perceived some bloody remains which looked to me to be human, but I passed on still incredulous. Presently we passed a woman who solved all doubt. She bore with her a piece of the thigh of a human body, just as we should go to market and carry thence a roast or steak. . . I was told by one of them afterwards that they had been busy dividing the body of a dead man, and that there was not enough for all. The head, I am told, is a royalty, being saved for the king."

Again : " Eating the bodies of persons who have died of sickness is a form of cannibalism of which I had never heard among my people, so that I determined to inquire if it were indeed a general custom among the Fans, or merely an exceptional freak. They spoke without embarrassment about the whole matter, and I was informed that they constantly buy the dead of the Osheba tribe, who in return buy theirs. They also buy the dead of other families in their own tribes, and besides this, get the bodies of a great many slaves from the Mbichos and Mboudemos, for which they readily give ivory at the rate of a small tusk for a body."

Other recent travellers confirm the statement, and Mr. W. C. Thomson, formerly, and for many years one of the United Presbyterian missionaries at Old Calabar, now settled and practising as a physician in Liverpool, leans to the belief that it is true. He says, in a letter addressed to my friend, the late Mr. Andrew Murray :—

"All flesh—human flesh, and that of the leopard or panther and the common vulture excepted—is edible in Calabar ; indeed, some of the imported slaves, and above all those who come from the Eboe country, do not except even flesh of their human kind, and boast of the sweetness of the human hand, and have been known to have their flesh-pots extra busy and extra well filled when the bodies of decapitated criminals have become accessible to them."

We all know how like in personal appearance the paws of a bear are to the hands of a man, and the paws of the bear, like the pettitoes of a pig, are esteemed the greatest delicacy of that animal, both in Europe and in North America.

Human flesh, therefore, I think must be reckoned an occasional article of food among the more savage tribes of Western and Central Africa, when accidental circumstances give them a supply, and when they have an excuse for eating it—such as tradition, custom, enmity, or hunger.

A paper in the "Journal of the Ethnographical Society" for 1869 testifies to the recent existence of communities of cave-dwelling cannibals in the territory of the Basutos, close to the frontiers of the Cape Colony.

Mr. Layland, the writer, after describing a cavern near to the mission station of Cana, the floor of which was strewn with human bones piled together and scattered about at random in the cavern, adds :—

"Skulls especially were very numerous, and consisted chiefly of those of children and young persons. These remains told too true a tale of the purpose for which they had been used, for they were hacked and cut to pieces with what appeared to have been blunt axes or sharpened stones. The marrow-bones were split into small pieces, the rounded points alone being left unbroken. Only a very few of the bones were charred, showing that the prevailing taste had been for boiled rather than roast meat. These people inhabited a fine agricultural country, which, moreover, abounded with game, yet they were not contented with hunting and feeding upon their enemies, but preyed much upon each other, many of their wives and children falling victims to the practice in times of scarcity."

They are reported to have abandoned the practice for a good many years, but Mr. Layland observed remains in which the marrow and fatty substances testified to a recent origin. He adds that thirty years ago the whole country from the Moluta to the Caledon River was inhabited by cannibals.

CHAPTER III.

FLESH FOOD FROM MAMMALS.

Flesh of Monkeys Eaten in Africa, the West Indies, South
America, Ceylon, and Borneo—The Lemurs in Madagascar
—Bats Eaten in the East and in Australia—Insectivora—
The Hedgehog—Carnivorous Plantigrades—Bears—Skunk—
Badger—Sea Otter—Civet Cat—Dogs' Flesh Eaten by North
American Indians, Chinese, Africans, and other People —
Foxes and Wolves Eaten—Lion's Flesh—Jaguar—Hyæna—
Lynx — Carnivorous Marsupials—Opossums — Bandicoots—
Kangaroos—Wombats—Phalangers—Marmots— Squirrels—
Rats—Rat Pie—Dormouse—Hares and Rabbits—Prodigious
Increase of Rabbits in Australasia—Flesh of the Beaver—
Porcupines—Agouti—Sloth—Anteater—Armadilloes.

I NOW proceed to notice some of the mammals whose
flesh occasionally serves as the food of man.

Monkeys.—The flesh of monkeys is more extensively
eaten as food than is generally supposed. African epicures esteem as one of their greatest delicacies, a tender
young monkey, highly seasoned and spiced, baked in a
jar or pan set in the earth, with a fire made over it,
gipsy fashion. Governor Connor, in one of his reports
to the Colonial Office, mentions that they are eaten on
the Gold Coast.

Young gorillas, it is said, are eaten when they can be
got, and their flesh, with that of the chimpanzee and
other monkeys, forms a prominent place in the African
bill of fare.*

Dr. Livingstone, in his last Journal, says, " The flesh "
(of the Soko, a species of Gorilla) "is yellow, and the
eagerness with which the Manynema devour it, leaves
the impression that eating sokos was the first stage by

* Cassell's " Natural History," vol. i., p. 9.

which they had arrived at being cannibals; they say the flesh is delicious."

But it is in Brazil, especially in the valley of the Amazon, that they are most eaten, for the animals found in the greatest numbers there are the monkeys.

Monkeys are said to be publicly sold in the markets of Rio Janeiro.

The barrigudo (*Lagothrix Humboldti*, Geoff.) is much persecuted by the Indians, on account of the excellence of its flesh as food. From information given to Mr. Bates he calculated that one troop of these Indians, numbering about 200, destroyed 1,200 monkeys a year for food.

Mr. Wallace tells us that having often heard how good monkey was, he had one cut up and fried for breakfast. He found the meat somewhat resembled rabbit, without any peculiar or unpleasant flavour. My friend, the late Sir Robert Schomburgk, told me that when travelling in the interior of Guiana he had often tasted the smaller kinds of monkeys, but could never bring himself to partake of the great spider monkey (*Ateles sp.*) and others eaten by the Indians, which approach so nearly to the human form.

It is a remarkable circumstance that among the South American Indians, monkeys are much more frequently used as food than among the inhabitants of the Old World, and on the Orinoco the broiled limbs of the marimonda (*Ateles Belzebub*, Geoffroy) was frequently seen by Humboldt in the huts of the natives; and at Emeralda he examined roasted and dried bodies in an Indian hut, which were prepared for an annual harvest *fête.*

Roasted monkeys, particularly those that have a round head, display a hideous resemblance to a child; the Europeans, therefore, who are obliged to feed on them, prefer separating the head and hands, and serve only the rest of the animal at their tables.

It is not at all improbable, from the close resemblance of a monkey, with the hair removed and ready to be cooked, to the human body, that with regard to some savage nations, accusations against them of cannibalism have been unjustly laid.

Dr. Vidal, speaking of the mammals of Japan eaten as food (Bulletin of the Society of Acclimatation, Paris, vol. 22, p. 436), says that the flesh of the monkey is publicly sold there. A large species he has seen exposed on the butchers' stalls of the markets, but he is not aware whether other kinds are eaten. Monkeys are, however, not very common there.

A French writer, speaking of monkeys as a dish, says, "They are excellent eating, and a '*soupe au singes*' will be found as good as any other, when you have conquered the aversion to the *bouillon* made of their heads, which look like those of little children."

In Ceylon some of the natives feed upon them. Several species of monkeys are relished as food by the aboriginal inhabitants of the Malayan Peninsula and the Dyaks of Borneo.

The Indians and some of the negroes of Trinidad, used to eat the flesh of the great red monkey, and reported it to be delicious, and yet it is the most vociferous and untameable of the Simian tribe.

Father Labat, in 1700, mentions the existence of monkeys in the West Indies. It was on this occasion, the good Father informs us, that he first ate monkey. "It is true," he says, "I was a good deal shocked when I saw four heads in the soup, very much resembling infants' heads, but when I tasted of the dish I had no difficulty in overcoming my scruples, and continued to eat with pleasure; for," he adds, "C'est une chair tendre, délicate, blanche, pleine d'un bon suc, et qui est également bonne à quelque sort de sauce qu'on la mette."

The worthy Father feelingly dwells upon the admirable qualities of young monkey in the form of soup or otherwise. The people of St. Christopher and Nevis might benefit by the experience and example of good Father Labat. Why not try young monkey as an article of diet generally? The planters would thus receive some compensation for the destruction of their canes and provisions by this troublesome mammal.

The flesh of the red fronted lemur (*Lemur rufifrons*) of Madagascar, is said to be as good as that of the hare, and the flesh of a large bat in the same island is very delicate eating.

Bats as Food.—We come next to the bats, the finger-winged animals, some of which are preferred to the finest game by the natives of the Eastern Archipelago, their flesh being compared to that of hare or partridge in flavour. The large flying lemur (*Galeopithecus volans*), though it diffuses a rank, disagreeable odour, is eaten. Yet bats must be palatable, since one species has been specially named by naturalists "the eatable" (*Pteropus edulis*). Its flesh is stated to be white, delicate and remarkably tender, and hence considered a dainty. The common Indian fruit bat, or flying fox (*Pteropus medius*) of Ceylon is eaten; but unless great care is taken in skinning them their flesh is said to acquire a musky and unpleasant odour, which is a matter of some importance, as the larger species constitute a favourite article of food in the countries which they inhabit. It is a great stretch of fancy, however, to imagine a frightful animal like a weasel, with extended leathery wings of about two feet each, being served up at table.

Dr. Leichardt found the fruit bat in Australia (*Pteropus Gouldii*) an excellent article of food. After it had fed upon the flowers of the so-called tea-tree it was unusually fat and delicate.

Dr. Oxley, speaking of the kalong (*Pteropus Javanicus*) says, "Their flesh is eaten by the natives, but no real fox smells, to my mind, so rank as they do. Methinks a rat would be palatable food compared with these."

The Mosaic prohibition of the bat as an article of food to the Jews, no doubt related to a species of *Cynonycteris*, which may have been commonly eaten in Egypt or in Syria.

Insectivora.—Turning from the Cheiroptera to the Insectivora, we find a few animals here applied as food for man. The mole is said to be eaten by some of those who trap them.

The Greeks devoured the flesh of the hedgehog (*Erinaceus Europœus*). When it has been well fed it is said to be sweet and well flavoured, and the flesh is eaten in many places on the Continent. It is during winter in his dormitory that the animal is fat and in good order. A gentleman who tried them stewed, says they reminded him a good deal of quail.

In the neighbourhood of Oxford I met an old gipsy woman, who, although squalid and dirty, was proud in being able to claim relationship with Black Jemmy, the king of the gipsies. She informed me that there were two ways of cooking a hedgehog, and seemed much surprised at my question whether her tribe ever eat them, as if there could exist a doubt on the subject. I expressed a wish to know the process, the receipt for which I subjoin in her own words :—" You cut the bristles off 'em with a sharp knife after you kills 'em fust, Sir ; then you sweals them," (Oxfordshire, burn them with straw like a bacon pig,) " and makes the rind brown, like a pig's swealings ; then you cuts 'em down the back, and spits 'em on a bit of stick pointed at both ends, and then you roasts 'em with a strong flare." It appears that hedgehogs are sometimes in season and sometimes out of season. My informant told me that they are nicest at Michaelmas time, when they have been eating the crabs which fall from the hedges. " Some," she added, " have yellow fat, and some white fat, and we calls 'em mutton and beef hedgehogs ; and very nice eating they be, Sir, when the fat is on 'em." The other way of cooking hedgehogs has gone out of fashion. The gipsy's grandmother used to cook them in the following manner, but it appears they are best roasted :—The exploded fashion is to temper up a bit of common clay, and then cover up the hedgehog, bristles and all, in it—like an apple in paste, when an apple dumpling is contemplated,— then hedgehog, clay and all, is to be placed in a hole in the ground and a fire lighted over it ; when the clay is found to be burning red, the hedgehog is done, and must be taken out of the hole; the clay-crust of the pie being opened, the hedgehog's bristles are found sticking to it, and the savoury dinner is ready.

The fashion of eating hedgehogs was not, in former days confined to gipsies. There was a farmer's family living at Long Compton, near Oxford, who were supplied with hedgehogs by our informant's grandmother; this family used also to breed them, keep and fatten several litters, "and," said the gipsy, "they used to eat up every litter they bred, dressing 'em just when they wanted 'em, like they did the fowls."

Sometimes a nest of young hedgehogs is found by the gipsies: if they are too small for eating, they are preserved till fit for use, or, as it is called in Oxfordshire, " flitted," that is, a string is tied to the hind leg, and the doomed animal is allowed to wander about the length of his tether, picking up what he can get; under this system, if well fed, he will fatten wonderfully.

Carnivora.—We next come to the animals of prey.

Bears.—Of the carnivorous Plantigrades, the flesh of our friend Bruin is occasionally devoured. The bear was eaten by the Romans, but it is clear that it was considered a rarity, and not relished by everybody. In the famous narrative which Petronius gives of the dinner at Trimalchio's, he represents a man who had dined at another house dropping in to dessert, and describing the feast enjoyed at the house he had just left. "We had," he said, "a joint of bear, which my wife Scintilla was rash enough to taste. On the other hand, I ate more than a pound of it, for it tasted like boar itself; and for my part, I say, that if bear eats man, man has a much greater right to eat bear."

The liver of the American bear is a peculiar luxury when dressed on skewers, kabob fashion, with alternate slices of fat. The liver, however, of the Polar bear is said to be unwholesome and dangerous.

Liver-sausage is regarded as an exquisite delicacy throughout Germany, and it would appear from a quaint

achievement recently effected in Berlin that its maximum
of toothsomeness can only be attained when the material
composing it is extracted from the carcass of a bear. At
an Exhibition of Culinary Art lately, at Hamburg, the
Berlin committee of restaurateurs, desiring to contribute
thereto an edible worthy of their gastronomic renown,
applied to Dr. Bodinus, the managing director of the
Zoological Gardens, for leave to purchase and slay one of
the Society's bears, in order to convert the ursine liver
into a sausage of paramount excellence. Having a bear
to spare, the learned doctor parted with one for the
moderate consideration of ten guineas, and the committee, twelve in number, proceeded to the doomed one's
den, where Herr Wiese, the proprietor of "Sommer's
Salon," shot Bruin through the head, and afterwards
narrowly escaped mutilation by venturing to stroke the
luckless beast's furry coat before it had quite given
up the ghost. The beast's liver was duly chopped up,
spiced, and manufactured into a gigantic sausage weighing twenty-five pounds ; and, his remains having been
artistically set up by a noted taxidermist, he was then
made to occupy an honourable and rampant position at
the chief entrance to the Hamburg Exhibition, support-
ing upon his fore-paws a silvern platter containing the
dainty comestible prepared from his own body.*

In Sweden the State pays for the destruction of a bear
nearly £3, for a wolf or a lynx half as much, and for a
glutton 12s. ; and this has greatly thinned them and
driven them off into the forests of Lapland and the
north. [See " Lloyd's Field Sports of North Europe."]

Bears are fast passing away both in Northern Europe
and America. Many hundreds used to be killed in the
winter in some of the American States. The mode of
serving up the bear as a first course was, to roast it
whole, entrails, skin, and all, as one would barbecue a
hog. Most of the planters preferred bears' flesh to all
other meat. Bears' paws were long reckoned a great

---

* *Daily Telegraph*, March 31, 1880.

delicacy in Germany, and after being salted and smoked were reserved for the tables of princes. The tongues and hams are still in repute when obtainable.

A species of black bear, of medium height, is common in the mountains of Japan, and is especially numerous in the island of Yeso. The flesh is much esteemed by the Japanese, who consider it an excellent game. But it is only in winter that it is chased, when the snow obliges it to descend into the valleys. It is during this season that it is found in the markets, and the price is high. The Europeans do not eat the flesh, except by way of curiosity.

The flesh of the Polar bear (*Ursus maritimus*) is eaten by the Esquimaux and the Danes in Greenland, and when young and cooked after the manner of beefsteak, is by no means to be despised, although rather insipid. Dr. Scoresby tells us that the muscular fat is well-flavoured and savory. "I once," he adds, "treated my surgeon to a dinner of bear's ham, and he did not know for above a month afterwards but that it was beef-steak." Some Russian sailors who wintered at Spitz-bergen found bears' flesh to be much more agreeable to the taste than the flesh of the reindeer. The Esquimaux prefer its flesh at all times to that of the seal.*

When care is taken not to soil the carcass with any of the strong-smelling fluid exuded by the animal, the meat of the skunk of America (*Mephites Americana*) is con-sidered by the natives to be excellent food.

The flesh of the American badger (*Meles Labradoris*) is said to be not inferior to that of the bear. That of the European species (*M. Taxus*) is reckoned a delicacy in Italy and France, and may be cured like hams and bacon. In China the flesh is a most common food, but in Europe, the hind quarters are the only parts eaten; the hams being considered by many superior in flavour to those of the hog.

In North America the flesh of the musk-rat (*Fiber zibethicus*, Cuv.), is occasionally eaten in winter, being out

---

* See Parry's "Fourth Voyage."

of season in summer, but it is insipid. With the Indians however, it forms a constant article of diet at their winter feasts. The animal is chiefly sought by the trappers for its fur, the carcass being mostly thrown away.

The flesh of the young sea otter (*Enhydra marina*) is reported to be very delicate food, not unlike lamb in flavour. I do not know that the flesh of the European land otter (*Lutra vulgaris*, Erkl.) is eaten, although many hundreds are killed yearly in Hanover and other States.

The Muskars, a low class of woodmen in India, eat the flesh of the Asiatic civet cat (*Viverra Zibetha*), and the Chinese the flesh of the wild cat of Formosa (*Felis viverrina*, Hodgson), although it has a strong civet odour.

Dogs' flesh as food.—Arriving at the canine animals of prey we find that among the ancient Greeks and Romans the dog was dished up at table, and, according to Pliny, roasted puppy dogs were considered excellent. Hippocrates was convinced that it was a light and wholesome food. They were served up at sumptuous feasts and at the festivals in honour of the consecration of the pontiffs. Dogs were regularly fed by the Romans for the table, and roast dog was one of the dishes most in vogue.*

Galen represents dog-meat as a highly desirable diet. M. E. Blaze, a French author, remarks :—" J'ai mangé plusieurs fois à l'armée du chien et du chat ; je préfère cette viande à celle du cheval."

Many of the North American tribes look upon an *entrée* of dog as the greatest possible *bonne bouche* they can set before a stranger. Sir Leopold McClintock relates that in the Sandwich Islands he had most profuse apologies offered to him because there was no puppy to be had for a feast to which he was invited. The Esquimaux, too, look upon a dish of young dog as a great treat ; and it is related that a Danish captain provided his friends with a feast of this kind, and when

---

* Martin's " History of the Dog."

they praised his mutton, sent for the skin of the beast and exhibited it to them!*

Many nations still consider the flesh of the dog excellent. In the Society Islands and parts of Africa, young puppies are considered a great delicacy.

In China the poorer classes eat the flesh of all dogs, but the rich only once or twice a year, under the idea that dog's flesh is a stimulant to the digestive functions.

"The dog mostly consumed by the Chinese is of a small size, and usually of a light brown colour, covered with a coat of soft, short hair, so thick as to look almost like wool. But the Chinese housewife refuses to cook dogs in the family pot, or in the domestic kitchen, and they are driven to the alternative of being boiled in the streets. On any morning, in certain open spaces at street corners, the execution of a certain number of unfortunate chow-chow dogs may be witnessed; after which, being skinned, they are forthwith placed in a suspended cauldron and the *disjecta membra* are then to be seen simmering, and inviting the passer-by to stop and dine, which they do, there and then." †

Captain Burton says the principal article of diet among the Warori is fattened dogs' flesh, of which the chiefs are inordinately fond. Schweinfurth states the flesh of the dog is not disdained by the Mittoo tribes inhabiting the territory within the 5° and 6° northern latitude. The Niam-niam also consider dogs dainty food. Lapdogs are fattened and used as food by the Western Balonda. The Somrais of Central Africa raise dogs, their flesh forming an article of food luxury.

Bosman, in his " Description of Guinea," says, " the negroes are great lovers of dogs' flesh, and they will willingly give a sheep for a good-sized dog. They prefer dogs' flesh for their eating to that of cattle, and accordingly esteem a meal of that the best treat they can take or give." The Africans of Zanzibar hold that a stew of

---

* Cassell's " Natural History " and Ellis's " Hawaii."
† Collingwood's " Rambles of a Naturalist."

puppies, as amongst us in the days of Charles II., is a dish fit for a monarch.

Humboldt tells us that, though the custom of eating the dog is disused on the banks of the Orinoco, it still exists in some parts of Guiana and Mexico.

In Australia the aborigines will even eat the wild dingo when hard pressed for food.

The Chinese, it is well known, have more curious habits and customs than any other people under the sun; fattening dogs for the purpose of human food is one of them, and in which a considerable trade is done. They are small, and fed on an exclusively vegetable diet. Mr. Cooper, who has been labouring to establish an overland route from China to India, says that one morning, as he was sitting down to breakfast at a "tea-shop" in Hung-zachien, in the country of the Upper Yang-tse-Kiang, he was informed that he was in luck, as the proprietor just then happened to have a dog-ham in cut, some slices of which he should have fried, a delicacy reserved only for mandarins like himself. At first he was on the point of ordering away the horrid dish, but, on second thoughts, he proceeded, with "stoical fortitude to taste doggie; one taste led to another," and, in summing up, he pronounced the dog-ham to be delicious in flavour, well-smoked, tender, and juicy. "It was small, not much bigger than the leg of a good-sized sucking-pig; the flesh was dark, and the hair had been carefully removed, while the paw had been left as a stamp of its genuineness, as the proprietor remarked. Dog-hams are justly considered a great delicacy in China, and as such bring a very high price, costing as much as five taels (1 tael = 6s. 6d.) per pound. They are chiefly cured in the province of Hoonan, where dogs of a peculiar breed are fattened for the purpose. Hoonan is also famous for its pigs, and possesses a large trade in bacon and ham, especially in pig-hams which have been cured in the same tubs with dog-hams, and are thereby considered to have acquired a finer flavour."

In Cochin-China also dogs and foxes are eaten.

Mr. Gray, in his work "Fourteen Months in Canton," thus speaks of cats and dogs as human food:—"The black cat is much more prized for food than any other of the feline race. We went upstairs leading to the saloon, where several small dining tables were placed. At one of these tables we saw a man with a little basin full of steaming stew. We went to him and said 'Meau?' (cat), and he answered 'Yau' (yes). It had a very dark appearance (warranted black cat, I should think), and had a most savoury smell. On the wall a bill of fare was placed, stating the cost of a repast of dog and cat. This is the correct rendering: 'One tael of black dog's flesh, 8 cash; one tael weight of black dog's fat, 3 kandereens of silver; one basin of black cat's flesh, 100 cash; one small basin of black cat's flesh, 50 cash; and one pair of black cat's eyes, 3 kandereens of silver.' These restaurants are crowded at the celebration of the Hachi, or festival of the summer solstice, by men of all ranks. To eat dog's flesh, especially black dog's flesh, on that day is to secure the eater against sickness for the summer."

The young dogs are brought to market in baskets made of bamboo, as also are young cats intended for the table. When delivered to the cook they are killed, scalded in boiling water, and the skin scraped with the blade of a knife to remove the hair, as is done with a pig.

When boiled, the flesh is cut up into small pieces that can be eaten with the chopsticks, each piece being dipped in soy and mixed with fish or rice. The young dogs and cats are highly esteemed as food dainties by the rich Chinese, while the poorer classes do not disdain the old animals. The Japanese eat dogs' flesh, but only exceptionally.

Never was the ancient adage, "there is no accounting for tastes," more quaintly illustrated than in a surprising story related in the London *Daily Telegraph* of March 20, 1880:—"One Peschka, an innkeeper of Neustadt, in Bohemia, was bitten some weeks ago by his own housedog. Unwilling to slay the animal on bare suspicion of

F

its sanity, he consigned it to the town grave-digger, enjoining that functionary to take care of it until further orders respecting its ultimate fate should be imparted to him. A few days later, however, Peschka was attacked by hydrophobia, of which horrible malady he died in excruciating agony. The sanitary authorities of Neustadt forthwith applied to the gravedigger for the mad dog committed to his custody, intending to have it destroyed. Their astonishment may be more readily conceived than described when the sexton, in answer to their requisition, calmly observed, 'The mad dog? I have eaten him!' 'You have eaten the mad dog?' incredulously exclaimed a horror-stricken sanitary official. 'Better that than he should eat me!' rejoined the philosophical grave-digger. It would appear not only that this man of strange appetites had swallowed and digested the rabid animal, but that it had agreed with him; for, as the story runs, he is still in the enjoyment of robust health, and pursues his professional avocations with unabated vigour."

In May, 1842, a butcher of Besançon was sentenced by the Tribunal of Correction to three months' imprisonment for selling *dog* instead of *kid* to his customers.

How the tastes of men differ! Forster, in his "Voyage Round the World," thus expresses himself: "In our cold countries, where animal food is so much used, and where to be carnivorous perhaps lies in the nature of man, or is indispensably necessary to the preservation of health and strength, it is strange that there should exist a Jewish aversion to dogs' flesh, when hogs, the most unclean of all animals, are eaten without scruple. Nature seems to have expressly intended them for this use by making their offspring so very numerous and their increase so quick and frequent."

Mr. Wilson, who quotes the above, adds: "There is no reason why it should not be more extensively practised in Europe. We know, for example, that Captain Cook's recovery from a serious illness at sea, if not entirely owing to, was at least greatly ameliorated by the broth and flesh of a dog." *

"Amongst the Society Islands," says Mr. Frederick Bennet, " the aboriginal dog, which was formerly eaten as a delicacy by the natives, is now extinct or merged into mongrel breeds by propagation with many exotic varieties. At the Sandwich group, where the inhabitants have been more remarkable for the use of this animal as food, and where that custom is yet pertinaciously retained, the pure breed of the Poe dog has been better protected, and although becoming yearly more scarce, examples of it are yet to be met with in all the islands, but principally as a delicacy for the use of the chiefs. As late as October, 1835, I noticed in the populous and well-civilised town of Honolulu, at Oahu, a skinned dog suspended at the door of a house of entertainment for natives, to denote what sumptuous fare might be obtained within." †

Anson, in his voyage round the world, speaking of Juan Fernandez, says: " These dogs, who are masters of all the accessible parts of the island, are of various kinds, some of them very large, and are multiplied to a prodigious degree. They sometimes came down to our habitations at night and stole our provisions, and once or twice they set upon single persons ; but assistance being at hand, they were driven off without doing any mischief. As at present it is rare for goats to fall in their way, we conceived that they lived principally on young seals ; and indeed some of our people had the curiosity to kill dogs sometimes and dress them, and it seemed to be agreed that they had a fishy taste."

Foxes as Food.—The flesh of the Arctic fox, particularly when young, is edible, whilst that of the red fox is ill-tasting, rank, and disagreeable, and eaten only through necessity. Sir John Franklin's party and other Arctic

* Wilson's "Essays on the Origin and Natural History of Domestic Animals."
† " Dogs, etc.," by Lieut.-Colonel C. Hamilton Smith, p. 211.

voyagers agreed with Hearne in comparing the flavour of a young Arctic fox to that of the American hare. Captain Lyon considered it to resemble the flesh of a kid. In Ross's voyage they were named lambs, from their resemblance in flavour to very young lamb.

"The flesh," observes Sir James Ross, "of the old fox is by no means so palatable, and the water it is boiled in becomes so acrid as to excoriate the mouth and tongue. During our late expedition they constituted one of the principal luxuries of our table, and were always reserved for holidays and great occasions. We ate them boiled, or more frequently parboiled, roasted in a pitch kettle."

Mr. Kennedy, in his "Voyage to the Arctic Regions," speaks of the delicacy of a fox pie, which was pronounced by competent authorities in his mess to be equal to rabbit, but then he honestly admits that there were others to whom it suggested uncomfortable reminiscences of dead cats, and who generally preferred the opposite side of the table when this dish made its appearance. Tastes, however, seem to differ, and much no doubt depends on the keenness of the appetite and the choice there may be at table.

At a dinner given after a grand wolf hunt at Genis (Dordogne) by M. Piston d'Aubonne, master of the wolf-hounds, a dish of cutlets was served from one of the animals killed, but they were found very tough and insipid.

At another sportsman's dinner in the department of Correze, fillets of fox flesh were cooked and declared to be excellent eating. They eat foxes in Italy, where they are sold dear, and thought fit for the table of a cardinal.

Passing now to the feline or cat-like animals of prey —the terrible wild hunters of the forests and deserts— we find many of these are in turn devoured by man.

Lions.—The flesh of the lion is eaten by the Hottentots; and a tribe of Arabs between Tunis and Algeria, according to Blumenbach, live almost entirely upon it when they can get it. After a lion has been killed and the skin removed the flesh is divided, and the mothers take each a small piece of the animal's heart and give it to their male children to eat, in order to render them strong and courageous.

It would seem from the Journal of the Marquis of Hastings, when Governor-General of India, that this superstition as to eating lion's flesh is as strong in India, for it is stated:—" Anxious interest was made with our servants for a bit of the flesh, though it should be but the size of a hazel-nut. Every native in the camp, male or female, who was fortunate enough to get a morsel, dressed it and ate it. They have a strong conviction that the eating of a piece of lion's flesh strengthens the constitution incalculably, and is a preservative against many particular distempers. The idea that a person imbibes the characteristics of an animal which he eats is very widely distributed. The Malays at Singapore used to give a large price for the flesh of the tiger, not because they liked it, but because they believed that the man who eats tiger's flesh will become as wise and powerful as that animal." The Dyaks of Borneo have a prejudice against the flesh of the deer, which the men may not eat, though it is allowed to the women and children. The reason given is that if the men were to eat venison they would become as timid as deer.

The Caribs will not eat the flesh of pigs or of tortoises, lest they should get small eyes. The Dacotahs of North America eat the liver of the dog that they may become as wise and brave as that animal.

The flesh of the lion has been eaten with gusto even by Europeans; for Madame Bedichon, in her work on "Algeria," states that at Oran a lion was killed which three days before had eaten a man, and the Préfet gave a grand dinner, the principal dish being part of the lion, which the French guests assembled ate with great relish.

More recently a magnificent quarter of a lion, shot in the neighbourhood of Philippeville, Algeria, by M. Constant Cheret, was sent to the Restaurant Magny, Paris, and served up to a party of nineteen guests, who enjoyed with gusto "Estouffade de leon à la meridionale," and "Cœur de leon à la Castellane."

The flesh of the American jaguar or panther is considered not bad eating, and that of the wild cat of Louisiana is also reported to be excellent. The former is eaten in Central and South America. Mr. Darwin, in his "Journal of a Naturalist," tells us that he supped on it, and found the meat very white and remarkably like veal in taste.

Mr. Wallace, when travelling up the Amazon, one day had some steaks of a jaguar (*Felis onca*) on his table, and found the meat very white and without any bad taste. "It appears evident to me," he adds, "that the common idea of the food of an animal determining the quality of its flesh is quite erroneous. Domestic poultry and pigs are the most unclean animals in their food, yet their flesh is highly esteemed, while field rats and squirrels, which eat only vegetable food, are in general disrepute."

Carnivorous fish are not less delicate eating than herbivorous ones, and there appears no reason why some carnivorous animals should not furnish wholesome and palatable food. The low Arabs do not object to the flesh of the hyæna, although the smell of the carcass is so rank and offensive that even dogs leave it with disgust.

The natives eat the flesh of the Canada lynx (*Felis Canadensis*, Geoffroy), which is white and tender but rather flavourless, much resembling that of the American hare. The European species (*F. lynx*) is also eaten in Switzerland and in Siberia.

Opossums and Bandicoots.—We have not quite done with the Carnivora, for the flesh of some of the carnivorous marsupials, such as the opossums, bandicoots and tiger cats, are eaten by man.

The vulpine or brushtailed opossum (*Phalangista vulpina*) is the staff of life to the natives of Australia. Mr. Gerardt Krafft says:—"I often admired my native friends, when, after a hard day's unsuccessful hunting, they dropped in at the camp empty-handed, how carefully they would examine the large flooded gum-trees fringing the river banks, how nimbly they would get a footing upon some hollow limb, and with what perseverance ' Possum' was dislodged and perhaps accidentally dropped into the river, whence it had to be rescued by the black fellow's better-half; for it was the question of ' to eat or not to eat.' "

The flesh of that most malodorous marsupial, the common opossum (*Didelphys Virginiana*) is eaten in some of the States of North America, and is said to be white and well tasted.

In Rio Grande do Sul and other provinces of Brazil, they bury it in the earth until the flesh is free from its characteristic offensive smell; before cooking, the axillary glands must first be extracted.

An American named Chancey has lately started a novel business at Hawkinsville, near Savannah, for raising opossums on a farm enclosed with wire fencing. As the average piney wood opossum finds a ready sale at about 2s., a fine fat stall-fed opossum will bring double that amount.

The flesh of the Australian bandicoot (*Perameles obesula*) is delicious, especially when done in the native style, that is, the hair removed and the game roasted upon the coals. The native tiger cat (*Dasyurus Geoffroyi*), the most bloodthirsty of the marsupial animals of Australia, is eaten by the natives.

Kangaroos.—The flesh of all the herbivorous marsupials is good. The forequarters indeed of the larger kangaroos are somewhat inferior, and are usually given to the dogs; but from the hinder quarters some fine steaks may be cut. These cooked in the same manner as venison collops, are, to most palates, very little inferior to the latter. The flesh of the large kangaroo, as well as that of the wallaby, is often dressed in the shape of a hash, and in this form also it is excellent. But the most admired part of the kangaroo is his tail. This is of enormous size in proportion to the rest of the body, the tail of a full-grown forester usually weighing ten or twelve pounds. It makes a superb soup, very much superior to ox-tail.

The wallaby, too, is most commonly used for soup.

The early settlers in the Australian colonies were more driven to eat kangaroo flesh than the present ones.

On the 21st April, 1806, we find the following entry in a book on Tasmania :—

"There being a necessity for making every possible saving of the salted meat remaining in His Majesty's stores, the commissary will receive kangaroo or emu at one shilling per pound, if brought to the stores on Mondays and Fridays, taking in only the hind quarters perfectly sweet, and issuing the same at the rate of two pounds of fresh for one of salted meat."

The forester is the largest of the kangaroo family, and is frequently found of two hundred pounds weight. The large male of the species is generally called the "old man kangaroo" by the colonists. The wallaby (*Halmaturus sp.*) and the pademelon (*H. thetidis*) are much smaller ; the average weight of the wallaby is about twelve or fourteen pounds, and that of the pademelon nine or ten pounds. The pademelon when cooked like a hare affords a dish with which the most fastidious gourmand might be satisfied.

The kangaroo rat (*Bettongia rufescens*) seldom weighs more than three or four pounds; it is not, as its name would import, anything of the rat species, but a perfect kangaroo in miniature. The flesh of the kangaroo rat resembles that of a rabbit, and it eats best when cooked in the same manner. This small animal is but little eaten, except by thorough bushmen, owing to the prejudice excited by the unfortunate name which has been bestowed upon it; but those who have once conquered this prejudice usually become fond of it, as the flesh is very palatable.

The flesh of the great red kangaroo (*Osphranter rufus*) is very palatable, indeed more so than that of *Macropus major*. That of the bridle nail-tailed kangaroo (*Onychogalea frœnata*) is white and well tasted.

The flesh of the hare kangaroo (*Lagorchestes leporoides*) is delicious ; in fact Mr. Kreft says it yields some of the best meat he ever tasted.

The wombat (*Phascolomys wombat*) is another Australian marsupial, which sometimes weighs 140 lbs. The flesh is said by some to be not unlike venison, while others compare it to lean mutton.

The flesh of the taguar or great flying phalanger (*Petaurista taguarioides*), a native of Australia, is said to be very good, and as the animal is a tolerably large one, it is a favourite article of diet among the white and black inhabitants of the country. It is, however, so extremely difficult of capture, that without the assistance of native aid, the white man would seldom be able to make a dinner on this creature.*

The oil which can be obtained from a fat woodchuck (*Arctomys monax*, Lin.) has some value, and when rightly killed the meat is relished by some as food ; the Indians consider the flesh of the hoary marmot (*A. pruinosus*, Pennant) as delicious food.

Considerable parties of Indians have been known to subsist for a time on the tawny marmot (*Arctomys Richardsonii*, Sabine) when the larger game is scarce ; their flesh is palatable when they are fat.

The flesh of the Hudson's Bay squirrel, or red chickaree (*Sciurus Hudsonius*, Pennant), is tender and edible, but that of the male has a strong murine flavour.

Among the squirrels which are eaten are the fox squirrel (*Sciurus cinereus*), the gray squirrel (*S. carolinensis*), the California gray squirrel (*S. fossor*), the tuft-eared squirrel (*S. aberti*), and the flying squirrel (*Sciuropterus volucella*). In the San Francisco market squirrels sell at 3s. to 4s. the dozen, and wild rabbits at 7s. to 8s. per dozen. The flesh of the squirrel is said to taste like that of the rabbit, but more juicy.

All the rodents are eaten by the natives of Australia,

---

* Routledge's "Natural History."

but only in case of no other food being at hand, as a large number of these little creatures are wanted to satisfy the hunger of a black fellow.

Rats.—Williams, in his Account of China, tells us that rats are very abundant, and furnish the common people with meat. Rats and mice, that shun the light of day, are not only eaten now by the Mongol races, but by other more civilised people. The Mongol fattens them like pigs, butchers them with care, and carries them on long white poles to market.

The wild cat is a very dainty dish among the West Indian negroes.*   The negroes in Brazil, like the aborigines in Australia, eat every rat they can catch.

It is a remarkable fact that there are no rats in the islands of the Pacific Ocean. Repeated attempts have been made to acclimatise the rodents there, as the flesh is much relished by the natives as an article of food, but the attempts thus far have failed, for they invariably die of consumption.

The mouse, to the Esquimaux epicure, is a real *bonne bouche,* and if he can catch half-a-dozen he runs a piece of horn or twig through them, in the same manner as the Leadenhall poulterers will larks; and, without stopping to skin or divest them of their entrails, broils them over the fire, and considers them a tit-bit.

I do not see why field rats should not be well tasted and wholesome meat, seeing that their food is entirely vegetable, and that they are clean, sleek, and plump.

The negroes on the West India plantations will often roast the cane-piece rats in the stoke-holes of the sugar-boiling houses, and those who have tasted them declare them to be very good eating.

So fat do the rats become in the West Indies, from feeding on the sugar canes, that most of the blacks esteem them highly, and, with the addition of chillies and other spiceries, make of them a delicate fricassee, not to be surpassed by a dish of frogs. As there is a rat-

---

* Brown's "History of Jamaica."

catcher on every estate, who is paid a reward of so much per dozen for the rats' tails he brings in, rats are very cheap. These rats' tails might perhaps be utilised, for a paragraph going the round of the papers tells us, that at a recent banquet at the Trois Frères, Paris, the novel feature of rats'-tail soup was introduced; but it did not come up to ox-tail by any means.

Everyone has heard of rats being eaten during the siege of Paris; but perhaps it is not known that in Belgium a society of rat-eaters has been formed.

After the siege of Paris, when rats' flesh was at a premium and the rodents were nearly exterminated in the crusade carried on against them, these animals once more increased prodigiously, until the great sewers which run beneath the streets of the city now swarm with them, and hence frequent battues have to be made with packs of terriers by the municipal authorities.

The Rev. J. G. Wood, a well-known naturalist, lecturing recently, spoke very favourably of rat pie.

" It is made," he says, "in precisely the same manner as rabbit pie, the only difference being that in the case of the rat pie the result is far more delicious. The cook should be careful to procure as fine rats as possible, cut off their tails, skin, dress, and wash them, then cut them into four pieces, and add a few morsels of pork fat. When cooked and cold the pie is full of the most delicious jelly." He had often, he added, been dining with his friends when they left the most delicious viands on the table untouched, while every scrap of the rat pie had been devoured.

Dr. Buller says a native rat formerly abounded to such an extent in the wooded parts of New Zealand, that it constituted the principal animal food of the Maori tribes of that period. The introduced Norway rat (*Mus decumanus*) has now exterminated and supplanted its predecessor.

The loir or dormouse (*Myoxus glis*, Lin., Desm.) was once in great request as a dainty for the table, numbers being cooped up and artificially fattened by the Romans. It is even now eaten in Italy.

Hares and Rabbits.—Of the rodents the hares and rabbits are, however, best known as food, and contribute very largely to the European meat supply.

In France about 70,000,000 of hares and rabbits are consumed annually, and in this country some estimates set the numbers down at 30,000,000. Those sold by the dealers form but a small proportion of what are eaten. A few years ago the average price of a hare was half-a-crown or three shillings; but it has now risen considerably, not owing to a decreased supply, but, as is the case in many other instances, to the increase of the number of persons who can afford to indulge in luxuries. It is a forbidden food to Jews and Mahomedans, and our British ancestors also refused to eat hares, from some religious objection to them.

The rabbit is very popular with the working classes, and in almost any form is good and acceptable food. The flesh in its general character more resembles that of a fowl than does the hare. Both wild rabbits and Ostend bred rabbits have advanced a third in price of late years.

Each case of Ostend rabbits contains, on an average, six dozen. They are sent from Antwerp, Flushing, and Calais, as well as Ostend, but are all sold as Ostend. About 200 tons come in weekly. About 2,000,000 rabbits were imported in the first five months of 1880 ; but this was far below the average of the previous years, the wet season of 1879 having killed large numbers of rabbits.

So rapidly have rabbits increased in the Australian colonies since their introduction, that the colonists find a difficulty in keeping them down, and they are slaughtered wholesale merely for their skins, their flesh being a drug. Some establishments have, however, set to work to preserve them in tins, and they are now shipped to England, stewed, boiled with onions, curried and fricasseed.

As an instance of how the work of rabbit extermination is going on in some of the up-country districts, the *Tuapeka Times,* of New Zealand, states that on one day

40,000 skins were brought to the railway station, there
to be despatched to Port Chalmers for shipment to the
London market. Those skins were brought from Strode
and Fraser's Earnscleuch Station, Clyde. These gentlemen employ eighteen poisoners on the station, while six
men with pack-horses (known as "packers") are engaged
in conducting traffic between the Home Station and the
rabbiters' camp in the ranges, carrying out poisoned
wheat and necessary supplies, and returning with the
rabbit skins. Two men and a clerk find full employment at the station in making up poisoned wheat, and
fixing up and despatching the bales. A waggoner is
engaged in conveying wheat to the Home Station, and
bales of skins from there to Lawrence. Some days previous he brought down 22,000 skins; on one day, as
we have said, he had 40,000, and at the station, when
he left it, there were other 40,000 in readiness to be
despatched to the railway; and still there are no symptoms of the traffic diminishing. Messrs. Strode and
Fraser supply the rabbiters with poisoned grain at the
rate of 8s. per 100 lbs., and purchase the rabbit skins at
2d. each. The men are earning from 20s. to 30s. a day,
and more men would be taken on, but cannot be had.
Some of the so-called "unemployed" were offered work,
but declined it, preferring their chance of loafing on the
industrious along the road. While these particulars
refer to Earnscleugh Station, it is only fair to mention
that the other runholders are pursuing similar measures
in concert, and by arrangement arrived at in public
meeting.

South Australia has gone in largely for preserving
rabbits for shipment to Europe. At Kapuna Factory
the rabbits are caught at night, disembowelled on the
ground, and then carried to the company's works. Here,
one after another in quick succession, heads (subsequently boiled down for jelly) and legs are removed, and
the skins pulled off in a twinkling. The bodies are
slightly salted (to remove the blood) and then washed.
Thirty men are employed by the company, and more lads

are required.   The tins are made by three or four men in the same room, each man turning out 300 or 400 tins a day.   These tins—the chopped up rabbits having been placed in them—are tied in a crate, and then lowered into a tank, where being hermetically sealed, they are boiled for eight hours by steam.   At the end of this period the tins are removed and the little hole at the top is reopened in order to permit the steam, which has accumulated during the process of cooking, to pass off. Before any air can enter, the hole is again soldered. The tins are then left to cool, and subsequently painted, branded, and boxed.   In 1877, 764 cases of these tins of preserved rabbits were received here from South Australia.

During 1881 8½ millions of rabbit skins were exported from New Zealand, valued at £84,744, and in 1883 we received from thence 12,361,224, valued at £119,461. From Victoria there were shipped in the same year 5,570,341 skins, valued at £67,271, but we have no information as to what quantity of the rabbits were consumed for food.   A premium of 3d. per skin is given by the Government.

Although rabbits are plentiful in the southern parts of Chili and on the islands of the coast, the Spaniards and Indians have as great a prejudice to their flesh as the Jews to pork; hence they are never eaten.   The negroes in the West Indies also dislike rabbits, while they will eat almost any other kind of animal food. The inhabitants of many islands in the Greek Archipelago live almost entirely on rabbits' flesh.

Beaver.—The flesh of the beaver is much prized by the Indian and Canadian voyageurs, especially when it is roasted in the skin, after the hair has been singed off.   In some districts it requires all the influence of the fur trader to restrain the hunters from sacrificing a considerable quantity of beaver furs every year, to secure the enjoyment of this luxury; Indians of note have generally one or two feasts in a season, wherein a roasted beaver is the prime dish.   The meat resembles pork in flavour, but the lean is dark-coloured, the fat oily, and it requires a strong stomach to sustain a full meal of it. The tail, which is considered a great luxury, consists of a gristly kind of fat, as rich, but not so nauseating, as the fat of the body.

Porcupines.—The Indians and hunters in the United States and about the Rocky Mountain ranges, eat the flesh of the Canadian porcupine (*Hystrix pilosus*, Catesby), but to a more refined taste it would be unpalatable.

The flesh of the common crested porcupine (*Hystrix cristata*), like that of most purely vegetable-feeding rodents, is considered very delicate food, and is often eaten at dinners in Rome, being sold at 5d. per pound, the porcupine being not uncommon in the Campagna. It is said there that they should be cooked like a hare, or with wine sauce, like a wild boar. Porcupines are common in Algeria and parts of the west coast of Africa, and their flesh is much liked. Porcupine and palaver sauce is an esteemed dish at Fernando Po.

The flesh of the young porcupine is very good eating and nutritious food. To be cooked properly it should be boiled first and roasted afterwards. This is necessary to soften the thick, gristly skin, which is the best part of the animal. The Dutch and the Hottentots in Southern Africa are very fond of it. The flesh is said to eat better when it has been hung in the smoke of a chimney a couple of days.

The flesh of the tree porcupines of South America (*Synetheres prehensilis* and *S. villosus*) is also said to be delicate and tender. If so it very much belies the odour which proceeds from the body.

There are two species of paca or agouti, the *Cœlogemys fulvus* and *C. subniger.* The flesh of the agouti is white, tender, and well-tasted, and when fat and well-dressed is by no means unpalatable food. Waterton, however, says its flesh is dry, with scarcely any fat. It has been sometimes termed the rabbit of South America. The flesh of the cavy, a smaller species, also resembles it. The paca or spotted cavy (*Cœlogemys paca*), is one of the best game animals of Brazil. Its flesh is said to be much esteemed, and forms a staple article of food in many parts of South America.

The flesh of the guinea pig is white and savoury. It used to be served up at table as a rarity in former times. That of the wild species (*Cavia caprera*), common in Central America, is very delicate.

The flesh of the biscacha (*Calomys bizcacha*), when cooked, is very white and good, but is seldom used, other animal food being so abundant in South America.

There are a few of the toothless animals (*Edentata*) which are laid under contribution for food. Wallace tells us he found the flesh of the sloth tender and palatable ; it is esteemed a great delicacy by the Indians, who hunt the animal for the purposes of food. The echidna, or native porcupine of Australia, which belongs to this order, is said to taste well.

The flesh of the great anteater (*Myrmecophaga jubata*) is esteemed a delicacy by the Indians and negroes in Brazil and Western Africa, and though black and of a strong musky flavour, is sometimes even met with at the tables of the Europeans. Feeding largely on the so-called ants' eggs, the flesh of the anteater of Australia is delicate meat, resembling that of a young sucking pig, and is considered superior to hare.

Most of the varieties of armadillo are used for food in South America. Waterton considered their flesh strong and rank, but throughout the whole of South America roast armadillo is highly esteemed, and may be seen in all the cafés and restaurants of the cities turned on their scaly backs feet uppermost, and the interior filled with a rich sauce composed of lemons and spices.

Peludos, or armadillos (*Dasypus sexcinctus*), are considered a very dainty dish by the natives and colonists when roasted in their skin, and served up in their shell or case. Mulitas (*D. hybridus*) are almost the same as peludos, and have such powerful claws, that if once they get their heads underground it is impossible to pull them out. The flesh of another species, the tatou

(*Dasypus villosus*), of the River Plate, is one of the most exquisite meats that can be eaten.

" Possessed of a most overpowering and unpleasant smell of musk, the taurec (*Centetes ecaudatus*) is not an animal which would be supposed to furnish an agreeable article of diet to any one, except to a starving man in the last extremity of hunger. Yet the natives of Madagascar esteem it among their rarest luxuries, and are so tenacious of this very powerful food, that they can hardly be induced to part with a specimen which they have captured, and which they have already dedicated in anticipation to the composition of some wonderful specimen of the cook's art."*

They hybernate from June to December, and as they are very fat when they first burrow, they are regarded as delicacies in Madagascar and Réunion, and pursued with great avidity.

---

* Routledge's " Natural History."

CHAPTER IV.

FLESH FOOD FROM MAMMALS.—*Continued.*

Pachyderms — Elephants — Hippopotami — Rhinoceros —Tapir—
Peccary—Swine — Immense Numbers in North America —
Our Large Imports of Bacon, Hams, etc., from the United
States—Wild Boars—Statistics of Swine in Various Countries
— Consumption of Pork in France — Horseflesh Eaten in
China, Europe, and America—Statistics of Horses—Increase
of Consumption of Horseflesh in Europe—Asses and Mules
also Eaten—Quagga and Zebra—The Ruminants—Statistics
of Horned Cattle over the World—Consumption in the United
Kingdom — Average Weights in Different Countries — Beef
Imported into England — Quantity Sold in the London
Markets—Average Prices — Buffaloes — Statistics of Sheep
in Various Countries—Large Imports of Carcases from New
Zealand — Imports of Sheep to the London Markets and
Comparative Prices—Average Weight of Different Kinds of
Sheep—Goats' Flesh—Flesh of the Camel Tribe—Alpaca—
Giraffe — Venison — Reindeer — Moose or Elk — Antelopes—
Eland—Bison—Marine Mammals—Whales—Seals—Sea Lion
—Sea Elephant—Walrus—Dugongs—Dolphins—Porpoises.

WE now have to treat of flesh food obtained from the
pachyderms, ruminants and amphibious mammals. We
will take first the thick-skinned quadrupeds.

The great pachyderms belong chiefly to the African
continent, although some are common to Asia. Among
them are the elephant, hippopotamus, and rhinoceros.

Elephants' flesh.—The flesh of this great animal, when it
cannot be eaten fresh, is in Africa, Asia and Ceylon either
simply sun-dried or salted and smoked. The whole of
the flesh is cut into thongs like the reins of a bridle,
which are hung in festoons on the branches of trees till
they become perfectly dry.

Gordon Cumming thus speaks of it :—" The flesh of
the elephant is cut into strips, varying from six to twenty

feet and about two inches in breadth and thickness. It is then placed on poles and allowed to dry in the sun for two or three days, after which it is packed into bundles, each man carrying off his share to his wife and family." He then speaks of the dainty dishes of baked elephant's feet and elephant's trunk.

The flesh of the elephant is relished by the inhabitants of many districts of Africa and Asia. Major Denham speaks of it as being esteemed by all, and even eaten in secret by the first people about the Sheik, and he adds that though it looked coarse, it was better flavoured than any beef he found in the country.

The ancient Romans considered the trunk as the most delicious part, but others fancy the foot to be the best. What are sheep's trotters and insipid boiled calves' feet compared to baked elephants' feet? Gordon Cumming thus describes the whole art and mystery of the process of preparing them :—

" The four feet are amputated at the fetlock joint, and the trunk, which at the base is about two feet in thickness, is cut into convenient lengths. Trunk and feet are then baked, preparatory to their removal to headquarters. The manner in which this is done is as follows :—A party, provided with sharp-pointed sticks, dig a hole in the ground for each foot and a portion of the trunk. These holes are about two feet deep and a yard in width; the excavated earth is embanked around the margin of the holes. This work being completed, they next collect an immense quantity of dry branches and trunks of trees, of which there is always a profusion scattered around, having been broken by the elephants in former years. These they pile above the holes to the height of eight or nine feet, and then set fire to the heap. When these strong fires have burnt down, and the whole of the wood is reduced to ashes, the holes and the surrounding earth are heated to a high degree. Ten or twelve men then stand round the pit and take out the ashes with a pole about sixteen feet in length, having a hook at the end. They relieve one another in quick succession, each man running in and raking the ashes for a few seconds, and then pitching the pole to his comrade, and retreating, since the heat is so intense that it is scarcely to be endured. When all the ashes are thus raked out beyond the surrounding bank of earth, each elephant's foot and portion of the trunk is lifted by two athletic men, standing side by side, who place it on their shoulders, and, approaching the pit together, they heave it into it. The long pole is now again resumed, and with it they shove in the heated bank of earth upon the foot, shoving and raking until it is completely buried in the earth. The hot embers, of which there is always a great supply, are then raked into a heap above the foot, and another bonfire is kindled over each, which is allowed to burn down and die a natural death; by which time the enormous foot or trunk will be found to be equally baked throughout its inmost parts. When the foot is supposed to be ready, it is taken out of the ground with pointed sticks, and is first well beaten, and then scraped with an assegai, whereby adhering particles of sand are got rid of. The outside is then pared off, and it is transfixed with a sharp stake for facility of carriage. The feet thus cooked are excellent, as is also the trunk, which very much resembles buffalo's tongue."

These certainly not "petit" toes when pickled in strong toddy, vinegar and cayenne pepper, are considered an Apician luxury in Ceylon.

Le Vaillant tells us that he found baked elephant's foot was food fit for a king. "I had often heard (he adds) the feet of bears boasted of, but I could not conceive how an animal so heavy and coarse as the elephant could produce so tender and delicate flesh. 'Never (said I to myself), never can our modern Luculli display upon their tables a dish like that which I now enjoy. In vain with their riches do they change and reverse the seasons; in vain do they boast of laying all Nature under contribution; their luxury has never yet attained to this gratification; bounds are prescribed to their sensuality.' And I devoured without bread my elephant's foot, while my

Hottentots seated near me regaled themselves with other parts, which they found no less excellent."

Opinions seem to differ on this head, for Captain A. Lindley, an African traveller, observes : " I cannot say much in favour of elephant's foot, though it is the *bonne bouche* of all Kaffirs. The Umzielas cooked it in an oven they made in the ground and then piled up fire on top. In flavour it was more like very soft leather and glue mixed together than anything else that I can compare it to."

Cuvier remarks that the trunk, being composed of a mixture of delicate muscular fibres and rich fat, would necessarily, when properly prepared, afford an article of food that might be very palatable. Pliny, in his " Natural History," having never perhaps tasted this viand, observes :—" Luxury has discovered even another recommendation in this animal, having found a particularly delicate flavour in the cartilaginous part of the trunk, for no other reason, in my belief, than because it fancies itself to be eating ivory." But ivory is absolutely frequently eaten now, for the ivory dust collected from the ivory turners is sold at about 6d. a pound and makes excellent jellies.

Hippopotami.—The ivory hunter on the bank of an African river having killed a hippopotamus for the supper of his negro attendants, leisurely watches their proceedings in preparing the feast, and observes that the entrails, without being cleansed, are carefully preserved as the choicest morsel, and subsequently cut up and distributed in shares to the party according to rank. When slightly roasted they are devoured with unmistakable signs of enjoyment. Being disposed, philosophically, to inquire into the nature of things, the hunter tries the taste of the extraordinary food, and leaves on record that the savages are certainly not without reason for their preference.

The flesh of the hippopotamus is much eaten by the natives of Africa, and even by Europeans it is not to be despised, although travellers seem to disagree as to its merits. Cumming says the flesh is excellent eating, and Baker appears to agree with him, while Dr. Livingstone speaks of it as being pretty good food when one is hungry and cannot get anything better, but that it is a coarse-grained meat, having a flavour something between pork and beef.

The flesh of the hippopotamus is well esteemed, and the meat, according to Du Chaillu, does not taste unlike beef. He considers it rather coarse-grained, and not fat, but a welcome and wholesome dish.

A fine young specimen which was exhibited in the Crystal Palace was roasted alive when the eastern wing of that palace was burned, in December, 1866. The hippopotamus was a black, leathery-looking, charred mass. Upon being more closely examined, it did not at all appear so distasteful a morsel as at a first glance. True, the skin was leathery and charred, but it had split in places, like cracknel, exposing a beautifully-delicate white meat or fat underneath. Dr. Crisp secured it, and he has given an account of his dissection of it in the "Proceedings of the Zoological Society, 1867," p. 601.

He there tells us that one side of the animal was well roasted, and that he supplied some of his friends with the meat thus cooked—gipsy fashion—and partook of it several times himself. He reports the flavour as excellent, and the colour of the flesh whiter than that of any veal he ever saw. The fat lay under the skin as in the hog, and not in the interior as in the elephant; it was about 1½ inches in thickness.

In South Africa hippopotamus meat is in request both among natives and colonists, and the epicures of Cape Town do not disdain to use their influence with the country farmers to obtain a preference in the matter of "sea cow's speck," (as the fat which lies immediately under the skin is called,) when salted and dried.

Dr. Schweinfurth says he always found hippopotamus bacon unfit for eating, and when cut into narrow strips and roasted it was as hard and tough as so much rope.

The same may be said of the tongue, which he often had smoked and salted. The meat is remarkably fibrous and is one continuous tissue of sinews.

Captain A. Lindley, in his work " After Ophir," says : " We dined off hippopotamus steak. It was not much relished, however, and we did not care to try it again ; but then the dark-coloured, coarse, and peculiarly flavoured flesh—a little more beef than fowl, and a little more fish than beef—though pretty tender and fairly succulent, could not be compared with the sweet wild-fowl and delicious venison we generally had at table."

The flesh of the rhinoceros is devoured in Abyssinia, and by some of the Dutch settlers in the Cape Colony it is held in high esteem. So is hippopotamus meat, as we have seen, which is eaten either roasted or boiled. The fat with which these animals are covered is considered delicious ; it is used in making puddings instead of butter. When salted it is greatly prized not only for the table, but for its reputed medicinal qualities. The Portuguese settlers on the east coast are permitted by their priests to eat the flesh of this animal in Lent, passing it off as *fish*, from its amphibious habits, and hence their consciences are at ease.

The flesh of the American tapir (*Tapirus Americanus*) although described by Europeans as unsavoury, coarse and dry, is considered palatable by the Indians. It somewhat resembles beef. The fatty protuberance on the nape of the neck is a delicacy which would do honour to the table of a modern Lucullus. The feet and groin cooked to a jelly are also morsels for a king. Most wild swine are, however, horribly rank, but by proper feeding they become delicious. A boar's head is, however, an appreciated delicacy of old reputation.

There are two species of peccary (*Dicoteles*) met with in South America. Both have on the back a fetid open gland, which must be cut out as soon as the animal is killed, for if allowed to remain the flesh would be uneatable. The peccaries are said by all those who have partaken of them to be excellent eating, and Sonnini frequently mentions his delicious repasts on them in the forest.

Swine.—The wild boar, the peccary, and other of the pig tribe are less common than the domestic hog, but the pig plays an extensive part in the culinary service of mankind in nearly all parts of the world; and a delicate sucking pig, a Bath chap, or a good rasher of bacon are tit bits not to be held in light esteem, common as they are with us.

There are nearly three million pigs in the United Kingdom, and about half of these are slaughtered annually. Ireland has nearly half the number—1,348,314.

Lord Brougham hoped to see the day when every man in the kingdom would read Bacon. To which Cobbett is said to have replied that it would be much better if his Lordship would use his influence that every man in the kingdom could eat bacon. The phrase of "going the whole hog" must certainly have originated in Chicago, for in that American city they slaughter annually four or five millions of pigs, and the inhabitants are therefore certainly the most hoggish community in the world. Pigs' ears, a dainty and gelatinous morsel, are at the pork-packing establishments in the United States preserved and canned.

American bacon is not so fat as good English or Irish bacon; it is better boiled than grilled or fried; when grilled it is apt to waste, and some of it also emits a peculiar flavour.

The pig may be considered quite a classical animal. The ancients sacrificed it to Ceres the goddess of harvests. In the island of Crete, the pig is considered sacred and honoured as such. It was highly esteemed in Rome, but not in a religious point of view, only for raising and fattening for food. Sensuality elevated it to such a point that the Emperors made a sumptuary law for it. The rich Romans cooked the animal in two very costly ways. The first consisted in serving the pig entire, cooked in such a way that one side was roasted and the other boiled, without the two modes being confounded. The second way was the Trojan, because it represented the wooden horse fraudulently introduced into Troy. The pig was gutted and cleaned, delicately cooked and stuffed with thrushes, beccaficoes, oysters, and a great quantity of birds or of rare and costly fish, soaked with exquisite wines.

Among the Gauls, pork was the principal article of food, and that most esteemed; of this many proofs may be cited.

The Salic law treated more at length of this than of any other animal, for there is an entire chapter devoted to laws against stealing pigs. The principal revenue of the Church consisted of the tithe of pigs. The dishes on which their flesh was served had a particular name, they were called baccon or bacconique, derived from baco, which signifies fat pork.

It was only permitted to eat pork in Egypt once a year, on the feast of the new moon, and the Egyptians vied with each other in sacrificing a great number to this planet.

The pig is not less honoured among modern nations; the taste of the Germans for fat pork has almost passed into a proverb. In Spain the sausage (chorigo) is a national meat. In France and in England it forms the base of public feasts. In Ireland the pig deserves even more public notice, for it is there the friend and the sustenance of the poor peasant; it shares with him his hut, and his potatoes, and its flesh affords the sole agreeable and strengthening animal food he can obtain.

The net weight of available flesh food in the pig is much higher than in the ruminants. The quantity will of course vary somewhat according to the breed. In well fed animals there will only be a total loss of 10 or 15 per cent. of offal not available for food, but then as the blood, intestines, liver and heart are eaten, this waste is reduced to about 6 or 7 per cent.

North America has more swine than any other country; nearly 44½ millions of pigs are officially recorded in the latest statistics of the United States. Russia stands second of all countries for its pigs, having about 12 millions. Pork raising is an important element in the agricultural wealth of the great transatlantic republic, and they ship annually for foreign consumption an enormous supply of pork products.

According to the Census returns of 1880, there was exported from the United States—

		Quantity.		Value.
Live hogs...		83,434	......	£84,000
Bacon and hams...	lbs.	759,773,109	......	10,200.000
Pork	,,	95,949,780	......	1,200,000
Lard	,,	374,979,286	......	5,600,000
				£17,084,000

rather a large figure for hog products.

The following are the official figures of the imports of foreign pork into the United Kingdom. We received from various countries in 1883 38,863 live pigs; and of—

				Quantity.		Value.
Bacon...	...	...	cwts.	3,080,162	......	£8,178,123
Hams ...	...	..	,,	602,025	......	1,823,352
Pork, salted ...	...	,,		328,768	......	635,280
,, fresh ...	...	,,		47,346	......	124,371
Lard ...	...	...	,,	852,150	......	2,243,956
				4,910,451		£13,005,082

Nearly all this came from the United States.

Now, judging from these imports (none of which are re-shipped, and adding our home production of pork, there are about 4,000,000 pigs in the United Kingdom), the flesh of swine enters more largely into the British food-supply than would be generally supposed.

More than 250,000 pigs are annually sold in the Paris markets, besides those killed annually for domestic use in the households, and some 500 tons of smoked flesh is disposed of at the annual ham-fair.

To give an idea of the importance of the elevation of swine in America, we have only to look at the figures of

the wholesale annual slaughter in the States, where pigs
are salted by millions.

Official data gave the following as the number of pigs
slaughtered in the different States in 1871, but the trade
has largely increased since then :—

Cincinnati and Ohio	626,305
Chicago and Illinois	1,425,079
St. Louis and Missouri	538,000
Milwaukie and Wisconsin	303,500
Louisville and Kentucky	302,240
Indianapolis and Indiana	196,317
Kansas City and Missouri	180,922
Total	3,572,699

At the Vienna Exhibition in 1873 many models of
special American slaughter-houses were shown, where
pigs are prepared for export in astonishing numbers.

The comparative number of hogs packed in

1860 were	2,350,882
1871 ,, ...	3,572,699
1880 ,, ...	6,950,451

Fifteen or sixteen years ago the swine in America
were nearly all of the white breed, now they are all
black. The Berkshire breed has been found to have
hardier skins, and are therefore less affected than the
white variety by exposure to sun and wind, mud and
frost, incident to their crude management in that
country.

Pork occupies the third place in nutritive value of the
animal food substances, ranking after beef and mutton.

All the world now-a-days knows that the nitrogenous
animal substances or meats are the most easy of digestion and the most nourishing, because they approximate
most closely to our nature, but occasionally there is a
necessity for special hydrogenous products, such as fat,
starch, etc., to assist respiration, and the development of
animal heat. For this object pork may be considered the
best of foods, because it contains both of these matters
—flesh and fat, while beef and veal contain more flesh

and less fat. The following comparative analysis shows the composition of pork compared with other flesh :—

	Beef.	Veal.	Pork.
Water	77·5 ...	79·7 ...	78·2
Fleshy fibre, vessels, nerves...	17·5 ...	15·0 ...	16·8
Albumine and red colouring matter	2·2 ...	3·2 ...	2·4
Non-coagulable matters soluble in water	1·3 ...	1·0 ...	0·8
Matters soluble in alcohol ...	1·5 ...	1·1 ...	1·7
Phosphate of lime	0·08 ...	0·1 ...	—

(Schlossberger, in Berzelius' " Annual Reports.")

Pork forms part of the food of the people in Greece, but it is chiefly consumed in winter, with the exception of sucking pigs, which are eaten in summer. In general, however, pork is not much eaten in Greece, but in the Ionian Islands and some of those of the Archipelago, smoked hams and sausages are eaten, and even exported.

In China the domestic pigs are believed to be derived from the stock of *Sus leucostymax*, Temm., of Japan. Pork is undoubtedly the favourite meat in China, and pigs are kept in great numbers.*

In the Austrian forests about 1,700 wild boars are killed yearly. Wild boars were formerly very common in Algeria. To the Arabs pork is forbidden meat. Numbers used, however, to be brought into the markets, and were sold to the French at 5s. or 6s. each. Although the Moors regard the boar as an unclean animal, many of them make no scruple of eating the flesh.

The proportion of foreign bacon and hams consumed per head in the United Kingdom is about 16 lbs. annually. The quantity of pork products imported into the United Kingdom have been as follows :—

	Pork, salted and fresh. cwts.		Bacon and Hams. cwts.		Lard. cwts.
1861...	...	136,416	......	515,953	324,691
1871...	...	296,144	......	1,093.838	477,568
1881...	...	381,526	......	4,627,484	854,322
1883...	...	376,899	......	3,695,992	853,541

* Collingwood's "Rambles of a Naturalist."

The aggregate value of these imports in 1883 was £13,045,213.

The average price of salt pork the last few years has been about £1 18s. per cwt.; of bacon, £2 13s.; of hams, £2 16s.; of lard, £3 10s.

The price of pork has not risen proportionately with other meat :—

					Large Hogs.		Small neat Porkers.
					s.	d.	s.	d.
1861	...	...	...	...	4	1	......	4	11¾
1871	...	...	...	...	3	10	......	4	8¼
1880	...	...	...	...	4	4	......	4	11¼

The number of pigs imported into London from abroad is about 20,000 annually.

The City of Rio Janeiro consumes about 18,000 pigs annually, besides bacon and salt pork, and 19,000 sheep, and 102,000 oxen.

It may be interesting to give the numbers of swine in various countries :—

AFRICA, &c.

Cape Colony	...	...	1875	......	132,373
Natal	...	...	1882	......	18,512
Mauritius ...	...	...	1875	......	30,318
Réunion	...	...	1874	......	71,490
					252,693

AMERICA AND THE WEST INDIES.

United States	...	...	1883	......	44,200,893
Dominion of Canada	...		1881	......	1,218,253
Newfoundland	...	...	1870	......	6,417
Uruguay	...	...	1874	......	12,000
Argentine Republic	...		1871	......	257,368
Falkland Islands ...	...		1875	......	6,000
French Guiana	...	...	1874	......	5,311
Jamaica	...	...	1870	......	9,086
Other British W.I. Islands		1874	......	20,000
Guadeloupe	...	...	1874	......	12,123
Martinique	...	...	1874	......	15,352
					45,762,803

EUROPE.

Russia	...	...	...	1877	10,839,093
Sweden	...	...	...	1882	430,648
Norway	...	...	...	1875	101,020
Denmark	...	...	...	1881	527,417
German Empire	...	...	...	1883	9,205,791
Holland	...	...	...	1882	403,618
Belgium	...	...	...	1880	646,379
France	...	...	...	1880	5,565,620
Portugal	...	...	...	1870	776,868
Spain	...	...	...	1865	4,264,817
Italy	...	...	...	1881	1,163,916
Austro-Hungary	...	...	...	1880	7,164,820
Switzerland		...	...	1866	304,428
Greece	...	...	...	1867	55,776
Roumania	...	...	...	1873	836,944
United Kingdom	...		...	1883	3,986,427
					46,273,582

INDIA, 1879.

Assam	...	...	...	...	...	293,677
Punjab	...	...	...	...	...	41,161
Central Provinces		...	...	...	...	93,681
Mysore	...	...	...	...	...	29,221
Coorg	...	...	...	...	...	10,551
Berar	...	...	...	...	...	2,726
Madras	...	...	...	...	...	232,174
						703,191

AUSTRALASIA, 1883.

New South Wales	...	...	...	...	154,815
Queensland	...	...	...	...	52,809
Victoria	...	...	...	...	237,917
South Australia	...	...	...	...	108,714
Western Australia	...	...	...	...	18,512
Tasmania	...	...	...	...	55,774
New Zealand	...	...	...	...	200,083
					828,624

In Tasmania and other Australian Colonies, there are
very fine breeds of pigs, and they are frequently fattened
up to 1,000 lbs. weight. Shepherds invariably keep pigs

and make a good addition to their wages, and their table thereby, as pork forms an agreeable change to continual mutton.

Pork is the meat most used in France, and, indeed, in most of the countries of Europe. Almost all the country people depend chiefly on pork. Some localities will not eat mutton, others do not like beef; but there is not a village or hamlet, not a cottage where pork is not the basis of the daily food. It is with pork that the soup is made, and with the fat that the vegetables are cooked.

The statistics give under 6,000,000 as the quantity of swine in France, but the number must be much larger than this, and may be fairly estimated at 8,000,000. Pigs are also imported, and much dead meat. There are about 12,000,000 heads of families in France, and there are very few that do not consume one pig a year. There are many that use three, four, or five annually.

In France the consumer of pork deems the lean part not so good as the fat. The Frenchman likes the firm and savoury fat of his prime Celtic pork, and not the oily, soft melting fat of the English breed. In many parts of France beef and mutton are beyond his means, and pork is his only meat; hence it is important that this should be of the best quality. The French peasant farmer prefers to sell his milk and his butter, and to supply his domestic wants with fat pork, or as it is termed, " lard."

Pig butchery in Paris is conducted upon a novel plan. The pigs are taken into a large round house, having a cupola in the roof to let off the smoke, the floor being divided into triangular dens. A dozen or so of pigs are driven into each den at a time, and a butcher passes along and strikes each one on the head with a mallet.

After being bled, the defunct porkers are carried to the side of the room and arranged methodically in a row. They are then covered with straw, which is set on fire, and the short bristles quickly burned off. After a thorough scorching the pigs are carried into the dressing-room, hung up on hooks, and scraped by means of a sort of drawing-knife, handled by a skilful operator, who performs his work at the rate of about one pig a minute. Then the bodies are washed, and the entrails taken out and cleaned.

Every part of the animal is utilised in Paris and much which the American throws away as worthless is made to subserve some use in the Frenchman's economy. The blood is employed in the manufacture of the large black sausages which meet with such extensive sale in Paris.

Roast pork, with its delicious crispy rind, is very generally relished. Pig once tasted could never hope for a reprieve from the butcher's knife. Though forbidden to the Jews by the Mosaic law, the Greeks ate him in the heroic ages, and before the advance of luxury had given birth to professional butchers the warriors of Homer killed their own pork as well as dressed and devoured it. With the advance of refinement came the butchers, who spared their patrons the disagreeable task of slaughter, and sold meat by the pound in the markets of Athens, weighed in the scale as now. The Romans were especially a pig-eating race, and retained their fondness for pork from the foundation to the decline of their empire. The Cretans abstained from it in order to offer it to Venus; the Egyptians fled from the sight of pigs as unclean beings whose presence defiled them. Neither the Phœnicians, the Indians, nor the Mahomedans would eat them. On the other hand, the Greek and Roman sages maintained that nature had created the pig for man's palate—that he is especially good to be eaten, and that there are many ways in which his flesh can be cooked —an opinion which seems to have been practically followed down to our own day. The Romans discovered fifty different flavours in pork, and under the hands of their skilful cooks swine's flesh was often transformed into delicate fish, ducks, turtle-doves, or capons. With them the Trojan hog, as we all know, was a favourite dish— it was a gastronomic imitation of the horse of Troy, its inside being stuffed with asafœtida and myriads of small game. The mode of its preparation is described by M Soyer, in his celebrated work.

The ancient mode of killing swine was as refined in barbarity as in epicurism. Plutarch tells us that the gravid sow was actually trampled to death to form a delicious mass fit for the gods. At other times pigs were slaughtered with red-hot spits, that the blood might not be lost.

The famous Hungarian pork sausage or "salami," as big as a man's arm, is very largely consumed throughout Austria. It is a great favourite with the poorer classes, who not only eat it at home, but take it to the beershops with them. Indeed, in the smaller suburban gardens it is the only solid food, besides bread and cheese, to be got, and is generally purveyed by a provision pedler, who carries Emmenthaler cheese and salami with him, together with an enormous pair of scales. A good deal of the salami comes from the Tyrol. With the prevalence of trichinous pork both in America and Europe, great care ought to be exercised in eating any products of swine not thoroughly cooked.

The number of "Wurst," or sausages, sold in Austria is bewildering to those who are unacquainted with the German love for this style of food: there are "Mett-Wurst," "Leber-Wurst" (liver sausages), "Blut-Wurst" (black puddings), "Hammel-Wurst" (mutton sausages), etc. In many country and farm-houses a "Rauchkammer," or smoking chamber, is frequently attached for the sole purpose of smoking sausages, but modern houses dispense with them, and modern science teaches the dubious substitute of brushing the sausages over with pyroligenous acid, so as to give the smoky flavour.

Many of the sausage-makers know that a small quantity of starch or ordinary flour boiled, absorbs a great quantity (about one-fifth) of the water, and forms a thick paste. They take advantage of this property to incorporate the paste in their sausages. To overcome the absence of colour in this fraudulent addition, they add fuchsine to the sausages. This food product, while con-

H

taining 27 per cent. of meat and 67 per cent. of a com-
bination of flour and water, has the appearance of a
perfect sausage. It is asserted by some that an addition
of flour is necessary, but this is not true. This addition
becomes unwholesome when the sausages are kept for
any time, for a fermentation is developed of the flour
and the water, and as the value of the sausage is largely
diminished, in Germany the sale of these adulterated
products is prohibited, when discovered.

Horseflesh.—We now come to speak of horseflesh, which
has of late years become largely utilised for the food of
man, instead of being given to the dogs. There is much
ancient testimony in favour of its use although repugnant to many minds. The nomad tribes of Northern
Asia make horseflesh their favourite food, though they
have numerous herds of oxen and flocks of sheep. The
flesh is eaten in China, and the leg and hoof are left on
by the butchers to indicate the animal.

Monseigneur Perny ("Bull. de la Société d'Acclimatation," 1884, p. 607,) tells us that in nine out of eighteen
provinces of China horseflesh is eaten by the poorer
classes, who let nothing go to waste, and its use seems
to be extending, as there are horse-butchers' shops in
all the principal towns.

Mungo Park mentions wild horses being eaten in
Africa. Dr. Duncan tells us, in "Cassell's Natural History," that "The horse was universally used for food by
man before the historic period, and would be used now
in Europe more generally than it is, were it not for an
edict of the Church in the eighth century. During the
Roman occupation of Britain, it formed a large portion
of the diet of the inhabitants. As Christianity prevailed
over the heathen worship, it was banished from the table.
It appears, however, that it was used in this country as
late as the year 787, after it had been prohibited in
Eastern Europe. The ecclesiastical rule, however, was
not always obeyed, for the monks of St. Gall, in Switzerland, not only ate horseflesh in the eleventh century, but
returned thanks for it in a metrical grace, which has

survived to our times on account of its elegance and beauty."

Mares' flesh is the choicest morsel, the daintiest bit, of the Chilian Indians, who do not eat cows' flesh except when pressed by necessity.

There is one fact connected with the use of horseflesh as an article of human diet, which, with other considerations, is likely to interfere with its general adoption. The Pampas Indians, who habitually live on mares' flesh, exhale a peculiarly disagreeable and even sickening odour. In the *saladeros* of Buenos Ayres and Montevideo, the Indian labourers are subject to the same nauseous emanations. At Buenos Ayres, when Rosas returned from his expedition against the Pampas Indians in 1835, bringing with him several young captives, these children, who were most hospitably received, severely tried the endurance of their protectors by the smell of the wild horse which emanated from their persons for several months. The Argentine General Mansilla, well known for his elegant and *distingué* manners, having on one occasion requested a young Corrientine lady to dance with him, was pertinaciously refused, and when he urged her to assign a reason for this affront she at last said to the General: "You smell like the Indians!" General Mansilla had that very day been making a repast of mare's flesh, not having been able to procure beef.

Sir John Richardson in his zoology of the northern parts of America, states that the Spokans, who inhabit the country lying between the forks of the Columbia, as well as other tribes of Indians, are fond of horseflesh as an article of food; and the residents of some of the Hudson's Bay Company's posts on that river were at one time under the necessity of making it their principal article of diet.

By way of curiosity we may give the number of horses in different countries, although but a very small proportion are consumed as food, especially in those countries where other domestic animals are plentiful:—

H 2

EUROPE.

Austro-Hungary ...	...	1880	......	3,282,790
Belgium	...	1880	......	271,974
France (with mules and asses)	...	1880	......	3,515,478
Germany	...	1883	......	3,522,316
Italy (with mules and asses)	...	1877	......	1,625,658
Russia in Europe	...	1877	......	17,589,188
Sweden and Norway	...	1882	......	621,519
Denmark	...	1881	......	347,561
Holland ...	...	1882	......	270,456
Spain and Portugal	...	1870	......	752,275
Turkey	...	1874	......	1,100,000
United Kingdom	...	1884	......	1,904,515

34,803,730

AMERICA.

United States ...	...	1883	......	11,169,683
Canada	...	1881	......	1,059,358
River Plate States	...	1876	......	5,600,000

17,829,041

AUSTRALASIA IN 1883

Victoria	...	...	...	...	286,779
New South Wales	...	...	...	...	328,026
Queensland ...	...	...	...	...	236,154
South Australia ...	...	...	...	...	164,360
Western Australia	...	...	...	...	32,884
Tasmania... ...	...	...	...	...	26,840
New Zealand ...	...	...	...	...	161,736

1,236,779

One of the most important revivals of late years is the use of horseflesh, which for centuries had been under ecclesiastical ban.

Curiously it was through the people whose prejudice against horseflesh remains most intense that the revival began. During the siege of Copenhagen by the English, in 1807, the scarcity of provisions compelled the Danes to eat their horses; and the practical knowledge of the quality of the meat thus gained led them to continue its use after the original necessity had passed away. Possibly the example of their Icelandic allies may have had a good deal to do with the breaking down of Danish prejudice in the matter. In Iceland, the practice had survived from the first. The islanders were willing to have their souls saved by the Church, but they would not submit to any interference with their stomachs; so, rather than lose them, the Church gave them special permission to eat the " execrable food," which they have continued to do to this day.

The first State to imitate the example of Denmark was Würtemburg, which legalised the sale of horseflesh in 1841. Bavaria followed in 1842, Baden in 1846, and Hanover, Bohemia, Saxony, Austria, and Belgium the year after. In 1853 the prejudices of Switzerland and Prussia were overcome, and two years later Norway and Sweden were added to the list of countries authorising the sale of the long rejected food.

The ancient Germans and Scandinavians had a marked liking for horseflesh. They possessed a certain race of white horses to be sacrificed to Odin, and after the sacrifice they boiled the flesh and feasted on it.

The struggle against religious prejudice continued long in France, and now an impression prevails that the revival is a Gallic eccentricity, rather than the result of Germanic good sense.

In 1841 horseflesh was openly adopted at Ochsenhausen, where it continues to be publicly sold under the surveillance of the police, and five or six horses are weekly brought to market. A large quantity of horseflesh is also sold at the Lake of Constance. In 1842 a banquet at which 150 persons assisted, inaugurated its public use at Königsbaden near Stuttgart. In 1846 Schaffhausen authorised its public sale, and in 1857 Weimer and Detmold witnessed public banquets of the hippophagists, which went off with much *éclat;* in Karlsbad and its environs the new beef came into general use, and at Zittau 200 horses are eaten annually.

At one time the feeling against the use of this heretical diet must have been exceedingly intense in the land of good cooking, for it is on record that as late as 1629 a man was condemned to death and executed in France for the crime of eating horseflesh on a Saturday in Lent.

A hundred and fifty years later, the use of the abhorred flesh was publicly advocated by a French physician. Not many converts to the doctrine were made, however, until the retreat from Moscow. During that terrible march, when the alternative was starvation, the French soldiery ventured to eat their disabled horses, and discovered that horseflesh would not only sustain life, but was really savoury and inviting. Several of the surviving officers afterwards endeavoured to break down the prejudice against horseflesh, and advocated its regular use in times of peace, but without much effect.

Hugard, an eminent veterinary surgeon, states, that in the scarcity which followed the Revolution of 1789, the greater part of the meat consumed in Paris for six months was horseflesh, and that it caused no ill effect on the public health.

In Russia the custom has always prevailed, the Greek Church never having meddled with the matter.

The distinguished army surgeon, Baron Larry, made his wounded patients eat horseflesh in the campaigns of the Rhine, of Catalonia and of the Maritime Alps, and he ascribes to it the cure of a great number of his sick in Egypt. The sale of horse-meat has now become a legalised and recognised trade in many of the Continental States, especially in France and Germany.

The Prefect of Police of Paris before legislating, appointed a commission of eminent and competent judges to inquire into the quality as human food, of the flesh taken from horses which had died, or were killed, in the city and its environs. Although prejudiced at first against horseflesh like the general public, the commission ultimately reported that the meat was good and savoury, and there was little sensible difference found between it and beef.

Since 1860, when the first slaughtering of horses for

food took place in Paris under the patronage of the
"Society for Promoting the Use of Horseflesh," the consumption of this meat has been steadily increasing.
About 66,000 horses were slain in Paris in 1871 to furnish food during the siege of the city by the Germans.

The *pièce de résistance* then was curried horseflesh, or
a cat's thigh, strong with garlic. The distaste for horseflesh among the besieged led to the invention of many
bouquets of garlic, peppercorns, cloves, coriander, and
ginger to impart a pleasant flavour to the insipid meat.

According to M. Decroix's full statistical tables published in the "Bulletin of the Society of Acclimatation,"
for February, 1873, p. 98, there had been slaughtered in
Paris from the opening of the first horse-butcher's shop,
in July, 1866, to the end of December, 1872, 83,071
equine animals for food, yielding a net weight of over
34¼ million pounds of meat. The net weight of meat he
calculated at 418 lbs. for horses and mules, and 110 lbs.
for asses, not including the offal, liver, heart, tongue,
brains, etc., which are sold like those of oxen.

In 1875 the horse butcheries of Paris furnished for
public consumption 6,865 horses, asses, and mules; in
1876 they supplied 9,271, giving over 3,700,000 lbs. of
meat. At Lyons the number killed for food in the two
years 1875 and 1876, was 2,350. There are sixty horse
butcheries in Paris, and seven in Lyons.

At Marseilles there were slaughtered at the horse
butchery in 1881, 321 donkeys, which were chiefly consumed in the town, and in the first three months of 1882,
182 horses, 140 mules, and 113 asses were killed for
food.

Some very interesting statistics have been published
by the Society for promoting the use of horseflesh and
the flesh of asses and mules as food, showing how steadily
the consumption of these articles of diet has been increasing in Paris and the provinces since the foundation
of the society in July, 1866. These show that 160,080
horses, 6,690 donkeys, and 395 mules, had been sold in
Paris alone for food up to the end of 1881, furnishing

67,809,460 lbs. of meat. The weight had increased from 171,300 kilos. (2½ lbs.) in 1866 to 1,789,010 kilos. in 1881. In the principal cities of the provinces the consumption of horseflesh may be considered to have fairly taken root. At Marseilles, in 1870, there were 599 horses eaten; 1,031 in 1875; and 1,533 in 1878. At Nancy, 165 in 1873, over 350 in 1876, and 705 in 1878; at Rheims, 291 in 1874, 423 in 1876, and 384 in 1878; at Lyons, 1,839 in 1873, and 1,313 in 1875. In both the latter cases some difficulties had been thrown in the way by the town authorities, as was the case recently at Châlons-sur-Marne, where the Mayor fixed the price of horseflesh at a higher rate than that of beef. Horseflesh is capable of being prepared in many by no means unappetising ways, such as *pot-au-feu*, boiled, roast, hashed, haricot, jugged, fillet, &c.*

The official calculation now is, net meat from the horses and mules, without including tongue, heart, brains, liver, and kidneys, 456 lbs.; for the asses, 120 lbs.

Horses which formerly were only worth 15 to 20 francs in the knacker's yard, now fetch 90 to 150 francs, according to the season and the condition of the animal.

Horseflesh is sold at half the price of beef, for corresponding pieces, thus fillet is 1s. 2d. per lb. instead of 2s. 6d., and pieces of the breast and other parts, 2½d. and 3d., instead of 5d. and 6d. per lb.

A banquet of horseflesh was served at the Langham Hotel, London, on 6th Feb. 1868, to about 150 persons, including Sir Henry Thompson, Sir John Lubbock, Dr. Buckland, and others. Attempts have been made to keep open butcher's shops for the sale of horseflesh in London, but they proved unsuccessful, and the endeavours to popularise the use of this meat in England have utterly failed.

The innovation gains ground rapidly on the Continent,

---

* An elaborate paper on "Hippophagy, the Horse as Food for Man," by A. S. Bicknell, in the "Journal of the Society of Arts," vol. xvi. p. 349, may be consulted with advantage.

and the public sale of horseflesh for human food is now
general in Austria, Bohemia, Saxony, Hanover, Switzerland, and Belgium.   At least ten thousand of the
inhabitants of Vienna are hippophagists.

A recent American paper says :—It may be demonstrated that, in not utilizing horseflesh as food,
we are throwing away a valuable and palatable
meat, of which there is sufficient quantity largely
to augment our existing aggregate food supply.   Supposing that the horse came into use here as food, it
can be easily shown that the absolute wealth in the
country would thereby be materially increased.   In
France the average price for horse-meat, as compared
with similar cuts from the steer, is about two-fifths less.
A horse is there sold to the slaughterer for from £2
to £3.

Estimating from this that £2 is the gross value of
every horse in the United States, over and above his
worth for working purposes, it remains to be seen how
much of that sum may be set apart as to be derived
from his utilization for food alone.   As will be seen
further on, the French butchers derive a revenue from
hide, hoofs, hair, etc., and, as is well-known, the same
portions of the animal find industrial uses here.   Placing
the value of these parts of the carcase at 30s., we find that
12s. is the net value of each horse for alimentary purposes.   In round numbers there are about eleven million
horses in the country.   According to the above showing, we
must add 12s. to the value of each horse, since, in addition
to his value as a worker or as a raw material for manufacturing, he now has a new one as food.   Consequently
the aggregate value of all the horses is increased by about
£6,000,000.   But this accretion to the wealth in the
country is of course not convertible into actual money,
for, so long as the working value exists, the food value
as well as the manufacturing value are practically at
zero ; neither could be realised without great loss, and
hence both are negatived.   But there is a certain easily
ascertained annual proportion of the horses of which the

working value becomes less than the sum of their food and manufacturing values, and this proportion includes the class of which the working value is more than their manufacturing value, but less than the above sum. We may estimate roughly that one-tenth of all the horses reach this condition yearly. Then, on this million animals, the food value is directly realisable, and therefore the wealth of the country may be considered as actually increased by the £6,000,000 derivable therefrom.

Moreover, in order that the horses should be available to the butcher, they must not be diseased or worn out. By this the owners are directly benefited, since, while on one hand they are obliged to sell their horses in fair condition, they are saved the expense of keeping the animals when the latter become used up and are unable to do but light work, though requiring more attention and more feed. So also with colts, which, whether they become good or bad horses, cost about the same to raise. If the animal bids fair to turn out poorly, he can be disposed of at once and at a remunerative price. The result of this weeding out in youth and destroying when old, coupled with the facilities which the former affords of selection of the best types, will naturally conduce to the improvement of breeds and a general benefit to the entire equine population of the country.

We can adduce no more striking example of the art of utilisation than the mode in which the French deal with their superannuated chargers. On the 1st of January last, France contained fifty horse abattoirs, and during last year consumed 2,850,144 lbs. of horse, mule, and ass meat. The flesh of each horse weighs about 450 lbs. The skin is sold to the tanner for 10s. 6d. The hair of the mane and tail fetches 1½d. The hoofs are bought by comb, or toy, or sal ammoniac, or Prussian blue, makers. The tendons are taken to glue factories. There are about ninety pounds of bone, worth 2s. 6d. The intestines, for purposes of manure, or as food for dogs, cats, and pigs, bring 2½d. The blood is purchased principally by the sugar refiners, but also by fatteners of poultry and fertilizer manufacturers. Twenty pounds of dried blood, which is the average, are worth nearly 2s. The fat goes to the soap kettle, or is transformed into genuine "bear's grease," which, delicately perfumed and elegantly put up, fetches some exorbitant prices in the apothecary stores of the United States; or else it is used as harness grease or as lamp oil. The yield is from eight to twelve pounds, at a value of 5d. a pound. Finally, it is said that even the waste flesh is allowed to decompose, and the maggots gathered as pheasant food, but this seems rather apocryphal. These utilisations are of course entirely outside the food supply.

Horse flesh, in comparison with the price of ordinary meat, is not dear. The relation of nitrogenous material is found by analysis to be higher in horse than in ox-flesh.

In two horses, both lean and healthy, the following was found by analysis to be the composition (the ash not estimated being about one per cent.) :—

CONSTITUENTS.	HORSE A.			HORSE B.		
	Neck.	Loin.	Thigh.	Neck.	Loin.	Thigh.
Water	75·02	76·0	75·22	75·1	77·3	79·28
Fixed material ...	24·98	24·0	24·78	24·9	22·7	20·72
Muscle-substance ...	22·85	21·76	23·26	22·16	20·64	18·35
Fat	0·95	1·24	0·52	1·76	1·06	0·86

M. Decroix, the strongest advocate for the use of horseflesh, says that this meat is to that of bullocks what seconds bread is to fine bread—not quite so palatable but more nutritious.

M. Engstrom, in his Consular report from Gothenburg, in December, 1855, stated that the great rise in the price of beef and other meats (averaging 5½d. per lb.), had led of late to the use of horse-flesh among the poorer classes, at a cost of 1¼d. to 1¾d. per pound. But the advance in the price of meat in the 30 years that have elapsed since then has been enormous.

At Gothenburg horseflesh is generally sold to the poorer classes, who cannot afford the higher prices of beef. In the last seventeen years nearly 30,000 horses have been killed and their flesh used as food in Berlin. In 1853 there were but five slaughter-houses, and only 150 horses sold ; in 1865 the number had increased there to 2,240.

Setting aside the prejudice against the flesh of the horse which most Englishmen entertain on the subject, we confess we see nothing that is repulsive in adopting it as an article of food. The horse, like the ox and the sheep, is granivorous and herbivorous, and a far more cleanly feeder than the pig, which will devour any filthy garbage ; and the flesh of a young horse cannot but be good eating. The mother of the celebrated William Godwin once had a fine young horse, three years old, that broke its leg in a gate. She instantly had it killed; and being a strong-minded lady, and free from prejudice, she directed a butcher to dress it and cut it up exactly as he would do a bullock. She then sent presents of it to her friends, requesting them to cook it the same as "other beef." Her request was complied with, and one and all pronounced it to be equal to any beef they ever partook of.

Whether this movement will be followed up by a partial adoption of horse-flesh in England, is a question that time alone can determine. There is, however, another view of it that must be decided before the middle and upper classes can be brought to patronise the plan. At what age then are horses to be fattened and slaughtered ? and is the slaughtering for sale to be confined to the poor, old, broken-down hacks of the cabs, omnibuses, and costermongers ? On the face of the proposition it appears so, for assuredly a horse under ten or twelve years, generally speaking, is too valuable for work, if he has been well treated by his owner, to be sold for such a purpose. Young horses are quite out of the question, unless, as in the case of Mrs. Godwin's horse, they by an accident are rendered unfit for work and useless. The slaughtering for the market will therefore, in England, be confined to the old and worn-out horses that are past work.

Ass's Flesh.—Mules and asses are numerous in many countries, but although in some parts of Europe their flesh is eaten, it is not usual. In Spain there are about 2,500,000 mules and asses, in the United States about 1,500,000, in Italy and Morocco each about 1,000,000, and in the South American States from one to two millions. The Greeks ate donkeys, and we must suppose they had their reasons for it. The flesh of the ass is still esteemed a delicacy in some countries. The northern climate, pasturage, and freedom may have some effect on the flesh. The Roman peasants found the flesh of the ass palatable, and the celebrated Mæcenas having tasted it, introduced it to the tables of the great and rich; but the fashion of eating it lasted no longer than his life. Galen compares the flesh of the ass to that of the stag. The flesh of the wild ass is said to be very delicate and good, but when killed in a tame state it is hard and unfit for food.

The skin of the wild ass is used for making a gelatine, which, scented with musk, is prescribed in chest diseases. It is sold in flat, rectangular, reddish pieces, translucid, and, like all the substances of great value, is wrapped by the Chinese in paper of vermilion colour. A gelatine made with cow-skin, is often substituted.

The wild ass, called Koulan by the Persians, is still common in many parts of Central Asia, from 48° North latitude to the confines of India. The Persians and Tartars hold its flesh in high esteem, and hunt it in preference to all other descriptions of game. Olearius assures us that he saw no fewer than thirty-two wild asses slain in one day by the Shah of Persia and his court, the bodies of which were sent to the royal kitchens at Ispahan; and we know from Martial that the epicures of Rome held the flesh of the Onager, or wild ass, in the same estimation as we do venison.

> Cum tener est *Onager*, solaque lalisio matre
> · Pascitur ; hoc infans, sed breve nomen habet.
> Martial, xiii. 97.

From a passage in Pliny (lib. viii., c. 44) it would appear that the Onager inhabited Africa; and that the most delicate and best flavoured *lalisiones*, or fat foals, were brought from that continent to the Roman markets. Asses' milk is universally known and approved of as a specific in many disorders. It is light, easy of digestion, and highly nutritious.

The Hottentots and other natives are very fond of the Quagga (*Equus quagga*, Lin.), the flesh of which, though coarse, is eaten.

Lieutenant Moodie ("Ten Years in South Africa") says —" Being one morning at the house of a neighbouring farmer who had just shot one of these animals, I requested that he would have a piece of the flesh cooked for my breakfast. His ' frow ' expressed some disgust at my proposal, but ordered a small bit to be grilled, with butter and pepper. I did not find it at all unpalatable, and certainly it was better than horse-flesh."

Capt. Burton, in his " Central Africa," says, " Of wild flesh the favourite is that of the Zebra ; it is smoked or jerked, despite which it retains a most savoury flavour."

Ruminants.—We come now to a better-known class of food-yielding animals, the Ruminants.

A writer in " The Farmer " well observes that " the consumption of meat increases with the increase of population, and in a higher ratio, as the world progresses in civilization, it consumes more animal food, as the best restorative of the daily exhaustion of bodily and mental forces. Farinaceous food and feebleness occupy the same zone. To get up and keep a good meat-appetite, man must live and work several degrees from the Equator. And in this truth the whole future meat question is contained. The Northern nations, who are the meat eating people, multiply and govern the earth, and thus the future demand must be immense, and such as the herds and flocks of the whole world will but satisfy. To English, Scottish, and Irish pastures and feeding-stalls, North and South America, Asia and Australia, may join supplies, but Europe is not likely to see over-cheap meat; and Christmas fat stock may always be looked for as a characteristic of the season."

Professor Atwater has tabulated the results of several authoritative investigations as to the nutritive value of different kinds of foods. As a basis the professor has taken medium quality beef—that is, beef neither very fat nor very lean—as having a nutritive value of 100, and upon this standard he forms the following table:—

Meat Game, and Fowl.	Nutritive Value
Beef (lean) ...	91·3
Beef (medium) ...	100·0
Beef (fat) ...	112·0
Veal (fat) ...	92·4
Mutton (medium) ...	86·6
Pork (fat) ...	116·0
Smoked beef ...	146·0
Smoked ham ...	157·0
Venison ...	88·8
Hen ...	93·9
Duck ...	104·0

There are probably two or three facts here which will surprise the uninitiated. Few, for instance, would imagine that smoked beef, or smoked ham, contained nearly twice as much nutritive value as venison or mutton, nor will the fact that pork is more nourishing than any other kind of meat not cured, be generally received as a truism. The great nutritive value of the smoked meats is due to the evaporation from them of all moisture, and the compression of the tissues, and the same circumstances apply in the case of other cured meats, of which the nutritive value averages very high. A second set of figures, computed on the same basis and proportion, shows the strength of various kinds of animal produce

—milk and its manufactured products and eggs, in the following table :—

Animal Produce.					Nutritive Value.
Cows' milk (normal)	...	...	...	...	23·8
Cows' milk (skimmed)	...	...	...	...	18·5
Cream from cows' milk	...	...	...	...	56·0
Butter	...	...	...	...	124·1
Cheese (from whole milk)	...	...	...	...	151·0
Cheese (from skimmed milk)	...	...	...	...	159·0
Cheese (from milk with cream added)	...	...	...		103·0
Hen's eggs	...	...	...	...	72·2

The salient feature here is the nutritive value of skimmed cheese, a food which in common with the fat pork whose great nutritive properties we have already mentioned, is most largely consumed by the rural classes. It is a little curious to note that the cheese made from skimmed milk is much more nutritive than the product of milk and cream mixed, and equally notable is the nutritive excellence of eggs, which weight for weight seem to be nearly equal to that of mutton. Professor Atwater states that the calculation as to the value of eggs is based upon several hundreds of analyses, which, however, only showed a variation of from 71·0 to 73·5, so that one egg seems to be practically as good as another.

Some fair idea of the amount of beef and veal consumed may be gained from the official returns of cattle in various countries. Thus, if we take Europe first, we find, according to the latest statistics available, the following numbers :—

HORNED CATTLE.

EUROPE.

United Kingdom	...	1884	......	10,422,762
European Russia	...	1877	......	27,323,219
Sweden	... ...	1882	......	2,257,048
Norway	... ...	1875	......	1,016,617
Denmark	...	1881	......	1,470,078
Holland	... ...	1882	......	1,427,936
Austro-Hungary	...	1880	......	13,181,620
France	... ...	1880	......	11,446,253
Italy	... ...	1881	......	4,783,232

Germany...	...	...	1873	......	15,785,322
Belgium ...	...	...	1880	......	1,382,815
Spain ...	...	...	1865	......	2,904,598
Portugal ...	...	...	1870	......	520,474
Switzerland	...	...	1866	......	993,241
Greece ...	...	...	1875	......	188,651
Roumania	...	...	1873	......	1,866,990
					96,970,856

AMERICA.

United States ...	...	1883	......	42,547,307
Dominion of Canada	...	1881	......	3,514.989
Uruguay	...	1876	......	6,092,488
Argentine Confederation		1876	......	13,493,000
Brazil ...	...	...	1880	......	20,000,000
Falkland Isles ...	...	1879	......	15,610
Newfoundland ...	...	1875	......	13,938
					85,677,332

For Paraguay, Chili, Peru, Venezuela, and other South and Central American States, there are no reliable data on which to form even an estimate. The West Indian Islands have about 500,000, of which 84,206 are in Jamaica.

AFRICA.

Egypt ...	...	...	1871	......	132,666
Algeria	...	...	1861	......	1,053,086
Cape Colony	...	...	1875	......	1,329,445
Dutch Republics and					
Kafirs ...	...	...	—	......	1,000,000
Natal	...	...	1882	......	545,010
					4,060,207

ASIA.

British India, about	...	—	......	50,000,000
Asiatic Russia (half in				
Siberia)	...	...	1863	......	2,628,000
Java ...	...	...	1873	......	4,358,105
Ceylon ...	...	...	1883	......	1,091,500
Mauritius	...	...	1875	......	29,545
Reunion ...	...	...	1866	......	6,000
					58,113,150

No. of Horned Cattle (Cows, Bullocks, and Buffaloes)
in 1879.

Assam	1,436,706
Punjaub	6,121,417
Central Provinces	5,374,234
British Burmah	1,404,168
Berar	1,728,786
Mysore	2,361,615
Coorg	116,419
Aymer and Mhaúwarra	143,161
Madras Presidency	2,938,838
Bombay „	2,808,794
	24,434,138

For Bengal there are no statistics available.

Nearly 25,000 head of cattle are imported yearly into British Burmah from countries beyond the border.

Of China, Tartary, Japan, and other Eastern States there are no returns to be obtained.

According to the census taken in the Punjab, Central Provinces, etc., in 1879, there were supposed to be in India about one head of horned cattle to every two human beings. This would give about 100 millions of cattle, worth at the very lowest calculation £75,000,000. But this assumption is clearly too high, and 50 millions of cattle may be a fair estimate. About 8,000,000 hides are annually exported, so that number must certainly be killed or die, exclusive of the hides locally tanned.

The River Plate Republics cannot consume their abundance of animal food; and they export largely dried meat, extract of meat, tongues, etc. In 1872 and 1873 as many as 19,000 tongues were shipped from Montevideo, but in 1875 this number had fallen to 7,000. From the republic of Uruguay there is also shipped annually from 30,000 to 40,000 tons of dried salted meat, known as tasago or charqui. It is estimated that the cattle slaughtered yield on an average 117 lbs. of meat when salted and dried.

The late Sir Harry Meysey Thompson, in a paper contributed to the Royal Agricultural Society's Journal in 1872, calculated that 25 per cent. of our entire stock went annually to the butcher, and Mr. J. W. Pease, M.P., in a later paper read before the South Durham and North Yorkshire Chamber of Agriculture at Darlington, in 1878, assumed the same proportion. This would give for 1883 2,600,000 animals, the whole number of cattle in the United Kingdom in that year being over 10,400,000. These may be estimated to weigh 600 lbs. per head, equal to 13,928,571 cwt. The total foreign imports in that year were 288,530 head of cattle. These would average 520 lbs. per head, or 1,339,603 cwt.; besides this we received 764,260 cwt. of dead meat from America and the Continent. This refers alone to the supply of beef.

Agricultural returns recently issued contain some interesting estimates of the respective average weights of the animals imported from various countries. Cattle: Danish, 560 lbs., French, 828 lbs., Schleswig-Holstein, and Netherlands, 680 lbs., Norwegian and Swedish, 624 lbs., Portuguese, 692 lbs., Spanish, 568 lbs., Canadian, 720 lbs., United States, 808 lbs.

CATTLE IN AUSTRALASIA (RETURNS OF 1883).

Queensland	...	...	...	...	4,246,141
New South Wales	...	...	...	...	1,859,985
Victoria ...	...	...	...	...	1,297,546
South Australia	...	...	...	...	319,620
Western Australia	...	...	...	...	64,558
Tasmania	...	...	...	...	130,525
New Zealand	...	...	...	...	698,637
					8,617,012
Hawaiian Isles	...	...	1866	......	60 000

The very large number of cattle and sheep in Australia not only makes meat cheap, but it is impossible to consume the flesh for food. Sheep are not now boiled down as formerly, simply for their tallow; strong efforts are being made to obtain a field for their consumption by exportation as frozen cargoes of meat, and preserved or tinned. The exports of preserved meat from the

Australian colonies were:—From New South Wales in 1879 to the value of £136,613, from Victoria in the same year to the value of but £69,054. The shipments which in 1871 were 14,876,000 lbs. from Victoria fell in 1879 to 2,867,633 lbs. Queensland shipped preserved meat to the value of £24,563 in 1879, against £79,962 in 1871. New Zealand shipped 20,815 cwts. in 1879, about one-third of what was exported in 1872.

The quantities of meat received in England from New Zealand were in 1882 8,839 carcases of mutton, in 1883 120,893 ditto, and 728 quarters of beef.

The shipments this year are expected to be about 300,000 carcases, and this will probably reach soon to 400,000 to 500,000 carcases per annum, a quantity that can easily be increased to a million a few years hence.

The salted beef imported into the United Kingdom is shown by the following figures :—

				Quantity. cwts.		Value. £
1861	...	...	...	141,683	......	231,502
1871	...	...	...	280,075	......	581,211
1880	...	...	...	290,564	......	535,213

Fresh or slightly salted beef—

				cwts.		£
1861	...	...	...	10,952	......	30,666
1871	...	...	...	22,004	......	54,142
1880	...	...	...	727,392	......	1,889,730

Of unclassed beef, salted or fresh—

				cwts.		£
1861	...	...	...	1,101	......	2,754
1871	...	...	...	42,340	......	107,814
1880	...	...	...	149,010	......	429,073

Preserved meat and tongues, etc.—

				cwts.		£
1861	...	...	...	4,334	......	15,944
1871	...	...	...	254,833	......	662,280
1880	...	...	...	655,800	......	1,905,717

The quantity of dead meat imported into the United Kingdom in 1883 was as follows :—

		Cwts.
Beef, fresh	... ...	804,794
„ salted	... ...	289,214
Mutton, fresh	... ...	236,496
Pork, fresh	... ...	47,346
„ salted	... ...	329,553
Bacon	... ...	3,089,830
Hams	... ...	606,162
Fresh or salted meat, unenumerated	... ...	36,353
Preserved otherwise than by salting	... ...	610,400
		6,050,148

The beef was principally from America, Russia, Germany, and Australasia ; the mutton from Australasia, Holland, and America. The fresh pork from Belgium and Holland, Germany and France ; the salted pork from the United States, Germany, and Denmark ; the preserved meat from Australasia, North America, and the River Plate States.

In 1864 we only imported 1,650,796 cwts. of meat of all kinds from abroad ; in 1883 the quantity had risen to 6,050,148 cwts., besides 6,283,472 cwts. of fish, lard, butter, and cheese, and a quantity of game, poultry, and eggs, valued at £3,323,950.

The number of live cattle imported into London from abroad in 1880 was 170,366, and the home supply to the Metropolitan Market then 173,290 beasts.

The quantity of each kind of meat and produce delivered at the London Central Meat and Poultry and Provision Markets in 1883 was as follows :—

		Cwts.
Country killed meat and produce	... ...	2,172,820
Town killed „ „	... ...	1,492,700
General Foreign killed meat and produce	...	228,280
American killed Fresh meat	... ...	535,980
Australian and New Zealand killed Fresh meat	... ...	93,420
		4,523,200

The fluctuations in the price of butchers' meat in the Metropolitan Cattle Market (at per stone of 8 lbs. sinking the offal) has been as follows :—

	1861. s. d.	1871. s. d.	1882. s. d.
Inferior beasts	3 3½	3 11¼	4 3¾
2nd class	4 0	4 10¼	4 9¾
3rd class, large prime ...	4 6	5 4½	5 7½
4th class, Scots	4 10¾	5 8½	5 10½
Coarse calves	4 3½	4 0¾	5 4¾
Small prime	5 2½	5 4¾	5 11¾

In 1883 the prices were as follows for live meat :—

	Foreign. s. d.	British. s. d.
Beef.		
Inferior	4 3	4 4
Second	5 1	5 7
First	5 6	6 1
Mutton.		
Inferior	5 6	6 2
Second	6 0	6 9
First	6 5	7 3

Taking the prices by the carcass, they were as follows in the London Central Meat Market, per lb. :—

	1864.	1883.
Beef	4⅜d. to 6½d.	5d. to 8⅛d.
Mutton	5⅜d. to 7d.	5⅝d. to 9¾d.

The imports into the United Kingdom of preserved meat, which in 1860 were only 6,131 cwt., advanced in 1870 to 83,081, and rose in 1880 to 655,800; much of this was, however, mutton.

The following were also other Foreign supplies we received in the same periods :—

	Salted Beef. cwts.	Fresh or slightly salted Meat. cwts.
1860	261,259	935
1870	215,748	34,300
1880	1,017,956	149,060

The beef product of the United States in 1873 was stated at 2,926,571 tons, of which 2,866,365 tons were consumed, leaving a surplus of 60,206 tons, of which about 12,000 tons were exported. Since then the horned cattle have increased by more than 6,000,000 head, and many live animals (in 1880 to the value of £3,177,000) are now shipped from thence to Europe. In 1880 there was exported from American ports 84,717,000 lbs. of fresh beef, and 45,237,000 lbs. of salted beef, or nearly 65,000 tons.

Very many of the European States besides our own are obliged to import supplies of foreign meat. France imported in 1880 55,400 tons of fresh and salted meat, Belgium 42,500 tons, Denmark about 5,700 tons, and Italy 6,000. Greece imported in 1875 about 4,500 tons.

Buffaloes.—This species of ox (*Bubalus buflus*) is found in large numbers in various parts of India and the Eastern islands, and to a limited extent in Eastern Europe and Africa. It is the chief draught animal of Asia. There are five or six millions in British India. In India animal food is hardly at all used by the natives, but in the large towns there are markets for buffalo beef for the low caste and poorer Mussulman population. The flesh is stringy, and gives off a musky odour; but the veal is considered good. The hump on the back is considered a delicacy. In Java the inhabitants cook the fresh hide for food, esteeming it a dainty beyond any other morsel. There are about 3,000,000 buffaloes in Java. In Sumatra they dress their meat immediately after killing it, while it is still warm, which is conformable with the practice of the ancients, as recorded by Homer and others, and in this state it is said to eat tenderer than when kept for a day; longer the climate will not admit of, unless it is preserved by the method of sun-drying and called "dendeng."

The flesh of the young yak or grunting ox (*Poephagus grunniens*), according to Sir J. Hooker, is delicious, much richer than common veal. Opinions differ as to that of the old yak. Pallas says the flesh is hard and bad-tasted; Huc, on the contrary, asserts it to be very good. The Lepchas eat not only the flesh, but the entrails, and singe and fry the skin. They also jerk the meat, which when dried is called "shat-chew," and is a very common and palatable food in Thibet. A large trade is carried on in dried meat from the islands of the Eastern Archipelago to China and Japan.

Sheep and Mutton.—Passing now to mutton supplies, I will start with the number of Sheep and Lambs in various countries.

EUROPE.

Russia	...	...	1877	......	51,822,238
Sweden	...	...	1873	......	1,388,329
Norway	...	...	1875	......	1,686,306
Denmark	...	...	1880	......	1,548,613
Iceland	...	...	1866	......	800,000
German Empire	...	...	1883	......	19,185,362
Holland	...	...	1879	......	745,187
Belgium	...	...	1880	......	365,400
France	...	...	1880	......	22,516,084
Portugal	...	...	1870	......	2,706,777
Spain	...	...	1865	......	22,054,967
Italy	...	...	1881	......	8,596,108
Austro-Hungary	...	...	1880	......	13,093,463
Switzerland	...	...	1866	......	447,001
Greece	...	...	1875	......	2,291,917
Turkey	...	...	1870	......	16,000,000
Roumania	...	...	1873	......	4,786,294
United Kingdom	...	...	1883	......	29,256,528
					199,290,574

AFRICA.

Egypt	...	...	1871	......	184,899
North Africa and Persia about		—		......	55,000,000
Algeria	...	...	1873	......	9,699,111
Cape Colony	...	...	1875	......	11,279,743
Natal	...	...	1882	......	454,235
					76,617,988

AMERICA.

United States	...	...	1883	......	50,626,626
British America	...	...	1881	......	3,048,678
Uruguay	...	...	1876	......	12,200,000
Argentine Confederation	...	...	1880	......	70,000,000
Falkland Islands	...	...	1875	......	60,000
Newfoundland	...	...	1875	......	28,766
Remainder of America	...	—		......	6,000,000
					141,964,070

ASIA.

India, estimated about ...	—	......	30,000,000
China, Japan, &c., ditto ...	—	......	20,000,000
Ceylon	1883	......	68,672
Mauritius	1875	......	28,036
			50,096,708

The following figures are from a census taken in 1879, but both sheep and goats are mixed up in the returns marked with a * :—

*Bombay Presidency	2,728,866
Madras...	4,544.904
*Mysore...	1,693,108
*Berar	391,959
*Coorg	6,373
*Aymer and Mhairwarra	186,823
*Assam	317,445
*Punjaub	3,864,013
*Central Provinces	702,359
*British Burmah	16,389
	14,452,239

No returns for Bengal.

AUSTRALASIA, 1883.

New South Wales	31,796,308
Queensland	11,507,475
Victoria	10,739,021
South Australia	6,677,067
Western Australia	1,315,155
Tasmania	1,831,069
New Zealand	13,384,075
	77,250,170

WEST INDIES.

Jamaica	1869	......	21,761
Martinique and Guadaloupe..	1865	......	23,607
			45,368

It was stated recently in *The Times* that in the nine months, January to September (1884) we received from Australia and New Zealand no less than 238,130 cwts. of frozen mutton, compared with 60,532 cwts. in the corresponding period of 1883, and 32,063 cwts. in 1882. Reckoning at 60 lbs. the weight of a carcass, this import is at the rate of 592,600 sheep in the year, or an average of 11,400 sheep per week. This is equivalent to doubling the number of sheep, though not doubling the weight of mutton, at the Metropolitan Cattle Market, as there were shown in that market in the year 1882 just 561,600 head, or 10,700 per week. The year's total of home and foreign live sheep at the Metropolitan and Deptford market together gives an average of 25,800 head per week.

The prices of sheep in the Metropolitan Cattle Market have been, per stone of 8 lbs. (sinking the offal), as follows:—

	1861.		1871.		1881.		1882.	
	s.	d.	s.	d.	s.	d.	s.	d.
Inferior	3	6¼	4	1	5	0½	5	7
2nd class	4	3¼	4	10½	5	8½	6	1¼
3rd class, long coarse wool	5	0¼	5	10½	6	6¾	6	9¾
4th class, Southdowns ...	5	5¾	6	5	6	9½	7	0¾
Lambs	6	5	7	3	8	1¼	7	10

The quantity of sheep imported into London from abroad in 1883 was 803,341, and the home supply sent to the Metropolitan Market was 465,450. Ireland exports about 500,000 sheep and lambs.

The average weight of the sheep we import is found to be about as follows:—Belgian 70 lbs., Danish 64 lbs., French 56 lbs., Schleswig-Holstein 64 lbs., Netherlands 70 lbs., Norwegian and Swedish 48 lbs., Canadian 68 lbs., United States 60 lbs.

In Spain and Southern Europe, the mutton is better than in the north, and replaces beef at the tables of the rich. Mutton is the flesh food almost exclusively of the pastoral people of Asia and Africa. In Holland and Germany mutton is held in disrepute.

Goat's flesh is much eaten by the Arabs in Northern Africa. Goats being very plentiful in Greece, their flesh forms the principal animal food in the provinces. That of the kid is considered as good as lamb, and the flesh of the she-goat and buck are both eaten.

Flesh of the Camel tribe.—Camels are less numerous than other domestic animals, and are limited to a few countries. Their flesh is not so generally eaten as that of other animals. In the north of Africa there are very many camels. Algeria has about 200,000, Tunis probably half as many. In Central Asia and parts of India there are large numbers; the Punjaub possesses about 130,000. Wild camels are met with occasionally in troops about Lake Lobnon in Asiatic Russia. Their flesh, which is fat in autumn, is eaten by the natives.

The flesh of the camel was eaten both by the Greeks and Persians. Heliogabalus had camel's flesh and camel's feet served up at his banquets, and by the Arabs the flesh of the young dromedary is considered equal to veal. The natives of Africa esteem camel's flesh more than that of any other animal, but in other quarters it is not held in equal favour, being considered hard and unsavoury and little esteemed even by the Tartars. They however use the hump cut into slices, which dissolved in tea serves the purpose of butter. In Barbary the tongues are salted and smoked for exportation to Italy and other countries, and they form a very good dish.

Alpaca Tribe.—The flesh of the alpaca of South America is but little inferior to mutton, and it yields about three or four times the weight of flesh that a sheep does. The meat of the fawn is best and most delicate, but it is used sparingly, the principal object being the wool. The flesh of all the tribe, either fresh or dried, affords a wholesome meal. That of the wild guanaco is the best of the class and is highly esteemed. The flesh of the vicuna, salted and dried under the name of " charqui," is eaten, but is not generally considered so good as that of its congeners the guanaco and alpaca. Opinions on this point however seem to differ, some considering the flesh of the vicuna equal to venison.

The giraffe is hunted in Kordofan chiefly for its flesh ; that of the young is said to be very delicate. The Hottentots in Southern Africa used to hunt the animal

principally on account of its marrow, which is a delicacy
they set a high value on.

Venison.—The deer tribe, both in their wild and domesticated state, contribute largely to human food, their
flesh being wholesome and nutritious. It will only be
necessary to instance a few of the least common.

The flesh of the little Japanese deer (*Cervus sica*) is excellent. They fatten well, and their legs contain layers
of fat, which are highly appreciated by connoisseurs.
Lord Powerscourt acclimatised them in Ireland, and has
more than a hundred head, and the young are sold in
the London market for venison. These deer, however,
attain rarely a weight of more than 100 lbs. in our
southern climate, while in the north they are double
that weight.

Reindeer.—In the winter many families of Laplanders
arrive in St. Petersburg bringing with them herds of
reindeer for sale to the rich proprietors. These are
killed, and the saddle of meat is considered an exquisite
dish; but the tongue is the most dainty morsel.

The stomach of the reindeer, distended with well
masticated willow sprigs in a half digested state, is
highly esteemed. This is dried over the fire or in the
smoke of the huts for winter use, and when mixed with
melted suet, oil and snow, is highly relished. It is
deemed a powerful anti-scorbutic.

Every part of the carcass of the reindeer serves the
natives of the northern regions for food. In the Russian
Empire there are computed to be about one million reindeer, in Norway about 100,000, one-fifth of the domesticated ones are yearly killed for food, and in North America
there are many thousands. A fine reindeer will sometimes
yield 120 lbs. of meat and forty of tallow. The Esquimaux
hunter breaks the leg of a recently slaughtered deer and
swallows the marrow still warm, with avidity; the kidneys and other parts of the intestines are also eaten raw;
the large gut, when roasted or boiled with all its fatty ap-
pendages, is one of the most savoury dishes that can be
offered, either to Indian or white settler in North America.

Some Indians and Canadians leave this savoury mixture to ferment or season for a few days before they eat it. The blood, if mixed in proper proportion with fat meat and cooked with some nicety, forms a rich and highly nutritious soup. After all the flesh is consumed the bones are pounded, and a large quantity of marrow extracted by boiling; this is employed in preparing pemmican.

Reindeers' tongues are much liked by many in this country, large quantities being imported annually from Russia. They are snow-cured, no salt whatever being used, the mildness and richness of flavour in the meat is preserved, and they are rendered extremely acceptable to refined palates.

The flesh of the moose or elk is more relished by the Indians and persons resident in the fur countries of America than that of any other animal. It bears a greater resemblance in its flavour to beef than to venison. It is said that the external fat is soft, like that of a breast of mutton, and when put into a bladder is as fine as marrow. In this it differs from all other species of deer, of which the external fat is hard. A buck in its grease will weigh as much as 800 lbs. without the offal. When in good condition the flesh is sweet and tender, and is highly esteemed as an article of food. The "moufle" or loose covering of the nose is considered by epicures the greatest delicacy of the North-west, contesting the palm with bear's paw, beaver tail, reindeer tongue, and buffalo boss.

In a few years, unless legislation interferes, there will be no elk, buffalo, mule-deer, or antelope left to hunt in the Western States and Territories. In Minnesota, Montana, and Wyoming alone 20,000 deer are annually slaughtered, and in one year between the Yellowstone and the head waters of the little Missouri 25,000 buffaloes were killed. Even if this extermination of the noble fauna of America was the result of legitimate sport it would be matter for regret. But sport has nothing to do with it. The price of an elk's skin is three dollars, and the trade in buffalo robes is always brisk. Hence all the resources of civilisation are enlisted in the cause of the almighty dollar against the wild nature of the New World. A large party of hunters with repeating rifles, each man killing from six to twelve beasts from every herd they come across before it can get beyond range, are calculated to thin the magnitude of those herds rather rapidly; and as the number of hunters increases annually while the herds decrease, it is an easy calculation to determine when the bottom of the basket will be reached.

There are a considerable variety of antelopes in South Africa, and a very great number of species in every district. The flesh of most is in universal esteem among all the people. It is well flavoured when fat, and of a delicate taste. It makes very fine venison when properly dressed, and the legs and shoulders of the anima are much esteemed as a relish when dried down into "biltong," a most convenient and palatable article of diet, perfectly familiar to the colonists. In this form it can be kept almost any length of time, and has frequently been brought to England. It is extremely nourishing and digestible, and can often be taken by individuals when other food is rejected by the stomach.

The flesh of the gemsbok (*Oryx Gazella*) of Africa ranks next to the eland, and at certain seasons of the year they are very fat.

Sir Cornwallis Harris, speaking of the Eland, says:— " By all classes in Africa its flesh is deservedly esteemed over that of any other animal. Both in grain and colour it resembles beef, but is far better tasted and more delicate, possessing a fine game flavour and exhibiting the most tempting looking layers of fat and lean, the surprising quantity of the former ingredient with which it is nterlarded, exceeding that of any other game quadruped with which I am acquainted. The venison fairly melts in the mouth, and as for the brisket, that is absolutely a cut for a monarch. During the greater part of our journey it was to the flesh of this goodly beast that we principally looked for our daily rations, both on account of its vast superiority over all other wild flesh, and from the circumstance of its being obtainable in larger quantities with comparatively less labour."

We have now to examine the food furnished by other mammals, which is an important necessary to many of the northern tribes.

Bison.—The existence of the North American Indians is bound up inseparably with that of the so-called "buffalo" (*Bos Bison*). These animals exist in vast numbers on the prairies, and it is computed that half a million are killed yearly, mainly for their furs or "robes" and the tongue, much of the flesh being wasted. The late Horace Greeley, writing from the plains, remarks, "What strikes the stranger with the most amazement is their immense numbers. I know a million is a great many, but I am confident we saw that number yesterday. Certainly all we saw could not have stood on ten miles of ground. . . I doubt whether the domesticated horned cattle of the United States equal the numbers, while they must fall considerably short in weight of the wild ones."

The flesh of a bison in good condition is very juicy and well flavoured, much resembling that of well-fed beef. The tongue is reckoned a delicacy, and may be cured so as to surpass in flavour the tongue of an English ox. The hump or flesh covering the long spinous processes of the first dorsal vertebræ, consisting of fat and muscles, is much esteemed. It is named *bos* by the Canadian voyageurs, and *wig* by the Orkney men in the service of the Hudson's Bay Company. The wig has a fine grain, and when salted and cut transversely it is almost as rich and tender as the tongue.

The flesh of the bison is largely used as food, and the hunch on the shoulders is esteemed a great delicacy. Each buffalo will produce from 50 to 70 lbs. of tallow, but a bull bison, when fat, will frequently yield 150 lbs. weight of tallow, which forms a considerable article of commerce.

One of the most useful applications of buffalo meat consists in the preparation of pemmican, an article of food of the greatest importance from its portability and nutritious qualities. This is prepared by cutting the lean meat into thin slices, exposing it to the heat of the sun or fire, and when dry, pounding it into a powder. It is then mixed with an equal weight of buffalo suet and stuffed into bladders. Sometimes venison is used instead of buffalo meat. One bison cow in good condition furnishes dried meat and fat enough to make a bag of pemmican weighing 90 pounds.

Marine Mammals.—The flesh of the whale has been already alluded to as furnishing food to the natives in many countries—New Zealand, Brazil, Japan, and especially the Arctic regions. In Barbados, when obtainable, the flesh of the hump-backed whale (*Megaptera Americana*) is eaten by all classes, being preferred to beef, which is there tough. The flesh of the whale is also eaten in Tobago, St. Lucia, and the Grenadines. A South Sea harpooner will tell you that, excepting the delicacy of a draught of the yellow, creamy milk taken from a freshly-speared she-whale, whale fins, properly cooked, are the greatest of conceivable dainties. The rank, rich, heat-producing flesh of the seal vies, in the opinion of an Esquimaux, with the merits of blubber cut from the flanks of a stranded whale. He will eat the raw flesh of the whale with the same apparent relish, when newly killed, or after it has been buried in the ground for several months.

There is no food more delicious to the taste of the Esquimaux than the flesh of seals, and especially that of the common seal (*Phoca vitulina*). Whales and walruses they capture when they come in their way, but the seal is their daily food. This animal is as useful to them as the sheep to us. This meat is so unlike the flesh to which Europeans are accustomed, that it is not surprising that we should have some difficulty at first in making up our minds to taste it; but when once that difficulty is overcome, everyone praises its flavour, tenderness, digestibility, juiciness, and its decidedly warming after-effects. Its colour is almost black, from the large amount of venous blood it contains, except in young seals, and is therefore very singular looking and not inviting, while its flavour is unlike anything else, and cannot be described except by saying "delicious." To suit European palates there are certain precautions to be taken before it is cooked. It has to be cut in thin slices, carefully removing any fat or blubber, and is then soaked in salt water for from 12 to 24 hours, to remove the blood, which gives it a slightly fishy flavour. The daintiest morsel is the liver, which requires no soaking, but may be eaten as soon as the animal is killed.

The heart is good eating, while the sweetbread and kidneys are not to be despised. The usual mode of cooking seal's flesh is to stew it with a few pieces of fat bacon, when an excellent rich gravy is formed, or it may be fried with a few pieces of pork.

The flesh of the hair-seals is said to be more juicy and sweet for food than that of the fur-seals, which are chiefly composed of blubber. The flesh of a young fur-seal, placed in running water overnight and then broiled, is, however, far from disagreeable, in fact it is said to taste exactly like mutton chop. The young sea-lion (*Otaria*), of which there are several species, is said to be even better eating. Anson, in his "Voyage Round the World," speaking of Juan Fernandez, writes:—

"There is another amphibious creature to be met with here called a sea-lion, which bears some resemblance to a seal, though it is much larger. This, too, we eat, under the denomination of beef. They are extremely fat, so that after having cut through the skin, which is about an inch in thickness, there is at least a foot of fat before you can either come at lean or bones; and we experienced more than once that the fat of some of the largest afforded us a butt of oil. We killed many of them for food, particularly for their hearts and tongues, which we esteemed exceeding good eating, and preferable even to

K

those of bullocks." The flesh of the female sea-lion is said to be delicate, while that of the cub can scarcely be distinguished from roast pig.

Capt. J. N. East, R.N., says that the tongues, fins, and kidneys of these enormous animals are excellent eating.

The flesh of the sea-elephant (*Macrorhinus angustirostris*) is not only black, oily and indigestible, but not easily separated from the fat. The tongues alone supply good aliment, and they are salted with care and sold in some markets. The heart is sometimes eaten, but it is hard and indigestible; and the liver, which is esteemed in some seals, according to Dr. Hamilton after repeated trials, would appear to be hurtful.

Among the savage inhabitants of the Arctic regions the flesh of the walrus (*Trichechus rosmarus*) is much valued and esteemed; it is greedily eaten along with the blubber, and even the skin. The flesh is strong, coarse, and of a game-like flavour, but the large tongue, heart and liver are often eaten by whalers for want of better provisions, and are passably good.

The animals of the *Sirenia* family are hunted for their flesh both in the eastern and western hemispheres. Being herbivorous animals their flesh is much appreciated. The dugong (*Halicore Indicus* or *H. Dugong*) is the eastern representative of the family, and it is captured about Ceylon and Northern Australia. The western species is the *Manatus Americanus*. The dugong is considered by the Malays a royal fish, and the king is entitled to all that are taken. The flesh when roasted has the flavour of pork combined with the taste of veal. It is esteemed a great delicacy by the Mahometans, who naturally seek a compensation in this dish for the prohibition under which they suffer respecting the porcine tribe terrestrial. When cured the flesh is considered in Queensland a relishing article of diet for the breakfast table, having the flavour of good bacon with just an agreeable "bloater" twang added. The tail, which is very fat, is much esteemed, and is generally soused or pickled.

The flesh of the full grown dugong is good and palat-able, resembling fair beef. The meat of the young animal, salted and cured with the flesh and fat in its alternate layers, produces excellent bacon which cannot readily be distinguished from the orthodox pig, and meets with ready sale in .Queensland. The oil properly boiled out from the fat and used on hot toast is equal to fresh butter, and it can also be made to serve exactly the same purpose in cooking.

The oil from the fat is free from that rancid odour common to animal oils, and is held in high esteem.

The flesh of this animal affords excellent food in the countries where it is captured. Humboldt compares it to ham, and Von Martius says he never tasted better meat in the Brazils. When properly dried and salted in the sun, the flesh will remain sweet for a whole year. Amongst the South American monks, it is regarded, from an ecclesiastical point of view, as a fish, together with whales, seals, and other water-loving mammals; hence they fare sumptuously upon its flesh during Lent. Mr. Bates describes the capture of a manatee or *vacca marina*, during his canoe voyage on the Upper Amazon; but does not praise the flavour of its flesh as other travellers have done. He says :—" The meat was cut up into cubical slabs, and each person skewered a dozen or so of these on a long stick. Fires were made, and the spits stuck in the ground, and slanted over the flames to roast. The meat has somewhat the taste of coarse pork ; but the fat, which lies in thick layers between the lean parts, is of a greenish colour, and of a disagreeable fishy flavour."

The flesh of the manatee of South America is edible, and pronounced by Humboldt and others sweet and palatable. When salted and sun dried it will keep for a year or more. The true manatees or lamantines are confined to the Atlantic Ocean. The largest species (*Manatus laterostris*) is found in the United States upon the Florida coast; another species inhabits the mouths of the rivers in South America.

In Africa, the *M. Senegalensis* and a second species,

provisionally named by Professor Owen, *Manatus Vogelii*, is a royal perquisite, like the sturgeon in Britain, and is generally taken to the chief's table. Dr. Vogel speaks of it as very good, its flesh and fat being like pork and very well flavoured. There is no reason why it should not be so. It reaches ten feet in length, and becomes very fat.

Dolphins and Porpoises.—At the Faroe Islands, the inhabitants of which principally live on fish, about 2,000 dolphins or bottle-noses (*Delphinus globiceps*) are taken annually; the flesh is eaten either fresh or salted, and tastes like coarse beef.

The fat is removed, some being used for domestic purposes. The flesh is cut into long bands as thick as the arm, salted, and hung around the houses in the air to dry. It has a black exterior coating and soon exhales a disagreeable odour, which passes away when it becomes thoroughly dried, and it may then be kept a long time.

In former years a dolphin was thought a fit and worthy present to be made to a Duke of Norfolk, who again divided its flesh among his friends; it was roasted and eaten with porpoise sauce.

The flesh and blubber of the dolphin (*Platanista gangetica*) are eaten by some low caste Indians. That of *Delphinus tursis* and *D. Delphis* is eaten along the coasts of the Adriatic.

Brand states that porpoises were sold for food in the Newcastle market in the year 1575. In the time of Edward I. the price for the best sea-hog was 6s. 8d.

At the dinners of the Goldsmiths' Company in olden times we find, besides ordinary fish, the seal and porpoise mentioned. The porpoise then constituted one of the standard dishes of a public feast. It was eaten with a sauce composed of sugar, vinegar, and crumbs of fine bread. Sailors will, however, scarcely eat it. M. de Bouganville, in his "Voyage to the Falkland Isles," writes: "We had some of the porpoise served up at dinner the day it was taken, which several others at the table besides myself thought by no means so ill-tasted as it is generally said to be."

Porpoise flesh is sold at Bridgetown, Barbados, to the negroes at 3d. to 6d. per pound, and the flesh of the shark at a penny per pound.

The porpoise was at one time, even in this country, esteemed a voluptuous article of food. Malcolm IV. granted to the monastery of Dunfermline, those which were caught in the neighbourhood; and it is said to have been introduced at the tables of the old English nobility as late as the time of Queen Elizabeth. Much later than this, it was a great article of consumption in some countries professing the Roman Catholic faith, especially during the season of Lent, and accordingly, in spring, it was the peculiar object of pursuit. Sailors on long voyages, in lack of fresh provisions, were often happy to have recourse to it. Thus, Capt. Colnett, in 1793, mentions that, when off the coast of Mexico in the Pacific, they saw porpoises in abundance, and took many of them, which they mixed with their salt pork, and so made excellent sausages : " They became," he adds, " our ordinary food."

Like most of the cetacea, its flesh has a very strong oily flavour, which, however, relished by an Esquimaux, is not very agreeable to the palate of a European epicure of the present day.

With modern times a change has taken place in the tastes of cultivated society; but in high northern latitudes porpoises are still, as they have ever been, highly esteemed as articles of food. Thus Egede states that " The flesh is by the Greenlanders reckoned a great dainty; and the oil they find a beverage, than which, according to their taste, nothing can be more delicious."*

° Naturalists' Library, Mammalia.

CHAPTER V.

FLESH FOOD FURNISHED BY THE FEATHERED TRIBES.

Buzzard, Kite, and Other Birds of Prey Eaten — Beccafico — Guacharo — Larks — Thrushes — Blackbirds — Buntings — Fried Canaries — Starlings — Rooks — Ortolans — Edible Birds' Nests — Statistics of Supply — Parrots — Toucans — Domestic Poultry — Fowls in Egypt and Morocco — Weight of Different Fowls — Statistics of Poultry in the United Kingdom — in France — in Austria — in the United States — Value of the Poultry Imported from Abroad — Turkeys — Christmas Supplies — Statistics of Turkeys in France — Wild Turkeys of America — Peacocks — Formerly Served at Royal Banquets — Bustards — Partridges — Game Birds Consumed in Great Britain — Snipes — Woodcocks — Grouse — Pheasants — Capercailzie — Game Birds of Sweden — Prairie Hens — Ruffs, Reeves, and Godwits — Quails — Game Pies of France — Patés de Foies Gras — Tragopins — Pigeons, Domestic and Wild — Ostrich Meat — Flamingoes, Cranes, and Herons — Ducks and Geese — Statistics of in France — Wild Geese — Swans — Plovers — Teal — Canvasback Duck — Pelicans — Penguins.

THE class of Birds, like that of Fishes, furnishes the most abundant resources to various people who depend a good deal for their daily food on the fisheries and the chase, and there are very few, with the exception of birds of prey, that are refused. The flesh of those birds which feed on grain or other vegetable products, is less strongly flavoured than that of carnivorous birds. One of the chief characteristics of the flesh of fowls (observes Prof. Church), notably those which are wild, is the almost entire absence of fat. When much fat is present the flavour of the meat is often less delicate and its digestibility, especially when roasted, decidedly difficult. As game, numerous wild birds, especially the water fowls, contribute largely to human food.

Raptores.—Among birds of prey there are not many that furnish food for man, or that are relished when they have been tasted. The buzzard (*Buteo vulgaris*) used to be commonly eaten in France, and the Pern or honey-buzzard was also there esteemed a delicacy. The Chinese and Japanese eat the flesh of the kite and other birds of prey. In the "Annals and Magazine of Natural History," for July, 1857, we read of the carrion kite of Northern Australia (*Milvus affinis*), which is hardly distinguishable from the common kite of India and China, that "these birds are excellent eating, and certainly excel any other game we have in flavour and tenderness." The kite stands A 1 as a table delicacy in the estimation of Dr. M. Elsey, surgeon to the North Australian expedition under Gregory. True he states that they feed entirely on grasshoppers; but what brought them in hundreds on the trees round the camp? Why to pick up all sorts of refuse undoubtedly that is edible by a carrion bird in any shape. The flesh of the hawk tribe is regarded by us as totally unfit for food, yet one species is so much in request in South Morocco, that the birds are sent from Mogador as presents to the Sultan; it is a small bird resembling the sparrow-hawk. (Leared's " Morocco.")

Passeres.—In this order we do not find many which contribute generally to human food.

The beccafico (*Sylvia hortensis*), a bird about the size of a linnet, is highly prized by the Italians for the delicacy of its flesh, particularly in autumn, when it is in excellent condition for the table. The Cypriots preserve them for winter use partially boiled in Commanderia wine.

The guacharo (*Steatornis caripensis*) is much sought for in certain caves in the West Indies and Central America for the fat obtained by melting down the young birds. The oil is semi-fluid, transparent, inodorous, and so pure that it will keep above a year without turning rancid. If eaten when taken from the nest these birds are pronounced by epicures unrivalled, and their flesh is also considered a delicacy when salted.

Preserved larks have been shown in the Italian section

at several of the International Exhibitions. They will keep good, it is said, for three years.

The griveas (*Alauda arvensis*) and thrushes are much in esteem and generally introduced at table at Nice, roasted on toast with a thin layer of bacon fat over them.

We have our delicate tit-bits in spitted larks; as many as four thousand dozen have been known to be taken in the neighbourhood of Dunstable between September and February. What the number sold in our metropolitan markets may be annually, it is impossible to say, but 400 dozen can be bought in one day. A few centuries ago larks were sold in London at 6d. a dozen, and blackbirds at 10d. a dozen. Larks are chiefly the produce of Cambridgeshire, with a smaller proportion from Bedfordshire. They are of easy sale now at about 1s. a dozen, and are generally roasted; at one time they were fashionable in pies. Larks are taken in much larger numbers in Germany, where there is an excise upon them, which has yielded as much as £1,000 a year in Leipsic. The larks of that place are famous all over the German Empire as being of a most delicate flavour.

In the Italian markets, besides carrion crows, strings of thrushes, larks, and even robin redbreasts are sold.

Each year in the autumn, in the south of France and Italy, there is an enormous destruction of small birds, which migrate to pass the winter in a warmer climate.

Owing to the number of robin redbreasts which are eaten in Lorraine, these pretty songsters are becoming scarce. Swallows, redbreasts, and larks are all shot for eating.

The flesh of the young fieldfare (*Turdus pilaris*) is accounted very good eating, and preferable to that of the thrush. It is much eaten in Germany. They migrate here in October staying till February, and are best in December and January.

The flesh of the white Lapland sparrow is so good that in Sweden it is considered equal to the ortolan.

The Italians are said to be fond of the flesh of the cuckoo, and those who have tasted it state that the young cuckoo is a most delicious morsel, but it has seldom or ever been eaten in this country.

The great spotted cuckoo (*Coccytes glandarius*) passes Greece in flocks from the north in August. This bird with the guepier (*Merops apiaster*, L.), and the hoopoe (*Upupa epops*, L.), are all sought for in Greece for food.

In winter they catch by thousands in Sweden, by means of hair springs or snares, a number of small birds which pass under the general name of grives, such as various species of thrush, the waxwing of Bohemia (*Ampelis garrulis*), the common bullfinch (*Pyrrhula europea*), etc.

There are annually sent to the Continent from Corsica between 350,000 and 400,000 blackbirds (*Turdus merula*). They come in vast numbers each winter to feed on the berries of the myrtle and arbutus, with which the mountains are covered. In the month of December they become very fat, and the flavour and perfume given by this food cause them to be much esteemed by the *gourmets* of Paris. A *pâte de foie de merle* is considered a great delicacy.

The common bunting (*Emberiza miliaria*) is often taken in nets and brought to market, where they are sold for larks. The snow bunting (*Plectrophanis* [*Emberiza*] *nivalis*) when fat is excellent eating.

When the ice on the Neva leaves St. Petersburg, innumerable flocks of snow buntings arrive. They almost line the banks of the river, and are killed in great quantities, being fat, but they do not merit the name of ortolans, given to them when served at table.

A favourite dish at some of the cafés of St. Michael's, Madeira, is "fried canaries" (*Fringilla canaria*, Lin.). They don't pay 10s. or £1 a piece for canaries there, only a dollar the hundred in the season. Was it not Vitellius who betrayed a weakness for a stew of nightingales' tongues? They are as materialistic in Madeira. It is some satisfaction to know that cooked canary is no better than sparrow pie.

Starlings (*Sturnus vulgaris*, Lin.) are frequently shot or trapped in the winter and eaten.

The flesh of the stone-chat (*Saxicola œnanthe*) is rather savoury, and that of the bristly-bearded mouse (*Calomophilus biarmicus*) is palatable.

Dr. Daubeny, in his "Lectures on Roman Husbandry," says:—"The ancient Romans had large preserves, not only of poultry and pigeons, but even of thrushes and quails enclosed in pens which were called ' ornithones,' from which they could draw their supply for the table at pleasure. We are told, indeed, of two sorts of ornithones, the one merely aviaries stocked with birds for the amusement of the proprietor; the other kind, constructed with a view to profit, which were often of vast extent, to supply the demands of the Roman market for such articles of luxury. In the Sabine country particularly, we read of extensive pens, filled with birds for the latter purpose. For thrushes alone there were large rooms provided, each capable of holding several thousand birds. As they were put in to be fattened, the place had only just light enough to enable the birds to see their food, but there was a good supply of fresh water accessible. And I may remark that, whilst nothing is said by the Roman writers about the fattening of oxen and sheep, particular directions are given for fattening poultry and other birds—a strong additional argument of the little importance they attached to the larger animals as articles of food."

One of the most delicious birds is the American rice-bunting (*Dolichonyx oryzivora*, Lin.).

This bird migrates over the continent of America, from Labrador to Mexico, and over the great Antilles, appearing in the southern extremity of the United States about the end of March. Towards the middle and close of August, they enter New York, and Pennsylvania on their way to the south. There, along the shores of the large rivers lined with floating fields of wild rice, they find abundant subsistence, grow fat, and their flesh becomes little inferior in flavour to that of the European ortolan, on which account the reed, or rice-birds, as they are then called, are shot in great numbers. When the cool nights in October commence, they move still farther south, till they reach the islands of Jamaica and Cuba in prodigious numbers to feed on the seeds of the guinea grass. Epicures compare the plump and juicy flesh of this delicacy to the ortolan.

As they go southward in the fall, the favourite meadow singers, the bobolinks, take to the marshes and become "reed-birds," much sought after by sportsmen and pot-hunters. At Chester, Delaware, the headquarters of the bird shooters of the State, there are forty professional "pushers." The shooting begins the 1st of September. The *Philadelphia Times* makes a brief estimate of the results of a month's shooting. "At Chester, at the Lazaretto, and the two hundred club-houses that line both banks of the Delaware from League Island to Marcus Hook, there will be at least nine hundred shooters daily. At the former two places 2,000 birds daily—taking the scores of those who push themselves and of the professional shooters—will be killed. Eight hundred gunners daily from the private club-houses is but a fair count, and, giving them each a score of 10 birds daily, the total will be 10,000 birds killed every day in the month of September, an aggregate of 300,000 scored at the above places alone. This is but a meagre approximation of the grand total, probably ranging over 1,000,000 when the marshes from Bombay Hook to Bordentown are included in the estimate."

Lawson affirms that the flesh of the Carolina crow is as good meat as a pigeon, for it never feeds upon any carrion.

Young rooks, when skinned and made into pies, are esteemed by some persons, but they are very coarse eating although wholesome food; rook pie can hardly compete with a pigeon pie, although it is said to have a fulness and lusciousness of flavour which excels any dish of graminivorous birds.

The ortolan (*Embiriza hortulana*) is much esteemed by epicures for the delicacy of its flesh. They are specially fattened in dark chambers till they become mere lumps of fat, and are so rich as soon to satisfy the appetite of a professed gourmand. A great traffic was formerly carried on from the Island of Cyprus in these birds. They are caught in vast numbers there, and pickled in casks, each containing from 300 to 400, prepared with spice and vinegar. In some years the number of casks exported has amounted to 400, or upon an average 140,000 of these highly-prized morsels.

In India they fatten what passes for ortolan, but are birds quite of another kind, being a species of the lark family (*Calandrella brachydactyla*, Temm). Those commonly served at table in Calcutta are mostly un-fattened birds, brought alive to the bazaar, of the species referred to when procurable in abundance, but often mingled with other kinds of larks and pipits, more especially the *Corydalla Richardi*, and not unfre-quently they are of this species exclusively.

Edible Birds' Nests.—There is a curious Chinese food dainty in the gelatinous nest of a species of swift, of which about eight millions are said to be annually sold in China. The nest and bird are figured in Gray's "Genera of Birds," where he names it *Collocalia Troglodytes*. Bonaparte names it *Salangana (Collocalia) fuciphaga*. Thunberg also gave it the name of *Hirundo fuciphaga* from the supposition that the mucilaginous matter em-ployed in the construction of the nests was obtained from seaweed eaten by the birds. But it is now ascertained beyond doubt that the substance in question is secreted by greatly developed glands. The most recent analysis of the nests we owe to Professor Troschel, of Bonn. He finds that the material does not consist of specially nourishing or stimulating substances, but is quite similar in composition to any animal saliva.

Whether *C. esculenta*, *C. fuciphaga*, and *C. nidifica* are one and the same species is not yet settled.

The bird producing this esculent nest is found all over the Malay and Philippine archipelagos, wherever there are caves to afford it shelter and protection. But Java and Borneo seem to be their chief resort. The celebrated caves of Karang-bolong, situated in the province of Baglin in Java, and on the shore of the Southern sea, may be taken as an example.

There are three periods for making the collection— April, August, and December. The nest gatherers are persons bred to their dangerous calling, and the nests are collected with long bamboo ladders. After the crop has been taken, the caves are hermetically sealed against human ingress. The whole annual gathering here, which is effected with little cost, amounts to about 28,000 lbs.

These nests are by no means confined to the sea coasts, for they are obtained in caves in the interior, both of Java and Borneo, and no doubt exist also in other islands. On the north-western side of Borneo, and not far from the banks of the river Baram, birds'-nest caves are found 140 miles from the sea by the course of the river.

The prices paid for these nests in the Canton market vary greatly, according to the quality. Williams tells us, in his work on China, that those of the best sort used to fetch the enormous price of 3,500 dollars the picul of 133 lbs., or more than £5 10s. the pound; the second quality produces 2,800 dollars per picul, and the third, or uncleaned, not more than 1,600 dollars. But the prices are now lower, viz., 2,500, 1,500 and 1,000 dollars. The nests resemble much a piece of fibrous isinglass badly cooked, of a reddish-white colour. They are little thicker than a silver spoon, and vary in weight from a quarter to half an ounce. When dry they are brittle and rough on the surface. In size they are a little larger than a goose egg. They are cleaned with great care, dried in the shade, and packed away. A large portion of the best quality nests are sent to Pekin for the use of the Court. In some parts of China as much as £9 per catty (rather more than 1¼ lbs.) has been paid for these birds' nests.

The value of the collection of these birds' nests in Siam, where it is a government monopoly, was stated by Crawfurd, many years ago, to be about £12,500 annually.

These expensive articles of food are principally employed in making soup, which owes most of its flavour to the ingredients that are added; but they are also made use of in various ways, and are regarded as a great delicacy by Chinese epicures. When newly formed these nests are perfectly clear, of a yellowish-white colour, and wholly soluble in water; but when old they become deeply soiled and mixed with feathers, and their value is immensely deteriorated. Hence they are broadly distinguished into white and black, of which the first are by far the most scarce and valuable, being found in the proportion of one only to twenty-five. The white nests sell in China for nearly their weight in silver. Besides birds'-nest soup, it is made into a jelly, prepared in the following manner:—They steep the nest in water during one night, then with great trouble clean it. This being done it is boiled in water, to which sugar candy is added till the whole forms a jelly. A single nest prepared in this way is enough for one person. These nests being very dear, only the wealthy Chinamen can obtain this delicacy. The rich opium smokers take in the morning a cup of it, for the purpose of refreshing and strengthening their debilitated frames. Persons attacked by consumption are advised by the Chinese practitioners to take these nests; they prescribe them also to those who are reduced by a protracted illness.

The birds which build these nests, of which there are two or probably more species, are found in great abundance in all parts of the Eastern Archipelago, and also on the Continent of India; the nests are collected in great quantities, and constitute an important article of commerce with China.

About 250 lbs. of these birds' nests are collected annually in Lower Cochin China, and fetch from 290 to 405 francs the kilo. The nests taken which are still inhabited by birds are clean, but those which have been abandoned contain a great quantity of agglutinated feathers and excrements.

The gelatinous substance of which they are composed

swells in cold water like gum tragacanth, and is only partially dissolved in boiling water. 120 grammes are required to make about half a litre of soup. They are washed in cold water, and cooked in a bain marie for about eight hours. A fowl is then boned and the flesh pounded, the gravy of which is added to the nests, with seasoning, and the whole is then boiled for a quarter of an hour.

Crawfurd in 1825 estimated the value of the nests annually imported into China at £243,000, but this appears excessive, judging by later returns. Some are imported from Caltura on the western coast of Ceylon, where the Chinese have rented caves from the Government. The average annual imports of birds' nests into China in the four years ending 1870 were 531 piculs, and in the five years ending 1875, 645 piculs (86,000 lbs.)

The value of these birds' nests exported from Bruni in Borneo in 1857 was £2,800.

In the three years ending 1865, edible birds' nests to the value of £2,880 were exported from Sarawak, and in 1880 to the value of £2,567.

There were imported into Labuan from Borneo and the Sulu Islands in the years 1869 and 1870, 26,730 catties of birds' nests, valued at £17,000.

In 1872 672½ piculs of birds' nests were imported into China in foreign vessels, which was a large increase on previous years. From Singapore the quantity reshipped to China in 1867 was 254 cwt., valued at £19,000.

Scansores.—Among the Scansores, or climbing birds, there are very few that have been tried for food. The Indians of Guiana find the flesh of the Ara very good.

The flesh of the macaw of the West Indies is hard, but it is in great esteem among many, especially the French. The green parroquet is a favourite food of the natives of Paraguay, who make an excellent soup with it, but the flesh is tough.

Parrots in Jamaica are generally reckoned very delicate meat, and are not unlike pigeons in flavour ; they are

frequently served up at table in all the country parts of
that Island.* Parrots in Australia are in considerable
estimation for food. Mr. Gould describes the flesh of
the ground parroquet (*Pezoporus formosus*) as excellent,
and much more delicate in flavour than that of the snipe,
equalling, if not surpassing, that of the quail.

Mr. Davidson, in his book "Trade and Travel in the
Far East," tells us that cockatoos make an excellent
dish, and that they occasionally furnished part of his
dinner when in Australia.

The bluish flesh of the toco toucan (*Ramphastos toco,*
Gm.), notwithstanding its enormous and unsightly beak,
is a wholesome and delicate meat; and there are no
birds that give the epicure a more delicious morsel. It
is one of the most omnivorous of birds, and its powers
of digestion and impunity to poisons are remarkable.

Waterton also says the flesh of the large toucan (*R.
maximus*) is delicate.

Domestic Poultry.—The great Gallinaceous tribe of
birds contribute most largely to human subsistence, and
all are esteemed, whether it be the domestic reared
fowls, turkeys and guinea fowl, the pheasants, partridges, grouse and ptarmigan, or the pigeon tribe.

It is curious to observe the change of taste that epicures have experienced with regard to different birds.
Even to-day the tastes of two neighbouring people—the
English and the French—are much more unlike in this
respect than one would imagine. In England, for example, the goose is held in almost as much esteem as the
turkey, while across the Channel the former is sold at
scarcely half the price of the latter, and is regarded as
nothing better than a vulgar dish. But if we compare
our present habits with those of seventeen or eighteen
centuries ago, the contrast will be much more remarkable
still.

To-day we never see a poulterer's shop adorned with
rows of peacocks; and should one of these beautiful birds

---

* Brown's "History of Jamaica."

appear upon the table at some grand public or private dinner, none of the guests would go into ecstasies over the dish, as if its delicacy was a fact universally known. But at Rome no banquet was complete without the presence of the peacock. Among the other large birds, the cranes, the swans, and even the ostrich, were held in high esteem. Geese were also greatly prized, and they were eaten not with a sauce, but stuffed with small green apples. The ducks and teal were served with the juice of the orange and not that of the lemon, and they were preferred to the heathcock and woodcock. As for larks and thrushes, they were usually eaten at the end of the meal, with the idea, true or false, that it would prove a sovereign remedy against affections of the bowels. But, as already observed, the bird most in esteem among all the subjects of the Cæsars was the common thrush. These birds were raised and fattened in large establishments near Rome, and brought very high prices. The artificial rearing of these birds, which are excellent for the table, would prove an easy matter.

Of all the conquests which man has made in the class of birds, and they have been numerous, the most productive and useful has been that of the cock and hen. The eggs and the flesh of this race constitute in many countries, and especially in France, an important part of the general food. The egg has a marked place in the most delicate dishes destined for the sumptuous table. It is also the simple resource of the peasant. Thanks to it, the labourer on returning from the fields can prepare promptly and readily an evening repast.

The details of the production and consumption of Eggs will be found in a subsequent Chapter.

All the world knows the excellence of the flesh of domestic poultry. Without a fowl no feast is complete, and the good King Henry, as a proof of his desire for the wellbeing of his people, wished that every peasant might be able to place a fowl in his pot.

In the early ages of the Church, poultry was regarded as food for fast days, the rule of St. Benedict interdicting

L

only the flesh of quadrupeds, and that of St. Columbanus permitting the consumption of poultry in default of fish. The cock was an object of worship in Syria; among the Greeks and Romans he figured more as a warrior than an esculent, but was gladly eaten by the lower orders. The hen was reckoned a bird of ill omen among the ancients, who sought to diminish the number by eating them. In Rome the art of fattening them, and of imparting a peculiar flavour to their flesh, was perfected by M. L. Strabo, a Roman knight. The rage for fat hens grew at length so great, that C. Fannius, the Consul, passed a decree forbidding the fattening process, fearing that not a living hen would be left in the Empire. Fortunately the new law said nothing about young cocks, and the capon was invented, and was received with such transports of delight that the destruction of birds was greater than ever, and the Consul repented too late that he had only named hens in his sumptuary law.

In old times the Egyptians hatched chickens in ovens; in the last century Réaumur recovered this art, which was thought to be lost, and it is practised at the present day with the most satisfactory results.

More than six million fowls and four million pigeons are artificially reared annually in Egypt.

The Romans were so fond of various birds that some Consular families assumed the names of those they most esteemed. Catius tells us how to drown fowls in Falernian wine, to render them luscious and tender.

The fowls of Morocco are of a very large size, often weighing 14 lbs. or more.

For the table the French breed of fowls is preferable to the Asiatic. They have small bones, well-developed muscles, the flesh is tender, white, and savoury, the skin white and thin; they fatten readily and attain to a remarkable degree of perfection. The pullets of Mans are noted for the delicacy of their flesh.

The average weight of barndoor fowls sold from farm-yards is 3½ lbs. From this must be deducted 3 ozs. for feathers, and 12 ozs. for offal, before they become food. The gamecock rarely exceeds 4½ lbs., but by crossing with the Malay they may be brought up to 6 lbs. or 7 lbs. in weight. Dorkings, when not inbred, but well and carefully fed as chickens, will reach to 7½ lbs. as pullets, and to 9 lbs. as cockerels ; higher weights, such as 10 lbs. for hens and 12 lbs. for cocks, can be obtained, but these are exceptional. The Dorking and Surrey fowls are beyond question the best for the table, in delicacy and weight of flesh; the game fowl the most savoury, although deficient in size; the Brahmapootra not so delicate in flavour as the others, but hardy, weighty, and easily fattened; the Houdan have the good without the bad qualities of the Dorking—are precocious and small boned. A fattened pullet of the Houdan breed killed at four months and a-half, weighs (the crop and intestines empty) 2 kilos. 200 grammes, or about 4½ pounds; thus divided :—

Intestines empty...	100	grammes.
Sand in the gizzard and feathers ...	50	,,
Bones	250	,,
Flesh, including the liver and gizzard...	1.800	,,
	2.200	,,

If we abstract the weight of the flesh of the head and feet, in fact all called "the giblets," or about one kilo. and a-half, we shall find that the bones of this species form barely one-eighth, while the bones in butcher's meat will average one-fourth of the weight.

It is difficult to arrive at any precise estimate of the number of domestic birds and poultry in various countries, but a few figures may not be out of place, although statistics are by no means pleasant reading.

The number of poultry in Ireland in 1883 was 13,382,430, composed as follows:—796,187 turkeys; 2,052,372 geese; 2,836,847 ducks; and 7,697,024 ordinary fowls. Estimating the geese and turkeys at an average market price of 3s. each, and ducks and ordinary fowl at 2s. 6d. per pair, the poultry in Ireland would represent a value of £1,085,651. The number of poultry was about 600,000 more in the two previous years. For Great Britain we have for the first time details this year (1884). The numbers were given as follows:—

			Great Britain.		Ireland.
Turkeys	...	...	500,770	....	706,567
Geese	...	...	888,313	....	1,183,518
Ducks	...	...	2,368,390	....	2,618,530
Fowls	...	...	12,303,539	....	7,537,433

Including the Channel Islands, the number for Great Britain is given at 28,944,249, but this must be taken with all reservation, and is certainly far below the real total. It can scarcely be believed that Ireland exceeds Great Britain in the number of turkeys and geese, considering that in the last two years there has been a very large decrease in the number of Irish poultry.

It is probable that few persons are aware of the extent of what may be termed the poultry industry, or can appreciate the contribution to animal wealth in various countries by the common barn-yard fowl.

According to official statistics published, the following was the number of poultry returned for France:

			1872.		1884.
Fowls	...	...	45,179,084	......	43,858,780
Geese	...	...	3,296,023	......	4,170,650
Ducks	...	...	3,522,292	......	3,600,500
Turkeys	...	...	1,073,898	......	1,800,500
Pigeons	...	...	5,212,042	......	—
Guinea fowls	...		—	......	2,588,700
			58,283,339	......	56,019,130

Mr. Masson, a French writer, estimated in 1884 the number of fowls in France at 43,858,780, which at the average price of 3 fr., is equal to 131,576,340 fr. Each year a fifth of these are sold for food, viz., 8,771,756, at 3 fr., making 27,855,268 fr. Also 2,100,000 cocks or capons sold at the same price for 6,300,000 fr. There remains, therefore, 32,982,024 hens, producing yearly 101,000,000 chickens, from which are selected 11,000,000 as reproducers, to replace those killed, and we may attribute to disease and accidents a loss of 11,000,000; in all 22,000,000 chickens have to be deducted from the 101,000,000 produced; ˙ there remains, therefore, 79,000,000, which sold at 1 fr. 75 c. each, yield a sum of 138,250,000 fr. To these figures must be added about 7,000,000 fr. for superior fowls, capons, and fat hens. The summary for these fowls is 179,405,268 fr. Furthermore, the 32,787,024 hens lay each year on an average 100 eggs each. From this we must deduct 100,000,000 eggs employed for hatching, which leaves 3,187,702,400 at ˙07 cents each, which gives a product of 223,139,168 fr. It may therefore be affirmed that the 43,858,780 fowls would yield on the one hand 179,405,268 fr. for poultry, and also 223,132,168 fr. for eggs, in all 402,537,436 fr.

Guinea-fowl are seldom met with on farms, and are chiefly found in the poultry-yards of amateurs or large proprietors; we are therefore surprised at the figures given by Mr. Masson, which can scarcely be correct. He states that there are in France 2,588,700 Guinea-fowls, worth 4 fr. each, equal to 10,354,800 fr. Of these, 647,740 are annually sold; at 4 fr. apiece, these will yield 2,590,960 fr. There remain 1,940,960 hens, producing annually 6,000,000 chickens. From these, 600,000 are chosen as reproducers, replacing those killed, and about 600,000 are carried off yearly by sickness and accidents. There remain, therefore, 4,800,000 young, which, sold at 2 fr. each, yield 9,600,000 fr. If we add 500,000 fr. for fine and choice birds, we have for those sold, 12,690,960 fr. Besides the eggs saved for hatching, the 1,940,960 hens will lay on an average 200 eggs each yearly, or 388,192,000 at ˙05 cents, equal to 19,409,600 fr., which, added to the value of the birds, makes 32,100,560 fr.

In Paris in 1883, 26,000 tons of poultry and game were sold. The price of poultry has increased very much during the last few years, and fowls, the wholesale price of which was rather less than 3 fr. in 1879, were last year over 5 fr. The wholesale price of ducks has gone up during the past ten years from 2 fr. 72c. to 4 fr., rabbits from 1 fr. 95c. to 3 fr. 50c., partridges from 2 fr. 10c. to 2 fr. 80c., and hares from 5 fr. 30c. to 6 fr., Pheasants, upon the other hand, have slightly fallen in price, from 6 fr. 90c. in 1873, to 6 fr. 25c. The largest portion of the poultry and game consumed in Paris comes from the provinces, but 1,200,000 pigeons, 40,000 quails, 24,000 turkeys, and 20,000 fowls came from Italy; 230,000 hares, 11,000 deer, and 200 wild boars from Germany; and a great number of partridges, woodcock, and snipe from Spain. Most of the game and poultry condemned as unfit for food are sold, according to the report published by the Inspector of Markets, by the railway companies, and this is accounted for by so many boxes of game and poultry being unclaimed or having had the addresses rubbed off. The contents are then sold, and, as may be imagined, they are generally very " high."

Summarising the total annual value of poultry in France we arrive at the following figures:—

			Francs.		Sterling.
Fowls	...	...	402,544,464	......	£16,021,780
Turkeys	...	...	33,701,120	......	1,348,045
Guinea-fowls		...	32,110,560	......	1,284,422
Geese	...	...	82,344,836	......	3,293,793
Ducks	...	...	23,277,020	......	931,081
			573,978,030		£22,879,121

When we consider that we derive from France poultry to the value of £130,000, and eggs to the value of £3,100,000, besides eggs from other European States, which bring up the total to close upon £9,000,000 yearly, the poultry trade of the Continent assumes large proportions.

The consumption of poultry in Chili is very large. There is not a family, rich or poor, that has not its boiled fowl (poule à pot or cazuela) at least once or twice a week. It is therefore no exaggeration to estimate the number of fowls, ducks, and pigeons at two millions, and these average in value about 10d. each.

The number of fowls in Austria is very difficult to be ascertained, but official authorities state that there may safely be quoted an average number of 60 millions, valued at 10 million florins. Those annually consumed are replaced, and 2,400 million eggs are supplied, representing a value of 4 millions sterling. They are chiefly consumed in Vienna, Prague, Steyer, and other large towns.

In Roumania the domestic poultry are reckoned at about 14,000,000, of which half are consumed yearly.

Thirty years ago the poultry in the United States were valued at £4,000,000. The statistics of poultry and eggs in the States were gathered for the first time by the census of 1880. The number of barnyard fowl reported, exclusive of spring-hatching, was 102,272,135 ; of other fowl, 23,235,187; the number of dozens of eggs, 456,910,916. At 12 cents. (6d.) a dozen, certainly a moderate estimate, the annual value of the egg product to the farmers would reach nearly £11,000,000 ; while we may suppose 150,000,000 to 180,000,000 pounds of meat sold annually out of the stock of fowls reported. There were twenty-seven States which reported more than 1,000,000 of barn-yard fowls each; seventeen which report more than 2,000,000 each; thirteen which report more than 5,000,000 each.

Not much can be said in praise of the poultry of the United States, with the exception of the turkeys, which are generally good, and are raised without much difficulty. They do not, however, appear to reach the great weight of our English birds, being of a slighter form, approaching that of the wild stock.

The fowls are exceptionally badly bred. If it may be said of the Texan cattle that they are all " legs and horns," the American fowl may be described as all "legs and elbows," and when plucked presents with his bright yellow skin a most uninviting appearance. They are, however, in request for a change from the perpetual repetition of tender loin and fillet of beef. In Detroit market ducks sell at about 1s. each, fowls 10d., and turkeys 6½d. per lb. At Lexington, Kentucky, when the loin of beef was from 5d. to 6¼d. per lb., turkeys ready for cooking were 5d. per lb., geese, good birds, 4d. per lb., and fowls 7½d. each.

On the Continent generally fowls are bred on a much larger scale than in England. In Egypt, China, and some other countries, the quantity of fowls and ducks used for food is so great, that it has been found necessary from time immemorial to hatch the young by artificial heat.

Our foreign supplies of poultry, etc., have progressed as follows :—

1861	...	...	...	...	...	£73,975
1871	...	...	...	...	...	174,518
1880	...	...	...	...	...	456,124
1883	...	...	...	...	...	591,367

The annual value of the poultry and game we import from abroad (including rabbits) now exceeds £600,000. In 1883 it came from the following countries :—

Belgium ...	...	...	...	...	...	£299,997
France	...	...	...	...	...	164,839
Other countries ...	...	...	...	...	126,575
						£591,411

Turkeys are supplied to the London market chiefly from Cambridge and Norfolk. Besides the general sale to the public, usually in the Christmas week 10,000 or 11,000 turkeys are sent as presents to the metropolis, and it is generally considered that a fine fat turkey with sausages and hamper, carriage, etc., costs about £1.

They are killed simply by breaking their necks, and the breast-bone is also broken before they are sent off to the poultry salesman, in order to give the breast a plumper appearance. The cocks, if sold out of their feathers to the neighbouring gentry, will fetch 1s. 2d. per lb., and the hens 1s., or sometimes only 9d., when a very plentiful season has knocked down prices, or they are not fed up to the mark. The larger they are, the higher their value per lb., on the same principle that salmon of 20 lbs. and upwards fetch 6d. more in the spring and early summer months for the large West-end dinner parties. The great bulk of these go in their feathers to the London salesmen; but the wives of the small farmers take them picked to Norwich, and sell them in the market, where very large ones, trussed and ready for the spit, have made 1s. 6d. per lb. at Christmas. Hen birds, which get fat sooner, and are generally killed off before the end of November, are thought to be a daintier morsel than the "gobblers." Some two-year-old cocks (beyond which age they are very seldom kept) have been killed at 30 lbs., when a heavy weight is wanted for an audit dinner; and with very high feeding, in one or two rare instances, prize birds have turned the scale at 40 lbs.

The turkey was long unknown to the Greeks, there being no turkeys in Europe during their palmy days. Sophocles is the first who mentions it. In Egypt it was still more rare. It was first introduced into Rome in the year 115 before our era, where it was regarded as an object of uncommon curiosity. A century later they had greatly multiplied, but afterwards declined again. Two were exhibited as curiosities at Athens about the middle of the sixth century. It is said that the moderns owe their introduction to the Jesuits, who imported them from America. Hurtant asserts that the first turkey was introduced in France at the wedding dinner of Charles IX., and that it was admired as a very extraordinary thing. Bouche, the historian of Provence, declares that the French are indebted for the turkey to King Réné, who died in 1480; and Beckmann again denies its existence in France previous to the sixteenth century. The English first tasted this new dish in 1525, the 15th year of the reign of Henry VIII.

There are about 1,800,500 turkeys in France, worth 8 frs. apiece, equal to 14,404,000 frs. A fifth of these with about 70,000 males, or 430,000, are sold for food, and, valued at 8 frs. a-piece, yield 3,441,120 frs. The 1,370,360 females remaining produce annually 16,000,000 young turkeys; 5,000,000 of these are reserved to replace those killed, and an average of 5,000,000 are carried off by disease. There remains, therefore, 6,000,000 turkeys which, sold at 3 frs. each, produce 30,000,000 frs. The higher price given for first-class birds may be estimated at 260,000 frs., which gives a total result of 33,701,120 frs.

The breast of the wild turkey of North America (*Meleagris gallo-pavo*), nicely fried in the oil of the black bear, would furnish a dish calculated to tickle the palate of a London alderman. Its flesh has a very characteristic flavour, different from that of the tame bird; it has a gamey taste, and the flesh after cooking is blacker than that of the domestic turkey.

"Always partridges" has become almost proverbial, and we find from Lawson ("History of Carolina") how a repetition of the most delicious food palls. "We cooked our supper," says that traveller, "but, having neither bread nor salt, our fat turkeys began to be loathsome to us, although we were never wanting of a good appetite, yet a continuance of our diet made us weary;" and again he adds, "by the way our guide killed more turkeys and two polecats, which he ate, esteeming them before fat turkeys."

The flesh of the turkey is unlawful food among the Mohammedans. The prejudice arises, it is said, from the tuft on the breast, which bears some resemblance to hog's bristles.

Peacocks were carefully reared by the ancients in the island of Samos. The guinea fowl was considered delicious by the Romans, but they knew not the turkey.

We no longer hear of peacocks and pies of cranes' tongues. As for peacocks, they have entirely gone out of fashion, and it is doubtful whether anyone living ever tasted peacock in England; yet peacock pies, with the heads and tails of the birds protruding from the crust, were formerly common enough at Christmas. William IV. is said to have partaken of peacock when dining with the Governor of Greenwich, and this is the last instance on record of peacock eating.

The peacock had prodigious success among the Romans. Quintus Hortensius was the first who had them served in a banquet; and the novelty made an extraordinary sensation at Rome, becoming so much the fashion that no feast was thought complete without them. Marcus Aufidius Livio contrived a way to fatten them, and made above £50,000 by the sale. Horace preferred them to the finest poultry. Tiberius reared them, and put to death a soldier who had the misfortune to kill one.

The peacock was considered during the ages of chivalry not merely an exquisite delicacy, but a dish of peculiar solemnity. After being roasted it was again decorated with its plumage, and a sponge dipped in lighted spirits of wine was placed in its bill. When it was introduced on days of grand festival it was the signal for the adventurous knights to take upon them vows to do some deed of chivalry " before the peacock and the ladies." Ultimately they were voted indigestible, and were served up in their skins and feathers to be looked at, but not eaten.

The peacock is stated to have been one of the famous dishes at the costly royal banquets of old, and the receipt for dressing it is thus given :—

" Take and flay off the skin with the feathers, tail, and the neck and head thereon; then take the skin and all the feathers and lay it on the table abroad, and strew thereon ground cumin; then take the peacock and roast him, and baste him with raw yolks of eggs; and when he is roasted, take him off and let him cool awhile, then take him and sew him in his skin, and gild his comb, and so serve him forth with the last course."

Game Birds.—The little bustard (*Otis tetrax, Tetrax campestris,* Leach) is taken in nets in France like the partridge ; it weighs about 25 ounces. The flesh has the appearance of a young pheasant. The Bengal floriken (*Sypheotides bengalensis,* Gm.), an Asiatic species, is much sought for by the Indian sportsman as a delicacy for the table.

Many of the family of the *Tetraonidæ*, called by the natives of Buenos Ayres partridges, are very much hunted on account of their savoury flesh.

Perdrix grises is a name adopted in commerce, and by cooks in France, for young partridges under a year old.

There are three stages very distinct in their culinary appreciation. In the first three months they feed only on ants' eggs, insects, and tender herbs—food which gives the flesh a bad taste; and they are only eatable about the end of July, or in August or September, when they have attained the fourth of their size, and have fed upon grains. But they are really not delicious till the close of the year, when they have amply fed on germinated grain and young buds. It is at this period their crop is filled with fermenting grain; this fermentation continues in their stomach and gives them that succulent gamey flavour. Their flesh is very delicate and easy of digestion.

Among the game-birds largely sold are grouse and blackcocks, ptarmigans, partridges, and pheasants, woodcocks, wild ducks, etc.

An estimate of the game birds consumed in Great Britain, made in 1880, gave the numbers and value as follows :—

510,000 grouse and black game, at 4s. ...	£102,000
376,000 partridges, at 2s.	37,600
335,000 pheasants, at 4s.	67,000
Woodcock, snipe, wild duck, &c.	30,000
	£236,600

Snipes (*Becassine* of the French), are sent in great numbers from St. Omer, in France, in the neighbourhood of which they are shot. They are generally fat and in good condition; their fat is of an exquisite flavour. This bird is always cooked ungutted.

The flesh of the woodcock (*Scolopax rusticula*) is esteemed a great delicacy, and they generally attract a good deal of the sportsman's attention. Woodcocks have occasionally been shot as heavy as 20 ounces, but 12 ounces is about the average weight. The curlew, common on our coasts, is often sold for woodcock when these birds are scarce. The American woodcock is *Philohela minor.*

The best woodcocks in France are sent to Paris from Nancy, Ardennes, Burgundy, and Berry. To ascertain their quality, the belly should be examined, this should be hard and full when they are fat. The rump and the loins should also be furnished with firm, white fat. Around the neck will be seen a vein of the same fat of the colour of ivory. In order to ascertain if the bird is young and tender, the bones at the extremity of the stomach should be tested; if these bend the bird is young and tender; if not, it is old and tough, and only fit to cook in a pasty or stew. Woodcocks weigh generally 450 to 500 grammes, or about one pound. The woodcocks sent from Nantes, Rennes, Brest, and all Brittany, are about one-third less in size, and are rarely fat. They are sent in great abundance to the markets of Paris in October and November. The woodcock may be kept fit for eating long after killing, and many prefer them high.

Of grouse, besides our home supply of red grouse (*Lagopus scoticus*) from the Scotch moors, we import immense numbers of ptarmigan or white grouse (*Lagopus vulgaris*) from the north of Europe, and some ruffed grouse (*Bonasia umbellata*) from the United States, but not in great quantity. Of European grouse one ship has brought over from Norway 24,000 ptarmigan, and one poulterer in London will sometimes receive 15,000 of these birds.

The Scotch grouse are smaller than those from Sweden and Norway. Their flesh, although of a grey colour, is excellent, and has a flavour very agreeable and aromatic.

The gelinotte (*Bonasa betulina*) or grouse of Russia is rather smaller than that obtained from Germany. The flesh is of a whitish-rose colour; when cooked it is of a darker colour but delicate flavour. It is esteemed for its good culinary qualities, and its property of keeping good long. The flesh is delicious and of easy digestion, and is good at all times.

The partridge (*Perdrix cinerea*) is common in Britain, but is also widely distributed, and there are many other species. The red-legged partridge (*P. rubra*), is delicate but not equal to the English bird; we get it from the eastern countries as from Russia and other parts of the Continent. The Greek partridge (*Caccabis saxatilis*, Meyer) is another European species largely sought for in the south.

Partridges and pheasants for the London market chiefly come from Norfolk and Suffolk; ptarmigan from the north of Scotland and Norway. About 150,000 to 200,000 partridges are sold in London annually.

The price of pheasants in England is very much affected by the great demand there is for them in France, where a great many are sold for their plumage, while they make the bodies into pies. From the Austrian forests about 70,000 pheasants and 700,000 partridges are annually obtained.

In severe winters 9,000 or 10,000 of ptarmigans have been received in a day from Norway. Holland contributes the great stock of wild duck for London tables. The duck decoys are objects of great care there. The largest supply of plovers and woodcocks is also from Holland.

The capercailzie (*Tetrao urogallus*, Linn.) may be called the king of the grouse or Tetrao tribe. He often weighs 8 lbs. and 10 lbs. The hen bird is much smaller, weighing only 4 or 5 lbs. This bird is delicious eating, feeding as it does on the cranberry, whortleberry, and bay leaf. Nor do the pine shoots or juniper give an unpleasant flavour. The same may be said of the black-game of Norway. Most epicures would, we should imagine, prefer the capercailzie, with its rare flavour, to the turkey. The black-game weighs 7 lbs. and 8 lbs. a brace. The capercailzie has been known to reach 14 lbs. in weight, and to attain the length of 2 ft. 9 in., whilst he is as plump as a partridge. The blackcock (*Tetrao tetrix*) are brought over in large numbers from Russia, Sweden and Norway.

In Sweden the following birds fit for food are the objects of chase more or less productive:—Large and small cock of the wood (*Tetrao urogallus*, and *T. tetrix*), gelinotte (*Bonasia betulina*), grey partridge (*Perdrix cinerea*), quail (*Coturnix communis*), plovers, as the guignard (*Charadrius morinellus*), the ordinary woodcock (*Scolopax rusticola*), snipes (*Gallinago major*, *G. media* and *G. gallinula*, *Totanus ochropus*, *T. glariola*, and *T. glottis*). These birds are chased with pointer dogs. The curlew (*Numenius arquata*), the whimbrel (*N. phæopus*, Lin.), which is often passed off to the unwary as a woodcock, and various wild ducks. The flesh of the curlew and whimbrel are alike excellent.

Hundreds of thousands of the large game birds are consumed yearly in the country, and sent to the southern provinces of Sweden and to England.

We get an abundance of prairie-hens and canvas-back ducks from the United States. These are frozen by machinery on the other side of the Atlantic, packed in barrels, and brought over in capital condition. In New York one man has been known to receive in a single consignment 20 tons of prairie hens (*Tetrao cupido, Cupidonia cupido*); allowing two pounds as the weight of each bird (a very fair average), the enormous number of 20,000 pinnated grouse would remain, received by one person in a single day.

Some of the large poultry dealers in the same city will sell in six months 200,000 game-birds; others 150,000, and others again 400 dozen, and so on downwards through the scale until the final result of all these amounts, if it could be accurately obtained, would make one stand aghast at the incredible numbers which are slaughtered every year.*

* "Report of Department of Agriculture, Washington, 1864," p. 383.

Ptarmigan, blackcock, and capercailzie are sent over in the winter from the northern countries, frozen naturally, in cases containing from eighty to a hundred each, shipped at Christiansund, landed at Hull, and brought up to town by rail. Holland is good enough to send us, sometimes forty or fifty baskets of two hundred each in one steamer, of her delicious wild ducks and those curious little birds the fighting snipes, called ruffs and reeves (*Machetes pugnax*), which are about the size of godwits, and the male of which has most wonderful plumage, with a pretty crown of grey feathers on his head, given to make him look handsome and attractive at courting time. These birds are good when fat. Though considerably larger than the ruff, the godwits (*Limosa ægocephala*, Lin.) are not in such high estimation as an article for the table.

Even wild turkeys and other birds from the backwoods of America are occasionally seen in the shops of our London poulterers, transmitted in a frozen state by the Atlantic steamers. St. Petersburg is supplied with game in a like manner, from the distant wilds of Tartary and Siberia.

But our most curious importation is the quail from Egypt and Algeria, which feeds us to this day as it fed the Israelites in the desert, and is brought over, alive, in consignments of from thirty to fifty thousand. These birds are shipped at Alexandria and Algiers, and sent on to Marseilles in charge of a native attendant to minister to their bodily wants. Thence they are "railed" across France in cages holding 100 birds each, lodged for the time at Smithfield, and then dispersed to all parts of the kingdom. So carefully are they transported that not more than seven per cent. of them perish by the way. Of the quail there are several species spread over Europe, Asia, and America, but that frequenting Europe, and especially the coasts of the Mediterranean (*Coturnix communis*, Bon.), is the best known.

They are easily taken in nets when they arrive in

August fatigued with their flight. The women in Greece pluck them and gut them, cutting off their heads and feet, flatten them between boards loaded with stones, and afterwards pack them in jars with layers of salt. They form an article of commerce, and are shipped in small casks. They are eaten in winter roasted on spits, or prepared in various other ways. In certain parts of the Peloponessus the quail forms one of the riches of the country.

The supply of live birds to our English markets is derived from Egypt, Italy, and Algeria. In Egypt, at the proper season, they are so plentiful that the people cannot consume, in a fresh state, the number captured, and therefore salt them down for future use or dry them in the sun. At the time of their migration the islands and shores of the Mediterranean absolutely swarm with them. Such great quantities used to be captured in the Isle of Capri, near Naples, as to afford the Bishop the chief part of his revenue, and he was called, in consequence, "the Bishop of Quail." An almost incredible number of quails is supplied to the great towns and cities of the Continent. Those imported into Paris from Italy alone are valued at about £50,000 annually. Leadenhall Market is the great depôt for the English supply, and as many as 200,000 are often brought there in a month during the season. Temminck tells us that hundreds of thousands arrive in Naples and Provence and are so fatigued that for some days they suffer themselves to be taken by hand.

It is almost impossible to speak too highly of the quail in a gastronomic point of view, though Yarrell considers it "heating food." The French proverb, "hot as a quail," probably had its origin in the pugnacious temper of the bird to which we have just alluded. Our opinion is, that the flesh of the quail is anything but "hot," and stimulating. It may lack what is considered a "gamey" flavour, but it is as delicate and succulent a morsel as the most educated *gourmet* can desire. Wither, in his Satires, says—

M

" He that feeds on no worse meat than quails,
And with choice dainty pleaseth appetite,
Will never have great lust to gnaw his nails,
Or in a coarse thin diet take delight."

The most approved way of cooking a quail is to envelop it in a very thin slice of bacon, tie it up in a large vine leaf, and then roast it. A cold quail pie is also a capital dish.

The Virginian quail (*Ortyx Virginianus*) is inferior to the European or African. Numbers are imported from America in barrels.

The pin-tailed sand-grouse, "el katte," (*Pterocles alchata*), of which enormous flights may be sometimes seen in the East, is believed to be the veritable quail of the Israelites. There is an Arabian quail, the bones and tendons of which are said to be so small and tender, that every part of the bird can be eaten.

Many of the towns of France have a reputation for their game pies. Chartres, which is situated in the centre of an abundant game district, is noted for these pies, which are composed of partridges, quails, larks, and hares, also for those made with plovers and dotterels. The town of Pithiviers is well-known for its *patés de mauviettes;* these are in season from the time of fogs or mist up to January. Rouen is renowned for its *patés de poulardes,* boned and seasoned with ham. Amiens is noted for its *patés de canards,* in originating which Degand, a man celebrated for his cooking, realised a fortune of a million of francs.

Montreuil on the sea has a high reputation for its " woodcock *patés,*" while Strasbourg is noted for its *patés de foies gras.* Formerly there was a strong objection among foreigners to eating these, from the cruel practice resorted to by the Jews to enlarge the liver at the expense of the other parts of the body. The geese were placed alive in an oven, which was gradually heated until the liver attained its greatest size. This has long been abolished, and the birds are now only shut up, like cloistered nuns, in small confined cells, which prevent their moving. They are fed with nourishing paste, and their drink is sulphurised water.

To Toulouse belongs the truffled *patés de foies de canard*, built up in the form of huge towers, which fetch £50 to £60, and are in demand for great occasions ; but those for ordinary consumption are prepared in earthenware pots. These *patés* are more unctuous than those of Strasbourg, but they are improved by adding a glass of sherry.

Périgord makes *patés* of truffled partridges in terrines, which, being well-seasoned, will keep for many months, and they have acquired a universal reputation. Courtoy, who gave his name to this delicacy, made a splendid fortune out of it.

The Tragopans (*Ceriornis satyra* and *C. temmincki*) are game birds of Asia, species of pheasants which are sought for by sportsmen. They make a near approach to the ordinary turkey and fowl.

Pigeons.—Of the domestic pigeons much need not be said, except that they are largely bred for food purposes ; but of some of the wild ones a brief mention may be made.

The passenger pigeon of America (*Columba* [*Ectopistes*] *migratoria*) is a very large and well-flavoured bird, which migrates in certain seasons in dense flocks. Wilson and Audubon describe having seen flocks which they computed to number respectively from thousands of millions up to upwards of a billion each. In one day seven tons of these pigeons have been brought into the New York Market by the Erie railroad. The Indians often watch the roosting places of these birds and knocking them on the head in the night, bring away thousands. They preserve the oil or fat for use instead of butter.

In their breeding places, herds of hogs are fed on the young pigeons or " squabs," which are also melted down by the settlers, as a substitute for butter or lard. The felling of a single tree often produces two hundred squabs, nearly as large as the old ones, and almost one mass of fat. They are very tender and delicate, and much more esteemed as food than the adult bird. Pennant, in his

Arctic Zoology, says, Sir William Johnstone told him, that at one shot, he brought down with a blunderbuss above a hundred and twenty pigeons. Wagon-loads of them are poured into the towns, and sold as cheap as a half-penny up to two-pence the dozen. The flesh, which is dark, tastes like that of the common wild blue pigeon, but is, if anything, better flavoured.

The wonga-wonga pigeon of Australia (*Leucosarcia picata*, Lath.) is not only of considerable size, but a first-rate bird for the table, possessing a whiteness and delicacy of texture in its pectoral muscles, which are unapproached by any other species of this widely spread and useful family, the one at all approximating to it being the *Geophaps scripta*.

The common bronze-winged pigeon of Australia (*Phaps chalcoptera*, Lath.) is a plump heavy bird, weighing when in good condition fully a pound; and is constantly eaten by every class of persons resident in Australia. The New Zealand wood pigeon (*Carpophago Novæ-Zealandiæ*, Gm.,) becomes exceedingly fat in the autumn. It is esteemed most by amateurs when feeding on the masts of the Miro, which imparts a peculiar flavour to the flesh. They are speared and snared in great numbers by the Maoris, an expert hand sometimes taking as many as sixty in a single day. These pigeons and the tui or parson birds, (*Prosthemadera Novæ Zealandiæ*, Gm.,) are potted for keeping by the Maoris, after their own elaborate and peculiar fashion. The birds, which are large, are denuded of their feathers and thoroughly cleaned; they are then carefully baked, in order to extract the oil, and closely packed in a species of basket woven for the purpose, the fat being poured over them. Secured in this manner from atmospheric influences, they are said to keep for years, and form a highly esteemed article of food amongst the Maoris. The appearance of these closely-woven calabashes, each containing upwards of 150 of these delicacies in the poultry department, is fanciful in the extreme, and the manner in which they are each mounted on what might be termed a tripod, and fantastically decked out with a variety of feathers, specially prepared for the purpose, is highly suggestive of the complicated Indian preserves of this nature.

The flesh of the passerine ground dove of America (*Chamœpelia passerina*, Linn.) is very delicate and much sought after in the Antilles.

Wood pigeons are so numerous occasionally in parts of Scotland that special funds are raised to promote their destruction. They arrive in great flocks from Norway, Denmark, and Sweden, and at least 17,000 are annually killed, according to the returns of the United East Lothian Agricultural Society. The fields of red clover are occasionally blue with the number of these pigeons feeding.

The flesh of the turtle dove (*Columba turtur*, Linn.) is considered much superior to that of the wild pigeon. Dampier, when he visited the Gallapagos Islands, in 1684, says " there are great plenty of turtle doves, so tame that a man may kill five or six dozen in a forenoon with a stick. They are somewhat less than a pigeon, but uncommonly fat."

The flesh of the Penelope is white, delicate and nutritious, and more tender and less dry than that of the hocco, or crested curassow (*Crax alector*), called the royal pheasant by the Mexicans, and for this reason esteemed more choice. It is to be feared that all kinds of these game birds will in time become very scarce. The flesh of the American guans, especially *Penelope marail*, Gm., is excellent, and resembles that of the pheasant ; it has been domesticated in France and England. *Penelope cristata*, furnishes an excellent dish for the table, and might advantageously be added to our domestic stock of poultry, as its flesh is delicate.

Ostrich-meat.—Those who have tasted Ostrich-meat state that it is both wholesome and palatable, although, as might be expected in the case of wild birds, it may be somewhat hard and tough. Where the birds have been domesticated, however, and fed on lucerne, clover and grain, the meat becomes juicy and tender. The fact of its prohibition by the Jewish legislation would indicate that ostrich-meat was employed as food in former times. Firmus, one of the kings of Egypt, it is said, used to dine off ostrich flesh; and according to Lampridius, the Emperor Heliogabalus, on the occasion of a great feast, caused the brains of six hundred ostriches to be served up in one dish. Africanus especially commends ostrich brains. It is related of Leo Africanus that he partook of ostrich-meat in Numidia, where it is said young ostriches were then fattened expressly for the table. Strabo gives a curious account of the Struthophages, a black tribe on the Upper Nile, who hunted and lived upon ostriches, and clothed themselves with the skin of this bird.

A recent observer, Canon Tristram, has remarked that the Arabs of the present day eat ostrich-meat, and that he himself has tasted it and found it palatable enough. Mr. John Parkes, of Wheatlands, in the Cape Colony in 1875, killed a young bird that had broken its leg, and had the meat converted into steaks and "biltong" or dried meat. It was said to eat "like young beef, juicy and tender, with just a suspicion of a sweetish flavour, usually undiscoverable in the legitimate article."

A kouskoussou surmounted by cutlets of fat taken from the breast of the ostrich, is said to be a royal dish of the desert; while the steam from the boiled fat imparts an unctuous taste and gamey flavour to the whole.

The best account, however, we have of the gastronomic flavour of the ostrich is furnished in the details of a dinner given at Marseilles in Nov., 1871, as recorded in the "Bulletin of the Society of Acclimatation of Paris" (vol. ix., p. 154). A young ostrich, one of a brood of eleven, which was being raised with care in the gardens of the Society there, had the misfortune to break its leg. Thereupon the President of the local Society, M. Ad. Lucy, summoned a meeting of the council to decide upon the food qualities of the young bird. Stripped of its feathers and cleaned, it weighed 73 lbs., and the interior parts 18 lbs.

The first surprise in cutting up the bird was that in place of what is known in the fowl as the most fleshy parts, the breasts and the wings, there was nothing but a bony skeleton with scarcely any flesh, more resembling the ribs of a lean sheep. But in place of flesh there were found two large masses of fat weighing not less than 12 lbs. The thighs, however, presented an enormous development, and could only be compared, when separated from the articulated joint, to a fat leg of Down mutton, the weight of each being not less than 12 lbs. The giblets, which could not be kept for the feast, were made into soup, and the liver, weighing over 2 lbs., cooked in a stewpan like that of a deer. The appreciation of the giblets, the wing pinions, the neck, etc., was general, and elicited the exclamation "It is remarkably good," whilst the liver resembled that of venison, of which it had the flavour and firmness, without being hard.

For the grand dinner, to which the chief magistrate of the town and other notabilities were invited, the menu was as follows:—

1. Tendons, façon filet de bœuf à la financière.
2. Cuissot en daube.
3. Paté en timbale.

The following were the opinions pronounced on these:—

(1.) *Financière.* If the meat had been well-kept, not one of the guests who partook of the dish would have doubted that it was beef served, the tenderness, succulence and flavour of the meat were generally acknowledged, and it was unanimously declared to be first rate.

(2.) *La Daube.* The vocabulary of praise for this dish was prodigious. On every side resounded, " perfect and excellent, rich, exquisite." The chief magistrate declared it recalled the flavour without disadvantage of "lange de bœuf à l'écarlate."

(3.) Then followed the *timbale*, which on being opened met with equal favour. A paté of Chartres or of Pithiviers could not have met with more compliments, each special dish having been successively put to the vote by the chairman. While agreeing that all met with approval, the daube was considered the best, the tendons à la financière second, and the timbale a good third.

It was thus proved that the young ostrich furnishes excellent food for the table, and in view of the progress making in domestication and artificial incubation at the Cape Colony, Algeria, Australia, and elsewhere, there is great probability of this bird appearing more frequently as a dish on the tables in Europe.

The young of the *Rhea* are eaten in South America.

The flesh of the Ibis is savoury and good, its eggs are nearly as large as those of the duck, and of a bright sky blue colour. The glossy ibis (*Plegadis falcinellus*, Linn.) is shot in Hungary and other parts in Europe.

The flesh of the flamingo (*Phœnicopterus antiquorum*) is pretty good meat, though rather fishy; the young are thought by some to be equal to partridge. This bird was not only esteemed as a bonne-bouche of old, but as most valuable after dinner; for when the gluttonous sensualists had eaten too much, they introduced one of its long scarlet feathers down their throats to disgorge their dinner. The flesh is red and coarse, and even the fat part partakes of the crimson hue.

According to Viellot, "the flesh of the *Phœnicopterus* is a dish more sought after in Egypt than in Europe; however, Catesby compares it for its delicacy to the partridge. Dampier says it has a fine flavour, though lean and black. Dutertre finds it excellent, notwithstanding its marshy taste; the tongue is the most delicious part."

Apicius has left receipts for dressing it with more than the minute accuracy of a modern cooking book, and the *Phœnicopterus ingens* appears among the luxuries of the table in Juvenal's eleventh satire.

The brains and the tongue figure as one of the favourite dishes of Heliogabalus, and the superior excellence of the latter was dwelt upon by the same Apicius,

and noticed by Pliny. Neither has it escaped the pointed
pen of Martial. Dampier does not forget this delicious
tongue of the flamingo, observing that a dish of these
tongues is worthy of a place at a prince's table.

The tongue is remarkable for its texture, magnitude,
and peculiar armature. The whole length of the tongue
is three inches ; its circumference two and a-half inches.
The substance is not muscular, but is chiefly composed
of an abundant yielding cellular substance, with fat
of an almost oily consistence.

In general, the flesh of the common heron (*Ardea
cinerea*) is good or bad according to the country where
they are bred, and the food on which they feed. It is
commonly said that the flesh of a young heron is food
for a king, but for what reason it is hard to say, for it
is usually fishy and of a disagreeable flavour. Leibaut
calls the heron a royal viand. It was formerly in considerable estimation as an article of food, and is still
eaten in some countries.

Soyer, in his "Panthropheon," tells us, "Some modern
nations—the French among others—formerly ate the
heron, crane, crow, stork, swan, cormorant and bittern ;
the first three especially were highly esteemed, and Tail-
levant, cook of Charles VII., teaches us how to prepare
these meagre, tough birds. Belon (*Hist. des Oiseaux*)
says that in spite of its revolting taste when unaccustomed to it, the bittern is, however, among the delicious
treats of the French. This writer also asserts that a
falcon or a vulture, either roasted or boiled, is excellent
eating, and that if one of these birds happened to kill
itself in flying after the game, the falconer instantly
cooked it.

Ducks and Geese.—We come now to treat of some of the
most useful of the class of birds in a food point of view,
the ducks and the geese. The duck, being such a good
swimmer, was sacrificed by the ancients in compliment
to Neptune. Ducks were always served at the tables
of the rich Greeks, but the more wealthy Romans only
offered to their guests the breast and head, returning

the remainder to the kitchen. The goose had its praises sung by Homer, and it was the favourite dish of the Egyptian monarchs. A sentiment of gratitude endeared them to the Romans, as by their noisy clamour they had formerly saved the capitol, and they were reared both in town and country to guard the house. At the anniversary of the deliverance of the capitol from the Gauls, the Roman people regaled themselves with boiled dog. At this solemnity a goose, laid on a soft cushion, was carried in triumph, followed by an unhappy dog nailed to a cross, whose loud cries amused the populace; thus they commemorated the signal service rendered by one animal, and the fatal negligence of the other. But time effaces the impression of gratitude, and for a century at least before the time of Pliny, the Romans had learned to eat goose; and by a perfidious art they fattened them delicately in darkness in preparation for the spit. The most luxurious eaters, however, valued only the liver, and this they contrived to increase to such a size that it often weighed over two pounds. Pliny says that Apicius found means to increase the livers to a size almost equalling in weight the whole body of the bird.

The modern gastronome will see, therefore, that it is to the Romans he owes these table luxuries of our day. Thus Horace says—

"Pinguibus et picis pastum jecur anseris albi."

Goose is eaten in England on Michaelmas Day, because, says report, Queen Elizabeth was dining on goose when the news was brought her of the defeat of the Spanish Armada.

According to the latest statistics there are in France 3,600,500 ducks, worth, at 3 fr. each, 10,801,500 fr. From these there are sold for food 1,720,100 ducks at 3 fr., equal to 2,160,300 fr.; 2,360,000 drakes, castrated, at 3 fr., equal to 1,080,000 fr. The 3,600,500 ducks will produce 10,000,000 ducklings in the year, from which 2,000,000 will be set aside for reproducing, and 2,000,000

more may be deducted as killed by disease and accidents. There will remain therefore 6,000,000, which,
sold at $2\frac{1}{2}$ fr. each, produce a sum of 15,000,000 fr. If
we add for extra fine birds an added value of 500,000 fr.,
we have a total of 18,740,300 fr. The 2,520,400 ducks
will lay on an average 30 eggs each yearly, in all
75,612,000 eggs, which, sold at 6 centimes each, yield a
sum of 4,536,720 fr.; this, added to the poultry value,
gives a total of 23,277,020 fr., or nearly £1,000,000 for
ducks and their eggs.

The best ducks of France are raised in the neighbourhood of Rouen. The ducklings of Rouen are sought
after for roasting, those of Amiens for their livers, which
serve to make excellent pâtés; those of Toulouse are
also in request for their fat livers which are of first-rate
quality; there is an enormous trade carried on in them
either in pâtés or in terrines with truffles, and in cookery
they are employed under a thousand names as entrées or
hors d'œuvre. When well hung, a Rouen duck is a
splendid table bird, but for maturity and delicacy in
early spring it must yield to its white rival—the Aylesbury. It is not an uncommon thing for a ton weight of
ducklings to be despatched from Aylesbury in a single
night. Now a ton of young ducks from six to eight
weeks old will comprise perhaps 450 birds, worth in
the best part of the spring, 6s. to 10s. a couple.

Considerable supplies of ducks are brought from
Holland, and some turkeys as well; but the Norwich
dealers' duck supplies are mostly gathered in the
county. Rouens and Aylesburies have not been much
used for crossing; and the supplies are generally of the
small mixed-brown-and-cinnamon sort, which has sub-
sisted since the flood. The cottagers do not force their
ducklings, but sell them to the dealers, one of whom
takes 30,000 a year, principally in the duck-and-green-
pea season. They come to him about 3 lb., in weight;
and after a week in the lean and three in the fat yard.
they are turned out in prime condition, with fully 1 lb.
gain in flesh.

In Brittany they have a plan of salting well fatted ducks after drawing them. When the flesh has been in a tub of salt with bay leaves and saltpetre about a fortnight, and has acquired a fine red colour, the bird is cut into four quarters, larded with cloves, and put into a pot with some spice. Geese and ducks' breasts are also pickled for three weeks or a month, then rolled in wheat or rye bran, strung together on long wooden skewers, and suspended in a light smoke for a week. They are then hung up in a draught for three days, after which the coating of bran is brushed off and they are stored in any suitable dry and airy place.

In Java and the principal Philippine islands, large flocks of ducks are kept for their flesh and eggs; the first being preserved by drying, and the last, when salted, forming a principal part of the stock of animal food in native sea voyages. Salted ducks form the basis of a large commerce from Cochin China to the Chinese Empire.

"In China ducks are usually cut open and made perfectly flat and then dried; and a man will hawk about near a hundred such dried ducks hanging on a pole across his shoulders. What particular delicacy there can be in ducks' bills I did not make trial of, but they are common articles hanging suspended in the provision shops. So also are dried rats, similarly split open and hung up in front of the shops for sale, their rodent teeth betraying them in their otherwise disguised condition."— Collingwood.

The tongues of ducks are among the dainties of Chinese epicures. A writer in the *Chinese Repository* says: "One article in the shop puzzled me much, and by inquiry I found it to be nothing more nor less than a string of dried tongues obtained from ducks. They were stretched out to the utmost length, resembling awls in shape, and hardened almost to the firmness of iron."

The great antiquity of the goose as an article of food, may be determined by examining some of the Egyptian monuments in the British Museum, or Rosellini's magnificent work on Egyptian antiquities, where we find geese represented alive, plucked, and prepared for the table.

Geese.— Mention has already been made of the fattening of the geese and of their livers carried on in Alsace and at Strasbourg. This fattening is also a speciality of Languedoc and Toulouse.

Geese are sometimes preserved for keeping either by smoking or boucanading, as they do hams; they are also cooked and then preserved by covering them with fat.

From recent statistics there are in France 4,170,650 geese, worth 4 frs. each, equal to 16,682,600 frs. A fifth of these are sold for food for a sum of 3,336,520 frs., as well as 834,131 ganders fattened and sold at 4 frs., equal to 3,336,524 frs. The 2,502,392 females will raise 37,535,895 goslings, from which 3,753,589 will be reserved for breeding; about 3,713,589 goslings will have to be deducted for losses by death and accidents; there will remain, therefore, 3,068,718 young geese, which, sold at 2½ frs., will produce 75,171,792 frs. If we add for fine and choice birds an increased value of 500,000 frs., this brings up the total for geese to 82,344,836 frs.

The French goose has of late years become a formidable rival of his fellow-geese from the Emerald Isle. Formerly there was a prejudice against French geese; the trade would not look at them, and the public would not eat them. But gastronomical prejudices are short-lived. Whether it be due to the soothing influence of sage and onions, or to the quality of the noble bird itself, it is certain that the French goose is now very popular on this side of the Channel, for the poulterers say that they sell large numbers of them at good prices. Indeed, so successful is the French goose that great quantities of his race are imported into England in an attenuated condition during the summer, and are sent into the country to be fattened for the London market at Michaelmas.

A large trade is carried on in France at Berry, Toulouse, etc., in geese. Their livers in patés and in terrines with truffles are consumed all over Europe. Geese are dressed in many ways in different countries for Michaelmas and Christmas; the fillets and pectoral muscles salted and smoked serve instead of ham ; the thighs cooked and covered with the grease keep well.

There are consumed annually in Paris about 150 tons of foie gras and truffled poultry, 30 tons of patés of Amiens, Chartres, and Pithiviers, and 539 tons of other patés. At Pau they boil down the geese for their fat but do not eat them.

In preparing the enlarged goose livers, when the birds are considered ripe they are killed, and the livers are conveyed to the· truffling house. The carcases, shrivelled out of all knowledge, are sold for about 1s. apiece to the peasants, who make soup of them. The livers are first cleaned and then weighed, and they will often scale two and a-half to three pounds each. The next step is to take each liver and to lard it with truffles in the proportion of half-a-pound of truffles to one pound of liver, and then to convey it to an icehouse, where it remains on a marble slab for a week, that the truffle perfume may thoroughly permeate it. At the end of a week each liver being removed is cut into the size required for the pot which it is to fill, and introduced into that pot between two thin layers of mincemeat made of the finest veal and bacon fat, both truffled with the liver itself, and one inch depth of the whitish lard is then spread over the whole that none of the savour may escape in baking. The baking takes about five hours, and the fire must never blaze too high or sink too low. When the cooking is over, nothing remains but to pack the dainty either in tin, earthenware, or wood, according as it may be needed for home or foreign consumption, and to ship it to the four points of the compass.

Enormous flocks of geese are bred in Lincolnshire, containing from 2,000 to 10,000 birds each; but it is to Norfolk and Suffolk that we look for goose-management on the largest and most economical scale. The goose trade of the great Norfolk dealers resolves itself into two branches—the green geese and the Michaelmas. In March and April they begin to get in their gosling supplies from farmers or cottagers near the commons, in both these counties. Most of these goslings are about five weeks old, and many of them in very poor plight; but six or seven weeks of feeding under stages, on barley-meal, maize, wheat-tailings, and brewers' grains mixed, make them all ripe for the green-goose market.

The Michaelmas geese take their places under the stages in August; and Norfolk and Suffolk are pretty well scoured before the dealers fall back upon the Irish, French, and Dutch supplies. The Dutch, which are principally grey, come from Rotterdam; and one of the largest Norwich dealers imports occasionally seventeen tons' weight of live birds in the year. They come over by steamers and sailing vessels, packed in big flat baskets, but not to any great extent after the 1st of October. In the dealers' hands they are fed on the same principle as ducks—low fare to begin with, and then on a gradually-ascending scale. The goose-pens of Messrs. Boyce, of Stratford, are capable of holding four thousand geese for fattening.

On the western moors of Cornwall everyone keeps geese; and they are bought up by jobbers in thousands, for the stubbers. Summer Court, on September 25th, is the "goose fair" of the county. Farmers all over England are supplied very largely both from Holland and Ireland. Geese are extensively bred in Moravia; and the hilly districts in Germany and Holland are peopled by numerous goose-farmers, who get their living entirely by them. The Hussenheim goose market is a very large one, and of great antiquity; and, according to local tradition, the town owes its name to the bird of its choice. The Dutch hucksters buy goslings from the cotters—who, like the burghers, are remarkable for turning the penny the right way—at prices varying from 1s. 6d. to 2s. They are driven to Rotterdam, where they are packed up in crates, which are capable of holding about fifty or sixty each.

Their voyage to Hull by the steamers is charged at 18s. per cwt., or about £5 for 300 or 400 birds; and they are not fed until they are landed, and then with oats. From Hull they are forwarded to central market-towns in railway trucks, each of which is capable of holding 230 birds. A small percentage of the more weakly ones die from being trampled on; and these casualties, with the expense of transit and sale, bring up the price to about 3s. 9d., when they are pitched in the market during August and September. The Irish collections are managed on a similar principle. If the goslings are purchased within reasonable distance of Dublin or Dundalk, they are driven to those ports; and if not, they are sent by rail. Liverpool, like Hull, is quite a "board of supply" for English dealers during the season.

There is a variety of goose called the snow goose (*Anser hyperboreus*), which is very general in the northern parts of America and in northern Europe, and is much prized for the delicacy of its flesh Dr. Richardson says it is much superior to the Canada goose (*Bernicla Canadensis*, Lin.) in juiciness and flavour.

In those countries where the latter abound they are killed in vast numbers by the natives, who pluck and gut them, and without any other preparation bury them in the ground. The earth freezing above them, keeps them perfectly sweet through the severe winter.

Dr. Richardson tells us that the arrival of the Canada goose in the fur countries is anxiously looked for, and hailed with great joy by the natives of the woody and swampy districts, who depend principally upon it for subsistence during the summer. It makes its appearance in flocks of from twenty to thirty, which are rapidly decoyed within gunshot, by the hunters, who set up stalls and imitate its call.

Two, three, or more, are so frequently killed at one shot that the price usually given for a goose is a single charge of ammunition. A Canada goose which, when fat, weighs nine pounds, is the daily ration of one of the

Hudson's Bay Company's servants during the season, and is reckoned equivalent to two snow geese, or three ducks, or eight pounds of buffalo meat, or two pounds of pemmican, or a pint of maize, and four ounces of suet.*

In favourable seasons there are as many as 6,000 or 7,000 killed and barrelled up for winter provision.

Among the animals forbidden to be eaten by the Jews (Levit. xi.) were the cormorant, swan, pelican, stork, heron, and lapwing; as well as the bat, lizard, snail, and tortoise. Sir Robert Schomburgk assured me that cormorants were very good eating after being skinned.

The swan was fattened for the table by the Romans, who first deprived it of sight.

The cygnet used to be a dainty dish, though now held in little esteem. They were fattened in London and Norwich for the corporation banquets. In the Mayoralty of Sir James Hawes (1575) we find in his tariff the selling price of the cygnet in the metropolis at 6s. till Allhallows Evetide, and 7s. from thence to Shrovetide. The flesh of the old swans is hard and ill-tasted, but among the items of consumption at the five days' open house feast given by the Serjeants at Law at Ely House, in November, 1531, twenty-four dozen of swans are enumerated.

There are a large number of swans on the Thames, which belong to the Dyers', Vintners', and other Livery Companies. These are all marked or nicked on each side of the bill, and an annual excursion is made, called swan upping, to nick or mark the young cygnets.

An island, called Kalguyef, in the Petchora River, north coast of Russia, is much resorted to by the fishermen, who wage an easy and inglorious warfare against the wild geese, swans, eider and other ducks which flock thither in vast numbers in spring time. The fattest and heaviest birds are driven into nets spread out to catch them, and they then fall easy victims. Ten men, in the

---

* Richardson's " Fauna Boreale Americana."

N

course of a month, will thus bag about 8,500 good-sized birds, some of which are generally retained for home consumption, the rest being exported. The brent goose (*Anas bernicla, Bernicla leucopsis*, Bechst.), a winter visitant, is a good bird for the table, the flesh being excellent and free from fishy flavour.

The grey duck of Australia (*Anas superciliosa*, Gmel.), as an article of food, is in its prime during the autumn and commencement of the winter; but the quality of the game differs according to the locality, those from the lakes and rivers of the interior (Dr. Buller tells us) having a richer flavour as a rule than birds living in the vicinity of the seashore, where the feed is coarser.

Few birds are better flavoured than a fresh snipe (*Gallinago media*), and they are most delicious eating. "Snypes" were among the birds admitted to the Earl of Northumberland's table ("Household," 1512); they were then charged 3d. the dozen.

The flesh of all the snipes is palatable and good, including the *Gallinago* species, many of which come from Ireland and Holland. Among these are the curlew (*Numenius arcuatus*), common on our coasts, and nearly the bulk of a chicken; the jack snipe (*Gallinago gallinula*), also called the judcock; the pool snipe (*Tetanus stagnatilus*); the strand snipe (*Tringa cinerea*); the stint (*Tringa minutella*), often sold for snipe when those birds are at a high price; and the blue-footed swordbill or European avocet (*Recurvirostra avocetta*, Lin.). The knot (*Tringa canutus*) visits our shores in large numbers in autumn, and the birds come to market mostly from Lincolnshire. The flesh is considered inferior to others of the tribe. The American snipe is *Gallinago Wilsonii*, and there is a red-breasted snipe (*Macrorhamphus griseus*).

The flesh of the Indian Jacana (*Hydrophasianus chirurgus*) is said to be excellent.

The moor-hen (*Gallinula chloropus*, Lin.), if killed in the autumn, is very good eating. The flesh of the rail (*Rallus aquaticus* is also palatable, that of the corn-crake or land rail (*Ortygometra crex, Crex pratensis*, Bechs.) is very delicate and good for the table. It bears the name of "king of the quails" in many countries.

The black-tailed godwit (*Limosa ægocephala*) is some-times caught and fattened, with the reeves, for the table, but though considerably larger it is not held in such high estimation.

Another family of wading birds is the Plovers, whose flesh is very good, and their brown speckled eggs are regarded as a great delicacy. The golden plover (*Charadius pluvialis*, Lin.) especially is an excellent bird for the table.

In the United States the following are the edible birds passing under the name of plover:—The black billed (*Squatarola helvetica*); the golden (*Charadius pluvialis*, var. *Virginicus*); the killdeer (*Ægealitis vociferus*, Lin.); Wilson's (*Æ. Wilsonius*); the ring-neck (*Æ. semipalmatus*); the piping (*Æ. melodus*); the ruddy (*Calidris arenaria*); and the upland plover (*Actiturus bartramius*).

The bustards form a kind of link between the Gallinacæ and the Plovers. The great bustard (*Otis tarda*, Lin.) is still plentiful in many parts of Europe. The large African kori bustard (*Eupodotis cristata*, Scop.) often weighs from 30 lbs. to 35 lbs., and is excellent eating. The flesh of the trumpeter of South America (*Psophia crepitans*, Lin.) is eatable.

The common teal and the Garganey teal (*Querquedula crecca*, and *Querquedula circia*, Lin.), are better than any other of the wild duck family, and are good game birds, but lean.

The flesh of the American species is excellent, viz., the green-winged (*Q. carolinensis*), the blue-winged (*Q. discors*), and the red-breasted (*Q. cyanoptera*).

The pin-tail (*Dafila acuta*) is abundant and its flesh better than that of the wild duck. Considerable num-bers of these as well as of teal are imported from Holland.

The clucking hen (a species of *Ardea*), is considered in Jamaica the best description of wildfowl. Some of the coots are occasionally served up, but they taste a little fishy. The flesh of the sand grouse (*Pterocles arenarius*) is good eating if kept long enough; at first it is rather hard and tough, but that of the young birds is delicious, and is much prized.

"The rotge is excellent eating, and is highly prized by every taste. I have heard the eider duck and the long-tailed duck and even the loon denounced by persons whose tastes were really fastidious, but I never heard a word against the little auk (*Mergulus alce*). Its flesh, and that of sea-fowl generally in the Arctic regions, improves very much by keeping for a few weeks after being shot; indeed, it is not uncommon to use them after they have been three months hanging to the booms around the ship's quarter."—*Sutherland's Journal.*

Captain Mark Law tells us that they feasted largely, in the Arctic regions, on loons (as Brunnock's guillemots are invariably called). In one harbour called Nameless Bay, a companion and himself, in less than two hours, bagged 600, and had they required it many hundreds more could have been obtained in the same space of time. The crew revelled for some time on such delicacies as "loon soup," "stewed loon," "curried loon," and other ingenious methods of cooking those birds.

The young of the albatross (*Diomedia*), when first taken from the nest, are said to be delicious.

The flesh of the Lapland duck or crested grebe (*Podiceps cristatus*) is stated to be tender. That of many of these water-fowls is, however, greasy. The smoked flesh of sea-birds with wild garlic, leeks and rice, forms an article of food with the Japanese.

Many of the islands in Bass's Straits are inhabited by men who follow the precarious trade of sealers and mutton bird procurers; this bird is a species of shearwater or petrel (*Puffinus sp.*). The immense number of mutton birds annually destroyed may be inferred from the fact that two and a-half tons of feathers formed the export of one season (each bird furnishing only the twentieth part of a pound weight) or 112,000 birds. The birds themselves are salted, dried and smoked for use in the winter, like the dried fish of the poor on the coast of

Great Britain, and sold in Launceston and Hobarton for threepence a-piece.

Three-fourths of the bird consist of pure white fat, and one-fourth of red meat and tender bones. The flavour is rather fishy, but if once used to it it is not bad at all, only rather too fat. They eat best when salted and smoked a little, then boiled a short time and afterwards eaten cold. If properly salted they might form an article of trade in that quarter, like herrings in Europe. The fat when clean is quite white, and looks like goose fat, but the taste is rather oily : however, it may be used for a good many other purposes than for food; it burns very well in small shallow tin lamps, which get warmed by the light and melt the fat.

One species of petrel (*Puffinus brevicaudus*) is very abundant on the coasts of Australia and New Zealand. At certain seasons the natives of New Zealand collect large numbers of these birds and preserve them in calabashes, potted in their own fat, either for future use or gifts to neighbours.

The canvas-back duck (*Fuligala valisneria*), which is lean on its first arrival in the United States, becomes in November about three pounds in weight, and in high order for the table; there are few birds which grace the board better. *Zostera marina* and *Ruppia maritima* form their food, as well as the fresh-water *Valisneria*, which last is limited in distribution.

The Prince of Musignano is eloquent in praise of this delicacy :—"Carne, della massima squisitezza, grandimente ricercata dai gastranomi. Le migliore della Anitre-Forse il miglior uccello d'America."

Everybody, says the Baltimore *Sun*, has heard of Chesapeake canvas-backed ducks and diamond-backed terrapins, and a great many people know something of how they taste when served up for the table, but not many are acquainted with the manner in which they are handled by the dealers in these and other famed gastronomic luxuries. There is an establishment in Baltimore which has been fitted up especially for this trade, where canvas-backs and all kinds of game are kept by the thousands, in apartments in which the temperature remains at 18° above zero, and where terrapins in multitudes live and grow fat on nothing. There are five large closets on the premises, built in the walls, similar to bank vaults, and these, by a scientific process, are arranged to keep their interiors at a very low temperature, by the use of ice, but in a different manner from the freezing process of a refrigerator. In one of these the canvas-backs and other wild game are kept perfectly fresh; in another there are all varieties of fish, including shad from Savannah, white fish from the lakes, rock and perch from the Chesapeake tributaries, and blue fish, haddock and codfish from the North. In another closet the smaller and more common fish are kept, and all of the closets are filled with some of the special products dealt in. Shipments of canvas-backs by the barrel are made to London, Liverpool, and Paris by the steamships from New York and Baltimore. The birds are taken from the cold closets, and, when on board the steamers, are put in ice and reach their destinations in excellent condition.

There is an enormous slaughter of pelicans in Cochin China for their feathers. As many as 2,000 are killed nightly for several nights in their great haunts. Most of the flesh of the birds is left to the crows, as there is no appliance for preserving it; some is, however, dried, and stated to be very good, and something like beef.

Cranes were by no means despised by people of taste among the Romans. The flesh of the young crane (*Grus cinereus*) is well flavoured and wholesome, for it does not feed on fish, but grain and seeds. According to Schweinfurth that of the West African crane (*Balearica pavonina*, Lin.) is more palatable than that of the goose.

Cranes, herons, bitterns and swans roasted, were served at table some five hundred years ago, and at the feasts in the time of Richard the Second.

The bittern (*Botaurus stellaris*) was formerly held in some estimation as an article of food for the table; the flesh is said to resemble that of the leveret in colour and taste, with some of the flavour of a wild fowl.

Young penguins are good eating, but the old ones are dark and tough when cooked. A voyager says :—

"The flesh of the penguin is black, and has rather a perfumed taste. We ate of them several times in ragouts, which we found to be as good as those made of hare." *

The penguins form regular rookeries, or perhaps they may be more correctly termed "penguineries," sometimes situated even miles from the shore and far removed from salt water. The breeding places are often of as great an extent as 500 yards by 50, the eggs being placed so close together that it is impossible to walk without treading on them.

Young puffins (*Fratercula arctica*, Lin.), though excessively rank from feeding on sprats and seaweed, are pickled and preserved with spices, and by some people are much admired.

---

* "Journal of a Voyage to the Falkland Islands."

CHAPTER VI.

EGGS OF VARIOUS KINDS AS FOOD.

Eggs of Domestic Poultry—Nutritive Value and Chemistry of Eggs—Average Weight of Eggs—Quantity and Values of our Imports of Eggs—Range of Prices—Number Received from France—Estimated by Weight on the Continent—Testing Eggs—Egg Traffic of the United States and Canada—Prices—Condensed Eggs—Various Modes of Preserving Eggs—Pickled Eggs—Easter Eggs—Ostrich Eggs—Emeu Eggs—Plovers' and Lapwings' Eggs—Eggs of Sea Fowl—Gulls—Terns—Penguins—Petrel—Albatross—Eggs of Reptiles—Turtles—Land Tortoises — Alligators — Lizards' Eggs — Snakes' Eggs—Insects' Eggs—Fish Spawn—Cod Roe — Herrings' Eggs — Sturgeon Caviare—Modes of Preparing—Roe of Sandre, Bream, etc.—Mullet—Fish-bread from Roes—Mode of Preparation—Eggs of Crustacea—Lobster Spawn.

OMNIVOROUS man feeds indiscriminately on a great variety of animal products; and among others, the eggs of Birds, reptiles, and fishes contribute somewhat largely to his sustenance. Let us first take a glance at those of Birds, which are the most important, and then notice some others.

It is a curious study to pass in review the number, size, form, weight and colour of eggs, according to the different species of birds, and the inferences we may draw in natural history from these oological characters in classifying the birds. According to the number of eggs they lay, birds may primarily be grouped into two great classes. Those which are destined to furnish food for man, as the Gallinaceous tribes, lay the greatest number of eggs; and when we find that in domestication the ostrich has laid as many as seventy-two to eighty-four eggs, we have reason to think it may shortly be ranked among regular domestic poultry.

The eggs of all domestic poultry are edible, but it is only those of the hen in which there is any very extensive commerce. The eggs of the goose, duck and turkey, when not employed for setting, are usually locally consumed. Turkeys' eggs are very good in pastry, and when mixed with hens' eggs they improve omelets. There is no egg of a bird which is not useful for food, or which could not be eaten by an hungry man.

Eggs are an article of cheap and nutritious food which we do not find on our tables in the quantity economy demands. Persons probably do not fully comprehend how valuable eggs are as food; like milk, an egg is a complete food in itself, containing everything necessary for the development of a perfect animal, as is manifest from the fact that a chick is formed from it. It seems a mystery how muscles, bones, feathers, and every thing that a chicken requires for its perfect development are made from the yolk and white of an egg; but such is the fact, and it shows how complete a food an egg is. It is also easily digested, if not damaged in cooking. A raw or soft boiled egg is always as easily assimilated as is milk, and can be eaten with impunity by children and invalids. The average egg weighing a thousand grains is worth more as food than so much beefsteak. Indeed, there is no more concentrated and nourishing food than eggs. The albumen, oil, and saline matter are, as in milk, in the right proportion for sustaining animal life. Two or three boiled eggs, with the addition of a slice or two of toast, will make a breakfast sufficient for a man, and good enough for a king.

The weight of an ordinary fowl's egg is one and a-half to two ounces, whilst that of the duck is two to three ounces; of the sea-gull and turkey, three to four ounces; and of the goose, four to six ounces. One reason why the eggs of wild birds are so highly esteemed is owing to the flavour acquired by the food consumed. Another is that the proportion of yellow in the eggs of wild birds is considerably larger than in those of domesticated ones, and this adds to the ratio of nutritive elements. The solid matter and the oil in the duck's egg exceed those in a hen's egg by about one-fourth. According to Dr. Edward Smith, in his treatise on "Food," an egg weighing an ounce and three-quarters consists of 120 grains of carbon, and eighteen and three-quarter grains of nitrogen, or 15·25 per cent. of carbon and two per cent. of nitrogen. The value of one pound of eggs, as food for sustaining the active forces of the body, is to the value of one pound of lean beef as 1,584 to 900. As a flesh-producer, one pound of eggs is about equal to one pound of beef.

The consumption of poultry and eggs is so large in this country as almost to exceed belief.

Besides our foreign supplies the home production is considerable. The Midland Railway brings up 150 tons of eggs, and the Great Eastern over 5,000 tons of poultry and game, annually. But this is a mere flea-bite in the course of the year. It is no uncommon thing in the early spring months for the Aylesbury Railway to carry two or three tons weight of ducklings and eggs in one night to London, and nearly £20,000 per annum is returned for ducks to the neighbourhood of Aylesbury alone. Ireland produces nearly 500,000,000 eggs, and the Continent supplies us with over 940,000,000; and if to this is added the annual production of Great Britain, the enormous consumption may be approximately estimated.

In 1850 we only imported 105½ millions of eggs from abroad; in 1870 this had risen to 431 millions, in 1878 to 784¾ millions, in 1883 to nearly 940½ millions, and probably as many more eggs are consumed of home production.

Value of the eggs imported into the United Kingdom :—

| 1861 | ... | £550,557 | 1881 | ... | £2,322,607 |
| 1871 | ... | 1,263,612 | 1883 | ... | 2,732,055 |

Eggs therefore form no unimportant item in the Englishman's bill of fare. On eggs and milk, indeed, man may not only live, but prosper exceedingly. But the price of a new-laid egg runs up to 2d. and 2½d. in the metropolis, and even then they are often difficult to obtain. High as this price is, it is not however so dear as the price of eggs in the city of Lima, where they fetch a dollar a dozen, or 4d. a-piece.

The average wholesale price of eggs per great hundred (120) in London was :—

			s.	d.				s.	d.
1861	...	...	6	5	1880	...	...	7	2
1871	...	...	7	7	1883	...	...	7	6

In 1873 and 1874 they were as high as 8s. 7d.

The already large and increasing consumption of eggs in England and France shows a growing appreciation of this form of food compared with any other.

Our consumption of foreign eggs is about thirty per head annually.

As a proof of the vast consumption of eggs in this country we may refer to the annual reports of our hospitals. In one of these it is stated that 800 dozen are required and made use of in the year, and taking into consideration the allowance of four eggs a day to some of the patients, the published statement does not cause so great amazement as at first sight it creates. Moreover, it goes to prove how important a part is played by our hens in keeping up or restoring strength in those who are suffering through some of the many ills to which flesh and bone is heir. Of course, such an item as that mentioned is something more than an atom of the annual expenditure; in fact, it is one of very serious amount. Eggs during the winter months are so extravagantly dear that people with large incomes have almost done without them; but their regular use in places devoted to the care and nurture of the sick seems to signify that no suitable substitute has yet been found.

Our receipts of eggs from France in the last five years have been as follows :—

Great Hundreds (of 120).

1878	...	3,734,920	1881	...	3,099,991
1879	...	3,441,131	1882	...	2,812,110
1880	...	3,151,158	1883	...	3,080,349

The import of eggs has about doubled in the last ten years and yet the price has risen. French eggs, which in 1864 were 5s. 11½d. the great hundred, were in 1883 6s. 0¾d. The total imports from the Continent were in 1864, 335,298,240, valued at £835,028, and in 1883, 940,436,160, of the value of £2,732,055.

The duty on eggs, which had been 4d. and 8d. per cubic foot measurement, according as they were of British or foreign produce, was repealed in 1860, involving a then loss to the Revenue of about £20,000 a year. The imports at that time were only about 203 millions.

France produces about 10 milliards (each a thousand million) of eggs annually; of this number about 400 millions are exported, chiefly to England. This commerce is very important for the northern departments. Paris consumes annually 400 to 500 millions : the quantity of eggs consumed in that city in 1883 was 40,000,000 dozen.

The French Customs estimates the shipments of eggs by weight. The exports were :—

		Kilos.			Kilos.
1870	...	24,969.000	1880	...	21,414,000
1875	...	34,417,000	1881	...	21,414,000
1879	...	22,887,000			

After repeated trials it has been decided in Paris that 20 eggs count as a kilogramme or 2⅕ lbs. In America there has long been an agitation for selling eggs by weight, and in Massachusetts a law has been passed to that effect.

The exports of eggs from Italy were, in :—

1870	...	...	...	...	4,876,798 kilos.
1875	...	...	...	...	9,071,000 „
1880	...	...	...	...	25,097,000 „

In France eggs are sorted and sized by passing them

through a ring. The average-sized ones must enter a ring 4 centimetres in diameter, the small ones a ring 3 centimetres 8 millimetres in diameter. The legalised charges in the public markets of Paris are; for mirage, or examining the eggs, 6d. the 1,000; testing their size by the ring, 1½d. the 1,000.

In a dark cellar in Paris, under one of the markets devoted to the sale of dairy produce, by the light of a candle, the troublesome operation of examining eggs is carried on, for not a single egg enters into consumption in Paris without having been thus examined. It is to be regretted that similar official scrutiny is not followed in London.

It is said that oval eggs are better than round ones. No less than 200 modes of cooking an egg have been published.

The fowls which lay large eggs, averaging about seven to a pound, are La Flèche, Houdans, Crèveceurs, and Black Spanish. Those laying medium eggs, averaging eight or nine to the pound, are Leghorns, Cochins, Brahmas, Polands, Dorkings, Games, and Sultans. The Hamburgs lay smaller eggs, eight or ten to the pound.

There are many debatable points yet to be settled about eggs. Has the hen in her ovary more or less than 600 eggs? Are there races of fowls which produce more eggs than others, and do hens lay in a short space of time all the eggs they will produce in the year.

The egg traffic of the United States is now exceedingly large. The aggregate transactions in the city of New York alone are said to amount to £1,600,000 in value. In Cincinnati and other cities the sale is proportionally great, and the total sales of eggs in the States have been estimated to reach £12,000,000 in value annually. Large as is, however, the indigenous production, the imports of eggs reach 5,000,000 or 6,000,000 dozen a year, chiefly from Canada.

The export of eggs from Canada doubles about every four years. In 1882, 10,500,000 dozens, valued at

£330,000, were shipped, principally to the American Republic, and 370,134 dozen to Great Britain.

Over 20,000 car-loads of live and dressed poultry are carried into New York city yearly, and 25,500,000 dozens of eggs go to the same market. According to the best estimates, the United States produce nine thousand million of eggs annually. This is a nice little item for the consideration of those who call chicken business—egg raising—a small thing. The American farmer, however, has been shrewd enough to discover that eggs pay better than birds, and he has turned attention to their production and preparation in large quantities for distant markets. The price paid by collectors seems good. In Minnesota, on the spot where fowls sold at 6s. 3d. a dozen, eggs made 5d. a dozen; while at Lexington, with fowls at 7½d. each, eggs made as much as 1d. each, and never lower than 4d. a dozen.

They are packed in millboard partitions, an egg in each square cell, thirty-six in each layer resting on cardboard sheets, one above the other, and the whole contained in a handy sized packing-case. The counting is thus made easy, and few eggs are broken. Another way is to pack seventy dozen in a wooden barrel in oats. These are treated as fresh meat, chilled and kept for months in cooled chambers; collected at about 3d. a dozen in the middle States, and thus preserved, they are sold in New York at from 11d. to 1s. a dozen when eggs are scarce; the oats making the cost price a gain to the packer. They come over 1,500 miles, and one dealer was known in 1878 to have cleared £3,000 by sales on a rise of prices. The abolition of slavery has affected the value of eggs, the free blacks keeping round their little houses a good stock of hens, but even now prices are sometimes remarkably high. In January, 1874, eggs sold at 20d. a dozen in New York, though before the month was out they fell to 6d.

The egg trade of Chicago is assuming large proportions. The average annual sales amount to 399,360 cases, which at thirty dozen each, makes the total number 143,769,600.

The perishable nature of eggs has naturally detracted from their value as a standard article of diet. The peculiar excellence of eggs depends upon their freshness. But lately the process of crystallising has been resorted to, and by this process the natural egg is converted into a vitreous substance of a delicate amber tint, in which form it is reduced seven-eighths in bulk compared with case eggs, and retains its properties for years unimpaired in any climate. This is indeed an achievement of science and mechanical ingenuity, and has a most important bearing on the question of cheaper food, by preventing waste, equalising prices throughout the year, and regulating consumption. In this form eggs may be transported without injury, either to the equator or the poles, and at any time can be restored to their original condition simply by adding the water which has been artificially taken away.

The chief American egg-desiccating companies are in St. Louis and New York. No salts or other extraneous matters are introduced in the process of crystallising, the product being simply a consolidated mixture of the yolk and albumen. Condensed eggs to the value of £400 are annually imported into America.

Mode of Preserving Eggs.—Immense quantities of eggs are preserved in the spring of the year by liming. Thus treated they are good for every purpose except boiling. A similar desiccating process is carried on in Germany. Herr von Effner's preserved eggs are put up much like other preserved articles of diet, in securely closed tins, and so protected from hygrometric variations in the atmosphere. They are prepared in three forms, the first containing the principles of the entire egg, while the others include those of either the white or the yolk only. When required for use it is only necessary to restore the water that has been eliminated, by moistening the flour till it has acquired the consistence of an ordinary egg as beaten up ready for the frying-pan in the preparation of omelettes. The dried yolk forms an agreeable adjunct to soups, or may be mixed with powdered biscuit, in which form it is particularly recommended by the inventor as a material out of which a palatable, wholesome, invigorating, and highly-nutritious cake can be quickly made for travellers or soldiers on the march.

In the counties of Hants and Dorset, pickled eggs constitute a very prominent feature in the farmhouse and store-rooms, insomuch that they would be considered by the industrious housewife but indifferently furnished without them. The mode in which the good dames pickle them is simply thus:—At the season of. the year when their stock of eggs is plentiful, they cause some four or six dozen to be boiled in a capacious saucepan until they become quite hard. They then, after removing the shells, lay them carefully in large mouthed jars, and pour over them scalding vinegar well seasoned with whole-pepper, allspice, some pieces of ginger, and a few cloves of garlic. When cold they are bunged down close, and in a month are fit for use. Where eggs are plentiful, the above pickle is by no means expensive, and, as an acetose accompaniment to cold meat it cannot be out-rivalled for piquancy.

At the London Dairy Show in 1884 there were upwards of thirty entries of eggs preserved in different ways, and there was a great variety of methods adopted. Quite a number were simply packed in common salt, and these were all sufficiently preserved for cooking purposes, and better than very many shop eggs, though the appearance was scarcely so good, for the salt had absorbed a rather large portion of the water of the albumen or white, consequently, there was a considerable air cavity at the larger end, the presence of which was evident by the sound produced when the eggs were shaken. The taste and smell were unobjectionable; but it is probable that these eggs would not sell well. The third-prize eggs, exhibited by Mr. C. W. Pearce, of Buckingham, packed by this method, and Dr. Benson's second-prize lot were first rubbed in butter and then packed in salt, but this made no difference to the preservation of the eggs, except that the white was more watery than when only salt was used. The other second prize was given to Mr. Percy Marigold of Edgbaston. These eggs were "preserved with beef and mutton dripping, melted together, a little painted over each egg, and then wiped with a cloth." They were quite fit for kitchen purposes, and equal to shop eggs, but, from the fact of the pores having been closed, there had been no evaporation, and, as in the case of the butter and salt system, the white was watery. The three lots of eggs preserved in liquids were good in quality, showing that this is a safe system, but those preserved in melted wax or paraffine were unfit for use.

The result of this experiment is that as yet no system has been adopted which will preserve the eggs equal to new laid. Most of the eggs were quite fit for cooking, and there are several systems equally good in this respect, but no one was fit for the table.

In China eggs are preserved after the following fashion:—They are covered with a paste of quicklime, sea salt and oak ashes, and thus packed away for three months in boxes, separated from each other by rice husks. As a matter of taste they are not nice, the white being coagulated, and the yolks having turned green, while the smell is anything but pleasant.

Easter Eggs.—In many countries there is a large consumption at Easter of hard boiled eggs, dyed red, or ornamented with designs caused by wax tracings.

The Easter eggs, otherwise called "Pâques eggs," whose life is so faithfully preserved by the French confectioner, are the commonest form of present in almost every country of the world. They are traced in Egypt, Persia, and Mesopotamia, in Greece and in Germany, and are extensively used to this day in Russia as a formal addition to the customary greeting and kiss of peace, "Christos vos Christe." In nearly every case they are ordinary eggs dyed red, and occasionally tinged yellow, as in the neighbourhood of Newcastle, with the

furze-blossom or "whin bloom." They are variously
decorated and inscribed by the simple process of mark-
ing them when hot with the end of a tallow candle,
and then steeping them with cochineal or some other
attractive dye. When elaborately designed or engraved,
the "Pace eggs" in old English times were preserved in
a deep long-stemmed ale glass, and kept in the family
corner cupboard as love relics or toys for the children.
At any rate, the religious significance of the Easter
egg in its connection with the deliverance from the
Deluge, the departure from Egypt, the Passover, and
the Resurrection, was soon lost sight of in Old England, for the boys used them as they do cob-nuts in
Wiltshire "to try the conqueror," the winning egg by
reason of hardness of shell over many smashed companions being considered by the boys of the village a
famous tough customer, and accordingly a valued prize.

The custom of giving Easter eggs to one's relations
and friends is a very old one in France, and there is no
fear of the usage dying out. But it has risen into an
expensive matter, for the imitation eggs are now of the
costliest kind, and made to contain all sorts of fancy
presents.

In 1533, an Archbishop of Paris, authorised by a bull
from Pope Julius III., being disposed to permit the use
of eggs during Lent, the Parliament took offence and
prevented the execution of the episcopal mandate. It
is this severe abstinence from eggs during Lent which
gave rise to the custom of having a great number of
them blessed on Easter Eve to be distributed among
friends on Easter Sunday, whence comes the expression
" to give Easter eggs." Pyramids of them were carried
into the king's cabinet after high mass. They were
gilded, or admirably painted, and the prince made
presents of them to his courtiers.

The origin of these Easter eggs is said to have sprung
from the fact that during several centuries no permission could be obtained from the clergy to eat eggs during
Holy Week. The rigid observance of that season pro-

duced the custom of preserving cooked those articles which could be neither eaten or sold. They were not coloured before the reign of Louis XIV. The first person who sold them red was a man named Solirène, established at "the descent from the Pont-Neuf, near the Samaritaine." That innovation had a great success, and St. Simon informs us in his "Mémoires," that the custom was on Easter Eve to raise in the cabinet of the Grand Monarque, pyramids of coloured eggs, which his Majesty afterwards presented to his courtiers. Since that period the community has undergone so many improvements that it is no longer eggs, properly so called, but boxes with unexpected contents, jewel cases, sometimes costing as high as two or three thousand francs, which are presented.

Macfarlane, in his "Southern Italy," mentions an amusing mistake of a hurried tourist, who, happening to be a day or two at Naples during Easter week, made a brief remark in his note-book that, contrary to the general habit of their species, all the Neapolitan hens laid red eggs!

Ostrich Eggs.—Passing from the ordinary domestic poultry, let us now glance at the huge eggs of the ostrich, which may ere long be more generally utilised for food.

As many as sixty eggs are sometimes found in and around an ostrich nest; but a smaller number is more common. Each female lays from twelve to sixteen, some say twenty-five to thirty eggs, in August and September. But it often happens that several couples unite to hatch together.

The eggs of each pair are disposed in a heap, always surmounted by a conspicuous one which was the first laid, and serves a special purpose. When the "delim," or male bird, perceives that the moment of hatching has arrived, he breaks the egg which he deems most matured, and at the same time he bores with great care a small hole in the surmounting egg. This serves as the first food for the nestlings, and for this purpose, though open, it continues long without spoiling, which is the more necessary, as the delim does not break all the eggs on the same day, but only three or four, and so on, as he hears the young ones stirring within. This egg is always liquid, but whether by a provision of nature in its original composition, or through the instinct of the parent birds in avoiding to keep it covered like the rest, is not ascertained. The young ones having received this their first nourishment, are immediately dried in the sun, and begin to run about; in a few days they will follow the parent birds to the pastures, always returning to shelter under their wings in the nest.

An ostrich egg is considered as equal in its contents to twenty-four eggs of the domestic hen. These eggs form a considerable item in the bushman's cuisine, and they are esteemed by the hunter, but in domestication they are too valuable for rearing in incubators to be handed over to the cook.

The eggs of domesticated ostriches are too costly at present to be given up for the table; their importance, however, can be estimated when we consider that the female occasionally lays 82 eggs (each equal to 32 fowls' eggs), that is above 2,624 of the latter, in the season. An ostrich egg roasted in the embers with truffles has been served up to august personages as a choice dainty, and in an industrial point of view the albumen they contain is considerable.

Emeu Eggs.—The eggs of the Australian emeu (*Dromæus Novæ Hollandiæ*) are nearly as large as those of the ostrich, but of a dark green colour. These birds, at one time abundant in Australia, are now becoming extinct, for natives and Europeans are fast thinning them out, the former eating the eggs and hunting down the birds for food, but they do not allow boys or women to partake of the flesh, it being reserved for warriors or counsellors. The eggs, although somewhat strong in flavour, are frequently eaten by settlers in the bush with great gusto. The flesh of the emeu is excellent, resembling good beef, and is dressed in a similar manner. The rump part is considered to be as delicate as fowl, the legs coarser in flavour, being more like beef, but still tender.

In the Pampas of South America, from 40 to 50 and even 70 eggs have been found in one nest of the *Rhea Americana*, the eggs lying on one another, tier upon tier. Perhaps twenty eggs will lie at the bottom of the nest, the others at the top of these. When fresh, the eggs are of a yellow colour, with clear white spots like wet lime attached to the surface. When stale the egg becomes white, and loses the spot-like appearance. These eggs form a staple commodity of food during the months of September, October and November.

Plovers' Eggs.—A popular periodical quaintly asks:— " Where do all the plovers' eggs come from ? They are seen at all sorts of meals—dinners, wedding breakfasts, show luncheons, pic-nics, evening-party refreshment tables, ball-suppers. In all sorts of forms, too, do they appear ; nestling in moss, held in bondage caressingly by succulent jelly, pearly and cool, the golden yolk just suggested through the semi-transparent white. Prodigiously good they are, in whatever shape presented, but prodigiously mysterious also, in their faculty of turning up in enormous quantities for the London season, and then disappearing with equally strange and inexplicable despatch. Very rarely does one encounter these plovers' eggs except during the London season ; and as to the plovers themselves, now and then, in crossing a breezy upland, the pedestrian's attention is caught by their shrill, plaintive cry, and their rapid flight round and round his head, as they seek to draw him away from the nest which lies close by ; but it is only now and then that the plovers are thus met with, and even where they are thickest, their numbers do not account for those innumerable dishes full of their eggs."

What are usually sold as plovers' eggs are those of the common lapwing (*Vanellus cristatus*, Meyer). The search for plovers' eggs is a science as well as a passion in Holland. Even from the flight of the bird some Dutch farmers deduce whether the plover has eggs, and whereabouts they are deposited. In Paraguay the eggs of the Tero-tero, or "pluvier armé," are good eating, but the flesh of the bird is said to be tough.

According to Father Huc, the Chinese make a great use of pheasants' eggs as a cosmetic to give their hair lustre and brilliancy.

Eggs of Sea Fowl.—The eggs of wild birds are not very generally eaten in this country, but in many localities those of sea-fowl are largely consumed, and a considerable trade is carried on in gulls' eggs. Those of the common foolish guillemot (*Uria troile*) seem to be accounted delicacies, notwithstanding their fishy diet. They are thick in the shell, which has a dull appearance. The bird only lays one egg, of a pale green, blotched and stained with black and dark brown. It may be incidentally remarked here that birds which build open nests uniformly have coloured eggs, and those which possess concealed or covered nests have white eggs.

Without going into the discussion of naturalists, who see in the different colours of eggs a certain relation to circumstances favourable to concealment, it may be observed that the blotched egg laid by the *Hydrochelidon fuliginosa*, usually known as the egg-bird, is found among sticks and dried leaves of the suriana, whilst the white eggs of the boobies and petrels are deposited in hollows of the coral rocks, amid sand and chalky dung. There is one curious coincidence between the eggs of the noddy tern (*Anous stolidus*, Linn.) and the peculiarities of the nest, that must not, however, be unremarked. The elaborate pile of sticks, slightly hollowed, in which they deposit their eggs, is always embellished with broken sea shells, speckled and spotted like the eggs. Audubon records the same occurrence in the nests of the noddy terns he inspected in the Florida Keys. The obvious suggestion for this curious prevalence of instinct is deceptiveness, arising from similarity between the egg shell and the sea shell.

For many kinds of cooking the eggs of wild birds are less valuable, though in the preparation of some sauces, where only the yellow portion of the egg is used, and when high colour and high flavour are both esteemed, two wild birds' eggs are considered equal to three domestic ones. The flavour of an egg is determined by the food of the bird, all or most of it residing in the yellow portion.

The number of eggs of the gulls—herring gull (*Larus argentatus, L. marinus, L. canus*, &c.,—sent to shore from the Fern Islands, off the Northumberland coast, for culinary purposes, is said to be prodigious.

From the cliffs of Bampton and Flamborough, men descend by ropes to obtain the eggs of the guillemots (*Uria troile* and *U. grylle*) and the razor-bill (*Alca torda*) or common auk. A good take will be 200 or 300 eggs at a time. They commence about the 14th of May, and go on for about nine days, and at the end of another nine days there will be a second run of successful collecting. These find a ready sale at Bridlington and other places in the neighbourhood. Innumerable quantities of the eggs of the gannet are obtained annually on the Island of St. Kilda. Incredible numbers of the eggs of the common auk are also collected on the coasts of Labrador and elsewhere.

So highly are the eggs of the sooty tern (*Sterna fuliginosa*, Gmel.) esteemed, that collecting them is quite a considerable trade. The eggs of the arctic tern (*S. arctica*, Tem.) and of the black tern or wideawake (*Hydrochelidon nigra*, Tem.) are excellent eating.

A great resort for the plunder of sea-fowls' eggs are the Pedro Keys, in the neighbourhood of Jamaica, which are annually visited by boats from Port Royal. The constant inhabitants of these rocks are several species of booby (*Sula fiber*), gannets, terns and petrels. The migratory visitors are ducks, herons, plovers, snipes, sandpipers, curlews, and ibises. The months of March, April, and May, are those of the egg harvest. The Keys are open to all adventurers, but the egg gathering is regulated by a custom which recognises the first arrival as the admiral commanding for the season, whose laws are to be obeyed; the second vessel is styled the commodore.

The peasants of Norway collect the eggs of the sea-birds, which are found in great numbers on all the coasts of their country. The eggs of the thick-billed or Brunnoch's guillemot are much sought after at the Farralones Islands, near San Francisco Bay.

At the island of Ichaboe, on the West Coast of Africa, large quantities of eggs are obtained. In the months of October and November the island is literally covered with jackass-penguins (*Eudyptes demersa*) and gannets (*Sula bassana*), which come here for the purpose of laying and incubation. The penguins lay three or four eggs, but the gannet seldom more than two.

At Cape Town some 30,000 eggs of the penguin are frequently received in a day from Jutten and Dassen Islands.

The island of Tristan d'Acunha is another great resort for sea-birds, numbers of penguins' eggs are obtained there at two great rookeries or nesting-places. The men who go to gather the eggs wear a large shirt tied round their waist, so as to form a great loose bag in front, and they pop the eggs in as fast as they can pick them up. They will gather from 200 to 300 in this way, no little load to carry, as they vary in size from a large hen's egg to that of a goose.

Funk Island has been visited from time immemorial by all the poor people of the northern part of New-foundland, for the procuring of eggs and birds which frequent the island in immense numbers, upon which they subsist for several months of the year, having no other animal food to use; they salt down the birds in barrels for preservation. The fishermen of all other parts of the colony, on their voyage to Labrador in the spring, regularly resort to Funk Island to procure the eggs of the sea-fowl, which there accumulate in vast quantities in the course of two or three days, and having supplied themselves with barrels full, they proceed on their voyage, and when arrived at their destination bury them in their salt bulk for use during the summer. Large quantities are also taken by the people of Conception Bay, Trinity Bay, Bonavista Bay, and of St. John's, where they find a ready market, and at the right season, when flesh meats are scarce and dear, they are quite a luxury for the poor.

In the high northern latitudes sea-fowls' eggs are a valuable article of food. In Greenland about 200,000 eggs of aquatic birds are consumed yearly. The eggs of the gannet or Solan goose are obtained for sale at great risk from the rocks, crags, and overhanging precipices.

Collecting the eggs of sea-birds forms a branch of considerable industry in many countries. The poor inhabitants of the Faroe Isles feed on the eggs of almost all the waterfowl which frequent their shores. The governors of the Isle of Texel have the exclusive right to all the eggs taken there, and they pay a considerable sum to secure this monopoly. It is asserted that 300 or 400 eggs of the silver gull (*Larus argentatus*) alone are gathered every day. After St. John's Day no more eggs may be taken, the birds being allowed to hatch in peace any they may lay after that period. Naumann says that 50,000 eggs of the large gulls are collected annually in the little island of Sylt, and quite as many of smaller species and of sea-swallows. Among the larger eggs there are at least 10,000 of the silver gull.

Three men are engaged in collecting these eggs from eight in the morning till late at night. They receive in payment the eggs of all the smaller kinds of birds.

In the islands of Bass' Straits a large harvest of eggs of the dusky petrel (*Puffinus brevicaudis*, Brandt) is obtained. The bird is called locally the "mutton bird." In shape and colour the eggs resemble those of the duck, but are larger in size, although the bird is smaller. The average weight of the egg is about three and a-half ounces, and the flavour, like that of most sea-birds, is strong. Early in December men, women, and children are engaged in the plunder, and one person will obtain five hundred eggs in a day. Not less than a thousand dozen of these eggs are conveyed to the port of. Launceston by boats in the season, and about as many more find their way to the capital, Hobart Town, by vessels calling at the islands, while large numbers are consumed on the spot, so that from two to three thousand dozen must be obtained annually. A few years ago nineteen hundred dozen were sent direct to Melbourne, but the shipment there has not been renewed.

The aborigines of Australia collect the eggs of wild fowl, and it is no uncommon sight to see a bark canoe so full of eggs that there is only just room for one person to stand in it. The eggs of the ibis or bran are those which are procured in the greatest number in New South Wales. They are of a white colour, rather sharp at one end and about the size of a turkey's egg. The albumen is, however, quite different from that of any other egg, being, even when boiled, pellucid, gelatinous, and fat in appearance, and very small in quantity in comparison with the yolk. It is not particularly palatable, and is only used as a makeshift when neither hen nor duck eggs can be procured.

The eggs of the albatross (*Diomedia fuliginosa*), which average about a pound in weight, are much esteemed by the sealers.

A large lake called the Hoister Meer, between Utrecht and Amsterdam, is much frequented ·by birds, and the nests of the cormorants and spoonbills are robbed of the eggs systematically twice a week during the months of May and June.

The natives of Celebes come for fifty miles round to a large bay to obtain the eggs of the Malee birds (*Megapode*), which are esteemed a great delicacy, and when fresh are indeed delicious. They are richer than hens' eggs, and of a fine flavour; each one completely fills an ordinary teacup, and forms, with bread or rice, a very good meal.

Eggs of Reptiles.—The eggs of most of the species of tortoises are excellent eating, being both nutritious and agreeable to the taste; but the albuminous portion, or white as it is commonly termed, does not acquire firmness by boiling.

The number of eggs which the female of the green turtle deposits every spring in the sand, is from 200 to 300, but scarcely does a thirtieth of that number of young turtles (supposing every egg to be hatched) reach the sea, or live for a week after gaining it. Turtles' eggs are held in great esteem wherever they are found, as well by Europeans as others; they have a very soft shell, and are about the size of a pigeon's egg. The mother turtles lay thrice a year, at intervals of two or three weeks, depositing in one night as many as a hundred at a time. An experienced eye and hand are required to detect the eggs, as they are always ingeniously covered up with sand; but when they are properly sought for very few escape.

Among the Florida Keys and in other places with the necessary sandy beaches and grassy foreshores, which the turtle selects for depositing her eggs, the fishermen are so expert that they can not only discern the track of a turtle from the sea to the higher sands where the nest is usually found—if the term "nest" be allowable—but they can tell whether or not eggs have been deposited; for sometimes the burdened animal is disturbed before she can deposit her eggs, in which event she turns, forming a semi-circle round the place of intended deposit which she is abandoning, and seeks the sea to look out for some more eligible spot. And so keen are the eyes of the fishermen, that they can always tell by this indication, which they technically express by the phrase that the turtle has made "a half moon," that no eggs have been there deposited. In such case they never search for eggs on the spot, for they know it would be fruitless. When, however, there are indications seen of a genuine deposit, the ramrod of a musket, or some other sharp pointed instrument, is thrust into the sand, drawn out, and the point examined, when they can decide by well-known appearances whether there are eggs in that place. A good "find" sometimes means the discovery of several hundreds of eggs in the same spot.

When this is satisfactorily ascertained, the man who makes the discovery waits till all the eggs are deposited and the turtle is about to cover them up, when he approaches, and turns the animal over—a feat that requires both dexterity and strength to perform, with a sharp look-out for the eyes, which are otherwise liable to be blinded by the sand which the turtle will scratch up.

It may not be out of place to say here, that though of the marine turtles the flesh of the green variety is the only kind suitable for food, yet the eggs of all are edible. At Key West, however, and perhaps in other parts of Florida, the loggerhead is eaten; but we do not consider it as legitimate human food.

Unlike his green congener, the loggerhead is not a purely grazing animal; in the Gulf of Florida, he feeds on that singular mollusc the nautilus—the "Portuguese man of war" of seamen—which abounds in those waters.

The Orinoco and Amazon Indians obtain from these eggs a kind of clear, sweet oil, which they use instead of butter. In the month of February, when the high waters of the rivers have receded, millions of turtles come on shore to deposit their eggs. The certainty and abundance of the harvest is such that it is estimated by the acre. The yearly gathering about the mouth of the river alone is nearly five thousand jars of oil, and it takes five thousand eggs to make a jar. A native of Brazil will consume as many as twenty or thirty turtles' eggs at a meal, and a European will eat a dozen at a breakfast. They make an excellent omelet. The Indians frequently eat them raw, mixed with their cassava flour.

There is some fear of the turtle supply falling off in numbers, owing to the reckless way in which the eggs are destroyed. These leather-cased eggs are deposited, like those of the crocodile and other reptiles, in the warm sand or mud, and left there to hatch out, incubation lasting three weeks or a month. Owing to the large destruction which takes place, and the fact that the turtles are more easily captured at breeding time than at any other period, it is proposed in Barbados to establish a "close time" for turtles, and to foster the industry which is thus threatened with extinction. Jamaica and other colonies will do well to take the hint and preserve a valuable industry which, if properly developed, would form a source of great and increasing wealth.

The only condition in which the egg of the turtle is fit to be eaten is, when taken from the slain animal before the formation of the glaze and the surrounding parchment-like skin, which answers the purpose of a shell. In this condition, the young egg consists entirely of yolk, and hundreds, perhaps thousands, in all stages of development, from the merest embryo upwards, may be found in the same individual. These imperfectly formed eggs are very often preserved by drying, and are considered a great luxury. In parts of India turtles' eggs are salted, by which means they keep fresh for three to five years. The process is very simple, and only requires a little knack in knowing when the egg is sufficiently salted. The shell, instead of being hard, is soft, and consequently when put together with others appears crumpled in all shapes. The process of salting is this; the fresh egg is well shaken, and thus the yolk is broken or addled, and the contents, i.e., the white and the yolk, blend together. It is then rolled by the hand on a board with salt till the whole shell shows a marked difference in appearance. This is allowed to cool, and is packed in fine salt. Eggs thus prepared are found to be plump, and on opening them of a pale yellow; from the fact of the contents all being shaken and mixed, they become of this uniform light colour, and not part yellow and part white, as eggs ordinarily are. A fowl's egg is equal to so many ounces of meat; but the turtle's egg is far more nutritious, and there are more of them.

In the Eastern Archipelago and about the Straits Settlements the eggs of the "pinnio," or sea-turtle, and of the "toontoong," or river-turtle (which last are of an oval shape) are eagerly searched for and sold at the rate of half-a-dollar the hundred. The eggs of the river-turtle are less oily than the round eggs of the sea-turtle. A single turtle will sometimes lay 250 to 300 eggs two or three times during the year. A considerable commerce is carried on in turtles' eggs at the mouth of the Amazon. The eggs are laid at different times according to the locality; in May and June at the Tortugas; that of June, according to Audubon, is the most considerable; from September to January on the coast of Isini, in Africa, according to Dampier. At the Tortugas certain parts of the sand are generally known to contain the eggs laid by hundreds of turtles.

The eggs of the greaved tortoise of South America (*Podocnemis expansa*) are large, spherical and white, and form an important part of the diet of the Indians. They dry these eggs by placing them on boards in the smoke of a fire.

The eggs of the river tortoises of Africa are as large as those of the pigeon. They have an excellent taste; the white, which never becomes hard by the heat of the fire, preserves the transparency of a bluish jelly. The close tortoise (*Testudo clausa*) is much sought for in North America on account of its eggs, which, like those of the African variety, are reckoned a delicacy.

The eggs of the long necked tortoise of Australia (*Chelodina longicollis*), which are deposited in the beginning of January, amount to about fifteen or twenty, perhaps even more, and are consumed in quantities by the natives.

The eggs of the terrestrial tortoises are generally spherical and covered with a calcareous shell of considerable firmness. Some species, however, deposit elongated eggs, and others eggs longer at one end than the other, resembling those of a bird.

The eggs of the box tortoises or terrapins (*Cistudo Carolina*) are accounted excellent, and are much sought after.

Alligators' Eggs.—The female alligator lays about 120

to 160 eggs, as large as those of the turkey, and these are much eaten by the natives.   Mr. Joseph, in his " History of Trinidad," states that he had eaten the eggs of the caiman (without knowing what eggs they were) and found them very good.   My relative, Mr. R. B. Walker, tells me he has often eaten them in Western Africa.   The shell of the egg is rough, and filled with a thick albumen without trace of yellow.

In Senegambia the natives are fond of these eggs, but they are said to have a disagreeable flavour, especially the yolk or yellow part.   According to Crawfurd they are eaten in Siam.

Lizards' Eggs.—The eggs of the large tree lizard, known as the Iguana (which looks like an alligator in miniature), are deserving the notice of gourmands.   One of these lizards will sometimes contain as many as four score eggs, about the size of a pigeon's egg, but with soft shell, which, when boiled, are like marrow.   It would be a refreshing sight to see some aldermanic dignitary who has gone the round of all the dishes which native and foreign skill have been able to produce, partaking for the first time of a dish of lizards' eggs garnished with anchovies.

Brown, in his work on Guiana, says :—" One of these reptiles captured at its burrow, when killed and cut for cooking, was found to contain ten eggs of an elliptoid form, shell-less, and midway in size between a pigeon and a hen's egg.   These are good eating when boiled for about five minutes and then allowed to get quite cold.   They then require some manipulation.   A hole is made in one end of the skin, and the albuminous part, which never coagulates, is squeezed out; then the skin is stripped off, and the semi-hardened yelk, of the consistency of butter, is eaten with salt."

The eggs of a large lizard (*Varanus bivittatus*), those of fish and of turtle, are eaten by the Malays and Chinese.   The large eggs of the boa constrictor are regarded as a rare dainty by the Africans from the Congo.   One of these snakes killed on an estate in

British Guiana, in 1884, had 50 eggs, which were eaten by the negroes.

The eggs of the common teguexin (*Teius teguexin*, Lin.), and other large species of lizards, are eaten in South America.

Insect Eggs.—The eggs of some insects are also eaten. The larvæ and nymphæ of ants are not only good food for poultry, but they are considered a choice relish by many people spread on bread and butter, and are excellent curried. They are eaten in Siam, forming, with edible birds' nests, an esteemed article of food, but being costly they are only obtainable by the rich. Ants' brood are subject to an import duty in some of the northern countries of Europe, especially in Denmark, Norway, and Sweden. In those countries they are steeped in boiling water, and a kind of vinegar or formic acid is obtained.

Among the other objects of insect products useful to man are the eggs obtained in Mexico from three species of hemipterous insects belonging to the group of aquatic beetles. These eggs are made into a sort of bread or cake called " Hautle," consumed by the people, and it forms an article of commerce in the markets. In the fresh waters of the lagoons, bundles of reeds or rushes are laid, on which the insects (*Corixa femorata* and *C. mercenaria*, Geoffroy, and *Notonecta Americana*) deposit their eggs. The bundles of rushes are then withdrawn, dried, and beaten over cloths, to detach the myriads of eggs. These are cleansed and sifted, and put into sacks and sold like flour, to form cakes, which are excellent eating, but have a fishy and slightly acid flavour. The custom seems to have been long practised, for it is mentioned so far back as 1625 by a missionary, Thomas Gage, who, travelling in Mexico, states that these cakes were being sold in the markets.

Brantz Mayer, in his " Mexico as it Was, and as it Is," published in New York, in 1844, speaks of having noticed on the Lake of Tescuco, men occupied in collecting the eggs of flies on plants and sheets. " These eggs, called axayatl, are a substance favourably known to the Indians long before the Conquest, and which cooked in cakes were not different from fish spawn, having the same appearance and flavour. After the frogs of France and the birds' nests of China, I fancy they would be considered delicacies, and I found they were not disdained on the fashionable tables of the capital."

The eggs of another species, *Corixa esculenta*, having the appearance of manna, are also eaten in Egypt.

In Mexico the dried insects themselves are sold in the streets and markets as food for birds, the dealers crying "Moschitos," "Moschitos," just as in Europe they cry "Food for your singing birds."

"A large fly deposits its eggs in the frothy edge of the surface of Mono Lake, in California, each of which when hatched becomes a larva of considerable size, and is called 'Ke-chah-re' by the natives. These larvæ when dried and pulverised are mixed with meal made of acorns, to be sun-dried or baked as bread, or mixed with water and boiled with hot stones for soup. The colour of the powdered larvæ being similar to that of coarsely ground black pepper, gives a forbidding appearance to the compound." *

Fish Spawn.—By those who have not looked into the subject, it would scarcely be conceived how extensive is the commerce, and how varied the uses of fish spawn. Even the variety in shape and extent of production of fish ova is a curious matter of investigation. The eggs of various fishes differ remarkably in external appearance. Some would scarcely be believed to be eggs at all ; take for instance the skate's egg. It looks like a flattened leather bag or purse, with four horns or handles at the corners. The yolk is the size of a walnut, larger or smaller according to the species. The yolk of the egg of the dogfish (*Galeus acanthias*), which is about the size of a pigeon's egg, is used in parts of

---

* Report of Commissioner of Agriculture for 1870. Washington.

Sweden as a substitute for other eggs in their domestic economy.

This subject of the eggs of fish is one that is as yet but imperfectly understood, although the late Mr. Frank Buckland, by his investigations, has thrown much light upon many disputed points, and accumulated a good deal of valuable information in his "Report on the Sea Fisheries of England and Wales," 1879, p. 240.

Cod-roe is sent off in tins to Australia and India in a salted state. It is sold in London in a dried form, smoked and thus darkly coloured. It is a delicious dish when partly salted, parboiled, and then fried. Mr. Frank Buckland states that in 1868 he examined a cod-roe weighing no less than $7\frac{3}{4}$ lbs.; they often weigh five pounds. By careful examination he found the average was 140 eggs to the grain. This gives 67,200 eggs to the ounce, so that in the whole mass of this one cod-roe, allowing three-quarters of a pound for skin, membrane, &c., there was no less than 7,526,400 eggs.

Herrings' eggs in North America are used for human food. In the spring of the year myriads of herrings, closely allied to our own species, arrive in shore to spawn. The Indian men, women and children scoop up the spawn in large quantities, and use it as food. Herrings' eggs are about the size of, and look very much like sago. Each egg has, like that of the salmon, its own oil vesicle. The roe of the ling is said to be better eating than that of the cod. The eggs of a species of herring (*Alausa macrurus*) are eaten by the Chinese.

The largest use of fish spawn is for bait on the French coasts in the sardine and anchovy fisheries, and preserved for food in the form of caviare and dried roes, &c. The export of cod-roe for fish bait from Norway averages 40,000 barrels annually.

Oviparous animals, it is well known, are the most prolific, and of these fish excel all others. A small cod-fish will produce two millions of eggs, and it is said that a single pair of herrings, if allowed to reproduce undisturbed, and multiply for twenty years, would not only supply the whole world with abundance of food, but would become inconveniently numerous. The average number of ova in a salmon is stated at twelve thousand; if it were possible that all those eggs produced fish and they arrived at maturity, there would be twelve thousand salmon, or six thousand pairs, whose produce, at the same rate, would be seventy-two millions. Were it not that vast numbers of the eggs are destroyed, fish would so multiply as to fill the waters completely.

There are many anomalies connected with the growth of fish which naturalists have apparently never been able to resolve. We know of the great waste of fish life which must take place in the sea, of the numberless eggs that are never impregnated by the milt, and of the countless millions which are devoured by enemies; we know also that out of a million of young codfish only a small percentage will ever reach the market or become of any commercial value; but what we should like to know is, how it comes that a fish counting its spawn by the million is scarcer than fishes which yield their eggs only in thousands? A codfish of fair dimensions sheds upwards of three millions and a half of eggs, a flounder also gives its eggs by the million. A small one of this species, which was weighed and the ova counted, actually spawned 1,351,400 eggs. The fish next in order as to quantity of spawn is the mackarel, which yields about 500,000 ova. The yield of a herring is 37,000 eggs. Now, the herring excels most of the fish we have named in plentifulness, and we have never yet seen an explanation of the cause. Can any naturalist tell us for certain that these large fishes deposit their spawn annually? We have some doubts of the fact ourselves, and for the very obvious reason that the herring, with its 37,000 eggs, is our most plentiful fish, whilst the cod, with its 4,000,000 or more of ova, is annually becoming less plentiful.

Sturgeon Caviare.—In Russia, when the eggs of the sturgeon have been taken from the fish, they are carried

in packets to the corner of the fishing stage set apart
for the preparation of caviare, of which there are four
kinds made :—

1. The grained spawn or eggs entire.
2. The hard, or pressed.
3. The salted.
4. The blind eggs.

The choicest caviare is made with the eggs of the
beluga (*Acipenser huso*), which are large and handsome.
Those of the common sturgeon (*A. Guldenstadtii*) the
sevruga (*A. stellatus*), and the bastard sturgeon, mixed,
furnish a less esteemed kind; while the eggs of the
sterlet (*A. ruthenus*), which are extremely small, do not
enter into commerce, but are used locally by the fishermen and workpeople.

In preparing caviare, the roe of the several kinds of
sturgeon is spread out on a net with narrow meshes
forming a sieve, and stretched over a wooden frame,
then the grains are passed through the meshes by slightly
pressing the whole mass till nothing remains on the
sieve but the cellular tissue, the fat, and the muscle.
The grains, which are black or brown, fall through the
sieve into a wooden receptacle placed underneath. For
manufacturing grained caviare the roe is sprinkled with
very clean and fine salt, and the whole mass is stirred
with a wooden fork having eight or ten prongs. The
less the fresh caviare is salted the more it is esteemed.
The roe mixed with the salt presents at first a doughy
appearance when it is stirred ; but when every grain has
been impregnated with salt, the whole mass swells, and
in stirring it a slight noise is perceptible like that of
stirring small grains of sand. This noise is the sign that
the caviare is ready.

In manufacturing pressed caviare the brine is made
stronger, and when the eggs are well impregnated with
salt, the grains are put into a sack made of the bark of
the linden tree, which is placed under a press, in order
to get all the brine out of the caviare, and to transform
it into a solid mass. In thus pressing the caviare, a

large number of the grains are crushed, and a portion of their contents flows out with the brine. After having taken the pressed caviare from the sacks, it is packed in casks containing 30 pouds (1,080 pounds), the insides of which are covered with napkin linen; this being the reason why the caviare is also called "napkin caviare." The finest quality of pressed caviare, that which has been less pressed and salted, is placed in straight linen bags of a cylindrical shape, and is then called cast caviare. Caviare is also shipped in tin boxes hermetically closed and soldered.

The exports of caviare from Russia in 1879 amounted to 201,746 pouds of 36 lbs. each.

Mullet Caviare.—The fishermen in the Gulf of Foz, the salt lakes of Caronti, Berre, and other bays and creeks of the Mediterranean, prepare a species of caviare with the roes of the mullet and other species of fish, which is called boutarge, or botargo. It is sold at from six to fifteen francs the kilogramme (2s. 6d. to 6s. 6d. the pound), according to the quantity obtained during the season.

It is thus prepared:—The fish is opened when the ovaries have reached maturity, and the roes are removed entire and cleaned. They are then placed between planks loaded with heavy weights, and the week following the roes are washed with brine and replaced under the press. It is then sold without any other preparation. This caviare is well known in Sicily, Greece, Syria and Turkey, and is much esteemed on all the coasts of the Mediterranean. At the tables of the rich it is served as a hors-d'œuvre; cut in small slices, steeped in olive oil, and before eating sprinkled with lemon juice.

The roe of the grey mullet is in great request all over the Mediterranean; 70,000 pairs per annum are collected at Tunis, and sent across to Italy, where they fetch 10d. to 1s. 8d. per pair. Under the general name of "botargo" the roe of the mullet and the spawn of the tunny fish are prepared on the coast of the Mediterranean and sold in Italy, Egypt, Turkey, and Barbary. The best is said to be made at Tunis, but it is also prepared at Cagliari. The mullet which is caught is the *Mugil cephalus*, Lin., and the eggs are salted, bruised,. and made into a cake, which is sometimes smoked and dried in the sun. In Honduras and parts of the West Indies, the roe of the callipeva (*Mugil liza*) is dried, and considered a delicacy.

The late Sir John Richardson tells us that very good bread can be made from the roe of the pollach (*Gadus pollachius*), and that when well bruised and mixed with a little flour, the roe of the methy (*Lota maculosa*) can be baked into very good biscuits, which are used in the fur countries as bread. The Chinook Indians collect the spawn of the herring, which they squeeze into balls and dry.

The roe of the sandre (*Leucioperca sandra*) is prepared in Russia for exporting to Greece and Turkey. This is done principally in the Sea of Azov, and especially by the Cossacks of Kouban, who make annually from 15,000 to 20,000 pouds (of 36 lbs. each), by leaving the spawn in the ovaries, which hardens, and is then packed in casks with layers of salt.

Of late years the Greek islanders have commenced to prepare the roes largely for shipment, as they obtain them from the fishermen for nothing. They use those of the lestiche or bream (*Abramis brama*), of the sandre, and of the vobla (*Leuciscus rutilus*). The little bags containing the roe are thrown together promiscuously, and each layer is covered with a certain quantity of salt. The whole is then pressed between boards weighed down by heavy stones as already described. This caviare remains thus for a month, after which the Greeks put it into casks, and ship it chiefly to Turkey and the mainland. Caviare which has been thus prepared, is cut into slices shaped like discs, and is much sought after in those countries bordering on the Mediterranean.

Formerly a kind of caviare was prepared for the Armenian and Turkish markets, by adding spices, cinnamon, cardamoms, nutmegs and cloves to the pressed kind, and drying it in the sun after salting, as is still done with the roes of the mullet, held in high estimation by the Greeks. The salted and dried roe, of enormous size, of the Trubu, a species of shad, which frequents the great rivers of Siak, in Sumatra, constitutes a considerable article of commerce in the western parts of the Malayan Archipelago.

The roe of the okorune (*Perca fluviatilis*), and of the Yerschi (*Acerina vulgaris*), is dried in ovens specially constructed for this purpose in Russia, and is used as a seasoning during Lent. The eggs of fish are sought for in the rivers of India and made into cakes. The eggs of the kari (*Labeo calbasu*) and kalmuri (*Discognathus larnta*) are highly prized.

There is also a destruction by mankind of the ova, or spawn, of the crustacea—lobsters, crabs and shrimps—which are carried under the tail. The lobster produces 15,000 to 20,000 eggs, the crayfish upwards of 100,000. The lobster is never so good as when in the condition of a " berried hen." Berried hens occur most frequently in April, May, and June. They begin to lose their berries about July. Almost the only use to which the berries are put is cooking. They are employed in many preparations by the West-end chefs, especially for the colouring and enriching sauces. The chefs are also fond of the coral out of the body of the lobster. As much as six ounces of berries can be taken off in May from a lobster weighing three to three pounds and a-half. There are about 6,720 eggs in an ounce of lobster spawn.

The eggs from female crabs are also used for colouring various sauces, they are mashed up with the sauce, a little anchovy added, and then it is called " lobster sauce."

The eggs of the king crab (*Limulus moluccanus*) are collected on the north coast of Java, and much esteemed by the natives. This crustacean is in some localities so plentiful as to be used for manuring land.

CHAPTER VII.

REPTILES, SNAKES, AND AMPHIBIANS EATEN AS FOOD.

Turtles and Tortoises—Land, Marsh, River and Sea Tortoises—
Flesh Largely Eaten in Various Countries—Terrapins of
America Great Food Delicacies—Turtle Soup and Dried
Turtle Flesh—Sources of Supply of Turtle—Recipes for
Cooking Turtle—Flesh of Loggerhead Turtle not Good—
Crocodiles and Alligators Eaten—Lizards Eaten—Monitors—
Iguanas—Snakes Eaten in Many Countries—Snake Wine—
Amphibians—Frogs Eaten in Europe, America, and Asia—
Modes of Catching Them—Recipes for Cooking Them—Sala-
mander and Aloxotl Eaten.

REPTILES.—Of these we find that many are eaten with
eagerness all over the world, and neither want of beauty
nor abundance of venom protect them against omnivorous
man. In vain they assume all manner of ugly shapes;
in vain they move, creeping and hopping and sliding,
although they suggest to us by form and motion all that
is false and unfair, hideous and horrid; even God's curse
of the serpent does not shield it; and from the humble
frog of the pond to the colossal crocodile of Egypt, they
are all but so much food for their master.

Taking the first order, Tortoises or Turtles, we find the
flesh of many kinds is tender and palatable, and the eggs
of most are much esteemed as food. Of the eggs we
have spoken in the last chapter. Professor Dumeril has
classed the tortoises, according to their habits, into four
families :—

1. *Chersites*, or land tortoises.
2. *Elodites*, or *Paludines*—marsh tortoises.
3. *Potamites*, or *Fluviales*—river tortoises.
4. *Thalassites*, or sea tortoises.

Speaking generally, it may be stated that the flesh of

all tortoises is edible, for there are people who eat different kinds in various countries, but as the flesh of some is better flavoured than others, those are necessarily most sought after.

1. *The Land Tortoises* (*Testudo*).—In Sicily and Italy land tortoises (*T. Græca*) are sold in the markets principally for making soup, in which mode of cooking it is more esteemed than prepared in any other way. The flesh of the gopher, or Florida terrapin (*T. polyphemus*, Holbrook, *T. Carolina*, Lecomte), is said to be excellent, and it is therefore sought after for the table. Certain species of tortoises (*Peltoastes*, *Chersina*, and *Homophus*) are eaten in the Cape Colony.

Darwin gives a good account of the great elephantine tortoise, which he terms *T. indicus.*

The flesh of this animal is largely employed, both fresh and salted, and a beautifully clear oil is prepared from the fat. When a tortoise is caught the man makes a slit in the skin near its tail, so as to see inside the body whether the fat under the dorsal plate is thick. If it is not, the animal is liberated, and is said to recover soon from this strange operation.

While staying in the upper district of St. James's Island, where a party of Spaniards were employed in catching tortoises, Mr. Darwin and his companions lived entirely on the meat of these animals. "The breast-plate roasted with the flesh attached," he says, "is very good, and the young tortoises make excellent soup, but otherwise the meat, to my taste, is very indifferent." Some of the largest of the land tortoises of the Gallapagos group weigh 300 or 400 pounds, but their common size is between 50 and 100 pounds. Capt. B. Hall, "Extracts of a Journal in Chili and Peru," gives a better opinion of the meat:—"Their flesh without exception is of as sweet and pleasant a flavour as any that I ever eat. It was common to take out of one of them 10 or 12 pounds of fat, when they were opened, besides what was necessary to cook them with. This was as yellow as our best butter, and of a sweeter flavour than hog's lard."

Porter, in his "Journal of a Cruise made to the Pacific Ocean in 1813," stated that some of the great land tortoises captured by him weighed from 300 to 400 pounds, and that on one island they were five feet and a half long, four feet and a half wide, and three feet thick in the body. He expatiates on the luscious and delicate food that the long-necked and small-headed and other kinds produce. They have been so hunted that at the present time it is most probable that the gigantic tortoises are very rare where they were formerly so abundant.

The land tortoise, or terrapin, which is brought from Aldabra, is a favourite article of food with the inhabitants of Mahe, Seychelles, but it has become scarce. Green turtle are, however, common there from November to April.

The turtle is unlawful food among the Mahomedans, but particular classes of Bengalis eat certain Emydes or terrapins, more especially the *Tetraodon Lessoni*, of Dumeril and Bibron, which is kept for sale in shallow tanks, many hundreds of them sometimes together. The eggs also of the different water tortoises are brought to the bazaar. In Greece the flesh of the tortoises is abhorred by the people as being that of an impure animal.

A large black terrestrial tortoise with red spots, which attains the weight of twenty pounds, is eaten in Brazil. In Japan some tortoises are met with in the markets; that principally eaten is a species of *Trionyx*, one of the mud or soft-shelled tortoises. The flesh of all are very nice. A Southern Indian kind (*Cryptopus granosus*, Bibr.) living in fresh water, is rather common on the coast of Coromandel. It forms an article of diet.

The flesh of the European box tortoise (*C. Europæa*), though not very delicate, is nevertheless eaten on the Continent. It is said, however, to be greatly improved by feeding the animals for some time on grain, bran, and other vegetable aliment.

2. Of the marsh tortoises we have no details to furnish.

3. The river tortoises of Africa, Asia, and America are highly esteemed by man as food.

Le Vaillant ("Travels in Africa," vol. i., p. 116) thus speaks of the tortoises there:—"Next morning, the weather being cool and cloudy, we marched six hours in order to reach the borders of a very large pond, abounding with small tortoises, of which we caught about twenty; we broiled them all in the same manner on the coals and found them excellent. They were from seven to eight inches in length and about four in breadth. The shell on the back was of a whitish-grey colour, inclining a little to yellow; when alive they had a disagreeable smell, but by roasting this was entirely destroyed."

M. da Silva Coutinho, a member of the Brazilian Commission at the Paris Exhibition in 1867, in an article on the tortoises of the Amazon,* states that "The flesh of the *Podocnemis expansa*, of the family of Emydes, is the most savoury of all. It is with this the best dishes are prepared, and it will of itself constitute the base of a repast the most delicate. According to the part of the body employed, and the manner of preparing the flesh, the flavour will vary and resemble either veal, fowl, or pork. The natives feed continually on it. When I made a voyage of exploration in the region of Para I lived on the flesh of this tortoise for more than two months without being surfeited. Its flesh is of such easy and healthy digestion that it replaces fowl for the sick, as is practised in the military hospital of Manaus." This species is the most abundant of all the turtles of the Amazon region. Its flesh is good for food, and its eggs are converted into an oil, which is generally used for burning, but when fresh it has little flavour, and might be utilised in preserving food, as it already is in the local preparation known as Mexira. A turtle of three feet, which costs in the Amazon region about 5s., will support a family of six persons for three days. The fat can also be employed, being more palatable and healthy than lard. An ordinary animal will furnish five pounds of fat, and as this is worth 1s. a

* "Bulletin of the Society of Acclimatation, Paris," vol. xv., p. 147.

pound, it represents the whole price of the animal; the flesh being obtained for nothing.

The salt water terrapin of North America (*Clemmys terrapin*, Schoepf) is in great request, its flesh being highly esteemed as a delicacy for the table, especially at the close of the summer, when the animals have retired to their winter dormitory. They are then fat, and considered as a delicacy.

The painted terrapin (*Clemmys picta*) and the red-bellied terrapin (*Clemmys Muhlenburgii*, Schweigg, *Pseudemys rugosa*, Shaw) are now less common in Central New Jersey, being sought after by restaurant keepers, who palm them off on their customers as the diamond-back terrapin (*Malacoclemmys palustris*, Gmelin), but no cooking, however skilful, can deceive those who are accustomed to the genuine article. The latter is met with on the American coasts, from New York to Texas, the red-bellied from New Jersey to Virginia. The Southern terrapin is *Pseudemys mobiliensis*, Hollbrook; the Florida river terrapin (*P. concinna*).

The American box tortoise (*Cistudo Carolina*) has a wide distribution. Its flesh is said to be excellent.

The terrapins inhabit North America, from Hudson's Bay to the Floridas. There are so many species that it is difficult to enumerate those which are eaten. They are found at the mouths of rivers and in salt marshes in North America, and their flesh is considered a very delicious article of food. To show the importance of the tortoise trade in the United States, I may quote the following account of a Baltimore establishment from an American paper:—

"The most novel feature in the house is the terrapin department. This room is kept warm and the terrapins luxuriate in air-tight chests, each from five to ten bushels capacity. These are packed full of terrapins, which number many hundreds in the aggregate. The most of them are the Chesapeake diamond-back variety, and all are at least seven inches across the under shell, that being the measurement the terrapin must reach before, in the opinion of the epicure, it is fit for the table.

" There are also kept in some of the chests hundreds of sliders or red fender terrapins, a fresh-water variety, chiefly from the James river. The habits of the terrapin have been made a study by the dealer. He keeps them in air tight chests without food, and says they not only exist deprived of air, but grow fat ; and if kept in the chests for six months, will each weigh four to six ounces more than when put in. If the terrapins are allowed to have liberty or free air, even in the most limited space, they become very poor, as they seem to draw sustenance from themselves, but do not take food. All the terrapins in the chests are in the enjoyment of vigorous existence, as proved by their movements when the lids are raised.

" The terrapins are principally sold to hotelkeepers to be served up at extra junketings, and they bring from twenty-five to thirty-six dollars a dozen during the season. In the terrapin season one house in Baltimore will sell a thousand dozens."

It is in Lent that terrapin commands its highest prices. A dozen terrapins consist of twelve diamond-backs, no one of which must be less than a "count terrapin," that is, should measure seven inches in length on the under shell. The largest known do not exceed ten inches in length and eight pounds in weight, and such prizes are extremely rare ; usually they weigh about $3\frac{1}{2}$ lbs. each. The seven-inch terrapin averages four pounds in weight. " Sliders," the common river turtles of almost all the rivers of the South, grow to a much larger size. They bring from 6 dols. to 9 dols. a dozen. The two or three men who control the trade in Baltimore say that they sell almost exclusively for private tables. Terrapin are caught all the way from Savannah and Charleston to the Patapsco and Gunpowder rivers, but the genuine diamond-back belongs almost exclusively to the upper Chesapeake and its tributaries. The majority of the sliders come to Baltimore from the James river and streams adjoining.   An active terrapin catcher sometimes makes fifty dols. a week, but the find varies, and often runs down as low as five dols.   The reptile is discovered by probing the mud in the shallows with a stick.   He is dormant and easily captured.

The females are more highly prized and are known as "cow" terrapin.   They are generally fatter and contain about thirty eggs, some of which a visitor has a right to expect to garnish the dish at 1 dol. 25c. a plate.   Many restaurateurs, reckless of their fair fame, have resort to the eggs of the pigeon made into a paste and rolled into a substitute for the genuine article.   Thirty years ago the largest dealer in Baltimore found it difficult to dispose of the terrapin he received at six dols. a dozen.   The negroes who bring them to market say that they are growing scarcer yearly, and nothing but the high price stimulates them to keep up the supply by a more extended and persistent search.

The painted turtle (*Chrysemys picta*, Henma and Gray) may be found in many of the American ponds, lakes, creeks and rivers, from New Brunswick to Georgia. Though not considered eatable, it is nevertheless sold along with several other tortoises, and figures as a "diamond-back" in the famous terrapin supper.   Indeed in some seasons there are more wood turtles (*Chelopus insculptus*, Le Conte) and red-bellied terrapins sold in the Philadelphia markets than edible salt water terrapins or diamond-backs.   In examining a netful of terrapins at a game store a short time ago, all of them were of the *rugosa* species.   Many of them were dead, and two were so "*very* dead" that their eyes had dried up and sunk deeply into their sockets.   And yet the wily caterer will buy them and stew them with wine and spices, and the epicure will smack his lips over this reptilian carrion, and exclaim, "How delicious!"

Emys tecta, Gray, abounds in the Hooghly, and is sold for food.   The flesh of an *Emys* is eaten in China, and is considered medicinally pectoral and emollient.   The shell cut up in small pieces is given in decoction.   The carapace is, however, carefully examined to observe if there are nine divisions or markings at the sides, for if so, its value is great. It is boiled in vinegar and water to form a jelly, much prescribed in rheumatism, debility, and other disorders. The flesh of the hairy tortoise is considered excellent in many maladies.

The long-headed Chinese tortoise (*Platysternon mega-cephalum*) is sometimes sold in Canton.

The flesh of the matamata terrapin (*Chelys matamata*, Brug.) is highly esteemed, and in Cayenne and Guiana, incessant warfare has been maintained against it, so that it has become scarce.

The flesh of the tailed tortoise of North America (*Chelydra serpentina*, Schweig.), and of the alligator snapper (*Macrochelys laxiutina*, Schw.), is considered un-palatable, and has a musky odour. That of the fringed snouted tortoise (*Chelys fimbriata*), is, however, excellent eating.

To the family of Testudo belongs the jaboty (*Testudo carbonaria*, Spix.), an exclusively terrestrial species, the flesh of which is much esteemed as delicate food, rivalling in flavour that of the *Podocnemis expansa*. The flesh fried is considered one of the best meats met with.

The greaved tortoises (*Podocnemis expansa*) are extremely numerous in the northern rivers of South America. Bates, when travelling on the Amazon, had to live for a considerable part of the year on this tortoise. It was the only animal food, except fish, which was to be had; and although all the arts of the native cuisine were employed, he got thoroughly tired of it, so that opinions differ regarding this food.

The flesh of many of the mud or soft tortoises (*Trionycides*) is very nice. *Trionyx sinensis* is eaten in China.

4. *Sea Tortoises.*—We come now to the marine turtles, and of these, in commencing his notice of them, M. Lace-pede well remarks:—" This is one of the best presents which Nature has given to the inhabitants of equatorial

countries, one of the most useful products which it has deposited on the confines of land and water." Of these we may notice the green turtle, the loggerhead or hawk-bill turtle (*Chelone imbricata*, Schweig), furnishing the tortoiseshell of commerce; and the luth or leathery turtle (*Sphargis coriacea*, Rondelet).

The flesh of some species of marine tortoises, but particularly of the green turtle (*Chelonia Mydas*, and *C. virgata*, Schw.), is in the greatest request as a luxury for the table, at least in England, and the animal itself is an object of commerce. The arrival of a cargo of "lively turtles" is by no means a thing of trifling importance. Of late years the flesh is imported dried, which has placed it within the reach of general consumers. The flesh is also salted in some quarters. All the turtles afford a considerable quantity of oil, which is employed for various purposes. In some of the West Indian islands, it supplies, when fresh, the place of butter or salad oil for culinary purposes, and it is also used for burning in lamps.

Turtle would seem to have been first introduced in England as an article of food about the eighteenth century, for a record in the "Gentleman's Magazine," under date August 31, 1753, shows that it was then a rarity; and they did not know how to dress it. It states:—"A turtle, brought by Admiral Anson, weighing 350 pounds, was ate at the 'King's Arms,' Pall Mall; the mouth of an oven was taken down to admit the part to be baked."

Steam communication has greatly increased the imports of this reptile. About 15,000 are now introduced into our ports, and from thence to our kitchens, every year. They are usually brought in casks open at the top, the sea water being replenished. They weigh from ¼ cwt. to 3 cwt. Not that all these shielded animals so arriving can be called "lively turtle," for the voyage has very often a damaging effect upon them, and they have to be brought into flesh before they can be used for the table.

Dr. Browne, in his " History of Jamaica," speaking of the turtle, says, " it is delicate, tender food while young, but as it grows old it becomes more tough and gristly, and is not so agreeable to the stomach in those warm countries ; the juices, however, are generally reckoned great restoratives, and often observed to heal and smooth the skin in scorbutic and leprous habits ; nay, it is said to cure even the most obstinate venereal taints."

In Portugal, syphilitic patients are often sent to the Cape Verde Isles to be cured by feeding on turtle flesh.

The flesh of the green turtle is eaten in the West India Islands generally, in all the maritime cities of the United States, Brazil and Peru, in England, in Africa, the Cape Verde Islands, and among the natives who inhabit the Western Coasts of Africa, Guinea, and Congo, the islands of Mauritius and Réunion in the Indian Ocean, at the English Presidencies of India, Java, and in Australia. There is not a four-footed animal, a voyager tells us, the flesh of which the Japanese esteem like that of the kecame or turtle.

The flesh of the turtle is thus, we find, a universal food, if we except some of the States of Europe, which do not seem to appreciate it as a delicacy. I may add that this has been so in all ages. Diodorus of Sicily, Pliny, and Strabo speak of it. The former named " Chelonophages " certain people inhabiting islands at the entry of the Red Sea, whose principal occupation was catching turtle.

There are in the turtle two pieces of flesh very white, compared to knuckles of veal. It may be larded and made into fricandeaux and patés, equal to those of Rouen or Pontoise. Every part of the flesh is edible. The bones being easily saturated with the gravy, are left in the ragouts which are made, and the fat, which is very fluid, serves instead of butter or lard. The two most choice preparations of the turtle in the West Indies are the soup and the boucan or plastron. The soup made there is flavoured with sherry, and seasoned with strong spices, capsicums, ginger, cloves, and nutmeg. It is considered

Q

to be excellent when, after having eaten, one is obliged to rest with the mouth wide open, and cool the fevered palate with Madeira or port. So that, to appreciate this fiery soup, the taste has to be acquired.

The plastron of boucaneered turtle is made by mincing the flesh fine, and cooking it in its own shell. Here is a receipt given for preparing and cooking it:—"The plastron or buckler is the shell of the belly, on which is left three or four inches of flesh, with all the fat, this being green, and of a very delicate flavour. The plastron is placed in the oven. It is seasoned with lemon juice, capsicum or cayenne, salt, pepper, cloves and eggs beaten up. The oven must not be too hot, as the flesh of the turtle being tender, it should be cooked slowly. While it is baking the flesh should be pierced from time to time with a wooden skewer, so that the gravy may penetrate all parts. It is sent up to table in the shell, and the meat carved out from it. I have never eaten anything more appetising or better flavoured." This is not the receipt of a royal *chef de cuisine*, or of an ordinary cook, but of Father Labat, a Dominican monk, and we know that in all that relates to the table, and especially the food of fast days, monks are good authorities. The old buccaneers from whom this dish was named, having no ovens, cooked their turtle in a trench covered with lighted charcoal, and this mode of cooking was said to be preferable. But in whatever manner dressed, all agree that the flesh of the turtle is an excellent and palatable food.

Griffith, in his "Animal Kingdom," says: "It would be quite superfluous to dilate on the enthusiastic veneration in which turtle soup is held by our wealthy and discerning citizens."

Dried turtle and the dried flesh for soup is now prepared in America and the West Indies. A manufactory at Key West, Florida, puts up in airtight cans for exportation 200,000 pounds yearly, and employs ten vessels and sixty men in collecting the turtle. It is sent to England and Cuba chiefly. At Jamaica some factories are also doing a good business in a preparation worthy of the gastronomic patronage of an aldermanic banquet, so rich is it in green fat and calipee, calipash, and those delicate gelatinous morsels appertaining to the fins. A steady supply of live turtle is obtained monthly through the West India and Pacific steamers from Colon, besides those brought from the Caymanas. 10,805 pounds of prepared turtle, valued at £660, was shipped from Jamaica in 1880.

Although all the varieties of the edible turtle are palatable, yet they are distinguished by the localities from whence they are obtained, and some are preferred to others. Those of the Bay of Honduras are most esteemed in England. Of the Cape Verde Islands, those of St. Vincent are considered the best. Dampier tells us that they are not so large as those of the American islands. The flesh is white, and intermixed with the green fat, which is firm and of good flavour.

Jamaica is the principal mart in the West Indies to which the turtle are brought from the coasts of the Gulf of Mexico, from Trinidad to Vera Cruz, principally from Honduras and the Tortugas. From Jamaica they are sent to England and the United States.

The island of Ascension ships about 3,000 turtle yearly, some weighing from 400 to 800 lbs.

Lemaire states that, at Cape Blanc, the turtles are of such a size that some with the bones removed yielded a barrel of flesh without the head, throat, tail, fins, tripe, and eggs, and would furnish a good meal to thirty men. (Firmin, " Voyage in Equinoctial Holland," p. 80.) But it is not these large turtles that are most esteemed; those of 10 lbs. or 25 lbs. weight are the best flavoured.

At Martinique the flesh of the turtle is cooked in various ways, and with different sauces. It is made into soup, roasted on a spit, stewed, fricasseed, in patés, etc. It may be said of the turtle as of the pig, that every part of it is good, from the head to the foot.

Here is a receipt; according to M. Chevet, senior, for making turtle soup in the French style, given in the

6th vol., p. 424, of the "Bulletin de la Société d'Acclima-tation," Paris.

"Soak in lukewarm water the fins and the plastron of the turtle to remove the shelly parts, then cut these in pieces and add the intestines and other flesh. Place in an earthen marmite about two lbs. of the turtle flesh with a litre and a-half of water. Cook it as for a pot-au-feu, skimming it with care. Add salt, ordinary vegetables, as carrots, leeks; let it boil on a moderate fire two hours and a-half. Add a little sherry or Madeira, and cayenne pepper, a little flour, tapioca, sago, or other fecula to thicken. An excellent bouillon is thus obtained, very refreshing, nutritive, gelatinous, and which leaves the mouth fresh.

"In place of water, bouillon may be added, and quenelles made of the lower flesh of the animal and the eggs when there are any. The eggs should be well washed, and cooked separately, so as not to discolour the soup. This soup we are told forms the principal dish of the dinner."

In whatever fashion cooked, the flesh of the turtle is very agreeable to the palate. And according to all voyagers it is so easily digestible that any quantity may be eaten without inconvenience. Dr. Rufz, in an interest-ing descriptive article from which we quote, states that during a practice of twenty years in Martinique, where it is largely consumed, he never heard of any accident arising from it. It is there in demand by all classes of the population, and within the reach of all; at Lent especially it is an invaluable food resource. It is sold in the public markets like beef and mutton, at about 1s. per pound. The flesh is much firmer than that of most fishes, and more nourishing. It approaches veal, of which one preparation, "tête de veau en tortue," gives the best idea of real turtle to those who have never tasted it.

In a compilation of Voyages and Travels, published in London in 1745, we find the following panegyric on turtle:—"The flesh is white, larded with a green fat, firm and well tasted, having this advantage over the fat of all other animals, that it is not cloying or disagreeable, but may be eaten alone. The delicacy of the flesh makes it not fit for salting; but when fresh it is highly nourishing, and of so easy a digestion, that, eat ever so much, it never incommodes you, being alike agreeable, dress it which way you will. The best piece is the belly, taking also the shell that covers it with the thickness of two fingers of the meat it contains. This they put in the oven whole, seasoning with lime-juice, salt, pimento, and common pepper mixed with cloves, and baked with a slow fire; it makes an excellent dish."

In Honduras and Jamaica the flesh of the turtle is cut off in strips and dried in the sun; that from the back being the calipash, and that from the belly the calipee, of a somewhat lighter colour. Its appearance and consistency thus dried is like that of thin cakes of glue, and it requires three or four days soaking in water before it can be made into soup, the processes of drying and soaking taking from it nothing of its real nutriment or flavour.

It is not the largest turtle which are the best for eating. Those of 10 to 25 lbs. are the most esteemed. "In this respect," says Audubon, at the Tortugas, "I could have had one weighing 700 lbs. for very little more than another weighing but 50 lbs. To every person of taste, there is not a meal to be compared to that of a turtle of 10 lbs. well dressed." It is said the flesh of the females is preferable to that of the males, but they are generally lean after depositing their eggs.

The flesh of the turtle is more or less green in different localities, and at various stages. Professor Dumeril distinguishes four varieties of the green or edible turtle, according to certain colorations of the shell; but these distinctions are not regarded by those who collect and eat them.

The English markets are principally supplied with turtles from the West Indies; about 200 are sent annually from Honduras; but the high price of the article would seem to indicate either that the natural supplies are not equal to the demand, or that the methods adopted for catching and sending over the produce, are not of the most economical kind. The turtles from which the highly-prized soup is made are sent over to this country in three different ways: either alive, or sun-dried, or preserved in tins like the Australian tinned meats. In all three branches the industry is capable of great extension, not only in the West Indies, but in Fiji, North Australia, and probably in other of our tropical or sub-tropical colonies. The market price of sun-dried Jamaica turtle is about 8s. per lb., while a tin of pre-served fat costs 4s. or 5s., and a small tin of soup ready for consumption as much as half a guinea. These prices must be very remunerative to either the producer or the middleman. Considering the little difficulty there is in catching these reptiles, which have only to be turned on their backs as they come to the surface or reach the shore, and considering the numbers in which they exist on the submarine plateaux off the shores of the numerous islands and continents within the tropics, the supply of turtles ought to be both regular and abundant; while as they may be kept alive for a long time with nothing to eat and without requiring any great attention, no branch of the fishing industry could well be more profitable.

Turtles are getting scarce in the Indian seas. They should be protected more than they are. Colonel Dove-ton, in his "History of the Burmese War," states when scurvy broke out among the troops, a ship was sent ex-pressly to Diamond Island, at the mouth of the Bassan River, Pegu, for a cargo of live turtle :—"The flesh was served out to the troops by the commissariat by the pound, as beef or pork. We usually dressed it like a beef-steak, which it much resembled, both in taste and appearance. What fell to my share was wanting neither in eggs nor green fat, though I suspect these dainty adjuncts were not duly appreciated by many of us, in the absence of those condiments so requisite for serving up the dish in the true aldermanic style." Ten years ago boats' loads of turtle eggs were taken to Moulmein ; now a man thinks himself lucky to get a few small basketfuls.   The turtle eggeries are sold by auction in the same manner as fisheries.

Thalassochelys corticata is sold as coarse food in the markets of Southern Italy.

The long necked tortoise (*Chelodina longicollis*) is found in considerable numbers in the Murray River, and its tributaries, Australia.   It affords food to the natives, especially during the summer, when the lagoons are dry, as it can then be procured in large numbers without difficulty.

The *Testudo lutaria* is found about the Ganges.   They are 18 inches in diameter, and weigh from thirty to forty pounds when full grown.   They are only eaten by the lower orders, being a dirty, omnivorous sort of animal.

The flesh of the Tyrse, or soft-shelled tortoise of the Nile, is considered good food.   That of the loggerhead, or hawk's-bill turtle (*Caretta imbricata*), is tasteless, and considered unhealthy.   The eggs are used for food, and the oil obtained from the flesh is used in the preparation of leather, etc.

Dr. Browne ("History of Jamaica") states he tasted the flesh of the loggerhead turtle, which agreed pretty well with his stomach ; it was fat and rich, but of a strong rank fishy taste.

The flesh of *Sphargis luth* is said to be excellent.

We know not why the flesh of the vegetable-feeding tortoises should not be adopted, as well as that of the green turtle, among the various articles which are in request for the table.   There is much in habit and association of ideas ; and though persons who would not refuse turtle might turn from tortoise with disgust, they may rest assured that, in Sicily and Italy, these land tortoises are sold in the markets principally for being made into soup, which is more esteemed than the flesh prepared in any other way.

Having dealt somewhat in detail with the Tortoises, we come now to treat of some other reptiles, Alligators,

Snakes, and Amphibians, whose flesh furnishes food to different people.

Crocodiles are highly valued in their native countries on account of their flesh and excellent eggs. Herodotus speaks with favour of the huge giants of Elephantine on the Upper Nile, where they are still caught with an angle and universally eaten, in spite of their strong musky odour. Even the alligator of the Southern States of America is by no means despised, and finds ready acceptance as food with the negroes and some white people.

Dr. Holbrook states that he found the flesh of the alligator tolerable eating, although Catesby considered its peculiar taste and odour disagreeable.

In Guiana the negroes do not disdain to eat the flesh of the caiman, or alligator, which is white but hard, and of a musky flavour. The alligator forms the chief food of the Indians of Brazil. The flesh is said to be like veal, and good eating.

In Siam the crocodile attains a length of 25 feet, with a voracity proportioned to its size. Its flesh is sold for food in the markets and bazaars. Pallegoix ("Siam," vol. i., p. 174) says:—" Un jour je vis plus de cinquante crocodiles, petits et grands, attachés aux colonnes de leurs maisons. Ils vendent la chair comme on vendrait de la chair de porc, mais à bien meilleur marché."

The flesh of the Nile crocodile (*Crocodilus niloticus*) is eaten by the negroes.

In Dongola the crocodile (*C. vulgaris*) is caught for the sake of its flesh, which is regarded as a delicacy. The flesh and fat are eaten by the Berberines, who consider these excellent, but both have a strong smell of musk. Dr. Madden tells us that in Egypt he tasted a piece of young crocodile broiled. The flavour a good deal resembled that of a lobster, and, though somewhat tough, it might certainly be considered very excellent food.

Crocodiles are very abundant in many parts of Africa. They are found in nearly all the rivers east of the Umzimvoobo in South Africa, and swarm especially in the waters running into Lake N'gami. The flesh has the appearance of veal and forms a royal repast for the natives.

A correspondent of the *Globe*, in December, 1881, writes of crocodile steaks:—"Some years ago, I, in company with others, was sent 400 miles up the Zambesi and Shire Rivers, in Central Africa. We were short of food; for a drought prevailed, and the domestic animals of the country had been eaten up. One of our party killed and landed a crocodile, and left it for the benefit of the starving natives. But I was caterer for our little community, and, unknown to my friends, cut from the tail of this creature two fine steaks. At dinner they were served up nicely broiled, and they looked nice. 'Hullo! what have you got there?' said one. 'Eat, and be thankful, and ask no questions,' said I, handing him a portion. I served out to others also, and then helped myself, and it seemed to me something like tough pork that had been fattened on fish. 'It is not so bad' was the general testimony. 'But what is it?' one and all demanded. 'Crocodile,' said I. The effect of prejudice upon the palate and the appetite was instantly manifested. One left the table, looking pale; another, the doctor, remembered that it was a reptile, and laid down his knife and fork; another thrust his plate from him in disgust; and, with the exception of myself, no one did justice to the provision. Well, it was tough, greasy, and fishy. Very hungry, one might eat it and be glad. Otherwise, I think very few would care for it. We did not try it again."

The flesh of the alligator was a favourite dish among the Port Essington settlers, and the seamen employed in the surveys of the northern coasts and rivers of Australia. It is, however, believed to have a strong liking for human flesh when that delicacy can safely be obtained.

Mr. Henry Koster, author of "Travels in Brazil," writes:—"I have been much blamed by my friends for not having eaten of the flesh of the alligator, and indeed I felt a little ashamed of my squeamishness when I was shown by the same friend a passage in a French writer, whose name I forget, in which he speaks favourably of this flesh. However, if the advocate for experimental eating had seen an alligator cut into slices, he would, I think, have turned from the sight as quickly as I did."

Waterton, speaking of his negro Quashi, says, "He had a brave stomach for heterogeneous food; it could digest and relish too, cayman, monkies, hawks and grubs. He made three or four meals off a cayman, while it was not absolutely putrid, and salted the rest." A cayman boiled was found sweet and tender, and Waterton remarks, he does not see why it should not be as good as frog or veal.

The Rev. Mr. Haensel, in his "Letters on the Nicobar Islands," tells us that "Part of the flesh of the crocodile or cayman is good and wholesome when well cooked. It tastes somewhat like pork, for which I took it, and ate it with much relish when I first came to Nancanweny, till on inquiry, finding it to be the flesh of a beast so disgusting and horrible in its appearance and habits, I felt a loathing, which I could never overcome; but it is eaten by both natives and Europeans."

The aboriginal natives of Trinidad considered a boiled slice of alligator as a dainty morsel, and Mr. Joseph, the historian, records having tasted it, and found it very palatable.

The Indians relish the white and savoury flesh of the yecaré, as it is called in South America, the spectacled cayman (*Alligator sclerops*) although it is dry and coarse. The flesh and fat are occasionally eaten by natives in Africa and other parts.

Alligators are killed in large numbers in the South American lakes and parts of the River Amazon for their fat. Mr. Wallace, in describing an alligator hunt on the lakes of Mesiana, an island lying off the mouth of the Amazon, states that about eighty were killed in two days. They are cut open, and the fat, which accumulates in considerable quantities about the intestines, is removed, and made up into packets in the skins of the smaller ones, taken off for the purpose. The fat is boiled down into oil and burned in lamps. It has rather a disagreeable smell, but not worse than train oil.

These various products render this animal much more valuable than it was supposed to be in the days of Romeo, when starved apothecaries, to show that learning and not beef was their aliment, hung up in their "meagre repertories" alligators stuffed.

Leaving the Reptiles we come now to Lizards and Snakes, which one would suppose to be the least acceptable of flesh food.

Lacerta.—Lizards are eaten by the natives of New Zealand, and the great Cyclodus (*C. gigas*, Bodd.) is prized by the Australian natives as a choice article of food. Lizards are dried and sent in packages to be used by the Chinese physicians in their practice.

The larger kind of lizards seem to have disappeared from parts of New Zealand. They appear to have been eaten in former times by the Maories. The Rev. J. W. Stack, in a paper in the "Transactions of the New Zealand Institute," records the following anecdote.

"Hakopa, a well-known Kaiapoi chief, who was taken prisoner by Te Rauparata, and spared on account of his great valour, while in captivity at Otaki, was invited one day by his masters to share the afternoon meal. When seated by the basket containing the food, his master asked him whether he would have some fish. 'Yes,' he replied, 'but where did you obtain it?' 'Ask no questions,' was the answer, 'taste and see how you like it.' He did taste it, and found it very good. When the meal was over his master told him he had eaten the flesh of a lizard."

He often joined afterwards in lizard hunts, when as many as forty were sometimes caught and eaten.

Kelaart says that the natives of Ceylon are partial to the flesh of the common Indian water lizard (*Monitor*

[*Varanus*] *dracaena*) and he once ate some excellent soup made from a guana, which tasted like hare. At Trincomalee they used to be hunted down by dogs, and sold in the market. Another monitor is also eaten in the East, *Hydrosaurus salvator*. The lowest castes of Hindoos capture these lizards by digging them out of their burrows on the banks of rivers for the sake of their flesh, which is greatly relished by these people. Some individuals attain to nearly seven feet in length.*

The meat of the *Amblyrhyncus subcristatus*, Mr. Darwin tells us, when cooked is white, and by those whose stomachs rise above all prejudices it is relished as very good food. Humboldt has remarked that in intertropical South America all lizards which inhabit dry regions are estimated delicacies for the table. The eggs of these animals, which are numerous, large and oval, are esteemed by the inhabitants of the Gallapagos islands as food.

Many of the lizard race, as the *Iguana delicatissima* have long held and still maintain a high rank as articles of luxury for the table; and the flesh and eggs of the common Teguixin, a large species, of Brazil and other parts of South America, are eaten.

The Salempenta (*Teius Teguexin*, Linn.) of South America, is a large species of lizard. Like the iguana, it affords very delicious food, which is thought to resemble the flesh of a very young chicken. New comers are at first averse to eating a lizard of any description, but they very soon find out their mistake, and would even prefer an iguana or salampenta cutlet to a chicken.†

The ugly looking large tree lizard called the Iguana, which is like an alligator in miniature, is certainly not very attractive in appearance, and yet by most persons in tropical countries its flesh is highly esteemed, being reckoned as delicate as chicken, and but little inferior to turtle in flavour. The eggs, which are somewhat smaller

---

* Cassell's "Natural History."
† Waterton's "Wanderings in South America."

than those of the domestic pigeon, are pronounced by Sir Robert Schomburgk and others to be delicious. These are deserving the attention of gourmands. One of these lizards will sometimes contain as many as four score eggs, about the size of a pigeon's egg, but with soft shells, which when boiled are like marrow. It would be a refreshing sight to see some civic dignitary who has gone the round of all the dishes which native and foreign skill have been able to produce, partaking for the first time of a dish of lizard's eggs garnished with anchovies.

The incessant destruction of the iguanas, for the sake of their flesh, has rendered them very scarce, if not altogether extinct in localities where they were once abundant. They were formerly so common on the Bahamas Islands, that Catesby tells us they furnished a great part of the subsistence of the inhabitants. They used to put them into the holds of the sloops and carry them alive for sale to Carolina, or salt and barrel them up for the use of their families at home. Browne, in his " Natural History of Jamaica," says, " The flesh of this creature is liked by many people, and frequently served up in fricassees, at their tables, in which state it is often preferred to the best fowls."

Iguanas are eaten in Brazil and Trinidad; indeed, we find these reptiles are eagerly hunted for food by the natives alike of Africa, Australia, America, and Asia.

Iguanas are very large and plentiful in the Bahamas group; they are hunted with a small kind of hound, and if taken alive, the mouth is sewed up with twine and they keep alive a month or six weeks without food. Nassau the capital is chiefly supplied with the iguana from the Berry Islands. This reptile is reported to be particularly plentiful in the Island of St. Vincent, and one was measured nearly ten feet from nose tip to tail end, the body being nearly as thick as that of a man. They do not usually, however, attain such dimensions. This lizard subsists on vegetables, earth-worms, and insects.

In Costa Rica the large iguanas attain the size of small crocodiles, and form a game which the people of the country highly prize. Although often roasted, a frequent native mode is to boil them, taking out the leaves of fat, which are melted and clarified, and put into a calabash or dish, into which they drop the flesh of the iguana as they eat it. The iguana and white-throated monitor (*Monitor albogularis*, Daud.) are sometimes employed as food at the Cape Colony, but their flesh, though white, is there thought to be dry and insipid.

The large saurian, *Cyclure pectine* (confounded with the iguana), is often eaten in warm countries. The flesh is white, tender, and very savoury; the tail and the lumbar regions have a fine flavour like eel, which Mr. Alfred Duges, of Mexico, says he has also tasted in the rattlesnake (*Crotalus rhombiferus*) and the *Pityophis* of Deppe, ophidians which attain a sufficient size to be served with white sauce like a fowl.

It was long before the Spaniards could conquer their repugnance to the iguana, the favourite delicacy of the Indians, but which the former had regarded with disgust as a species of serpent. They found it, however, to be highly palatable and delicate, and from that time forward the iguana was held in repute among Spanish epicures. The story is thus related by Peter Martyn:—"These serpentes are lyke unto crocodiles, saving in bygness; they call them guanas. Unto that day none of owre men durste adventure to taste them, by reason of theyre horrible deformitie and lothsomnes. Yet the Adlantado being entysed by the pleasantnes of the king's sister Anacaona, determined to taste the serpentes. But when he felte the flesh thereof to be so delycate to his tongue, set to amayne without al feare. The which theyre companions perceiving, were not behynde hym in greedynesse; insomuche that they had now none other talke than of the sweetnesse of these serpentes, which they affirm to be of more pleasant taste than eyther our phesantes or partriches."

Ophidians.—We now come to snakes and serpents, which one would suppose to be even more repulsive and objectionable as food than alligators and lizards, but tastes differ, and we are told of an innkeeper in some tropical country who used to inquire of his guests which they would have served, land eels or water eels. Snakes are frequently, however, eaten by civilised and savage man, but not always from choice. Seeing the loss of human life occasioned by snakes, any means of destroying them is useful. Official accounts state that 19,519 persons were killed by snakes in India in 1882, and 3,000 by wild animals; 212,776 snakes were killed in 1880, and 59,488 in 1882.

Mr. Frank Buckland tells us that he once ate a piece of a boa-constrictor; it tasted, he says, like veal, the flesh being exceedingly white and firm. A narrative in the " Penny Magazine " describes a supper off fried rattlesnake, which was served up under the name of " Musical Jack." The flesh of serpents was held in high repute by the ancients medicinally, and when properly prepared seems to have been a very agreeable article of food, corresponding with the turtle soup of the present day. Vipers are much used on the Continent, whether for food or for medicine, I cannot tell. The Italians, however, regale themselves with a jelly made of stewed vipers.

There is a large edible snake spoken of as found in Kiang-se, China, which being dried and smoked is pared off in thin slices, like smoked beef, and is found a convenient condiment by travellers. Several kinds of snake wines are sold in the apothecaries' shops, and used in palsy. The snake thus employed appears to be peculiar to the mountains of Kiang-se. To assure purchasers that the article is genuine, a strip of the skin of the animal is fastened to the top of the containing vessel. This wine is in high esteem as an anthelmintic, and is an antidote to malaria. Wulu, on the Yang-tse, produces a snake wine which is in high repute. An adder wine is also used in paralysis and insanity.

Sea snakes (*Hydrophidæ*) are eaten by the inhabitants of some of the countries on whose shores they are found.

The Indians of Western Nevada eat snakes of different kinds. The reptile is, while yet alive, impaled lengthwise on a stick, and held writhing over the fire until broiled.*

Browne in his "History of Jamaica" tells us (p. 461) that "many of the negroes eat the yellow snakes, and look upon them as a rich and delicious food; but they generally preserve the fat, which is considered as a good resolutive, and highly recommended for such purposes."

In an account of Jamaica, published in 1683, it is related that "the snakes were eaten by the Indians as regularly as the guanas by the Spaniards. The latter is but small, and of the shape of an alligator; the flesh is sweet and tender." Many lizards are sought for on trees, and in their holes in the sand by the borders of moors.

McFarlane in his "Southern Italy" says:—"Although no Roman or Neapolitan peasant will eat of a tame goose, I have seen great black snakes fried and eaten both in Calabria and Sicily to this day. Celsus recommends vipers as wholesome and luscious; in China they are salted and pickled. The lizards of the American Continent are a most delicate dish, and not long since the leguana of the Antilles was brought in large numbers to South Carolina. At home they are raised and fattened upon chicory and rice. Snakes also find a ready market in Eastern countries. The giant snake of Java, well nigh ten feet long and of the thickness of a man's arm, infests the pepper plantations, and its venom is fatal; still it is caught and eaten with relish. The huge boa-constrictor is said to furnish an exceedingly fat meat, and the negroes of its native country prefer it to the daintiest food of the white man. The anaconda of Brazil supplies the table of the poor, though the

---

* S. Powers, in "Smithsonian Report for 1876," p. 453.

Portuguese only use the rich fat it contains. The natives of South America eat almost all snakes, and the far West has taught many a fastidious palate from over the sea to relish, with the Red Indian, the fatal rattlesnake."

Kaempfer tell us that snakes are eaten in Japan, and Anderson states that the Battus of Sumali, in Africa, eat snakes and alligators.

The flesh and skin of several serpents is employed in China as medicine, care being taken to cut off the head and tail, where it is supposed their poison accumulates.

A kind of adder, 8 or 10 feet long, is eaten by the people, although it is believed to be rather poisonous.

A species of serpent from one to three feet long is caught, and after being gutted and washed is shaped into a circle with bamboo pins and dried on a slow fire. It is made into medicine.

The *San Francisco Bulletin* remarks :—" The ingredients of a witch's cauldron, as described by the poet, could not have been more repulsively disgusting than are the articles and compounds shipped to the Chinese physicians of this city from their native country and used as medicines here. There seems to be just at the present time an extra demand for a venomous serpent closely resembling the rattlesnake, of which hundreds are received constantly. A Custom House official brought a specimen of these cheerful looking creatures to this office yesterday—a coiled snake of about four feet long, fanged, and with hideous head scales like a crest. How these animals are taken by patients of Chinese doctors is not known. One would be a fair dose if disguised in a coating of sugar. They are to be taken in sections three times a day, as they are desiccated, or they may be boiled down or pulverised, and taken in powders or rolled into pills."

Among the Amphibians we have Frogs, the Salamander, and Axolotl utilised. Frogs are eaten in many countries, not only in France and the United States, but also in South America, China, and the Indian Archipelago. The

R

species most esteemed is the green frog (*Rana esculenta*), but others are eaten, as *R. Catesbiana* and *R. clamitans.* Frogs are considered an excellent food dish by some in Brazil. The American green frog (*Rana halecina*), is eaten in Guatemala. The Indians catch them to eat, spearing the larger ones, and netting the larvæ. In Surinam and other parts of South America the flesh of *Rana paradoxa* is eaten. In the Antilles bull frogs (*Rana pipiens*) are reared in a state of domestication for the table, and the hind legs are said to afford excellent eating.

The matlametlo of the Africans (*Tomoptera adspersa*) is edible, and according to Dr. Livingstone, is said to resemble chicken in flavour.

It is usual to associate frog-eating with Frenchmen, as the people of that nation were, without doubt, the first to make use of them as a table dish, and to introduce them to the epicures of other countries, who were not long in acquiring an appetite for these dainties, and soon grew as fond of them as their neighbour. It is more than three hundred years since they were first placed among the dishes at the nobles' feasts, and the favour which they found has been continually increasing until now, when they are used as food in nearly all the countries of Europe and America.

The frog, as an article of food, has not, however, been introduced in the London Market. We have not yet thought of this way of manifesting the friendly feelings and intimate union existing between England and France. We have adopted many French tastes and customs, but the frog must hop about a little longer before it can mount on the table of the average Englishman. He has, however, his eye upon us, and we shall have to eat him yet. He has tempted successfully our cousin ; how can we hope to resist much longer ?

The *New York Times* informs us that frogs are now inscribed daily on the bills of fare of the most prominent restaurants of that city, and are becoming a favourite dish among the epicures and gourmands whose purses correspond to their tastes. What can be more emphatic than this? Not only do the Americans eat the frog, but they pay a high price for the privilege. These are our cousins who are thus distinguishing themselves by their adventurous spirit. They were allied to France in the time of Lafayette—before we were—and they are the first to eat the frog.

The physicians of Europe early made use of the nutritious properties of the flesh of the frog in their practice, prescribing it generally in the shape of broth for various affections of the chest, and particularly consumption. This practice is still in vogue throughout the sparsely-settled districts of North America, and in the Western States it is a common occurrence for those who are affected with diseases of the chest to live on a frog diet. Frogs cooked in oil and salt were considered by the ancients an excellent antidote to the poison of serpents, and when boiled in vinegar were used as a remedy for the toothache.

Of the dozen or more varieties common to the United States and Europe, only a few are considered edible and used as food by man. The celebrated edible, or green frog of Europe, which naturalists call *Rana esculenta*, is the greatest favourite and the most sought after in the European countries. In the United States the species called bull-frogs or shad-frogs, are about the only kinds that are used for culinary purposes. The European edible frog is of a bright green colour above, with round circumscribed black spots, a light coloured line along the back, and of a yellowish colour underneath. The American bull-frog is familiar to almost every one who has been in the tropics, and somewhat resembles the common European frog.

As a general rule, only the hindquarters of the frog are eaten, but in Germany every part, with the exception of the intestines and skin, is made use of as food. Many persons will not eat frogs, believing that they are unclean, yet they have no hesitation in partaking of crabs or lobsters that feed upon the refuse animal matter which they find in the water. The flesh of the frog is very white and tender, nutritious and delicately flavoured, and when nicely cooked is one of the most dainty dishes that the gustatory sense of an epicure could desire, surpassing in flavour any of fish, flesh, or fowl. They are cooked in various ways, in all of which their extreme delicacy is apparent. They can be made into a broth, fried, stewed, or fricasseed, as the eater may desire; but most people who eat them prefer to have them fried. The manner in which they are fried at the prominent American restaurants is very simple. The legs, after being well skinned, are parboiled for about five minutes in slightly salted water; they are then plunged into cold water for a few minutes, and are taken out to drain, after which they are placed in a hot pan and fried in the usual way. The broth can be made in the same way as chicken or beef broth.

The marshes between Detroit and Lake St. Clair in North America are the resort of millions of frogs; and it is asserted that more frogs are sold in Detroit than in any other city of its size. During the frog season heavy shipments are made to New York, Boston, and other Eastern cities. The *Free Press*, which pronounces the commercial frog as suspicious as a wolf, as wild as a deer, and as shrewd as a fox, describes the work of frog hunting as follows :—

" Most of the frogs are caught for this market by men. One or two boys have some fame as successful frog catchers, but it has been demonstrated that the average boy lacks the necessary qualifications to make the business of any profit to him. We know of one old fisherman and hunter who has followed the frog catching business for the last twelve years, and he has sometimes made it pay as high as 15 dollars per week. While there is only one way of killing a goose there are several ways of killing a frog. Frog hunting would be a great financial success if the jumpers would take a seat on a log and permit a man to walk up and crack 'em over the head with a club, but the frog is utterly opposed to any such proceeding. His eagle eye detects the enemy afar off, and the approach must be cautious. The outfit consists of a frog spear, a hook and line, a fish pole with a pointed iron in the end, and sometimes a small shot gun is taken along. First discover your frog. He may be sitting on a log ten feet from shore. He feels quite safe at that distance and will probably wait for developments. The hook and line can be used here. The line is stout and the hook big enough to hold a twenty pound bass. The idea is to fish for the frog without bait. A careful hand will manœuvre the line until the hook is under the frog's throat, and then a sudden jerk takes him off his meditative roost and gives him into the power of his enemy. The spear, which is provided with a long handle, can sometimes be used, though a frog will dodge a sudden thrust as quick as a pickerel. If the shot gun is used it is with a light charge of powder and very fine shot, and the head is the point aimed at. Some of the froggers work the banks and are provided with boats, but success depends a good deal on circumstances. A good hunter has been known to bag 200 frogs per day, but three or four dozen legs are called a fair day's catch. A frog will probably live ten or fifteen years if steering clear of accidents. They are not worth catching until they are two years old, and are not "prime" until they reach the age of five. A frog sees his palmy days from five to ten. Before reaching five he is giddy and thoughtless. After that he settles down to a life of ease and contentment, and the days come and go and leave him no sorrow. Frogs have been caught in the St. Clair marshes weighing as high as seven pounds and having legs almost like drumsticks. One was caught at the head of Belle Isle two years ago which kicked the beam at nine, and one weighing only half a pound less was on exhibition at the Central Market last spring."

In America the season for frogs extends from March until November. They are in the best condition for table use in the fall, just before going into winter quarters, although more are eaten in the spring and early part of the summer, because they can be caught much easier at this season of the year. They are taken sometimes by beating them with long poles as they sit on the banks of the streams and ponds. The extreme voracity of the frog is easily taken advantage of, as it will leap after and seize almost anything that floats on the waters near the banks, having the appearance of life, and in motion. A hook and line, baited with an insect, or covered with a piece of red flannel, serves as a good tempter to the frog, who will generally seize it without hesitation or difficulty. After being caught, they are preserved in large frog ponds, or froggeries, as they are called, until they are required for the market. There are a number of these froggeries on Long Island, in Westchester county, and in New Jersey, from whence the city markets are supplied. The proprietors of these froggeries send the frogs to market at regular intervals, and they are kept alive until the customers purchase them. The principal places where they are sold in quantities in New York city are Fulton, Catherine, and Washington markets, where they can be obtained from a number of dealers. The prices range from 50 cents to 2 dollars per dozen, according to the size, appearance, and quality; but when they reach the restaurants their value becomes much greater, depending upon the purses and appetites of the customers. Several of the hotels and large restaurants are supplied directly from the froggeries, and do not purchase from the market dealers, but the majority obtain them from the marketmen as their demands require them.

A correspondent in a Troy newspaper states that he watched two men catching frogs in a swamp. "They would strike them with clubs where they could reach them, but most of them they caught with a wire snare. They had a large basketful, more than a hundred pounds in weight. One of them said he made a good deal of money catching frogs for the New York market, having in one month last season caught 1,600 lbs. of dressed frogs, for which he got 30 cents a pound, making 480 dollars for his month's work. Part of the time he had two boys to help him. One week, near Hudson, he caught upwards of 500 lbs., and sold them for 160 dollars, or at an average of 22 cents a pound. These stories seemed to me incredible, and yet he assured me it was truth. He can clear 28 cents a pound, he says, easily. He seemed to be an honest man, and from the ease with which they caught the frogs, I was led to believe that he had not stretched the truth much, if at all."

The question whether any four-legged creature can properly be described as a fish may not at first sight seem very debateable, and yet it has occupied for some time past the serious attention of certain transatlantic authorities. The discussion arose out of a rather curious trade which has been going on for years between Canada and the cities of the Republic. Our American cousins have, as it seems, quite got over those prejudices which in this benighted island still militate against the admission of frogs to the *cuisine*, and they are now so fond of the delicacy which was once considered the distinctive food of Frenchmen, that the produce of their own ponds and ditches does not suffice for the demands of the market. Accordingly, the Canadians, whose waters seem to be specially prolific in these creatures, have been driving a large and flourishing trade with the towns across the border, and especially with New York, in supplying them with the edible parts of the frog, which until lately were transported free of Customs duty under the designation of " Canadian fish." Some official busybody at last found fault with this easy-going definition, and claimed duty on the imports; and the Treasury on appeal decided that frogs are not Canadian fish within the meaning of the Washington Treaty, and therefore are not free of Customs duty. The Canadians were, however, not discouraged, and possibly may have thought that as the mummy of a Pharaoh travelled under the name of salt fish in Egypt, so a dead frog might fairly be allowed to travel in America as fresh fish. As " fresh fish destined for immediate consumption " they accordingly essayed to pass their valuable commodities, but without success,

as the Secretary of the Treasury at Washington has
again rejected their claim. Still the exporters are not
convinced, and are now hoping to get their goods admitted as "fish to be used for bait," which is also
exempt by virtue of the treaty. So obstinate a conviction that the creature which " would a wooing go "
belongs to the tribe sometimes described as " finny,"
seems to show that the distinction between beasts,
reptiles, and fishes is not quite so clear as naturalists
ought by this time to have made it.*

From a recent article in the *St. James's Gazette* we
quote the following remarks:—" De la Reynière, in his
Annual for 1806, said frogs were only good in spring;
and the late Mr. Dallas, in his ' Book of the Table,'
copied this statement in 1877. It may have been true
that, as Lenten fare, they were formerly only seen on
Parisian tables during those forty days; but they are
decidedly at their best later on, and are essentially a
light summer dish. Indeed, the French gourmet we
have already quoted goes on to point out how in
Auvergne, one Simon of Riom had amassed a couple of
hundred thousand francs by serving them in fricassee all
the year round, at the price of three a penny. It is
absolutely impossible, says this enthusiastic gourmand,
to bring on an indigestion of frogs, no matter what
quantity you eat; and this fact is thought to have
turned much to Simon's advantage. He had such an
enormous custom that he could not afford to trust to
markets; and so he filled his cellars with tanks, his
tanks with water, and the water with the ' pretty little
things;' and there fed and fattened them, and fricasseed
and sold them, until he distanced all competition. And
although he went by the nickname of ' Old Simon the
Frog,' and although, too, his surname—as we believe on
the word of Hebrew scholars—means snub-nosed, neither
he nor any of his customers had cause to turn up their
noses at frogs, as too many do even at the present day.

---

* The *Globe*.

In his time people who drew the line at frogs put oysters
and snails too at the far side of it; 'so voluntarily de-
priving themselves of three great pleasures,' says De la
Reynière. But the brave have shown the way to oysters,
and snails and frogs are now eaten in all parts of France
where vines flourish or have flourished, and reeds grow
in ponds.

" There are many ways of cooking a frog, or rather the
only joints of him that are eaten—namely, his hind-legs,
to which a portion of the back is left attached, chiefly to
hold those limbs together. Old Simon's way is as good
as any. The edible portions should first be thrown into
plenty of fresh cold water to blanch ; next, they should
be drained and dried; then put to soak awhile in white
of eggs well beaten up ; now powder them over with
flour ; and finally fry them in plenty of fine olive-oil
until they are crisp as 'the whitebait of the Minister,
that treasure of the sea,' and the bones are changed into
something so rich and strange that they melt in the
mouth. Add a lemon, red pepper, brown bread and
butter, to complete ' the loaves and fishes ' illusion, and
say if a ' fricassée de grenouilles ' be not much easier to
eat than to pronounce, and a species of 'small deer ' by
no means to be abandoned to Poor Tom. You can devil
them like the ' bait,' too, if you like ; and they make a
tip-top curry. Or they fry well in batter ; or you stew
them in butter and white wine, with parsley and enough
garlic to swear by chopped up fine. But, no matter how
they be cooked, they are very pretty eating, and make a
delicious *entrée*—tenderer than the youngest chicken, and
still with a flavour and a velvety texture all their own.
There is a painful French proverb—'il n'y a pas de
grenouille qui ne trouve son crapaud '—and it has a
dreadful double-edged explanation. It means that there
is no girl so—well, so unbeautiful that she cannot find
an uglier husband. We put something like it long ago
in a much prettier way when, in ' Froggy would a wooing go,' we sang, 'A lily-white duck came and gobbled
him up.' But, ugly or not, froggy ' eats ' well ; as we

shall all probably acknowledge some day when we have sufficiently overcome our insular prejudice about him."

At Paris there is a regular market held once a week in the Rue Geoffroy St. Hilaire for the sale of this Batrachian. The vendors bring their merchandise in large casks pierced with holes, in which the frogs are packed in hundreds in wet moss. They are sold, if of good size, at 75 to 85 francs the hundred, a good price for this wretched animal. Many are bought by gardeners, as they are great destroyers of insects.

In France efforts are being made to prevent cruelty in supplying this table delicacy. The Société Protectrice des Animaux has issued a strong protest against the present mode of providing frogs for the dinner table in France. It appears that the poor creatures when caught, have the upper part of their legs, or edible portion of their bodies, ruthlessly cut off with a pair of shears. The frogs in their mutilated state being useless, they are thrown aside. Numbers of them are stated to have been found eight or ten days after their mutilation crawling about on their forelegs in a pitiable condition. The Society, therefore, recommends that some plan of killing them in the first place should be adopted.

Many of the frogs brought to the markets in Paris are caught in the stagnant waters round Montmorenci, in the Bois de Vincennes, Bois de Boulogne, etc. The people employed in this traffic separate the hind quarters and legs of the frogs from the body, denude them of their skin, arrange them on skewers, as larks are done in this country, and then bring them in that state to market. In seeking for frogs, these dealers often meet with toads, which they do not reject, but prepare them in the same way as they would frogs; and, as it is impossible to determine whether the hind quarters of these creatures, after the skin is stripped off, belong to frogs or toads, it continually happens that great numbers of the supposed frogs sold in Paris for food are actually toads.

"The exportation of frogs from Belgium to France," says the *Echo du Luxembourg*, "has developed considerably of late. A man named B., of Vance, has forwarded 200,000 in the last three weeks; on Thursday he sent off 30,000. They are chiefly sent to Rheims, Nancy, and Paris. A thousand frogs fetch 13 francs (10s. 6d.), and weigh 50 kilogrammes (1 cwt.). They enter France duty free. At Rheims 25 pairs of frogs' legs can be bought for 60 centimes (6d.). The thighs, as everyone knows, (*des succulents rôtis*) are served with white sauce and in a *fricassee*. They are thus a dish by no means to be despised." But the rest of the body, and the skin—the sticky, slimy skin—what is done with that? Why they make—turtle soup of it! Yes, that savoury *mock turtle* over which gourmands lick their lips, has for its chief foundation the amphibians which haunt the marshes and the fields of Luxembourg. The autumn and the spring are the best time of year for frogs. In Vienna, where the consumption of frogs is considerable, they are preserved alive and fattened in froggeries (*grenouillières*) constructed for the express purpose.

Wallace, in his "Travels on the Amazon," states that "his Indians went several times early in the morning to the gapo to catch frogs, which they obtained in great numbers, stringing them on a sipo, and boiling them entire, entrails and all, and devoured them with much gusto. The frogs are mottled of various colours, have dilated toes, and are called jui."

The large frog, or crapaud, of Dominica (*Cystignathus ocelatus*), is a part of the dietary of the people of all classes in that colony. According to Dr. Imray it is very wholesome and much relished. It is much esteemed as an article of food, the flesh when fricasseed being preferred to chicken, and made into soup, it is recommended for the sick, especially in consumptive cases. Its extensive destruction by the mischievous opossum has been a great evil to the country, but its extermination would be a serious loss. Happily, however, it appears to be gaining ground of late, though it can never abound as formerly, while the "Manicou," or opossum, which feeds upon it, exists in the woods.

Frogs are considered an excellent food dish by some in Brazil.

In America, the flesh of the huge bull-frog (*Rana pipiens*, Harl.; *R. mugiens*, Catesby) is said to be tender, white, and affords excellent eating. Some bull-frogs weigh as much as half a pound, but the hind legs are the only parts used as food.

The natives of parts of Australia when pinched for food, capture large numbers of the common golden tree frog (*Hyla aurea*) by the light of a torch at night. Other tribes in Western Australia eat a species that burrows in the sand, the aboriginal name of which is Guya or Goya. It is in season in the months of April and May.

There is also a frog called Tolun-jar, eaten about King George's Sound, and another called Tuck, from the noise it makes. Thus the taste for this food extends to the East.

Mr. R. Fortune, in describing a Chinese market, observes:—"Frogs seemed much in demand. They are brought to market in tubs and baskets, and the vendor employs himself in skinning them as he sits making sales. He is extremely expert at this part of his business. He takes up the frog in his left hand, and with a knife, which he holds in his right, chops off the fore part of its head. The skin is then drawn back over the body and down to the feet, which are chopped off and thrown away. The poor frog, still alive, but headless, skinless, and footless, is then thrown into another tub, and the operation is repeated on the rest in the same way. Every now and then the artist lays down his knife, and takes up his scales to weigh these animals for his customers, and make his sales. Everything in this civilised country, whether it be gold or silver, geese or frogs, is sold by weight." *Rana tigrina* is the frog eaten in China.

Many kinds of toads are believed by the Chinese to have medicinal properties. Dr. Soubeiran, in his "Materia Medica of the Chinese," states that several species of frogs are used by them. They prepare soups with them, and a gelatine considered excellent for convalescents. A brown frog with black spots on the head is especially esteemed for making broths and soups.

The eating of frogs seems to be indulged in in the Philippines, for a traveller tells us that—

" After the rains there may generally be procured, by those who like them, frogs, which are taken from the ditch round the walls in great numbers, and are then fat and in good condition for eating, making a very favourite curry with some of the Europeans, their flesh being very tender." (McMicking's " Manila.")

Frogs are occasionally eaten also in Japan.

The spotted salamander (*Salamandra maculosa*, Laur.) is in high repute in China as an aphrodisiac, and is also prescribed against epilepsy. The old Mexicans loved the speckled salamander, and ate it with capsicum or Spanish pepper ; the Spaniards learned the odd fashion, and as late as the sixteenth century this ugly creature was brought to their markets and roasted for the table. The axolotl (*Siredon Mexicanus*, Shaw) is commonly sold in the markets of Mexico, and dressed in the manner of stewed eels, it is esteemed a great delicacy.

CHAPTER VIII.

FOOD PRODUCTS OF THE SEA—SOME FISH DELICACIES.

The Harvest of the Sea—Nutritive Value of Fish—The Office of the Food Taster—A Chinese Fish Dinner—An American Fish Dinner—Supply of Fish to London—Imports of Fish in the United Kingdom—Supply of Birmingham, Dublin, etc. —Imports of European States—Supply to New York—Commercial Classification—The Cod Family—Statistics of the Fisheries—Norwegian Fisheries—Capelin—Fish Flour and Bread, Extracts, and Other Preparations—Fish Sauces—Flat Fish—Soles, Turbot, Plaice, etc.—Herrings—Extent of the Fisheries—Pilchards—Whitebait—Fish Supply of Paris —Statistics of the French Fisheries—Sardines—Anchovies—Skates—Mackerel—Mullet—Tunny—Conger Eels—Fresh Water Eels—Large Consumption in Italy.

THERE is a great difference in the production of animal food on land and in the sea. Poultry, game, and live stock derive their food from the produce of the earth; but the produce of the sea fisheries, whether fish, crustacea, or shell fish, can be obtained in illimitable quantities by the sole resources of the sea, and at little or no expense to man. In respect of fish, no natural causes prevent their co-existence, in the greatest abundance, with man in the highest state of civilisation and refinement, in the midst of the greatest agricultural and manufacturing opulence.

The fishery has over agriculture one great advantage —nature alone is charged with sowing the field which the fisherman reaps. The products of the sea, like those of the land, enter largely into the food resources of man. The fisheries supply our markets for daily consumption, and also furnish to commerce articles for export. The fisheries have their regional coasts, which are regularly fished, and their great seas which are explored, and have the distinction applied according to the field worked, the different means employed, and the capital required. It is the coast or the sea fisheries, as we speak of small or large farms, when treating of the soil. In the one case, it is the nature of the banks or depths and the instincts of the fish which have to be studied; in the other, the composition of the earth and the requirements of plants.

This is found to be true at the present time in a better appreciation of the grand industry of the waters, as shown by the coining and adoption of two new words now applied to the fisheries, *aquiculture* and *pisciculture*. Hence the fishery is the agriculture of the sea; and science has now consecrated the use of this definition, which is not new, but which had for a long time wanted application.

Every sea and every marine shore has its special inhabitants, and the main point is, to ascertain how far these may be made to subserve the wants of man.

The number of savoury species of fish is so great, that there are few persons so fastidious as not to be satisfied with some one or more kinds of fish.

Man treats with carelessness and neglect a food supply sufficient for the sustenance of millions—perhaps hundreds of millions—of human lives. Enormous quantities of food-fishes are given the go-by altogether. Numberless species, which are both palatable and nutritious, are left untouched.

That the sea and the lakes and the rivers already teem with fish suitable for human food, and that vast districts of the earth's surface which are covered with water are capable of being made to produce food equal in nutriment and money value to the product of the same number of acres of land, scarcely admits of a doubt Nearly all the species of fish are edible, and those only are refused which are absolutely poisonous, or the flesh of which has a disagreeable flavour.

The value of fish as an article of food is very generally under-estimated. In many parts of the world, and especially along the northern shores of Europe, Asia, and America, where vegetation is of the scantiest description, fish forms the chief, if not the only, food of the inhabitants.

Some pertinent remarks on fish supply were lately made in the *Lancet* :—

"Whatever may be the nutritious value of fish as food —and we believe that to be very great—it must be evident that a full and cheap supply of fish would react so as to produce a lowering of the price of butcher's meat. The 'purveyors,' as they like to be called, are encouraged, and, in truth, enabled, to keep up the price of flesh because there is nothing to compete with it as a staple of the common food of the people. A revival of the old and healthy habit of living largely on fish would place the meat supply on an entirely new footing. This is manifest on the face of the facts ; but what may not be equally apparent, though it is scarcely less noteworthy, is the consideration that nervous diseases and weaknesses increase in a country as the population comes to live on the flesh of warm-blooded animals. This is a point to which attention has not been adequately directed. 'Meat'—using that term in its popular sense —is highly stimulating, and supplies proportionally more exciting than actually nourishing pabulum to the nervous system. The meat-eater lives at high pressure, and is, or ought to be, a peculiarly active organism, like a predatory animal, always on the alert, walking rapidly, and consuming large quantities of oxygen, which are imperatively necessary for the safe disposal of his disassimilated material. In practice we find that the meat-eater does not live up to the level of his food, and as a consequence he cannot, or does not, take in enough oxygen to satisfy the exigencies of his mode of life. Thereupon follow many, if not most, of the ills to which highly civilised and luxurious meat-eating classes are liable. This is a physiological view of the food question, and it has bearings on the question of fish supply which ought not to be neglected."

The prejudices of some people in regard to food are curious. The celebrated Erasmus, though a native of Rotterdam, had such an aversion to fish, that the smell of it threw him into a fever. Ambrose Paré had a patient who could never see an eel without fainting; and another who would fall into convulsions at the sight of a carp. What would have been the effect of an electric eel on these gentlemen? Joseph Scaliger and others could never drink milk. Gardan was disgusted at the sight of eggs.

Professor Atwater, of the Agricultural College of the State of Connecticut, gives us the following as the relative nutritive value of fresh and prepared fish and shell fish :—

FISH (FRESH).				Per Cent. of Edible Solids.	Nutritive Value.
Halibut...	...	...	...	21·45	87·9
Flounder	...	...	...	5·97	82·4
Cod ...	...	...	...	11·45	68·2
Haddock	...	...	...	8·88	74·9
Eels ...	...	...	...	22·50	95·6
Mackerel	...	...	...	15·48	90·9
Salmon ...	...	...	...	32·99	107·9
Salmon trout ...	...	...	14·38	95·7
Brook trout	...	...	...	10·77	84·2
White fish	...	...	...	13·69	104·5
Smelt ...	...	...	...	12·51	73·8
Herring...	...	...	...	11·52	100·4
Turbot ...	...	...	...	15·61	84·4

PREPARED FISH AND INVERTEBRATES.

				Per Cent. of Edible Solids.	Nutritive Value.
Boned cod	...	...	...	30·91	106·9
Salted cod	...	...	...	20·45	102·5
Smoked halibut	...	...	31·63	102·2
Smoked herring	...	...	28·66	163·2
Canned salmon	...	...	29·95	107·2
Salt mackerel ...	...	...	30·97	111·1
Lobsters	...	...	...	7·98	50·3
Scallops...	...	...	...	17·47	68·8
Oysters ...	...	...	...	—	21·8

It must be noted in this table that the percentage is given of edible solids, i.e., the actual amount of nutritive materials in the samples analysed, as well as the nutritive value. The nutritive value in all these cases is therefore only that of the fish after bones and non-edible parts have been removed. The fact makes all the difference in the world in a consideration of the nutritive value of fish proportionately with that of other foods. White fish, as an instance, is returned in. the table a nutritious value of 104·5, but this is only a value based upon 13·69 of the whole fish. And herring, which is returned as being a somewhat higher nutritive value than medium beef, is seen, if allowance be made for the consideration we have named, to be little more than one-tenth as nourishing. Some other facts are noticeable in this table. The small nutritive value of lobsters, scallops, and oysters is remarkable. Oysters are commonly enough spoken of as being notably strengthening, and having other special virtues. Yet here we find that the nutritive value of this. food is in point of fact less than that of the same weight of milk.

The occupation of the food-taster is not yet extinct, but it is now chiefly restricted to securing the safety of monarchs of savage tribes.

The late Captain Pilkington, R.E., when at Lagos, on the Western coast of Africa, some years ago, and visiting its King, had practical demonstration of the custom much to his disgust.

Rising to take leave of the sable monarch, he asked permission to bring fowls for an evening meal, upon which the king promised to send him his supper. In due time appeared a jet black man, carrying something on his head, which he solemnly placed upon the table. It proved to be the promised supper, in a tray covered with a white cloth, which had obviously been just unfolded. This fair promise of cleanliness prepared the captain's mind for a well served supper, which after his long journey in the canoe, was no ungrateful anticipation.

"When uncovered by the bearer, a delicious looking fish presented itself to view, which I eagerly surveyed from side to side; but had scarcely expressed my entire willingness to accept it, ere the cook resumed possession of the dish, stooped his head, and put out his huge tongue, with the too evident intention of licking it from head to tail. I interposed, of course, in great alarm, and, seizing the dish with one hand, and his woolly head with the other, I struggled hard to prevent the execution of his foul design, which he, on the other hand, seemed equally resolved to accomplish.

"The interpreter, who had followed him, interposed at length, saying, imploringly, which heightened not a little the comedy of the whole scene—

"'Pray, Massa, let he lick the fish!'

"'Oh no!' I exclaimed, 'I really will not.'

"'If you do not, Massa, he no leave de fish!'

"'Why so?' said I, in undisguised astonishment.

"'Cause, Massa, if you go dead, King will kill he, suppose he no lick um, Massa.'

"'Oh,' replied I, 'I am not at all afraid; I know it is not poisoned.'

"'No, no, Massa; cook won't trust a dat, for you can get sick in the night, may be you catch one cold, and you die. Den King ask me, if cook lick de fish. Suppose I say, No, King; den King cut the cook's head off.'

"Seeing therefore, no alternative, I let go my hold, consoling myself with the reflection that the other side of the fish would be, at all events, free from this ungainly process; but Sir Cook had no sooner carefully finished that side of the fish than he immediately proceeded to operate upon the other. In great dismay, I turned from this exhibition, the strangers took their leave, and when the gate had closed upon them, I proceeded, with the help of James, to strip the skin from the devoted fish, and after making the best meal I was able, retired to my basket bed."

This same operation is performed upon every article of food prepared for the King. The whole suspicious process is the result of that tyranny which authorises the odious traffic in slaves; and the monarch who thus, instead of being the protector of his subjects, betrays

them to the agony of expatriation and a servitude more
terrible than death, finds the system in some degree
recoil upon himself, becoming the slave of his own fears,
and thus living in perpetual dread of poison or assas-
sination.

Here is a way of cooking a fish to make it taste excellent, at least when you are camping out far-a-field, in
some distant quarter :—

"Take some nice clean clay and work it up a little,
then, without either scaling or dressing, plaster your fish
all over with the clay, about an inch thick, and put him
right into the hot ashes. When 'tis done the clay and
scales will all peel off, and you'll have a dish that would
bring to life any starved man, if he hadn't been dead
more than a week. That's the ordinary way ; but if
you want an extra touch, cut a hole in him, and stick
in a piece of salt pork, or bear's fat if come-at-able, and
a few beech nuts or the meat of walnuts, or butter nuts,
and you'd think you were eating a water angel." *

The fish culturists, when in session at the Centennial
Exposition, in 1876, treated themselves, during their stay
in Philadelphia, to a fish dinner, which was certainly extraordinary and unique in its way. The bill of fare em-
braced fifty-eight different kinds of fish, and in its en-
tirety is much too long for publication here. Some of the
delicacies, however, were remarkable. Under the head
of *hors d'œuvres froids* (the *menu*, by the way, was organised
with the utmost elaboration) were Norwegian pollack
fish, Portuguese conger eel, and Spanish conger eel, with
tomatoes, Turkish botargo or mullet roe, Japanese shaki
or dried salmon, cray-fish from the Cape of Good Hope,
French tunny fish, Chinese white and black shark fins,
Alaska oulachans, Portuguese sword-fish and squid,
Russian caviare, Chinese dried fish-maws, and, most
astonishing of all, "desiccated octopus eggs." Noted
scientists were honoured by having their names applied
to the various sauces. Thus there was *filet* of English soles

* Mayo's Kaloolah.

à la Buckland, sheepsheads with Agassiz sauce, aspic of eels *à la* Huxley, and *bisque* of lobster, Seth Green style. It was a memorable feast, and taxed the culinary skill of the cooks at the Centennial to the utmost. One particular dish seems to have puzzled even the most ingenious *chefs*, and that was kanten (Japanese seaweed) *à la* Sekizawa Akekio. The aid of the Japanese cook in the employ of the Japanese Commission was at last invoked, and he proved equal to its toothsome preparation.

The bill of fare of a regular Mandarin supper given by Sir Charles Macdonnell at Hong Kong in 1867 to the Duc de Penthievre, the Comte de Beauvois, and some other French gentlemen, contained the following items: fish roe in sweet caramel sauce; shark's fins in gelatinous sauce; cakes of coagulated blood; hashed dog with lotus sauce; bird's-nest soup; whale's nerves with sweet sauce; sturgeon's gills in compote; croquettes of fish and rat; shark's fat soup; stewed sea snails with tadpoles; and a sweet course composed of fish fins, fruit, ham, almonds and essences.

Mr. J. Bertram published some ten years ago a work, under the title of "The Harvest of the Sea" (London: Murray); but it was more descriptive and theoretical than practical, or useful as to details concerning the general supply of fish, and was restricted to the British food fishes. Mr. Buckland's reports on the sea fisheries of England and Wales were much more full and important, and from these I have been able to quote largely.

The fresh fish supply of London, in 1880, was thus officially returned:—

Brought in by rail...	...	...	...	87,884	tons.
„	at the wharves	...	...	5,487	„
„	by water	...	...	37,258	„
				130,629	„

The following table gives the sources whence drawn,

by rail or water, with a comparison of the quantity received in 1875 :—

RETURN OF THE QUANTITY OF FISH DELIVERED AT BILLINGS-GATE MARKET, OR ITS IMMEDIATE VICINITY, IN 1875 AND 1880.

DELIVERED BY RAILWAY.

	1875. Tons.		1880. Tons.
Great Western	5,039	......	6,724
Great Northern	24,501	......	26,543
Great Eastern	25,977	......	30,381
South Western	3,556	......	2,297
London, Chatham, and Dover ...	2,984	......	2,530
London and North Western ...	5,477	......	8,089
London and South Western ...	1,663	......	1,623
London, Brighton & South Coast	1,094	......	605
Midland	1,076	......	9,092
	71,367	......	87,884

LANDED AT WHARVES.

General Steam Navigation Company (estimated)	1	......	2,580
Nicholson's...	211	......	872
Aberdeen Steam Navigation Company	1,194	......	2,001
Millwall Dock	67	......	34
	1,473	......	5,487
Water-carriage Fish landed at the Market	22,109	......	37,258

TOTALS.

Delivered by Railway	71,367	......	87,884
Landed at Wharves	1,473	......	5,487
Water-carriage Fish landed at the Market	22,109	......	37,258
	94,949	......	130,629

A reference to the monthly returns of the Fishmongers'' Company shows that the imports of fish into London have been as follows :—

	Tons.
1882 (4 months to December)...	52,543
1883	125,428
1884	129,099

The average imports seem to be about 11,000 tons per month. The quantity of spoiled fish seized is proportionately very small, only about 10,000 to 12,000 cwt., and the same of shell fish per month, except perhaps in the exceptionally hot months of summer, when it may reach a somewhat higher figure.

The total imports of fish into the United Kingdom were in :—

	Cwts.		Value.
1861	337,517	......	£376,561
1871	605,330	......	711,295
1881	1,530,219	......	2,332,605
1883	1,295,754	......	2,311,966
1884 (Cured)	814,648	......	1,493,485

In 1883 we imported 427,826 cwt. of fresh fish not of British take, valued at £522,445, and of cured or salted fish 868,125 cwt., of the value of £1,773,027.

The supply of fresh fish to the London market does not keep pace with the increase of population and wealth, and may be said to be less by about 20,000 tons than what it was ten years ago. It appears to be now about 130,000 tons in quantity, and as the largest portion of what is caught on our coasts comes to London, the consumption of fish is not as great as it might be if the fisheries were better carried on, and the prices reduced by retailers, instead of maintained, by frequently destroying wholesome fish, rather than selling it below a certain price.

According to Mr. W. Smith Scott, fish-salesman of Birmingham, about 100,000 tons of fish per annum reaches that town for the use of its population and that of the surrounding districts, which have a population numbering about two millions. Deducting one-third for weight of packages and waste, this leaves a little over 60,000 tons as food, or about twenty ounces per head of the population. The heaviest weight is herrings and mackerel and salmon from Ireland and Norway, the Scotch salmon going principally to London and Manchester.

The sale of fish in Dublin, in 1878, was stated as follows :—

		Value.
Salmon, 2,880 cwts.		£16,128
Herrings, 19,920 mease		19,920
Mackerel, 4,900 packages		4,900
Haddock and cod, 3,000 packages		6,000
Eels, 1,000 packages		1,500
Prime trawl fish, 2,304 hampers		6,912
Offal, 8,856 hampers		8,856
Lobsters, crabs, shrimps, cockles, &c.		1,500

£65,716

What is termed " offal fish " by the dealers, are had-docks, sprats, herrings, mackerel, skate, and perhaps cod.

There is nearly double the quantity of fish brought into Liverpool that used to be. The demand has in-creased, and the supply has kept up with the demand. Soles are nearly twice as dear as they were formerly.

In 1880 we imported of fresh fish (not of British taking) 550,737 cwt., valued at £438,789, and of cured or salted fish from abroad 792,697 cwt., valued at £1,227,921. The fresh fish was mostly consumed in the kingdom. The exports consisted of 6,333 cwt. of salmon, 41,259 cwt. of cod, 1,072,397 barrels of herrings, and 11,770 head of pilchards—the latter to Italy.

The value of the herrings exported in 1883 was £1,643,622, and of the other fish sent away £466,334. We import about 130,000 cwt. of fish from France, of the value of £400,000.

Owing to religious observances, fish is more in request in Catholic countries than in England.

150,000 cwt. of fish were consumed in Berlin in 1873.

According to the latest statistics the following were some of the imports of fish into different countries in 1880. Germany 737,137 tons of herrings, Spain 44,203,000 kilos. of codfish, Italy 43,204,000 kilos. of fish of all kinds, Russia 350,000 to 400,000 barrels of salted herrings yearly. Sweden imports 775,000 to 1,000,000 cubic feet of herrings annually; a curious trade measure.

The undeveloped fishing resources of North America

are very great. Many of the fishes and invertebrates which in Europe are highly valued by the poorer classes, are never used there; only about 150 of the 1,500 species of the fishes known to inhabit the waters of the United States are ordinarily found in the markets.

The following statement compiled by Mr. G. M. Lamphear was read at a recent meeting of the American Fish Culturists' Association. It shows the amount of the various kinds of fish, tortoises, crustacea, etc., received in the wholesale markets of New York for ten months, from March 1, 1880, to Jan. 1, 1881:—

	Pounds.		Pounds.
Flounders	1,186,469	Pickerel and pike ...	516,317
Halibut	2,211,742	Yellow pike... ...	151,001
Cod	5,269,607	Sisco...	435,988
Pollack	611,295	Whitefish	872,144
Haddock	1,643,554	Brook trout... ...	5,995
Frostfish or tomcod	58,831	Salmon trout ...	35,720
Blackfish	184,171	Catfish	36,267
Mackerel	3,236,197	Small freshwater fish	394,358
Spanish mackerel ...	346,678	Terrapin	1,219
Weakfish	1,213,141	Green turtle ...	2,494
Kingfish	10,732	Lobsters, No. 1,311,981	
Sheepshead ...	55,586	Scallops, gallons 29,499	
Porgies	1,565,836	Turbot	86
Sea bass	284,602	Redfish	22,854
Striped bass ...	478,716	Perch	143,332
Bluefish	4,284,613	Buffalo fish	3,398
Smelt	575,005	Pompano	1,768
Salmon	150,642	Swordfish	1,285
Shad, counts 923,474		Small salt water fish	393,325
Herring „ 463,884		Mullet	11,658
Eels...	993,248	Bonita	67,231
Sturgeon	46,170		
Black bass	36,943	Total... ...27,540,218	

The value of the fish, fresh, dry, pickled, etc., imported into the United States in 1880 was returned at 3,403,000 dollars.

After these few preliminary and general remarks, let us pass on to consider the fish-capture of various countries, and the groups or families that furnish the chief supply.

Commercial fish may be divided generally into "round fish" and "flat fish."

The round fish include the cod, conger, haddock, hake, herring, ling, mackerel, torsk, pilchard, whiting, etc.

The principal flat fish are soles, turbot, halibut, plaice, skate, and brill.

The fish families that yield the largest food supply are the *Gadidæ*, embracing the codfish, the haddock, ling, hake, whiting, etc.; the *Pleuronectidæ*, embracing the turbot, sole, brill, flounder, and other flat fish; the *Clupeidæ*, furnishing the herring, sardine, sprat, etc. Then we have the family of the skates, known scientifically as the *Raiidæ*. The mackerel is also a plentiful fish, and when procured in a thoroughly fresh state, it is of excellent service for table purposes. The *Murenidæ*, or eel family, is also in great demand.

It is scarcely possible to follow any systematic classification in treating of the catch and consumption of fish in various countries, nor can they be arranged entirely under families, hence the remarks and descriptions must, to some extent be disjointed and discursive.

Codfish.—The following was the take of cod, ling, and hake by the Scotch fisheries in 1878. Number of fish taken and cured in vessels, 2,560,142 fish, of which were cured and dried 55,257 cwt. Number cured on shore 3,658,583, of which 128,552 cwt. were cured and dried, and 9,219 barrels in pickle. This shows a total of 6,218,725 fish taken. The exports were 94,970 cwt. (out of 183,809 cwt.), which is the largest export for many years.

Iceland appears to be a more reliable field for the cod-fishing than either Faroe or Rockall. At Stornoway, and upon other parts of the west coast of Scotland, the fishery did well.

The fish are cleaned, split, slightly salted and packed in barrels, twenty to twenty-four fish in a barrel. They are sold at Aberdeen at 40s. to 55s. a barrel.

The flesh of the cod contains a large quantity of creatine. The fish are in best condition from October to January. It has been remarked that the immense fecundity of the cod seems to be an appointment of Providence in affording a supply of food to bleak and frozen countries that are unfit for the production of grain ; not only so, but the cod supplies all Europe with a considerable quantity of provision.

The black cod (*Gadus carbonarius*), formerly called coal fish, abounds in the waters of the Pacific, on the coasts of North West America. This fish is highly spoken of in America, and is considered far superior to the cod of Newfoundland, the flesh being richer and of finer fibre. It received its popular name of coal fish from the dusky pigment which tinges the skin and soils the fingers when handled. In England it is considered a coarse fish and principally eaten by the poor, but in America it is salted and sold by the hundredweight.

The hake (*Merlucius vulgaris*) is an excellent fish, and considered good eating, especially when cut in fillets and fried in butter.

The fish which passes under the name of hake on the coasts of America is the *Phycis chuss*, Wall., *P. americanus*, Storer. This is sometimes called ling by the fishermen, but differs in many points from the ling of Europe. The squirrel hake is *Phycis tenuis*, Mitchell, and there is another American species, the long-finned hake, *P. chesterii*, Goode and Bear.

The whiting (*Merlangus* [*Gadus*] *vulgaris*), a small delicate fish, seldom exceeding a pound and a half in weight, is one of the cod family. In Devonshire and Cornwall whiting are salted and dried in the sun immediately after being caught, and when sufficiently dry are tied up in bundles of six or upwards ; but most of those caught are now sent fresh to the London market by the fast trains.

The whiting of North America is *Menticirrus nebulosus*, [Mitch.] Gill, also known as the king fish.

The fish which pass under the name of whiting in India are *Selago schama*, Forsk., and *S. pama*, the flesh of which furnishes a light and nourishing diet.

The haddock (*Gadus* [*Morrhua*] *œglefinus*) fishing is of

great importance to this country, inasmuch as it affords
occupation to a large number of poor fishermen during the
winter months. They are in the greatest perfection for
the table from October to the beginning of January,
just before they are about to spawn. A great many
small haddocks are sometimes caught by the trawlers;
they are largely sold to the poor, and fetch from 8d.
to 1s. 6d. per basket, weighing three stones. In some
of the Scotch cities these small haddocks dried are sold
under the name of "speldrings," and also under the name
of "Finnon haddocks," from the name of the village near
Aberdeen, where they were first cured and smoked by
burning the green branches of fir. Thousands and tens
of thousands of haddocks are cured in every possible
state of freshness ; but none are equal in quality to the
Scotch cured. The fish there are cured all but alive.
Some are dried with peat smoke instead of sawdust,
which is used in the London curing. The Norway haddock is *Sebastes Norvegicus.*

The cod (*Gadus morrhua,* Lin.) and its allies, *G. navaga,*
G. virens, contribute largely to human food. The
annual average catch on the great breeding grounds
of the species, and where the finest fish are obtained,
as on the banks and shores of Newfoundland and
the coasts of Labrador, is about 4,000,000 cwt. Assuming fifty fish to the cwt., this gives a yearly take of
200,000,000.

In 1872 the take of cod in the Gulf of St. Lawrence
and the Lower British American Provinces (exclusive of
Newfoundland and Labrador) was 824,411 quintals.

In 1880 Canada exported 996,870 cwt. of dried fish,
and 27,084 cwt. and 264,953 barrels of pickled fish. In
1882 the value of the fisheries of Canada was given at
£3,217,734.

The export of cod-fish from Newfoundland of British
take in 1874, reached a total of 1,250,000 cwt., worth
more than one million sterling ; in 1882 it was 1,463,439
cwt., valued at £1,170,751.

The cod fishery, which is the staple produce of Newfoundland, is prosecuted from June till October, and affords occupation to the mass of the population, who carry on this fishery around the shores of the island and on the coast of Labrador, from whence one-third of the annual catch is now, during a prosperous season, taken. The fishery on the banks is almost exclusively confined to the French and Americans. It is remarkable that the cod fishery shows very little progress, and the fluctuations are considerable. In 1820 there were exported 901,159 cwt.; in 1850, 1,089,182 cwt.; in 1866, 716,690 cwt.; in 1874, 1,240,320 cwt.; in 1878, 694,339 cwt.; in 1879, 994,334 cwt.; and in 1880, 1,419,503 cwt. Thus, while the population has more than doubled, there has been scarcely any increase in their chief means of support, which, it will be observed, is precarious. Cod to the value of £59,000 are caught by the French in Newfoundland.

The largest export of the cured fish is made to Spain, Portugal, Italy, and Greece, which, together, take about half the catch, and Brazil one-fourth : the rest goes to the West Indies, the British North American provinces, and the United Kingdom. The local consumption of fish in the island of Newfoundland is estimated at $1\frac{1}{4}$ to 2 cwt. per head of the population per annum.

Of cods' tongues and sounds salted, about 3,000 barrels are sent away annually from each of the provinces of Nova Scotia and New Brunswick, besides large quantities from Newfoundland.

At Archangel, if the fishing is good, every fishing boat can gather, in the season, about 3,500 lbs. of cod fish tongues. They are salted separately, 15 lbs. of salt being used to 100 lbs. of tongues. These tongues sell at about $1\frac{1}{2}$d. a pound.

The coasts of Norway are another great haunt of the edible fish of the cod family, as well as of herrings. The yield of cod in Norway in 1877 was the most abundant of which we have any record, the catch having been 76,000,000 fish, of the estimated value of £1,220,000. The total value of the Norwegian fisheries averaged in

1876 and 1877 nearly £3,500,000—a large amount for a country having hardly two millions of inhabitants.

The following was the export of fish from Norway in 1878 :—

Dried codfish	...	...	...	320,511	centners.*
Klip fish, salted cod	...	...	...	819,221	,,
Fresh or living fish	...	...	.·.	44,420	.,
Other salted fish	...	...	...	61,644	tondes.
Spring herrings	...	...	...	35,534	,,
Other herrings	...	...	...	641,467	,,
Anchovies	...	...	...	201,081	duntres.

Salt fish is prepared there in two ways, as klip fish flattened, or as stock fish and round fish. The preparation of klip fish was first introduced at Christiansund, in Norway, by the English about the close of the eighteenth century. In preparing it in this way it is cleaned soon after it is caught, salted and carefully dried. If the fish remain more than ten days in the wet they are unfit for klip fish. The best salt is required to prepare cod fish properly. Stock fish is not salted, but merely dried in the sun and wind for local consumption.

The old-fashioned plan of keeping the fish in brine has been nearly abandoned since the more general adoption of salting and drying.

About two-thirds of the fish caught are salted and prepared as klip fish, and one-third sun-dried, known as round fish. The quantity of cod fish taken annually ranges from fifteen to seventy-six millions. In 1871, 24,000 tons were caught at the Lofoden isles, which is the largest and most renowned of the Norwegian fishing grounds.

The Russian fishermen buy annually from the Norwegians twenty-six to thirty-six million pounds of cod and other fish. From Iceland five to seven million pounds of cod fish are annually exported.

---

* The centner is not quite 1 cwt., but only 109¾ lbs. The tonde of fish is 3·186 bushels. The duntre is a small keg.

Besides the smoked, salted, and fresh fish locally consumed in Norway, about 250,000 lbs. is sent annually to
England, packed in ice ; 1,000 to 1,200 barrels of salted
salmon is exported, and the sale of salmon brings in
about £100,000.

Norway exported in 1880—

Dried or split cod	...	...	... kilos.	72,215,000
Herrings	...	...	hectolitres	536,333
Other salted fish	...	...	„	118,348
Anchovies	...	...	„	11,755

And fresh fish to the value of £51,000.

For home consumption in Iceland, under the name
of heingefish, the cod is split along the back and hung
up unsalted to dry, in sheds, when it has a shrivelled
up appearance. It is eaten uncooked by the natives,
who likewise dry and eat the refuse heads with great
relish.

The export of fish products from Norway averages
about 170,000 tons per annum, of which $1\frac{1}{2}$ per cent. is
fresh or iced fish, and the remainder salted, dried, pickled,
spiced, or smoked fish, roe, and fish oil. The value of the
exported fish will average now about £2,500,000 ; and
if all the fisheries are put together, there is an average
export dried and dry-salted fish of 75,000,000 yearly,
which would answer to about 375,000 tons of live fish,
leaving out of account the home consumption.

The number of species of known fish in Swedish waters
is at present about 170, of which, however, only fifty are
commonly caught.

The Baltic herring (stroemming), a smaller variety of
Clupea harengus, Lin., is sold either fresh in the towns
along the coast, or else salted in barrels. The barrelled
article is generally sold in Sweden, salted herring being
the daily food of the Swedish peasant, but of late years
it has also been exported to Germany.

In Northern Europe the herring of the second year is
called "Christiania herring," in the third year "middle
herring," in the fourth "merchant's herring," and in the

fifth "spring herring." There is no essential difference
between these varieties, except the size and the greater
or less development of the sexual organs. There are also
some other classifications, as boundary herring, winter
herring and fall herring.

Sprats are partly sold fresh and partly pickled or
spiced, while some are prepared as "anchovies," and
sold under that name, although of course they are a
different kind of fish to the true anchovy.

Capelin.—In the month of June, each year, the shores
of Newfoundland are visited by enormous shoals of
capelin (*Mallotus arcticus*) for the purpose of spawning.
The masses of them in the various bays and harbours are
so great that two men with a small landing-net will fill
a boat in a couple of hours. So little account is taken of
this delicious little fish that it is largely employed in
manuring the fields and gardens, as sprats often are in
England.

The flavour of it, when fresh, is delicious, and its size
is about that of the sardine. There is little doubt that,
if properly cured, the capelin might compete with either
sardines or anchovies, which are so profitable to the fishermen of the Mediterranean. If merely pickled and dried
it is worth more than a dollar per barrel. But no attention is paid to this little fish, the supply of which seems
inexhaustible. It is principally used by the fishermen
as bait for the cod. About 100 barrels of capelin, salted
and dried, are sent to England.

In Switzerland the imports of fish amount to about
45,000 lbs. annually, chiefly fresh fish.

It is an incontestable fact that although since 1830
prices have at least doubled, the sale of sea-fish has
grown enormously in Belgium. Fish always abounds in
the markets of Ostend, and the supply reaches 2,000 tons
yearly. The annual proceeds of the sale of fish at the
Ostend market averages about £140,000.

The fishery products on the coast of Spain for the
year 1882 were estimated at about 8,000 tons weight;
half of the catch was salted and preserved; about fifty-

five tons of fresh fish were exported and the same quantity of pickled fish; 380 tons of sardines were salted and pressed, and 100 tons of shell fish exported.

In some countries, fish when tainted, or even putrid, is preferred to that which is fresh. The inhabitants of the banks of the Senegal and Orange rivers in Africa pound some small fish of the size of sprats in a wooden mortar, as they are taken from the stream, and afterwards make them up into conical lumps, like our sugar-loaves, which they dry in the sun. In this state they soon become slightly decomposed, and give out a most unpleasant odour; notwithstanding which these people consider them a luxury.

Several northern nations possess the art of preparing fish in a variety of ways unpractised in Europe, such as in the form of flour, bread, etc. Sir John Richardson mentions that a very good bread may be made from the roe of the pollack (*Pollachius carbonarius*) and of the methy, and this is used in the fur countries as tea bread. A kind of fish flour or powder is made from the stock-fish in Norway, which has a high nutritive value. It may, therefore, when compressed into the form of biscuits realise, under certain circumstances, the problem sought by armies in the field, of having the largest amount of nourishment in the smallest compass and least weight. There are at present two houses which make this fish-flour at the Lofoden Islands, but the manufacture is likely to extend. About 2,000 packages of fish flour (of 2 lbs. each) were made at the factory of Llyngvær, Norway, in 1876, and 2,424 packages in 1877. Crackers of fish-meal made by Mad. Rosing, Christiania, were shown at the Philadelphia Centennial Exhibition in 1876.

The biscuit is made in Norway out of this fish-flour in the following manner:—500 grammes of the dry fish-flour are mixed with three litres of water, and $4\frac{1}{2}$ pounds of oatmeal are added and all well kneaded. The paste is then rolled out and cut into squares and cakes. These are pierced with holes and dried in an oven, but

T

not at a sufficiently high temperature to cook or bake them. They should be turned several times while in the oven. From the experience of M. Rosing, Professor of Agricultural Chemistry at the Royal model farm at Aas, it results that these biscuits are very nutritious, being four times richer in albuminoid principles than beef, four and a half times than fresh cod, and six times richer than milk or rye bread. And it has also the advantage of being very rich in phosphates. The Siberians also bake bread with a meal formed by grinding down the dried remains of fish.

An extract of fish is now made from the juice of the flesh of the menhaden (*Brevoostra tyrannus*), also called the ocean trout, by S. L. Goodale, Saco, Maine. Professor Johnson, of the Sheffield Scientific School, Yale College, formerly a pupil of Baron Liebig, writes of it, " I find your extract of fish both by actual use, and by chemical analysis, in all respects equal to the best Liebig's extract of beef." The menhaden is unknown in Europe, but in the herring, its near relative, Professor Almen, of the University of Upsala, reports finding eighteen per cent. more of extractive matter, and fifty per cent. more of soluble salts (these two together constituting flesh extract) than in beef.

Mr. Goodale states : " From each barrel of menhaden fish as taken, I get three pounds of extract when flesh alone is used, and four pounds if the spine is retained in dressing. Considering the large amount of fish annually taken and hitherto treated for oil and manure alone, the juices of which have been allowed to run back into the ocean as a worthless bye-product, I cannot avoid the conclusion that a new source of food is within reach, which at no distant day may contribute materially to human welfare." Mr. Goodale estimates that the fish used by the oil factories in the towns of Bristol and Booth Bay, Maine, in 1873, 1874, and 1875, allowing the product to equal one-fifth of the weight of the live fish, would have yielded in either year upwards of a million of pounds, or 500 tons of extract of fish.

Carrying out the same calculation for the entire catch of the Atlantic States, the potential yield of the menhaden fisheries would exceed ten millions of pounds of "extract of fish."

Among various food preparations of fish and other sea animals put up in America are the following:—

Cod-fish balls, canned fish chowder (cod and haddock), smoked smelts and canned smelts (*Osmerus mordax*), canned mackerel (*Scomber*), smoked Spanish mackerel (*Cymbium maculatum*), smoked halibut (*Hippoglossus vulgaris*), pickled clam chowder, pickled scallops (*Pecten irradians*), pickled mussels (*Mytilus edulis*), pickled oyster crabs (*Pinnotheres ostreum*), and devilled crabs.

Some of the purely national dishes of different nations are most extraordinary things, such as the Swedish lutfisk on Christmas eve.

Lut-fisk is the salted stock or cod fish steeped in a solution of potash until, in fact, decomposition takes place. On Christmas eve, the great evening of Sweden, this mess is boiled and eaten with oil, and this and grot, which is simply boiled rice, are the Christmas dishes of Sweden, just as roast beef and plum pudding are with us. The smell of the lut-fisk is terrific, but a true Swede clings to his national dish on Julaften as much as any beef-eating Englishman does to his.

Very many food fishes are preserved in oil, and thus form considerable articles of commerce and food dainties, such as the tunny, the halibut, the sardine, menhaden, and small pilchards.

Fish Sauces.—We have our anchovy, lobster, and shrimp sauce for fish, but the ancients and some of the Eastern nations also indulged in fish sauces, as their garum, balachong, gna-pee, and other condiments prove.

Balachong is a compound made of prawns, sardines, and other small fish, pounded and pickled. This article, is of universal use as a condiment, and one of the largest articles of native consumption throughout both the Malay and Philippine Archipelago. It is not confined indeed as a condiment to the Asiatic islanders, but is also largely used by the Burmese, the Siamese, and Cochin-Chinese.

The garum, or celebrated fish sauce of the Romans, was principally made out of the *Sciæna umbra* and the mackerel, the entrails and blood being macerated in brine until they became putrid :

> " Experantes adhuc scombri de sanguine primo,
> Accipe fastosum munera cara garum."—*Martial.*

Galen affirms that this disgusting preparation was so precious, that a measure of about three of our pints fetched two thousand silver pieces. So delightful was the effluvium of the garum considered, that Martial informs us it was carried about in onyx smelling-bottles.

Flat Fish.—Let us now glance at some of the principal flat fish used for food. For the London market, and the British public in general, soles (*Solea platessa*) are the most important of sea fish. They are required by all classes of society; the higher classes get those of the best quality, the poorer, the smaller fish known in the trade as " tongues " and " slips." Two thousand tons of soles are sent up by the railway from Brixham in a year. In " London Labour and the London Poor," Mr. Mayhew stated that in 1864 the number of soles sold at Billingsgate Market was 97,520,000, and that the weight was 26,880,000 lbs., or 12,000 tons. Another good authority, Mr. Poole, gave the number of soles sent to the London market a quarter of a century ago as 100,000,000.

The turbot (*Pleuronectes maximus*) is the rich man's fish, its flesh being delicate, sweet and fine, and being so valuable, the fishermen pay rather more attention to its abundance or scarcity than to that of almost any other sea fish. Six to seven hundred tons of turbot are received yearly in London.

The Jews are forbidden by law to eat anything that has no scales; the question is whether the turbot has or has not scales, and upon this decision depends whether the Jews may or may not eat turbot.

When turbots are scarce, hotelkeepers frequently serve up brills (*Rhombus vulgaris*) as turbots. Many persons prefer them to turbot if taken before spawning. The brill is distinguished from the turbot not only by size and quality but by the perfect smoothness of its skin, which is covered with scales of a moderate size. These fish have been caught of very large size in the North Sea, near the Silver Pits; sixteen pounds is about the largest seen at the Yarmouth fish market.

The best are caught by the Dutch off their coasts. The American turbot is *Platessa oblonga*, Dekay, which is fully equal to the English turbot. The fish known as turbot in Newfoundland is *Reinhardtius hippoglossoides*. In Scotland the halibut is called a turbot.

Of the smaller flat fish the flounder (*Pleuronectes flexus*) is perhaps the best for the table. In North America the common flounder is *Pseudo-rhombus dentatus* [Lin.] Gunther; the southern flounder *C. oblonga*, the smooth flounder *Pleuronectes glaber*, and the sand flounder *Lophopsetta maculata*. On the west coast of England these flat fish are generally called "flukes," the white fluke is the flounder, the gar fluke the dab (*Platessa limanda*), and the plain fluke the plaice. Plaice (*Pleuronectes platessa*) at certain periods fetch high prices; as much as 7s. 6d. each has been paid. The plaice is a favourite fish with the Jews, being a food which they are permitted to eat at all their feasts and fasts. Eaten cold, dressed as the Jews cook this fish, it is a most delicious article of food, and they usually lay in a stock sufficient for several days' con-·sumption.

The plaice may be considered the poor man's fish; it is nevertheless highly nutritious, and affords good, wholesome and cheap food. They are in season from May to December, but are finest at the end of May although sold all the year round. To ensure firmness in this fish it should be powdered with salt and hung up for a day. Enormous quantities of plaice are sold all over the country. Mr. Mayhew reports that there were sold in Billingsgate in 1864, chiefly to the costermongers, over 33½ millions, averaging one pound each. A large number are also consumed in the shops that sell fried fish. The plaice is there cut into junks, and sold from a half-penny to two-pence a junk. The fish is first dipped in batter and then fried in boiling oil.

The John Dorey (*Zeus faber*) is also called St. Peter's fish, on account of the dark mark on each side, like the impression made by the human thumb. The common name is said to be derived from the French *jaune* (yellow) and *doré*, referring to the golden yellow of the fish when fresh. Although an ugly fish, it is thought a delicacy by epicures.

The dorey is a very voracious fish, and the more a sea fish is carnivorous the better will be its flesh. That of the dorey is not unlike that of the turbot, and is especially good from January to March.

The most important members of the *Clupediæ* are the common herring (*Clupea harengus*), the sardine (*C. Sardina*), the sprat (*C. sprattus*), and the pilchard (*C. pilchardus*), the whitebait and the anchovy.

Herrings.—The Dutch became a great nation principally by the herring fishery, and Amsterdam, they say, is built on a foundation of herring bones. Even at present the Dutch herrings, though caught on the same ground as the English or Scotch, bear a higher price than any other in the world, and are eaten raw as a relish in Holland and Germany. The first barrel of new herrings that is taken, is forwarded to the King at the Hague. It is carried in procession with banners and military music—the day is one of public rejoicing, and a few of the new herrings are sent as presents to the nobles of the land. The captured herrings are for the most part cured almost immediately they are taken and on board ship, while another portion are first salted prior to being smoked and sold as red herrings to the trade. Those gutted and salted on board, are acknowledged to be much superior in quality, being more tender and fatter than all other kinds, preserving their agreeable flavour even till the following year.   The first Dutch herrings in former times frequently brought £60 per barrel, and were sold by small quantities from 2s. to 3s. a piece. In the year 1815 the first 195 barrels were sold for rather over £3,450, thus averaging about £17 per barrel.   Banquets were held, of which herrings formed the principal dish, and the hosts sang their praises :

> " Who first between his teeth
> The dainty morsel takes
> Enjoys a glorious treat."

The production has of late years remained prosperous, reaching in .1880 about 227 million, and in 1881 197½ million of fish, representing a market value of from £250,000 to £330,000.

The principal destination of the salted herrings is Germany, the smoked ones being sent to Belgium.   The export of cured herrings increased from 80,000 barrels in 1872 to 139,500 barrels in 1882.   The quantity of fresh fish exported chiefly to Belgium ranges from 4½ to 7 million kilos., 10,000,000 to 15,500,000 pounds.

The herring fishery of Ireland in 1878 resulted in a catch of 193,606· mease, valued at £220,278, or an average of £1 2s. 9d. per mease of say 630 fish.   In 1883 the Irish herring fishery only resulted in 109,250 mease, valued at £105,738. The number of fish landed at Tynemouth, North Shields, in 1878-79, was 2,785 lasts of herrings and 2,286 tons of white fish.   The "last" is 100 long hundreds of 132, or 13,200 fish.

The herring fishery of Scotland in 1878 resulted in 905,768 barrels being cured, which proved the fishing of the year to have been remarkably good, and so much above an average fishing as to have been exceeded only by the great fishings of the years 1873, 1874, and 1875. Of the quantity exported (623,934 barrels) 608,970 barrels went to the Continent, principally to Germany and Russia.

It was stated in the Report of the Herring Fishery Commissioners for 1878, that 2,400,000,000 herrings are caught annually by the British, French, Dutch, and Norwegian fishermen.

The take of herrings in Scotland varies from 600,000 to 1,000,000 barrels, that is, reckoning the quantity cured, exclusive of those eaten fresh. The quantity sent abroad ranges from 500,000 to 700,000 barrels.

The Norfolk fishery obtains about 64,000 tons of herrings, and the Dutch catch about 35,000 tons.

Spiced herrings, known as kryddsell, are much sought after in some places of Sweden, and especially in North Germany. They are thus prepared. The fresh-caught herrings are immediately put into vinegar, with one-fourth water and some salt. After remaining in this mixture for twenty-four hours, the herrings are taken out and the vinegar drained off. The fish are then placed in a keg with a mixture of the following spices, reckoning these quantities for every fourscore herrings : one pound fine dry salt, one pound pulverised sugar, half an ounce each of pepper, bay-leaves, and saltpetre, a quarter of an ounce of ginger and a very little hops and cloves; others add double the quantity of pepper, allspice, and cloves. The herrings must be left in this mixture for two months before they are fit for use.

Pilchards.—The pilchard fishery (*Clupea pilchardus*), which is confined to the coasts of Cornwall and Devon, is variable in its yield, reaching sometimes 47,000 hogsheads, as in 1871, and at others not a fifth of this quantity are caught, as but 9,477 hogsheads in 1877. It takes nearly 4,000 summer pilchards and 3,000 winter pilchards to fill a hogshead, which will weigh when well pressed 467 pounds gross.

Besides what are consumed locally fresh, the shipments, when salted, go almost entirely to Italy, where they are largely consumed during Lent.

Whitebait.—The whitebait which are reported so great a delicacy in London are composed in reality of the fry of various small fish, but they consist chiefly of those of sprats and herrings. Their capture has hitherto been confined to the neighbourhood of London, but it is now rapidly extending to other places, and continually increasing quantities of young herrings and young sprats are annually consumed in various parts of this kingdom.

There are tons of whitebait caught in the Thames about Greenwich and Gravesend. They are much more numerous than they were. At one time they were confined to the estuary from Blackwall to Gravesend; now they have extended to the Medway and the Crouch to Harwich.

The fishery for whitebait commences when Parliament meets, and ends with the session, or from February to August. About £40 a week for twenty-six weeks is paid at Queenborough for wages in catching whitebait. From £1,500 to £1,800 is expended in catching whitebait. The average quantity of fish caught during the season is about half a ton a day. It fetches from 1s. to to 2s. a quart wholesale, and a pint will weigh about eighteen ounces.

Twice a year the coasts of the South Sea Islands are visited by innumerable hosts of tiny fish, which, from their resemblance to the small fry caught in the estuary of the Thames, and so highly prized during the " London season," have been christened by the general name of " whitebait." Nobody knows really of what species this little fish consist; but there is no doubt that, like their English prototypes, they consist of the young of many different varieties of fish in the earliest stages of their growth. Their appearance is hailed with delight by the natives, who are inveterate fishermen, and who take advantage of the harvest while it lasts. The waters of the South Pacific teem with many kinds of edible fish, and most of the other islands of the Pacific are visited by shoals of these " whitebait " in one form or another.

The Fiji islands boast of a special delicacy in the shape of a species of annelid, known to the natives as " balolo " (*Palolo viridis*, Gray), which swarms round their coasts about September, and is eagerly sought for by both the natives (who cook them in ovens dug out of the earth) and by European settlers and visitors. Although not an actual "fish," these little marine worms are as highly esteemed as any Thames whitebait, which they closely resemble in flavour; and both they and the various forms of fish life are eagerly sought for. Fortunately the destructive powers of the natives—terrible "poachers" as they are, killing the fish by means of poisons and explosives, and using old sails, baskets, and all kinds of instruments of a very unsportsmanlike character—are out of all proportion to the productiveness of the waters, and as the disappearance of the "whitebait" is as sudden as their appearance, they have not much time to make any impression on the stock of fish in the sea. The Maori is looking forward to the time when he may be able to supply England with salmon; and the Fiji islanders may possibly some day be sending us over supplies of "whitebait" to grace the table of the English epicure.

France.—Much as fish is appreciated in France, and essential as it is as food, owing to their fasts and religious observances, the consumption is after all comparatively small.

In a paper by Captain Lemonssu, published in the "Bulletin of the Society of Acclimatation," Paris, in 1860 (vol. vii. p. 332), he stated that the average annual consumption per head was about as follows :—

> 250 grammes of fresh fish ;
> 1   „   prawns :
> 1 decagramme of crayfish or lobsters ; and
> 3 oysters.

or about nine or ten ounces in all. Of other molluscs the consumption is also very small, although they might be cultivated and multiplied extensively.

Of fish preserved in oil, or marinaded, the consumption is equally limited. Each individual uses of

Sardines ...	...	...	...	...	6 decagrammes.
Anchovy ...	...	...	..	...	2 „
Tunny ...	...	...	...	...	3 grammes.

From this it will be seen how restricted is the consumption of sea fish, etc., notwithstanding the increasing price of the other food necessaries of life. And yet this providential manna passes and repasses the coast, and might be taken and utilised at a price four or five times below that at present charged. In 1860 the sales of fresh fish in the Paris market were to the value of £450,000. The quantity was about 12,000,000 kilos.; 2,000,000 kilos. of salted fish is consumed in Paris, and 500,000 kilos. of marinaded or fish preserved in oil. The value of the fresh water or river fish sold is set down at about £80,000.

The weight and kinds of fish consumed in Paris in 1877 were given as follows :—

						lbs.
Eels	...	...	...	...	...	328,000
Barbel	...	...	...	...	...	23,826
Bream	...	...	...	...,	...	94,176
Pike	...	...	...	...	...	354.232
Smelts	...	...	...	...	...	290.454
Gudgeon...	...	...	...	...	...	39,060
Lampreys	...	...	...	...	...	286
Perch	...	...	...	...	...	28,738
Tench	...	...	...	...	...	154,674
Trout	...	...	...	...	...	5.128
Various small white fish		...	...	...	...	1,157,434
						2,476,008

There was sold of sea fish at the central markets 31,500,000 lbs. From four to five million pounds of salted and smoked cod, herrings, mackerel, and salmon is also sold in Paris. The trade in sea fish in that city has doubled in value in the last ten years, and now amounts in value to about 40,000,000 frs. (£1,600,000).

The consumption of fish in Paris in 1883 was about 22,400 tons, or 1,000 tons more than in 1882, and nearly a fourth of the whole were herrings, sold at an average wholesale price of 3d. per lb. About a fourth of the whole supply of fish came from abroad, chiefly from England.

The official statistics of the French fisheries gave as
the total value of the catch for—

	1876.		1878.
Boat fishery	£3,341,220	......	£3,239,276
Angling or hand fisheries	218,405	......	239,600
	3,559,625		£3,478,878

The aggregate quantity of codfish sent from France to
her colonies in the five years ending 1876, was close
upon 41,000,000 kilos., or over 8,800 tons per annum.
The shipments were less in 1877, and have been on the
decline since. The quantity of herrings, fresh or salted,
brought into French ports in 1877 was 361,574 metrical
quintals. The total weight of fish caught by the French
fishermen averages about 120,000 tons.

The following was the weight and kinds of fish
obtained by the French sea fisheries, in kilogrammes,
in—

	1876.		1878.
Cod, Newfoundland ... }	27,886,472 {	......	16,070,560
„ Iceland		......	12,951,751
Herring	26,061,536	......	21,764,707
Mackerel...	11,863,478	......	7,368,143
Anchovy	1,167,728	......	860,347
Other species	42,577,902	......	44,134,983
	109,557,116		103,150,497
Sardines ... No.	1,198,402,181	......	1,919,302,829

In 1878 the French had 685 vessels engaged in the
Newfoundland cod fishery, employing 13,217 men, who
received in premiums of fifteen to fifty francs each a
sum of 594,120 francs (nearly £24,000).

The shipments of cod were from the seat of the
fisheries—

	Kilos.
To the French Colonies...	1,689,344
From French ports to foreign countries ..	1,337,196
To Algiers and Sardinia	1,879.139
Cod roe imported	273,970
	5,179,649

The aggregate premiums paid by the State on these were 786,201 francs for the fish and 54,794 francs on the cod roes imported for bait in the sardine fisheries.   The bounty varies from twelve to twenty francs per 100 kilos.

The total value of the fish taken by the French fisheries in 1883 was £4,289,076, being £570,000 more than in 1882.   The quantities caught were 34,000 tons of cod, 36,000 tons of herrings, and 6,000 tons of mackerel. The catch of sardines was also nearly double that of the previous year.

In Newfoundland 17,683,289 kilogrammes of cod were caught by the French in 1881, and in Iceland 9,695,411 kilos.

The take of fresh table fish (usually called " La Marée fraîche ") in 1881 was about 50,000,000 kilos., which comprised turbots, brill, soles, plaice, flounders, rays, gurnets, mullets, whiting, conger, salmon, lampreys, sturgeons, &c.   The sea fisheries for the whole Republic in 1881 resulted in sales of fish of the value of nearly three millions and a quarter pounds sterling.

The fresh-water fish of France are divided into two categories, according to their degree of utility for public consumption.   The first comprises the shad, the pike, carp, chevenne (chub), sturgeon, lamprey, ombre (*Thymallus vexillifer*), perch, salmon, tench, trout, eel, barbel and bream.   The second includes the bleak, dace, bullhead, stickleback, roach, gudgeon, loach, rotengle (*Leuciscus erythrophthalmus*), vandoise (*L. vulgaris*), veron (*L. phoxinus*), &c.

Besides the cod, herring, mackerel, and sardine coast fisheries, the "other species" of fish comprised in the French returns are "barbues" (brills), turbots, soles, carrelets (flounders), limandes (dabs), merlans (whiting), skate, rougets, mullets, congers, salmon, lampreys, sturgeons, &c.   Of these there were caught in—

1875	...	...	...	...	...	41,300,121 kilos.
1876	...	...	...	...	...	42,557,902 ,,
1878	...	...	...	...	...	44,134,983 ,,
1879	...	...	...	...	...	47,207,964 ,,
1880	...	...	...	...	...	48,324,308 ,,

Sardines.—Few have any idea of the great importance of the fishing for that diminutive fish the sardine, or the extent of the commerce in it. The largest shoals of these fish are found on the coasts of Sardinia, whence the popular name they bear, which has been incorporated into the specific name, *Clupea sardina*, Cuv. The preserved sardine is said to have been brought into fashion by Henry IV. The sardine is a dainty morsel in any way, whether delicately cooked, fresh in his paper-casing like a mummy embalmed in spices, preserved in oil, or salted as in Italy. In Norway they are put up spiced, and also preserved in sugar. The French fisheries on the coast of Finisterre and Morbihan are of very great importance. In some years the sardines are very plentiful; in others they are more scarce.

The sardine fishery is eminently French, although also prosecuted in Italy. It is carried on from the Gulf of Gascony to the east. The fish are sold all over France fresh (when this is possible), half salted, and salted pressed in barrels. But the preservation of sardines in oil forms the most important branch of the trade, the shipments when prepared being usually estimated to be over one million sterling in value. Indeed, the annual value of the French fisheries on the western coast are stated at twelve to fourteen million francs, divided among about 140,000 inhabitants.

This delicate fish has been termed "the manna of the sea." On the French coasts it gives employment to no less than 13,000 boats in Vendée and Brittany. Concarneau alone has 500, which in 100 days' fishing will bring in on an average of years one million and a half of fish.

The little tin boxes with French labels are found all over the world, and the fish is everywhere held in good repute. They are mostly put up in what are called half and quarter tins, weighing sixteen or eighteen ounces and seven ounces. If properly prepared, and not too salt, the longer the tin is kept unopened the more mellow do the fish become.

Sardines and anchovies to the value of 723,000 dollars are imported into the United States. The whole boxes of sardines are 5 × 4 × 3½ inches; the half boxes, 5 × 4 × 1⅝ inches; the quarter boxes, 4¾ × 3½ × 1½ inches.

Over 10,000,000 tins are yearly exported from the coasts of Brittany to other countries. The fish as brought in are taken to the market, and either sold to dealers, who pack them off by rail to Paris and other towns, where they are used fresh, or they are bought by the local factories for preserving in oil. The average annual value of the sardines caught on French coasts, in the three years ending 1870, was officially returned at £400,000, but this was only the nominal declared value, and of late years the amount is much larger. The sardine fishery increases every day in importance, and so do the preserving establishments. At D'Auray, in 1870, there were about twenty of these. The number of fish tinned was 17,300,000; pressed and salted, 774,000; consumed locally, 1,500,000; and sent fresh into the interior, 10,000,000; and yet in that year it was only half an average catch. At the port of Croisic, where the value of the catch was returned in 1870 at £8,000 for the fresh fish, they sold at twenty francs (16s.) the 1,000, and were readily bought by the preserving factories at Tremblade, Croisic, and Polignen. At Sables d'Olonne the five or six preserving establishments at Gujan, Mestres, &c., put up annually about 1,000,000 lbs. In some years the porpoises are very destructive, frighten off the fish, and break the nets.

In 1883 the total number of sardines caught on the French coasts was 1,148½ millions, or rather more than twice the take of 1882.

The sardine fishery in Tuscany is carried on chiefly around the islands of Elba, Giglio, Orbitello, and Grossito, and produces about 450,000 lbs. of fish. They are generally salted and shipped in barrels of about 130 lbs. The sardines of Gallipoli are excellent, but badly prepared. The quantity of sardines and anchovies caught on the coast of Italy amounts to about 1,600,000 lbs., to

which has to be added the product of the fisheries of
Genoa and Sicily. Other countries have attempted to
enter into competition in the preservation of fish in oil.
Brazil, Spain, Italy, and the United States have tried;
but their efforts, more or less successful, have not been
able to compete with the French production. In North
America they have tried to preserve in this manner the
young of a species of herring, the *Alosa menhaden*. Lately,
too, a company was formed in Cornwall to convert young
pilchards into sardines; and no doubt a good many sprats
are occasionally put up in tins as sardines.

Anchovies.—The anchovy (*Engraulis encrasicolus*) is
another fish, the catching and preserving of which gives
extensive employment on the French Atlantic coast and
in the Mediterranean. The value of these fish caught
on the French coasts is returned at about £16,000 per
annum. The fishing is carried on from May to October.
Bayonne, Port Vendres, St. Jean de Luz, Marseilles,
D'Agde, Douarnenez, and L'Orient are the principal
ports for anchovies. At Marseilles the annual average
value of fresh fish caught is over £1,000. A smaller and
more delicate kind of anchovy (*E. meletta*, Lin.), is also
caught in the Mediterranean. Small sardines are very
often put up as anchovies. After gutting and removing
the head, they are washed and simply placed in barrels
with layers of salt, and a little reddish ochrous earth
added to give them colour. The mineral used to colour
the fish is rather dangerous, but fortunately the fish
are never used without being previously well washed in
water, which removes most of the colouring substance,
that might otherwise prove injurious. The Romans used
to prepare with the intestines of the anchovy a sauce of
a detestable odour, and so strong that it burnt the tongue
and the palate.

Mr. Couch, in his "Cornish Fauna," says the anchovy
abounds there towards the end of summer and if attention were paid to the fishery, enough might be caught to
supply the consumption of the British Islands; and also
adds that he has seen it in the Cornish seas of the length

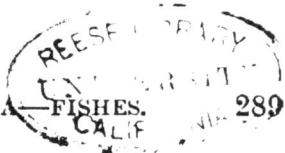

of seven inches and a half. Anchovies are also caught in the Zuyder Zee, Holland.

The catch is, however, extremely uncertain, for while in abundant years it sometimes amounts to over 70,000 baskets, each of about 3,500 fish, in poor years the whole may be put down at 1,000 baskets.

If the fisheries on the Spanish coasts cannot compete in importance with those of some of the other European States in the supply to foreign markets, they at least furnish sufficient for the interior consumption. There are about 37,000 fishermen employed in boats, and the fish taken averages about 78,700 tons per annum, of which half is consumed fresh and half is salted, some few hundredweight being marinaded. At Corunna there are 220 establishments for salting and pressing sardines and pilchards, a trade of much importance. In 1871 salt pilchards sold there at 1½ to 2½ dollars per thousand. They are caught very largely on the coast in favourable years, and promptly cured or salted for removal. The value of the fish caught in 1871 was estimated at £350,000.

Many of the skates and rays are caught by our fishermen, but for some reason the British public do not readily eat this fish, and they are therefore exported in large quantities to France and Holland. The French chefs have many ways of cooking rays, of which " Raie au beurre noir " is about the best. The commonest of these fish in the British markets is the blue skate (*Raia batis* or *vulgaris*), and the thornback or rough ray (*R. clavata*). Another, the Homelyn ray (*R. maculata*), is also generally sold as skate in the London market. The sharp-nosed ray (*R. oxyrhynchus*) is the favourite species with the French. In Iceland they eat the ray when it is half rotten. At Nantes, under the name of "goules rondes," the heads of rays are sold separately in bundles of twenty, and they are regarded as dainty morsels, somewhat as their backs were esteemed by the ancients according to Antiphanes.

Mackerel.—The mackerel (*Scomber scombrus*) fishery is prosecuted on many parts of the British coasts, but it is difficult to state with precision the quantity taken. On the Cornish coast about 1,600 to 2,000 tons are caught in some years. In 1875 about 4,000 long hundred (120) were taken on the Norfolk coast. In 1876 the Irish mackerel fishery yielded 139,000 boxes of six score fish each. The mackerel fishery in 1878 resulted in a take of 92,626 boxes, as compared with 114,562 boxes in 1877. In 1883 the catch of mackerel in Ireland by 270 boats amounted to 242,975 boxes, averaging 14s. per box, and realising £170,624, the largest amount ever received in one year.

On the Sussex and other coasts they are also taken ; 10,000 to 12,000 tons are sold annually in London. The average catch on the French coasts is greater than that of Ireland. A large quantity are sent from Norway in ice. On the North American coasts a very extensive trade is done in pickled mackerel. About 200,000 barrels are taken there yearly in British waters, and 350,000 barrels in American waters. In 1870, 16,000 barrels of mackerel were cured in Prince Edward Island, and in 1883, 93,000 barrels in New Brunswick and Nova Scotia.

Fishing for mackerel and herring is not pursued to so great an extent as might be the case if the demand were greater and the expense less. The fishery returns for 1872 were—

	Herring. Barrels.		Mackerel. Barrels.
Nova Scotia	170,657	......	115,833
Quebec	29,069	......	1,759
New Brunswick... ...	124,157	......	2,217
Ontario	6,974	......	—
	330,857		119,809

Besides the salted mackerel a good many are put up in hermetically sealed tins, about 351,000 cans were exported from New Brunswick and Nova Scotia in 1883 valued at 7½d. per can.

From a careful diagram of the mackerel catch of Massachusetts it appears to have grown steadily from 7,000 barrels in 1804, to 385,000 barrels in 1831. In the next ten years it declined to 50,000. The scale has since been fluctuating, being for 1880 about 150,000. This account is only of salt mackerel, and is not appreciably affected by the use of pounds, weirs, and traps, all caught thus not exceeding 5,000 barrels yearly, most of which are consumed fresh. The number of barrels used in this way, in 1876, was for the whole United States but 27,000. Evidently causes different from mere methods of capture must account for the partial disappearance of mackerel, and much is yet to be learned as to this valuable but singular fish, upon whose migratory movements so many depend for a living. In early spring they strike the coast of Virginia, moving northward in immense shoals, visiting successively Cape May, Sandy Hook, Block Island, Cape Cod, and various points as far as Labrador. Captain N. E. Atwood, in illustration of the vicissitudes of mackerel fishing, states that with the help of a boy he has caught in one night off Cape Cod 2,050 fish, and the next night 3,520; but on another trip he fished all the way from the Grand Bank to the Azores and caught only one mackerel!

The mackerel is much esteemed, its flesh having an excellent flavour, but it is fat and not easily digested.

Mullet.—There are several kinds of mullet. Those principally seen in the markets are the grey mullet (*Mugel capito*), an excellent fish, and the red mullet (*Mullus surmulletus*). The grey mullet is an estuary fish. The name mullet is said to be derived from *mullus*, the scarlet sandal or shoe worn by Roman consuls. This fish is also termed the woodcock of the sea.

The red mullet seldom come into the market with their scales on, as the fishermen generally scrape them off with their thumb nails immediately they are caught, else the rich crimson hue invariably fades, but the bared skin becomes brilliantly red.

This fish is also called the striped surmullet, from the circumstance that its bright red colour is relieved by three longitudinal stripes of yellow. The flesh is white, firm, and remarkably free from fat, and has always been esteemed one of the epicure's greatest luxuries. Its flavour improves with the size, and small fish deprived of the liver are more or less insipid. The method of cooking by rolling them in paper to prevent injury to the skin has been observed for at least two thousand years. The red mullet was held in such a distinguished category among the genteel fishes of the Romans, that three of them, although of small size, were known to fetch upwards of £200.

Mullus surmulletus is called on some of the French coasts " barbarien," and *Mullus barbatus* "rouget," or " le barbarien petit."

The mullet was one of those fish which was most sought for in Rome. It is difficult for us to realise the enormous value which the Romans placed upon this fish, for as it never reaches any great size, they did not hesitate to pay its weight in gold if it was unusually large. Seneca and Suetonius have given us in their writings descriptions of the extravagant taste in the preparation of the mullet for the table of the rich. According to Seneca (Epistle 95) the Emperor Tiberius sold at auction a mullet, weighing four pounds, to Apicius and Octavius jointly for the sum of 4,000 sesterces (£32). In this country they do not usually exceed three pounds and a half in weight.

The scarus, muræna, tunny, and sword-fish were other esteemed fishes among the ancients. They knew how to preserve some, first frying them in oil with bay leaves, salt, and spices, and then pouring boiling vinegar over them. They were more appreciated when brought alive and gradually allowed to die immersed in the delicious garum, when the Romans feasted their eyes in the anticipated delight of eating them, by gazing on the dying creature as he changed colour like an expiring dolphin. Seneca reproaches them with this refinement of cruelty, " Oculis quoque gulosi sunt." The most renowned of Apicius's culinary discoveries was the alec, a compound of their livers.

Several fishes were immortalised by the ancients ; the *Murœna Hellena* was raised in their ponds, and rendered so tame that it came to be killed at the tinkling of his master's bell or the sound of his voice, " Natat ad magistrum delicata muræna," says Martial. Hirtius ceded six thousand of these fish to Cæsar as a great favour, and Vitellius delighted in their roe. One of the mullets, *M. cephalus*, and its roe are now largely employed in the Black Sea and the Mediterranean coasts, and the prepared roes have been mentioned in the Chapter on Eggs, *ante*, p. 213.

The mountain mullet of Jamaica (*Dajaus monticola*, Cuv. and Val. ; *Mugil monticola*, Bancroft) is a very delicate fish. The flesh is remarkably sweet and white, and the roe is a most *recherché* morsel. In general it is found nearly as large as the fish itself. There are two modes of dressing them for the table, first wrap them up in a plantain leaf and put them in hot ashes, and there let them remain for an hour, or they may be fried. The fine large roes should not be treated in any other way for the gourmet. It is the best mode of preparing them for the table. The mountain mullet weighs from half a pound to a pound. The long-nosed mullet (*Mugil albula*, Cuv. and Val.) is the largest and perhaps the sweetest. In the month of September they are in prime order for the table. The king and queen mullets of Jamaica are species of *Upeneus*, a sub-genus of *Mullus*.

The callipeva, or Jamaica salmon as it has been called, and the sea mullet, are rich and well tasted, and abound with a thin yellow fat that gives them an excellent flavour. The head and neck are a mass of rich, sweet gelatinous substance, and scarcely any other fish can compare in flesh and flavour with this fine delightful specimen of the finny tribe.

The callipeva (*Mugel liza*) is a river mullet, seldom extending further than the embouchure of streams or into the ponds and marshes. It is met with in some other of the West Indian islands and Central America.

Tunny.—The fishing for and employment of the tunny

(*Thynnus vulgaris*, Cuv.) as food is principally on the shores of the Mediterranean, but the use of its firm flesh is spreading a little over the Continent. In America and England it is held but in low estimation. It is eaten fresh, salted, preserved in oil, or pickled like salmon. Some parts of the fish are said to resemble beef in flavour, and others veal and pork. In Italy it is boiled down into soup and made into pies, which will keep, it is said, for two months. The average exports from Sardinia are about 3,000,000 lbs. The fish which are to be preserved in oil, then called "scabeccio," are first boiled for an hour, then allowed to cool and dry, when they are packed in barrels, two gallons of oil being poured into each barrel, so as to well permeate the fish. Those tinned are prepared in the same way. While the tunny is wholesome and agreeable when used fresh or salted, it at once becomes hurtful when it begins to ferment or at all approaches decomposition. The police of Venice examine carefully the boats that bring in the fish, especially when the sirocco has delayed their arrival—and even if ever so little touched, they throw them into the sea. The fresh tunny ought to be sold within twenty-four hours.

The fish averages about four feet long, but sometimes attains ten to fourteen feet.

Although the common tunny (*Orcynus thynnus* of some authors) is the most important special sea fishery in Italy, not a few allied species are also caught, such as *O. brachypterus, O. germo, Thynnus thunnina,* and *Auxis Rochei,* all sea fishes, which periodically and successively visit in large numbers different parts of the coasts.

The Dorade (*Coryphæna suerui*, Cuv. and Val.; *Sparus aurata*), a very excellent sea fish, sometimes called the dolphin, is eaten fried in butter, but it ought to be cooked immediately.

Congers.—The sea eel or conger (*Muræna conger*) is very abundant on the coasts of England and France, in the Mediterranean sea (where it was much sought after by the ancients), and in the Propontis, where it is held in considerable estimation; those of Sicyon were especially esteemed. The flesh of this fish is coarse, but white and well-flavoured; as it is however very fat, it does not agree with all stomachs. In many places the conger eels are dried for exportation. For this purpose they are cut open in their underpart through their entire length, the intestines are removed, deep scarifications are made upon the back, the parts are kept separate by means of small sticks, and they are suspended by the tail to poles or the branches of trees. When they are perfectly dry, they are collected in packets, each weighing about two hundred pounds.

The extensive fringes of reefs and rocks encircling all the Channel Islands, the shallows and banks between them, are grand habitats of this species of the genus eel, and nowhere on our British coasts are they so numerous, so · huge, and so generally utilised for food. In the markets of Guernsey and Jersey they may constantly be seen in larger or smaller quantities, their coarse, repulsive, snake-like carcases selling readily for three halfpence, twopence, or threepence per pound, according to the " take " and the condition ; for, coarseness and uncomeliness notwithstanding, your *Conger vulgaris*, as some naturalists call him, is esteemed delectable and nutritious fare by the Channel Islander. He swears by the toothsomeness and restorative properties of his conger eel soup, and seems to have inherited the taste from many a bygone ancestor. So far back as King John's time we hear a something of this predilection, for conger fishing and salting were included in the charter of privileges which that monarch granted to the Channel Isles. A duty on this fish and on mackerel—" esperkeria " is the old name of the tax—was, we may also find, paid to the Crown in 1331, for in Edward III.'s *Extent*, or rent roll for Guernsey, one of the articles says, 'Our Lord the King also has a revenue from a certain custom called the fishery of congers and mackerel, and on all fish of the islands, the whole extent of which is 210 livres 13 sous and 4 deniers.' Then, after mentioning who might or might not carry on the fishery, and to whom the fish might or might not be sold, the arbitrary Royal document continues, 'The fishermen may do what they like with congers that are so small that they may span them round the middle with the fist, and they may reserve from the large as well as the small as much as may be sufficient for their diet.'

"But even previously to 1331 we get an inkling of the magnitude and value, pecuniary and gustatory, of this fishery, for Mr. Falle, another writer, says that one Otho de Grandison, governor of these islands (*tempore* Edward I. and II.) 'forced an impost upon congers salted for transportation, and that at one penny only per conger above 10 lbs. so salted and transported, he raised yearly 400 livres Tournois.' Until the beginning of the seventeenth century, when the Newfoundland cod fishery materially interfered with that of conger in Guernsey and Jersey, it remained a source of much industry and profit to their inhabitants; at present, however, its export is nothing, and its consumption is limited to home appetites.

"The particular family, the *Murenidæ*, or eel tribe, is not a large one, the common fresh-water eel being its type, but in many respects the conger differs from this well-known slippery gentleman. His average length is between three and four feet, his weight from 15 to 20 lbs., but we read of him growing much longer and weighing very much heavier. Not unfrequently he has measured six or eight feet, and has turned the scale at 50 or 60 lbs.; and now and again piscatorial records note his attaining the huge size of ten feet, and the heavy weight of 90 or 100 lbs.; but, under those gigantic conditions, the 'monstrum horrendum, informe, ingens' is an 'anak' of his race, and fame deals with him as such."*

Congers are in some parts of England, especially where the coasts are rocky, an important sea fish. At Fowey, Mevagissey, and other parts of Cornwall, they have been

---

* The *Globe.*

taken weighing seventy to eighty pounds. They are not particularly common in the London markets, but may often be seen in the markets at Liverpool, Birmingham, &c. The French and Italians are particularly fond of congers. According to M. Court, congers were formerly cut across in such a manner as to allow of their being sewn five or six together in the form of a sheet. In this condition they were dried in the sun without salt, and under the name of "conger douce" formed a profitable article of commerce with Spain and Portugal. They are sometimes exported to those countries in the dried state, where they are ground down into a kind of powder, and used for enriching soups. An excellent soup is thus made in the Channel Islands, and is called "Bouilli Baisse." According to the late Mr. Buckland, from whose report on the sea fisheries I quote, a large quantity of them are exported from the Channel Islands for soup-making, and they form the basis of a very large proportion of London-made soups, especially mock turtle.

Eels.—The fresh-water eel is valued very highly, as it forms the principal flesh food of large populations in Europe, and salted, smoked or pickled it is an important article of trade. The skin and fat are used for technical purposes. At one period there was a strong prejudice against eels, which still prevails among some people.

There is an excellent eel fishery in the Parret, large numbers of elvers or young eels are caught when ascending this river in the spring months; these are boiled, compressed into cakes, and sold in the neighbouring markets, where they form palatable and nutritious food.

The price of eels varies from 2d. to 9d. the pound. The broad-nosed eel is caught in the summer, and the sharp-nosed eel in the fall of the year.

Eels were once a staple of English diet, since they supplied almost the only animal food to which the poor could aspire. The rich and oily flesh was a welcome addition to their daily fare of rye-bread and beans.

The England of the Middle Ages, abounding in lagoons and ponds, and full of sluggish streams and sullen

marshes, was a very paradise for the eel-fisher, notably
so the flat fen counties lying to the east.

Eels appear to have been early favourites, particularly
in the monasteries. The cellaress of Barking Abbey,
Essex, in the ancient times of that foundation, was,
amongst other eatables, " to provide russ aulx in Lenton,
and to bake with *elys* on Shere Tuesday :" and at Shrovetide she was to have ready "twelve *stubbe eles* and nine
schaft eles." The regulation and management for the
sale of eels seems to have formed a prominent feature in
the old ordinances of the Fishmongers' Company. There
were artificial receptacles made for eels in our rivers,
called *anguilonea,* constructed with rows of poles, that
they might be more easily taken.

" In Scotland few people can be found who will venture
to partake of eels. Whether the prejudice against this
kind of food is founded on the resemblance which the
eel bears to the serpent, or is a remnant of the ancient
Jewish prohibition of its use as an article of diet, we
will not venture to say. The most important eel-fisheries
in England are those situated in the estuary of the
Severn and the streams which run into that arm of the
sea, and here not only full-grown eels, but the fry of
eels, called 'elvers,' are captured in large quantities.
Like almost every other fish, eels are oviparous, the
spawning usually taking place in the brackish waters of
estuaries, whence the young fry, called 'elvers' or 'eel-
fare' soon migrate up-stream in countless myriads. In
the Severn this fact is taken advantage of by the fishermen, who reap an abundant harvest of delicious food
during the months of March, April, and May, when
other kinds of fish are scarce. The adult eels are caught
in their progress down the streams in the later months
of the year, in most parts of England ; but it is principally in the Bristol Channel and its tributary streams
that the capture of 'elvers' is practised."*

The best kind, the silver eel, is that found in the

* *Chambers's Journal.*

clearest waters. The dingy yellow and the deep sallow green are very inferior to the clear coppery brown-backed eel, and even to the bronze-coloured. Welled vessels often bring over a cargo of 15,000 to 20,000 eels from Holland. The consumption of eels in Great Britain is very large, amounting to 4,000 or 5,000 tons a year. We get the largest portion from Holland, but the best come from Ireland. One thousand packages of eels were sold in Dublin in 1870, worth 30s. a package.

The eel is the oiliest of all fishes, but is correspondingly deficient in nitrogenous matter, containing only 10 per cent. of the latter, but having at least 14 per cent. of fat. The Jews were prohibited from eating eels by the Levitical law, which forbade the eating of "whatsoever had no fins nor scales in the water," although in other fish-eating countries they form a favourite dish. Especially is this the case in England, where the demand for eels always exceeds the supply, and where no fewer than ten millions of them are annually brought to Billingsgate for the supply of the Metropolitan market. The eel is also a special favourite with the Italians, who cultivate it in the great lagoons of the Adriatic, and the Neapolitans import it to the extent of a million pounds annually.

The eel, with its many varieties and sub-species, is one of the most common fishes in Italy; it is caught in the sea, in brackish waters, and in fresh water, but more especially in lagoons and estuaries, and forms one of the most important items of the local fisheries. In the valley of Commachio are extensive salt and brackish waters, lagoons about thirty miles in length, at the delta of the Po; eel fishing there is an ancient and important industry. The mean annual produce there is about 2,000,000 lbs. of preserved eels. In 1871, nearly 3,000,000 lbs. of eels were got there. They cultivate here also soles, plaice, chub, dory and other fish. In 1878, 44,000,000 kilos. of fish of different kinds were imported into Italy.

There is a large trade carried on in this valley of

Commachio in eels, transported either alive in viva-
riums, salted, dried, pickled, or marinaded, and sent
across to the Naples market. About 1,300,000 lbs. are
annually caught there, and half as much more in other
districts. The produce of the lakes, in fish of all kinds,
is about 5,000,000 lbs. Many of the eels are cooked
before being sent to market. The heads and tails are
taken off, and the larger ones are cut in joints. They
are roasted on spits, and the fat which drops from
them is saved. Some which cannot be spitted are
fried. They are then packed in barrels with layers of
grey rock-salt, and strong vinegar is then poured on.
A barrel of pickled eels weighs about 150 lbs. Sometimes the eels are merely salted and dried by the heat of
the kitchen fire. The eels are sold at about 5d. per lb.
when marinaded, and 4½d. salted. The fish are sometimes five or six lbs. in weight.

In Italy eels are eaten for breakfast, dinner and
supper, by the masses; they grow to a large size and are
reputed to be of excellent flavour.

The Neapolitan of the lowest class has his winter
dish of roasted sea-eel, when his summer dinner of
sliced melon goes out of season. The great capitone,
often of 30 or 40 lbs. weight, is to the lazzaroni, what
solid beef is to the Yorkshireman.

In New Zealand eels reach nearly six feet long and
are as thick as a man's thigh, weighing between 20 and
25 lbs. They are dried and cooked as wanted. In India
eels also attain a large size. Being seldom eaten except
by the lower classes, there is but little demand for
them.

Eels of a large size and of the finest quality are
abundant in all the bays and creeks of Prince Edward
Island. Twenty-eight tons were taken in 1883 for consumption fresh. They might be sent in large quantities
pickled or fresh, to New York, where there is a good
demand. Two thousand three hundred and eight barrels
of eels, valued at nine dollars a barrel, were shipped from
Nova Scotia in 1883.

Minnows.—The Staffordshire people, so late as the time of Walton, and even of Pennant, reaped a harvest of minnows from the meres for which their shire was famous. The silvery shoals of tiny fish were surprised in the shallows, and caught, in sheets and sail-cloth instead of nets, in incredible quantities, then cooked and compressed into a sort of fish-cake, flavoured with herbs, under the name of minnow-tansies, a local phrase that still lingers. The dwellers beside Windermere and Ullswater used to capture, at certain seasons, enormous numbers of a small bluish fish popularly known as the skilly, or fresh-water herring.

CHAPTER IX.

FOOD PRODUCTS OF THE SEA—FISHES.

Fisheries of Sweden — Of Roumania — Lampreys — Sturgeons— Balyk—Mode of Preparing—Russian Fisheries—Fisheries of Tunis—Of Egypt and West African Coasts—Indian Fisheries —Choice Fish—Statistics of Imports and Exports—Trade in Sharks' Fins and Fish-maws — Bonito — Gourami — Fish of Guadaloupe—Consumption of Fish in West Indies—Barbados —Jamaica—Honduras—Sharks as Food—Their Flesh Eaten in Various Countries—Swordfish—Oulachans, Large Fishery for—Carp Family—Trout and Salmon—Statistics of British Trade — Salmon Fisheries of Canada — Tinned Salmon, Enormous Trade in—Halibut—North American Fisheries— Fish Preserved in Ice—White Fish (Coregonus) and other Lake Fish—Flying Fish—Consumption of Fish in Zanzibar —New Zealand Fish — Tasmanian Fish — Fish of Ceylon, China, and the Indian Seas—Of Japan—Brazilian Fish—Fish of River Plate and Paraguay.

Swedish Fisheries.—The lake and river fisheries of Sweden furnish the perch, the sandre, the pike, the bream, and other cyprians, the *Lota vulgaris* and the common eel. The fishery for the lavaret, the *Coregonus albula* and the alpine salmon (*S. Alpinus*) in the Vitter bring in annually about £5,600. The largest salmon fisheries are those of Elfkarleby in Uppland and Morsim in Bletinge, which yield annually a revenue of about £4,000; but the aggregate returns of the salmon fisheries in Sweden are set down at £41,000. The greater part of the fish is consumed locally, but some is sent fresh in ice to England and Germany, and some to Denmark, where it is smoked. About 150,000 barrels of herrings are salted annually on the Baltic coasts of Sweden, but these are insufficient for the home demand, and large quantities are imported from Norway.

The Baltic herrings are partly sold fresh, or smoked in the towns on the coast, partly salted, packed in casks, and sent all over the country. As salt herring constitutes the daily food of the Swedish peasants and the lower classes in general, the amount secured in the country is not sufficient, so that a considerable quantity has to be imported from Norway. On an average the total annual yield of herring on the Swedish coasts of the Baltic amounts to 150,000 tons, of which about half is sold fresh to the inhabitants and the other half salted.

The gar-pike or gorebill (*Esox belone*) is excellent eating, when cut in pieces and fried as eels; but the public do not seem to like it, because the bones are of an emerald green, and erroneously supposed to be poisonous. The Jews are very fond of this fish.

The maigre (*Sciœna aquila*), although not a common fish, is sometimes seen in the English markets. It is very like a huge bass, and good eating, having a flavour between sturgeon and salmon.

Of the 460 species of fish known to inhabit the Mediterranean and Adriatic Seas, most are sought for by fishermen and used as food. The Elasmobranchs are all eaten, even the larger species of sharks, which are sent to inland markets, and, when cut up, sell well.

In Roumania they prepare their fish for keeping in the following manner: A series of stages of osier-work are built up, which are covered with walnut leaves, in these trout, barbel, and other fish are wrapped; the building is then filled with the smoke from burning wood for several days, and the fish acquire an amber colour and an exquisite flavour. They are then made into packets, and surrounded with pine branches, which adds a new perfume to them. The quantity of fish, fresh and salted, locally consumed in Roumania is valued at twenty million piastres, and about one million worth more is exported.

There are four kinds of gurnards sold in the markets. The grey gurnard (*Trigla gurnardus*), the piper (*T. lyra*), the red gurnard or ellick (*T. cuculus*), and the sapphirine gurnard (*T. hirundo*). The gurnard is an excellent table fish. Much of the fish which is now sold as " offal "—such as latchets, which are a species of large gurnard—is equal in quality to turbot, or any other of the fish called " prime " which swim the sea.

Lampreys.—The lamprey is abundant in many parts of the Caspian Sea, and yet is almost entirely neglected, or only dried to be burnt as a candle.

The fame of the lamprey—the *Mustela* of Ausonius and Pliny—is generally known; that and the sturgeon (*Acipenser sturio*) were served at table with triumphant pomp; but the turbot, one of which was brought to Domitian from Ancona, was considered such a present from the gods that this emperor assembled the Senate to admire it. The dorade (*Sparus auratus*) was even conse-crated to Venus; the *Labrus scarus* was called the brain of Jupiter, and Apuleius and Epicharmus maintain that its very entrails would be relished in Olympus.

Many kinds of sea-bream (*Sparus*) are sold for food in the London market. The commonest is the *Sparus auratus*, a very brilliant fish.

Sturgeons.—The sturgeon is still considered a royal fish in Britain, but it is not common or much esteemed. It was highly appreciated by the ancient Romans and Greeks, and was the principal dish at all great dinner parties. Cicero reproved epicures on account of spend-ing so much money for this fish. Pliny tells us that the sturgeon was served at the most sumptuous tables, and always carried by servants, crowned with garlands of flowers, and accompanied by a band of musicians. Even at this time the fish is rare and dear at Rome. Pickled sturgeon is a favourite food of the colonists of Spain and Portugal in South America, as well as of the in-habitants of the West India Islands, principally during Lent.

The sturgeon abounds in British Columbia, and in Quebec, and other parts of Canada; it differs from the fish of the same name of the European waters. It is caught as large as 800 lbs., and frequents not only the seas and rivers, but the lakes of the country. The flesh is by some considered excellent; it is dried by the Indians, and is also salted. Generally speaking, however, the flesh of the sturgeon is dry and tough, nor could we expect aught else from a fish weighing several hundred pounds. Specimens reaching from 800 to 1,000 lbs. have frequently been caught in the Danube in olden times.

It is said that a good cook can obtain beef, mutton, pork, or poultry from the flesh of the sturgeon, which is very likely, as some of its flesh is quite white and some the colour of rump steak. The sturgeons have, instead of bones, soft flexible gristle.

There are few other fishes which are of greater use to man than the sturgeon. In Russia a large proportion of the population is supported by the sturgeon fisheries, and they live chiefly on it. The flesh is there considered to combine a certain firmness with excellent flavour, and is even preferred to veal by many persons. They are either salted, dried in the sun, or smoked, and thus shipped to a great distance. The choicest species is the sterlet (*A. ruthenus*), which seldom weighs more than eight or nine pounds. It is in the Russian rivers that the different species of sturgeon most abound, the principal ones taken are *Acipenser huso*, *A. Guldenstadtii*, Brandt, *A. schipa*, Guld., and *A. stellatus*, Pallas. Besides their flesh, other products obtained from them, as caviare, isinglass, and vesiga, form a considerable portion of their value.

The flavour of the flesh and the quality of the products of the four species named differ very little. The aggregate value of these may be estimated at £1,200,000, more than half being made up of the fish frozen, salted, or prepared in balyk, weighing in the aggregate perhaps 75 million pounds.

Besides the sturgeon, there are numerous other fishes caught in Russia as the sander (*Leucopercus sandre*), of which 60,000,000 to 100,000,000 are taken; the ordinary

x

herring in the White Sea and the Baltic; the herring of the Volga and the Sea of Azov (*Clupea pontica*, Eichu), of which from sixty to one hundred millions are salted; the bream, of which upwards of fifty million are caught in the Lower Volga, and large quantities in other quarters; the lake smelt (*Eperlanus*), of which nine million pounds are obtained from the Lake of Peypons alone. The cod, carp, silurus, salmon, coregonus, and many other fish are also caught in different localities.

The aggregate value of the Russian fisheries was officially estimated in 1867 at 20,000,000 of silver roubles (about £3,000,000 sterling), and the quantity of fish taken annually from the waters of Russia, at 1,000 million pounds' weight, without counting those locally consumed at the seats of the fisheries.* This amount far surpasses the catch of the Newfoundland and other large fisheries; and with this enormous take of fish it may well be asked why so little fish is exported from Russia. The answer to this is that Russia has but little sea coast, and that there is a very large demand for supplying the population of 72,000,000.

It may also be added that during the greater part of the fasts (which amount to over one hundred and fifty days in the year), the Russian people have only fish as their animal food, hence large imports have even to be made to supply the demand. The import of salted herrings yearly into Russia is from 300,000 to 500,000 barrels.

Not less than 396,000,000 pounds of fish are annually caught in the waters of the Caspian Sea. Of this total 36,000,000 lbs. is sturgeon; 7,200,000 lbs. carp; sander and pike, 95,400,000 lbs.; bream, 49,500,000 lbs.; shad, 108,000.000 lbs.; and the rest is made up of other fish, perch, silurus, coregonus, etc.

Besides the ordinary mode of salting, fish are prepared in other ways in Russia, they are smoked, marinaded, and simply dried in the open air or in an oven. This

---

last method of drying in a furnace is only employed for
the lake smelt, the cod is dried in the sun in spring,
when the weather is still cold. The lampreys are alone
marinaded in quantities sufficient to be sent into commerce. There are smoked about a dozen million of small
herrings of Saroka, two species of mullet (*Mugil saliens*
and *M. auratus*) taken on the southern coasts of the Black
Sea, and particularly about the Crimea, in millions, and
the chemaia (*Aspius clupeoides*, Pall.) which is in great
repute, and of which 1,500,000 to 2,500,000 are prepared.
They are preferred to red herrings, and appear on the
best tables from St. Petersburg to Astrakan and Odessa.
The reputation of this fish is indicated by its popular
name, which is a corruption from the Persian *chach-
mahé*, signifying "royal fish."

Balyk.—A considerable quantity of sturgeon and of
the so-called white salmon (*Coregonus leucichthys*, Pall.)
is prepared in what is called "balyk," the Tartar word
for fish. This is only salted and dried, but so much care
and precaution is taken in the preparation, that the fish
acquires a special and exquisite flavour. As balyk is
only made in Russia, some details as to the processes
adopted may be interesting. Balyk is always prepared
in spring before the great heat commences, for later on,
it would be necessary to salt the fish more to prevent
its spoiling. At the fisheries on the northern part of the
Caspian Sea and those of the Sea of Azov, they only
employ for balyk the sturgeon (*Acipenser Guldenstadtii*,) and the belouga (*A. huso*), but on the Koura
in Transcaucasia they employ annually 300,000 sevrugas
(*A. stellatus*) to make an inferior quality of balyk called
"djirim."

It is hard and necessarily salt; but this is its chief
merit with the inhabitants of Kakhetie, the principal
market for it, as it incites thirst, which they quench
with the excellent wine of their country.

The fattest fish are chosen, and they commence by
removing the head and tail, and then the entrails and
lateral parts of the body, leaving only the back, which

forms what is properly called "balyk," that is, fish of excellence, balyk implying refined or prepared fish. The parts of the fish removed, are salted in the ordinary manner and employed as food by the fishermen and working classes; but the coats of the stomach, which are very fat, are sometimes prepared like balyk and called tiochka. The backs of the sturgeons (*A. Gulden-stadtii*), are left entire, each forming a balyk, but those of the large huso are divided lengthwise and crosswise, in many parts, to form balyks; for they would else be too large and too thick for the salt to penetrate. The backs are then placed in troughs, or wooden reservoirs, well covered with salt, care being taken that one balyk is separated from another, and does not touch the wood, or it would infallibly be spoiled or tainted. They are left in the salt for nine or ten days, or for fifteen, if the weather is hot, and the pieces large. To the salt, saltpetre is added, in the proportion of 2 lbs. to 1,500 lbs. of balyk, to give it a red colour. There is also added the best kind of pepper, cloves, and bay leaf. When it is thought the fish is sufficiently penetrated with salt, it is removed from the troughs, and is steeped for two days in fresh water, or in the water of the sea of Azov, which is preferred. When the steeping has removed the surplus of salt, the fish is suspended in the air to mature, and remains exposed to the direct rays of the sun; after which it is hung in sheds open at the sides, so that the air may freely reach the rows of fish hung to dry. Here it is kept for a month or six weeks. When it is ripe, or properly cured, it will be found covered with a sort of mould, if this does not form it is an indication that the fish is too salt. Notwithstanding all the care given to the preparation, the balyks will not all cure equally well; and there are those who at a glance, from experience, will detect which are the best by their deeper colour.

Good balyk, such as is prepared near the embouchures of the Don and some parts of the littoral of the sea of

Azov, especially the northern and eastern coasts of the peninsula of Kertch, is almost as tender as salted salmon, of an orange brown colour, and translucid. Its smell is peculiar, and has nothing disagreeable about it, resembling a little the odour of fresh cucumber; it should not have an after-taste at all rancid or putrid, nor be too salt. It is only skilful men who can give to their balyk these good qualities, and although it is bought cheap wholesale at the seat of production, it is often sold to consumers as high as 3s. a pound.

Vesiga.—Another edible fish-product of Russia is "Vesiga," which is the dried dorsal cord of several species of sturgeon. When the fish has been gutted, and the roe and the swimming-bladder removed, a small incision is made in the flesh, and by inserting the finger, the dorsal cord is removed in the form of a long and straight ribbon. This is carefully washed, and by squeezing, the soft matter it contains is removed, and it is then left for from three days to a week to dry in the sun, according to the temperature. When thoroughly dry, it is made up into packets, fifty of which weigh about 36 lbs. A packet of vesiga of the great sturgeon or belouga (*A. huso*) will only consist of a dozen dried dorsal cords, while there may be twenty in a package of the vesiga of the common sturgeon (*A. Guldenstadtii*) and other small species.

A thousand belougas of average size will furnish ordinarily 180 pounds of vesiga, while the same number of common sturgeon and sevruga will only yield about thirty or forty pounds. When the vesiga is boiled it swells, and in this state it is cut into small pieces, which enter into the composition of excellent fish-cakes.

The following is an estimate made in 1873, of the products of the fisheries of the Caspian Sea and its principal affluents, or one fishing district alone of Russia.*

---

* A. Schultz, President of the Administration of Fisheries, Astrakhan.

	Pouds of 36 lbs.		Value, Roubles of 3s.
Belouga (*A. huso*)	475,000	...	1,288,000
Sturgeons (*A. Guldenstadtii* and *A. schipa*)	405,000	...	1,620,000
Sevruga (*A. stellatus*)	65,000	...	1,962,000
Sterlet (*A. ruthenus*)	50,750	...	275,000
Carps	200,000	...	120,000
Sanders (*Lucioperca sandre*) and Pikes	2,650,000	...	2,450,000
Bream	1,375,000	...	1,275,000
Shad	3,000,000	...	1,050,000
Voblas (*Leuciscus rutilus*) ...	600,000 } ...		500,000
Perch and other small fish ...	760,000 }		
Siluruds	185,000	...	315,000
Salmon	33,000	...	106,000
Whitefish (*Coregonus*)	32,000	...	103.000
Isinglass	5,500	...	600,000
Vesiga	4,000	...	70.000
Caviare of sturgeon	139,000	...	1,390,000
Do. of the sander and bream ...	300,000	...	300,000
	10,279,250		13,424,000

Equal to about 185,000 tons, value £2,000,000.

Africa.—The fishery is important on the coasts of Tunis. About 1,000 cwt. of dried fish is shipped annually to Greece. The lake of Beguta abounds in fish; the right of fishing is let, and about 600,000 fish of from three to six pounds weight each are sent from there to the Tunis markets yearly. Another lake which separates Tunis from Goleta, is also full of fish.

The tunny fishery is carried on in summer from May to July off Cape Bon and the island of Tonera, and 9,000 to 10,000 fish taken, which yield from 1,200,000 to 1,400,000 lbs. of fish annually; this is chiefly sent pickled in barrels to Genoa, Leghorn, and Malta, but some small portion is salted and put up in oil in tins.

The value of the maritime and private fishery in Egypt is estimated at three million francs (£120,000.) There are mullets and many other very delicate fish, which are slightly smoked, or dried in the sun. The

roes of the mullet are made into the botargo of commerce.

Senegal, and the sea which waters its coasts, abounds
in fish. The negroes take great quantities, which support the population, and a considerable quantity, sun-
dried, is carried into the interior.

Fish abound also in the archipelago of the Canary
Islands, and the inhabitants derive much of their food
from the fish, while large quantities salted are exported.

Teneriffe has important fisheries. Cod, sardines, herrings, and tunny are caught.

The number of fishing establishments which cover the
River Gaboon, evidence the occupation of the natives.
They load their pirogues with dried fish, which they sell
on the upper part of the lagoon, exchanging it for palm
oil. As a rule, it may be said of the Tropics that fresh fish
to be enjoyed, must be consumed on the day of the catch.

The population of the Gold Coast colony, with Lagos,
is estimated in round numbers at 400,000, and as these
live chiefly on fish, some conception can be formed of the
considerable catch there must be annually to supply such
a mass. The curing shrimps and herrings forms a large
industry, and represents a considerable trade within the
colony and beyond its border. The people suffer much
from cutaneous diseases and ulcerations, which are attributed to the bad condition of the fish diet on which
they, as a rule, have to depend.

Indian Seas.—The seas which surround the island of
Ceylon contain an enormous quantity and variety of
fish; hardly any place in the world has been so richly
endowed in this respect by nature.

The Maldive islands, under the protection of Ceylon,
maintain a large fishing industry, and yield considerable
exports. In 1882 they exported to Ceylon 1,600 tons
of dried and salted fish, worth £27,000. India also sent
to Ceylon 2,800 tons of salt fish, worth £47,000. This
salt fish is used all over Ceylon, as a relish with curries,
by the natives. Fresh fish also finds a ready market on
the sea coast, but the want of means of quick transport

inland confines its consumption to a distance of a day's journey from the coast.

In India and Burmah only a proportion of the people consume fish as food, or rather, are able to do so without infringing caste prejudices. Dr. Day tells us that in the Punjâb comparatively few of the inhabitants are thus prohibited, although Brahmins and the rural population in some places reject it; but among the residents of hilly districts and towns its consumption is only limited by the paucity of the supply and the cost of the article. In the North-west provinces, Hyderabad, Mysore, and Coorg, more than half the population are permitted by their religion to consume fish. In Oudh the majority can do so; in Sindh, nearly all except the Brahmins; in Bombay, by far the largest proportion of the people; in South Canara, 89 per cent.; in Madras, the majority, the exceptions being Brahmins, goldsmiths, high-caste Sudras, the followers of Siva, Jains, etc.; in Orissa, more than half the people; in Bengal proper, from 90 to 95 per cent.; in Assam and Chittagong, almost the entire population; and in Burmah, in the form of *ngapee*, its use is universal.

The sea-board of India and Burmah extends for about 4,611 miles, and the seas are much more abundantly stocked with fish than are those of Europe. The dried and salted fish sold in the different districts on the west or Malabar coast of Madras is from £17,000 to £18,000 in value.

Wherever any quantity of water is present in the East, there we are almost certain to find fishes, and this from the sea level to nearly the summits of the highest mountains. As soon as young fish are moving about, or shortly after the monsoons have set in, men, women and children obtain myriads of fry from paddy fields and every sheltered spot to which they have retired for shelter and security.

In Asia nearly every kind of fish that swims either in salt or fresh water is greedily eaten by most natives; and as many as 200 or 300 kinds of dried fish and different preparations of them are to be found in the bazaars. Owing to the high price of salt, which is a Government monopoly, the cured fish have a very unpleasant odour and flavour, for very often they are merely rubbed with saline earth. The fish most in repute among Europeans are the seer (*Cybium commersonii*), the pomfrets (*Stromateus niger* and *S. argenteus*), and the mullets. The seer is sold in cutlets, like salmon in Europe, and is in some respects perhaps superior to salmon, more especially as regards digestibility. Hilsah (*Clupea ilasah*) is a delicious fish, either boiled, baked, or fried. When cured with tamarinds it forms a good substitute for herrings.

Pomfrets are also prepared in this way, and much esteemed as a breakfast relish. The fish are cut in transverse slices, and preserved in kegs with the acid pulp of the tamarind fruit.

Burtah, the salted and spiced flesh of the suleah fish (*Polynemus sele*) is a piquant relish well known at the breakfast tables of Bengal.

The dried sounds or swimming-bladders of many fishes are largely shipped to China and other parts under the name of "fish maws," singally and sozille; *Polynemus plebeius* and *P. indicus* seem to furnish the greater portion. These fish are caught of a great size and sold in the Calcutta bazaar during the cold season.

The larger part of the salted fish imported by the Burmese and Arabs was formerly re-shipped, chiefly to Ceylon, 3,000,000 to 5,000,000 lbs., but much is now used at home. The following figures give the Indian trade of the last few years ending 1st April, in pounds weight.

	Imports. lbs.		Exports. lbs.
1876	3,615,373	......	3,569,150
1877	3,556,508	......	5,222,889
1878	5,105,957	......	4,633,987
1879	6,710,842	......	2,817,580
1880	10,157,408	......	1,810,850
1881	7,125,927	......	3,335,281
1882	12,811,805	......	4,324,769
1883	10,621,929	......	4,681,881
1884	11,660,485	......	7,890,854

Of the imports in the last-named year, 5½ million pounds came from the Straits Settlements.

The following figures show the trade in fish-maws, shark's fins, singally and sozelle, all species of isinglass or fish glue.

				Imports. lbs.		Exports. lbs.
1877	...	...	...	966,658	......	483,150
1878	...	...	...	1,082,681	......	411,895
1879	...	...	...	1,238,728	......	438,849
1880	...	...	...	1,145,968	......	523,658
1881	...	...	...	979,014	......	569,843
1882	...	...	...	972,912	......	447,340
1883	...	...	...	1,080,470	......	494,100
1884	...	...	...	1,126,372	......	1,612,014

The exports are made principally to Hong Kong and Singapore, and some to Great Britain.

There is a considerable local trade in salted fish between the ports in the Bombay Presidency, and a good deal is imported into the province from Diu, Goa, and Katheawar. From Madras also some is sent to Burmah and there is a large local trade in that province, much of it being what is known as *gnapee*, fish in the form of paste, generally used as a condiment with their rice by the Burmese.

The imports of salted fish into India in 1883-84, 11,660,485 lbs., were valued at £105,000. The fish brought from Mekran and Sonmiani is salted whole and is consumed in Western India.

The exports of salted fish from India by land in 1883-4 were 61,240 cwt., value £93,813, almost all to Upper Burmah, the Northern Shan States, Karennee and Siam. It is principally imported from the Straits Settlements. Ngapee was also exported to those countries to the extent of 282,951 cwt., value £92,141.

Ceylon imported in 1879 74,322 cwt. of salted and dried fish. The Cape Colony exported in that year four million pounds of cured fish, principally to Mauritius.

In the Maldive Islands the flesh of the bonito (*Thynnus pelamys*) is thus prepared. The backbone is removed and the fish laid in the shade and occasionally sprinkled with sea-water. After a certain period has elapsed, the flesh is wrapped up in cocoa-palm leaves and buried in the sand, where it becomes hard. Fish thus prepared is known in Ceylon and perhaps all over India by the name of "cummelmums." The pieces of fish, as brought to market, have a horny hardness, and are rasped or grated on rice to render it savoury.

One of the most exquisite of the Indian fresh-water fish is the Gourami (*Osphromenus olfax*) a native of Cochin China and the Eastern islands. It has been introduced into Penang, Malacca, Mauritius, Reunion, Cape of Good Hope, Australia and Cayenne, but has not yet been successfully acclimatised in Europe. It somewhat resembles a carp and is covered like that fish with large round scales. It is not less remarkable for its size than for its excellent flavour, being usually larger than a turbot and sometimes attaining twenty to fifty pounds weight.

Its flesh is delicious. Commerson tells us that he never ate anything more exquisite in the way of fish, whether of the sea or of the fresh water. He adds that the Dutch in Batavia rear these fishes in large earthen vessels, renewing the water every day and feeding them on nothing but fresh-water plants. It is served in the East at the tables of the most opulent and sumptuous, and at St. Denis, Reunion, a young gourami will sell for 15s. or 16s.

West Indies.—In Guadaloupe they have several river fish which are esteemed, among others the Dormeur (*Philypirus dormitator*), a sluggish fish with few scales, its flesh is white and delicate, and transparent when young. It attains a weight of six or eight pounds.

The Loche (*Eleotris guavina*) has a white, fine and delicate flesh, but is rather inferior to the Dormeur. It is only eaten fried, but like most of the river-fish has many bones.

The Pancou (*Gobius martinicus*) has white flesh, with somewhat of the flavour of the eel, and resembles that of the Loche, but is more firm and less delicate, and one of the smallest of the fishes.

The Tetard (*Eleotris gyrinus*) is, of all the river-fish, that of which the flesh is most esteemed and sought after. The liver is large, and when cooked, has a slight perfume of orange flowers.

The Sarde (*Pagellus calamus*) is a large fish which somewhat resembles a mullet, and will weigh six to eight pounds.

The West Indies require large supplies of cured fish for the negro population. In 1880 the imports into Jamaica were,—dried or salted fish, 11,500,000 lbs.; pickled fish, 50,000 barrels; besides 100,000 lbs. of smoked fish.

Barbados in 1879 imported 90,574 cwt. of dried fish; Trinidad, 6,500,000 lbs. of dried, and 1,200 barrels. of pickled fish; British Guiana 81,832 cwt. of dried fish.

In Honduras two-thirds of the population, numbering 24,000 souls, live on fish, fresh or salted. Around Cuba about 125,000 cwt. of fish are taken annually, and at Porto Rico 9,000 cwt.

The import of fish into Jamaica in 1880 was to the following amount, at invoice value:—

Saltfish	...	...	...	...	...	£106,336
Herrings	...	...	...	...	...	28,968
Mackerel	...	...	...	...	...	20,309
Shad	...	...	...	...	...	2,729
Salmon	...	...	...	...	...	1,800
						£160,142

and other foreign fish to about £40,000. But there is a very fair supply of fresh fish and turtle brought into the markets by the native fishermen. The approximate value of the coast fishery of Jamaica is about £30,000.

The callipeva, or Jamaica salmon (*Mugel liza*) as it has been called from its appearance, is classed with the mullets, and generally held to be the finest fish of the island. It ranks among three specially Jamaican dainties, the other two being the ringtail pigeon and the mountain or black land-crab. Almost all writers on Jamaica have united in praising the variety, abundance and superior quality of its sea and river fish.

Sharks as Food.—Sharks are more commonly eaten as human food than is generally supposed. In parts of India their flesh is much valued and said to be very palatable and nutritious. By seamen they are often eaten as a change of food on board ship.

The picked or common dog-fish (*Acanthias vulgaris; Squalus acanthias*), if salted and dried, affords very fair food. At Folkestone it is known as "Folkestone beef." In the west of Cornwall the flesh of the rough-horned or lesser spotted dog-fish (*Scyllium catulus*) is used sometimes to make what is called "Morghi" soup.

The flesh of the picked dog-fish is also sometimes eaten in the northern countries fresh, but must be skinned before being cooked. It is also dried like split stock fish for consumption in Norway as well as for export to Sweden, where it is greatly appreciated. The fishermen on the coasts of France salt the flesh of *Squalus caniculata* and *S. galeus* for winter use.

At Morecambe Bay the fishermen contrive to sell all the dog-fish they can catch, which are sent to Blackburn and Preston for food, and are known as "Darwen salmon." It is stated that the people of these two towns like them much, and the fishermen obtain as high a price for them as for skate.

In Norway the flesh of the Greenland shark (*Scymnus borealis*) is occasionally used for human food, being cut up into long strips and dried in the open air or buried in the ground until partially decomposed, when it is taken up and prepared in a peculiar manner, so as to become edible. It requires, however, an Arctic stomach to digest it.

Bosman tells us that the negroes eat sharks on the Gold Coast and to make their flesh tender they "lay them a rotting and stinking for seven or eight days after which they are greedily eaten as a delicacy."

Sharks of various species are plentiful about New Zealand. They are taken in thousands by the Maories and dried on poles for winter use. The species most valued is the "smooth hound" (*Mustelus antarcticus*), which is the only shark that is properly edible, as it subsists on shell fish and crabs, and has clean feeding habits. Sharks are eaten in Japan.

There is a large trade carried on from India to China in the fins of sharks and fish-maws, which are considered by the Celestials as a great food delicacy From Bombay about 5,000 cwts. are annually shipped, and from Madras 250 to 300 cwts. The shipments from India of sharks' fins, fish-maws, and other species of fish isinglass have been already given. Sharks' fins are also sent from Akyab, Sumatra, Manilla, Borneo and the Sandwich Islands. There are two qualities, the white and the black fins, the former being the dorsal fins which are uniformly light-coloured on both sides and are reputed to yield more gelatine; the black are the pectoral, ventral and anal fins, which being less esteemed sell for a lower price. The species of sharks taken in the Indian seas and from which the fins are obtained are chiefly *Rhyncobatis pectina*, *R. lævis* and *Galiocorda tigrina*. The flesh of these sharks is also cut off in long strips and salted for food by the natives.

We have a few more miscellaneous fish to speak of.

On the Atlantic coasts of the United States the flesh of the sword-fish (*Xiphias gladius*, Lin.) is eaten, both fresh and salted. Before being pickled the flesh is cut into slices, and it is said to keep good for a year; in Massachussetts several hundred barrels are put up annually. The flesh is much esteemed in the Mediterranean; it is of a dull red colour, but very palatable, and a sword-fish steak makes an excellent substitute for a salmon cutlet.

Oulachan.—The ulikon or oulachan (*Thaleichthys pacificus*, Gerard). This has long been an ichthyological curiosity, and has been noticed by almost every traveller who has visited the coasts of British Columbia and

South Alaska. It is a small silvery fish, averaging about fourteen inches long, and in general appearance much resembling a smelt. They are the fattest of all known fish. Dried they serve as torches; when a light is needed, the tail is touched with a match and they will burn with a bright light for some time. No description can give an adequate idea of their numbers when ascending the rivers from the sea. The water is literally alive with them and appears to be boiling. Many native tribes come to these fisheries, which begin about the third week in March. The first fish is addressed as a chief; apologies are made to him by the Indians for the necessity of destroying his kindred for the supply of their own wants; a feast is given with appropriate speeches, songs and dances in his honour, and after that the fishing goes on. The fish are caught in wicker baskets, and are dried or smoked as much as their oily nature will allow. The fishery lasts a fortnight or three weeks, and supplies many hundred aborigines with food for a considerable period.

They enter the Fraser river in millions about the first of May. They are delicious when fresh, smoked or salted, and their oil is considered superior to cod-liver or any other fish oil known. It is of a whitish tint, about the consistency of thin lard, and is a staple food and article of barter between the Indians of the coast and the interior tribes. The fish are taken in purse nets, frequently a canoe load at a single haul, and are piled in heaps on the shore. They are then placed in bins made of plank and having sheet iron bottoms holding from three to five barrels, and are boiled in water about four hours. The concoction is then strained through baskets made from willow roots, and the oil is run into red cedar boxes of about fifteen gallons capacity each. When the run of fish is good each tribe will put up about twenty boxes.

The surf smelt is almost as numerous as the oulachan, and about the same size, eight inches long. It is an excellent table fish. The very common smaller smelt is prized at table, but the flesh is softer than that of the surf smelt and oulachan. Anchovies are only second to the oulachans in abundance, and may be taken with great ease during the autumn.

Carp.—The family of the Cyprinidæ is so large that it embraces nearly half of all the fishes of Europe. It consists of more than fifty genera; but there are not more than a dozen of any real importance.

The carp may be considered the head of this large family. Dr. Horach possesses in Bohemia carp ponds covering more than 100 hectares (about 250 acres). He finds that between April and September the fish increase 10 per cent. in weight.

The carp, after the *Salmo hucho,* is one of the largest producers of flesh, for it is gluttonous and feeds on everything, and is a great purifier of the waters. Its colour varies with age, season, and the chemical composition of the water in which it lives.

The weight of the carp from Upper and North Lusatia, represented at Cottbus by their breeders, is 8,000 to 10,000 cwt., and every year on the first Monday of the Cottbus fall market, there is a so-called carp exchange for selling the fish, which are mostly sent to Berlin by water. The carp in beer is a favourite dish there, and about 500,000 lbs. are annually consumed in that city.

Recently three species of carp have been introduced into the United States, the mirror carp, the scale carp, and the leather carp.

In a recent communication Professor Baird expresses great faith in the future of this new fish. He is satisfied that within ten years it will constitute a very prominent portion of the animal food of the North American continent. Although scarcely known in the United States, and but little more, as an article of extended application, in England and France, the carp is in Germany and Austria cultivated to the highest degree, so as to constitute a notable article of the market supply.

The carp will have 100,000 eggs per pound weight of

the female.   Mr. Niklas (p. 17 of his " Treatise on Fish
Ponds ") confirms this, for he found 650,000 eggs in a
carp of $5\frac{1}{2}$ lbs. weight.

The carp is much esteemed in France; it is seldom
obtained there heavier than 15 lbs., but on the Oder
they have been caught weighing 60 lbs.   On draining
the marshes of that river, the carp were found in such
quantities that they employed them to fatten pigs.   The
carp of the Saone in its fifth or sixth year is reported
to be excellent eating, while that of the Loire living in
clear and running waters is vile.

The carp is said by Rondolet to have been brought
into Europe from Persia, and introduced into Italy by
Lucullus.   It was introduced into England by Marechal
in 1514, in Denmark by Oke in 1560, and into France
it is mentioned as early as 1312.

The tomcod (*Gadus gracilis*, Tilesius; *Microgadus proxi-
mus*, Guard.), serve the natives of Alaska for food, either
boiled or in the frozen state.   They are preserved by
removing the intestines and drying in large bunches
strung on seal line, or by throwing them as they are
caught in seines, and preserved frozen, in great heaps
upon staging erected for the purpose.   They are among
the most palatable of the many fish found in those seas,
and the number preserved is so great as to be almost
incalculable

The most abundant of the fresh-water fish in Finland
is the lavaret argente (*Coregonus lavaretus*, Lin.), which
salted constitutes the principal food of the people in the
interior.   The roe is sold largely at the markets of Hel-
singfors and other principal towns, and is considered a
food delicacy.

Trout.—The common trout (*Salmo fario*, Lin.), a well-
known fresh water fish of the rivers and lakes of Europe,
is an excellent fish for the table.   They are finest in
flavour from the end of May till the end of September.
The variations of its tints and spots, from golden yellow
to crimson and greenish black, are almost infinite, and
depend in a great measure on the nature of its food, for

the colours are always the most brilliant in those fish that feed on the water shrimp ; and these are also the most highly prized for the table. The flesh of the gray trout (*Salmo ferox*) is very inferior in quality to this species. The lake trout (*Salmo lacustris*, Lin.) and the Swiss charr (*S. umbla*, Lin.) are both esteemed fish of the lakes of Switzerland.

The bull trout (*Salmo esox*), according to Mr. Buckland, are not such good eating as the salmon proper ; their flesh is white and not so tasteful as that of the salmon. The reason of this is as yet unexplained. In the local markets in Wales the price is slightly less per pound for bull trout than for salmon, but the great market for them is in France. The fish hawkers sometimes clip the round tail of the bull trout into a square shape, and sell the fish for salmon. The bull trout of the Cognet sometimes attains a considerable size ; one was caught in 1878 which weighed 22½ lbs.

The delicate flavour of the brook trout or American charr (*Salmo [Salvelinus] fontinalis*, Mitchell), is known to all. As Aldrovandus quaintly expresses it, " The salmon, the grayling, and the trout, all fish that live in clear and sharp streams, are made by their mother Nature, of such exact shape and pleasant colours purposely to invite us to joy and contentedness in feasting with her." St. Ambrose of old called the grayling the " flower fish."

Salmon.—Formerly the salmon of the Tweed was all pickled and salted, after being boiled, and sent to London under the name of Newcastle salmon. Within the memory of some old people, salted salmon formed a material article of food in the farmhouses of the Vale of Tweed, insomuch that indoor servants often bargained that they should not be obliged to take more than two meals of salmon weekly. It could then be bought fresh at 2s. per stone, now it is usually that price per pound.

The average value of *Salmo salar* sold in London may be stated at £250,000. In 1869 32,450 boxes of

120 lbs. were sold in Billingsgate Market.   In 1870 and 1881 the supplies were drawn from the following sources:—

	1870.		1881.
Scotch	20,648	......	23,905
Irish	9,211	......	10,633
Dutch	626	......	638
Norwegian	852	......	573
English and Welsh	3,120	......	3,709
	34,457		39,458

In 1871 35,275 boxes, weighing 1,7 64 tons, were disposed of at Billingsgate, and besides this some 14,000 boxes were sold in the Midland to wns and other places.

In 1879 24,422 boxes of salmon were received at Billingsgate, in 1880 31,471 boxes.

ARRIVALS OF SALMON IN LONDON.

In Boxes, averaging 2 cwt.

	1881.	1882.	1883.	1884.
Scotch	23,817	22,968	34,506	27,219
Irish	10,633	4,720	9,033	5,979
English	1,875	2,186	2,261	1,591
Berwick	1,692	1,412	2,263	1,774
Norway	466	167	345	426
Sweden	107	52	50	531
Dutch	370	1,402	2,026	1,497
	38,960	32,907	50,484	39,017

The average annual value of the salmon caught in the Severn in the last ten years was over £12,000; 19,500 fish were taken in 1881, 15,500 in 1882, and 30,000 in 1883, weighing 174 tons.

In the district of the Tyne the take of salmon has been as follows :—

	No.				No.
1870	36,450		1877		41,300
1871	120,600		1878		48,150
1872	129,100		1879		20,670
1873	86,792		1880		45,688
1874	21,746		1881		45,946
1875	23,290		1882		41,110
1876	24,840		1883		32,566

About 250,000 salmon, weighing in all 1,418,000 lbs., were taken in England and Wales in 1883, against 1,000,000 lbs. weight caught in 1882. These figures do not, however, represent the aggregate catch in the whole of the salmon rivers.

The quantity of salmon from the Irish fisheries sent off in 1870 was as follows, to—

	Boxes.	Value.
Nottingham	250	£1,750
Wolverhampton	300	2,100
Bradford	800	5,600
Sheffield	800	5,600
Leeds	1,000	7,000
Birmingham	2,000	14,000
Manchester	3,500	24,500
Liverpool	2,138	14,966
London	9,211	73,688
	19,899	149,204

Each box then weighed on the average 120 lbs, and was priced at 1s. 2d. per lb.

The salmon sent to England from Ireland in 1878 was 44,637½ boxes, computed at 1s. 3d. per lb., value delivered £418,476. The proportion was, to London 4,378 boxes, to Nottingham 2,793, Bradford 3,679, Manchester 6,555, Sheffield 4,641, Wolverhampton 3,110, Leeds 4,000½, Liverpool 8,761 boxes, Birmingham 6,720. In 1877 the total quantity sent from Ireland was rather larger, namely, 47,934 boxes.

Besides the above shipments, 2,880 boxes were sold in

the Dublin market, and no doubt much also in other large towns, and the aggregate value may be set down at nearly £200,000. In 1880, 9,660 boxes were sent to London.

Salmon Fisheries of Canada.—The salmon and trout fisheries have greatly increased under careful cultivation. Many salmon ladders have been built, and thousands of ova have been hatched artificially and distributed through the Dominion. In streams that till lately were devoid of salmon these fish are now to be found in abundance. The captures were in 1872:—

Nova Scotia	...	6,690 barrels, valued at	144,195 dols.
Quebec ...	...	4,153 ,,	,,	65,830 ,,
New Brunswick...	8.291 ,,	,,	210,386 ,,
Ontario ...	...	7.586 ,,	,,	60,688 ,,
Total	...	26,720 ,,	,,	481,099 ,,

The Californian salmon, the *Onchorhynchus quinnat,* (*Salmo quinnat,* Rich) is a handsome fish, with silvery scales and a deeper body and less delicate look than the salmon of Europe; but the quality of the flesh is quite equal to the latter.

From the annual report of the Oregon Board of Trade we learn that the salmon catch of the spring and summer of 1880 yielded 530,000 cases. In 1875 a catch of 231,500 cases was considered enormous; 1877 yielded 400,000 cases, and 1879 as many as 435,000 cases. This rapid increase shows the vast extent and financial value of the Oregon salmon fisheries. Of the half million and more cases packed in 1880, 211,522 cases were sent to San Francisco, and 239,241 cases shipped direct to Great Britain.

The fisheries of British Columbia are among the richest in the world. They are probably only equalled by those on the eastern coast of Canada. The most important fish is the salmon, of which there are six species or varieties. Those of Fraser river are justly famous; they make their way up the river for 1,000 miles. The silver salmon begin to arrive in March or early in April, and last till the end of June. Their average weight is from four to twenty-five pounds, but they have been caught weighing over seventy. The second kind are caught from June to August and are considered the finest. Their average size is only five to six pounds. The third coming in August, and continuing till winter, average seven pounds and are an excellent fish. The noan, or humpback salmon, comes every second year, lasting from August till winter, weighing from six to fourteen pounds.

The hookbill arrives in September and remains till winter, weighing from twelve to fifteen and even forty-five pounds. Salmon is sold in the capital, Victoria, at 3d. to 4d. per pound and there seems to be no limit to the catch. The salmon fisheries in the province now employ about 5,000 men during the season.

It is while making their annual pilgrimage from the sea that the salmon are caught, generally near the entrance to the streams, though often many miles inland, and prepared for market. The salmon has always been one of the most important of the various forms of food used by the Indians of the Pacific coast, who annually gather along the streams and catch thousands of them, drying them in the sun for winter use. Long ago the Hudson's Bay Company began salting them for its own use, and of late years many canning factories have been established at favourable points, where thousands of cans are prepared for market annually.

The salmon packed on the Columbia river (American section), in 1883, was 629,438 cases, from the Californian and Alaska fisheries 210,978 cases, and from British Columbia 196,292 cases, making a total for the Pacific coast of 1,036,708 cases of four dozen pound cans each.

Preserved Salmon is conspicuously the poor man's luxury, and with the capacity of purchase by the lower classes in England and on the Continent of Europe, the rise or fall of the market must materially depend.

The first cargo of canned salmon of the catch of 1880, from the Columbia River, when cleared from Portland, Oregon, for Liverpool, England, comprised 56,756 cases, each containing four dozen one pound cans, or their equivalent. The gross weight was over 1,400 tons. Two other ships followed soon after, both taking nearly full cargoes. Large consignments were also received at San Francisco, for reshipment to England, Australia, and New York. The steamer Oregon, from Portland, June 25th, brought 22,546 cases, the largest invoice of the season if not the largest single shipment ever made to San Francisco from the Columbia River.

The business has grown rapidly, until now salmon-packing is the largest industry, save wheat-growing, in the north west, and more salmon is put up on the Columbia river than in all other localities in the world. In the year 1881, the quantity packed consisted of 540,000 cases at 5 dollars, against 4,000 cases in 1866 at 16 dollars. Between Cape Disappointment and the Cascades there are thirty-five canning establishments and more than a dozen fishing stations. The greater part of the indoor work is done by Chinamen, of whom about 4,000 are employed on the river.

The Californian salmon is one of the largest of this family. Its average weight in the Sacramento River is twenty pounds, while in overgrown individuals it is as high as 100 pounds. Its flavour when fresh, and properly cooked, is scarcely inferior to that of the Atlantic coast salmon, (*Salmo salar*), and in the markets of California and as far eastward as New York, it is sought as a luxury and commands a high price. Prepared in cans it finds a wide market throughout the United States and Australia. In the season of 1875, 13,000,000 lbs. were put up at the different canning establishments on the Columbia river, worth on the average 6d. per pound.

In 1876, twenty million pounds of salmon were exported. The catch of salmon in the rivers Sacramento and San Joachim in the year ending, August, 1879, was 4,432,250 lbs. The river Columbia furnishes 45 million pounds annually. Astoria, in Oregon, is the centre for canning, there being seven establishments there. The principal one, that of Mr. Booth, sends away 2½ million pounds annually. There are over forty establishments in all on the Pacific coast, and for 100 days in the year they work night and day in putting up fish. The principal catch is in June. It is estimated that in the province of Alaska alone, 12 million salmon are taken yearly; two million are dried annually in the river Yukon, this fish forming the chief food of the Indians.

The spring salmon, as it is termed, is the principal kind used on the Pacific coast for canning, as it is the best of the family; its flesh being rich and delicate, and by many considered far superior in flavour to any of the European varieties. This species averages ordinarily from 15 to 40 lbs. in weight, and is only valued at 1s. the fish when sold in the market fresh. A person can stand at any of the cataracts above the river Columbia, and with a scoop net capture from thirty to fifty in an hour, as they crowd each other, while preparing for a leap. They are also speared by the Indians and netted. In about four months, four to five million pounds weight of salmon will be taken.

The fish are either salted, sent to the smoke-house, or prepared for canning. This latter process is now the means generally adopted for exportation, and is the most successful, as the packages are of convenient size, portable and sold at such a price as to enable even the foreign labouring classes to indulge in the luxury of fresh or spiced salmon on festal occasions.

To prepare the fish for canning they are first cleansed in the most thorough manner, and cut into slices of one or two pounds, according to the size needed. These pieces are then put into a can of the required size, and with them is placed some spice to flavour them. They are then covered up, except a small hole in the top of the can to allow steam to escape, placed in a boiler filled with boiling salt water and allowed to remain there a specific time; they are then taken out and boiled for half-an-hour in fresh water; the cans are then soldered air-tight, and are ready for shipment. Some persons boil the can in three waters, but two is the usual number. This canned fish is now eagerly sought for in the principal markets of Europe and Asia for its excellent flavour. A large quantity is also smoked and barrelled, but this is used at home, except a small portion which is shipped to the Sandwich Islands.

Salmon canning is one of the most valuable industries of British Columbia, and there seems to be no limit to its extension. In 1876 there were only three canning establishments, which put out 8,300 cases, each containing four dozen one pound tins. In 1883 there were thirty-one canneries, with an out-put of probably 320,000 cases, or 15,360,000 lbs.

The king salmon (*Onchorhynchus orientalis*, Pallas), is the chowicpee of the Russians and the largest and finest of the Alaska salmon, reaching a weight of sixty to ninety pounds. It is dried for winter use by the natives All dried fish is called Ukali, or Yookalee, by the Russians. This is prepared by cutting the fish in three slices, after removing the head, leaving the backbone in the middle slice, and all three connected by the tail. Two or three dry chowicpee ukali will weigh at least fifty pounds, and one is accounted sufficient for a day's food for six men. The more northern the ground where the fish are taken, the finer their flavour; and the chowicpee of the Yukon were held in such esteem that several hogsheads were annually salted for the Emperor's table by the Russians.

The salmon fishery of Newfoundland is abundant, but of secondary importance to the cod fishery. The method of taking the fish is generally in nets. So plentiful is the supply of fresh salmon during the season in St. John's, that it is often sold at 2d. to 3d. the pound. Salmon abound in many of the rivers, and the innumerable streams and lakes teem with trout, which are frequently of large size, five or six pounds.

About 3,000 tierces and barrels of salted salmon are shipped annually, chiefly to the States and the United

Kingdom, and preserved salmon to the value of £400 or £500. Six or seven hundred barrels of trout are also sent away to Spain and the United States, and 400 to 500 kegs of cod's tongues and sounds, 1,300 barrels of mackerel and 700 cwt. of halibut.

The fishing of salmon in the Dutch rivers is large. In 1874, 77,070 fish were caught at Krelingen, a village in the neighbourhood of Rotterdam, which is the centre of the trade. There were sold in 1882, 55,079 fish.

In 1877 the produce of the salmon fishery in Norway was 905,454 pounds. It is exported almost exclusively to England fresh, preserved in ice. The smoked salmon is equally esteemed; it is consumed for the most part in Norway, but a certain quantity is exported to Denmark and Germany. The price has gone up considerably; two years ago a pound of fresh salmon was rarely worth more than 3d. or 4d., while now it brings from 6d. to 7d.

The preparation of salmon in oil commenced in Sweden in 1864, and is carried on for about three months of the year. The quantity put up by one firm in 1877 was 29,140 boxes or tins, sold at 1s. 3d. per box.

Enormous quantities of salmon are caught in the Petchora, Mezene, Dwina, Onega, Vazoukha and other affluents of the White Sea. It is rarely smoked, but generally salted. The best is that of the Onega and the Dwina.

Halibut.—On the coast of Mommane very many halibut (*Hippoglossus maximus*) are taken, and salted down for consumption in the interior.

Halibut are found in great numbers on the Pacific coast of North America, especially off the west coast of Queen Charlotte Island, where they are frequently taken upwards of 100 pounds in weight, and often twice that size. The Indians of that region catch and dry them for food.

Halibut in America are to some extent salted (especially the heads), some parts are smoked (principally the backs and the bellies). The cheeks are considered a delicacy. Salted halibut heads are sold at 20s. to 26s. per

barrel. The white naped halibut are worth 100 per
cent. more than the black naped.

In London this fish is occasionally seen in the markets
in the months of March and April; it is sold in slices at
a low price by the pound. The Jews are very fond of
it. The flesh, though white and firm, is dry, and the
muscular fibre coarse; the head and fins are the best
parts.

United States Fisheries.—The export of American
fishery products is comparatively small, owing to the
fact that the demand for home consumption is really
greater than the supply, and is constantly on the increase.
In 1880 the total value of exported fish products
amounted to £1,550,000 of which England received about
half, consisting chiefly of canned preparations. In 1882,
according to the returns of the census, the value of the
fisheries of the sea, the great rivers, and the lakes of the
United States was placed at $43,046,053, and that of
those of the minor inland waters at $1,500,000; in all
$44,546,053. These values were estimated upon the basis
of the prices of the products received by the producers,
but if average wholesale prices had been considered, the
value would have been much greater. In 1882, the yield
of the fisheries was much greater than in 1880, and prices
both at first hand and at wholesale were higher, so that
a fair estimate at wholesale market prices would place
the value of the exports at that time rather above than
below the sum of £2,000,000.

The practice of setting aside the surplus of the city
fish markets in seasons of plenty to meet the demand
when fish are scarce or entirely out of season, has led
to the establishment in New York of enormous re-
frigerators, or buildings for "cold storage," in which
tons of fresh fish are securely locked up in ice and kept
for months. The magnitude of this cold storage business and its relative novelty have attracted to it no little
popular attention.

Less generally known, but probably of greater financial and economic importance, is the business that has

grown up there in drying, pickling, and smoking fish. For the most part the city cured fish are taken by fishermen under contract, and roughly salted at sea. They are mainly cod, mackerel, and salmon. Other establishments are directly engaged in sea and shore fishing. One firm, which cures from 15,000 to 40,000 pounds of fish a week, makes a speciality of smoked shad and sturgeon. The sturgeon are taken in drift nets off the coasts of Florida and Georgia. The nets are 100 fathoms long and 20 fathoms deep, the sturgeon often weighing from 300 to 500 pounds each. Occasionally the capture of a large shark or alligator gives serious and unprofitable diversity to the work of the fishermen. When caught the sturgeon are cleaned, the back bone is cut out, and the sides packed in ice and sent to Savannah. There the fish is packed in fresh ice and shipped by steamer to New York. The sides are cut in slices, pickled in brine for four hours, dried, and smoked. The drying takes about six hours and the smoking fourteen hours. The smoke is made from hickory wood and cedar sawdust, and the smoking room is hot enough to thoroughly cook the fish. Other fish are smoked in substantially the same way. The sturgeon roe is immediately treated to successive washings, passing each time through sieves to cleanse it thoroughly, and is then packed in salt. The same parties have sturgeon fisheries in Delaware, and eel fisheries there and in New Jersey. The best and fattest eels are said to come from the mouth of the Shrewsbury River. The eels are thoroughly scrubbed to remove the slime, and either smoked or put up in jelly. Herrings are smoked and also put up in kits in pickle. Considerable quantities of smelts from the coast of Massachusetts are smoked, also many lake whitefish, which are accounted particularly fine in flavour. Mackerel smoked round when fresh— Boston smoked—is becoming a popular preparation. All the fish to be smoked are brought to the city fresh, packed in ice, except salmon, which during part of the year is pickled.

The home and foreign demand for fish cured in New York is large and rapidly increasing. The industry promises to become very great.

The pompano (*Trachynotus carolinensis*), a member of the mackerel family, is the champion of the sub-tropical waters, and so esteemed as a delicacy that it fetches as high as 4s. a pound in New York. There sre several other species, as *T. ovatus, T. glaucus,* &c.

Another much hunted fish is the Spanish mackerel (*Cybium maculatum*), which is fat, delicate and savoury.

In North America the losh (*Lota maculata*) grows to a very large size, sometimes weighing sixty pounds, and forms an acceptable dish in the absence of the white fish of the lakes, which are usually also fat and excellent eating. The flesh of the losh is comparatively hard and dry, and the fish are chiefly valued for their livers and roe. The liver is of a triangular shape, weighing a pound or two, and is an extremely rich and delicate morsel when broiled. It affords a pint or so of sweet rich oil, used by the Russians in cooking, and which doubtless might be employed instead of cod liver oil.

White Fish and other Lake Fish.—No more delicious repast can be offered than a fine Mackinaw trout, caught from the depths of his cool retreat; but when pickled and packed for future market, much of the flavour is lost, or so incorporated with the brine, that they lose caste in comparison with their smaller and more numerous rivals the white fish. These fish range in weight from three to six pounds, and in some rare instances attain treble that weight. In size and general outline, they resemble the eastern shad, but upon close examination prove more symmetrical and striking.

It would be useless to give the names of all the prominent kinds caught in the American lakes, but among the different varieties of trout, maskalonge, siscowet, white fish, bass, perch, cat fish, and sturgeon, enough are found to hold strong competition with the best taken along the Atlantic. There are innumerable species of small fish to be found in the lakes which are highly prized, but for extensive packing and profitable investment as an article of traffic, white fish stand conspicuous.

The excellence of the white fish as an article of food is described by all travellers in the Northern regions of America, where it forms the staple diet of the Indians and trappers during a large part of the year. It is a plump-bodied fish, free from small bones, with firm, delicately flavoured flesh in large white flakes. As an article of food it is highly nutritious; but at the same time free from the rich oil which renders the salmon so cloying to the appetite if constantly used as food. The size of the full grown fish is pretty uniform if caught in the same locality; but in some places they reach a weight of 20 lbs., and even 40 lbs., while in others the average is about 2 lbs. weight, the difference being no doubt due to the paucity or abundance of their favourite food, which consists of small crustaceans and shell fish. They grow rapidly and are very fertile, the number of eggs deposited by the female being about 10,000 for every pound weight of fish. They have the great advantage of being in season and procurable at all times of the year, although they have regular migrations from the shallows to the deeper waters of the lakes for the purpose of spawning.

One of the most valuable fish of Canada is this white fish (*Coregonus albus*), a species of salmon common to most of the lakes in the North-West and called by the Indians "attehawmeg." It is esteemed the prince of fresh-water fish, and affords the staple food of thousands in the remoter parts of the country; it varies in size, and is caught principally in the autumn, when it is spawning, and is consequently in its worst condition. These fish are hung up in bunches of a dozen, by means of sticks passed through the tails, and dried and frozen; when sufficiently solid they are brought down and stored. The value of these fish annually cured on the American and Canadian lakes has been estimated at about £200,000, besides the larger amount consumed fresh. The winter supply is caught with nets in the shallow water on some of the lakes, between October and November. This practice is injurious and a reduced capture has ensued.

An ice factory in New Orleans has introduced a new way of shipping fish, particularly red snappers. · They are frozen in cakes of ice, or rather cakes of ice are frozen around the fish, and in this condition they are forwarded to all sections of the country.

Flying Fish.—There is a sea fish which must not be passed over without notice, and that is the flying-fish (*Exocetus volitans*). Of this there are three species or varieties met with in the North Atlantic, the large double-winged, the smaller double-winged, and the single winged, but there would seem to be other varieties.

In the ocean near the frontier island of Barbados they are very plentiful, and are a source of profit to the negro fishermen, who take them with the cast net; they are afterwards baked in a plantain leaf and sold to the ships in harbour. Some of these fish are fourteen inches in length. They have been likened to the herring, but except in size there is not much resemblance.

The species *Exocetus Robertii* is that caught in large numbers about the island of Barbados from the 1st of November to the end of July by about 250 boats, manned by three or five men. In a few hours they will get fifty or sixty fish, with which they will return; these are sold at about 1d. each, but often if the fish are abundant they will not fetch more than 2s. the thousand, and often they are only useful for manure. In 1880 they were selling at 2d. the 100. The best time is from March to May, when the fish are fat and succulent, and they are then called gulf fish. These fish are occasionally preserved in oil or vinegar to be sent to other islands, and it is strange that a larger export trade is not carried on.

Zanzibar has a large import trade of dry and salt fish, principally shark and seer fish. The import of cured fish averages in annual value £30,000, representing about 500 tons, the greater part of which comes to the capital.

There is a fish custom-house at Zanzibar, and a regular salt fish market, where the fish is sold wholesale, fetching on an average 12s. per cwt. It is afterwards retailed to the working population at about 2d. per lb. Dried fish is the staple animal food of the poor and labouring population there, both free and slave ; it is either grilled or cooked with a little roughly prepared curry, and served as a relish with the evening meal of rice, or more commonly meal porridge, in every hut and cottage, two or three ounces sufficing for each person. Any other description of animal food is rarely within the means of natives of the labouring classes, except in the case of those residing on the coast, who at times can procure fresh fish at equally low prices, as well as a great variety of shell fish during the spring tides. There is a considerable quantity of sharks and small fish cured in the coast villages, principally for home consumption. The price of fresh fish may be considered high, being fully half as much as is paid in London for fish of similar quality. The octopus is also dried in great quantities by the native fishermen, and being sold at a very low price is largely eaten by the natives. Its use is liable to cause a very unsightly disease.

The unctuous lumpsucker (*Cyclopterus lumpus*) is not much used in this country for food, although it is said to be considered a great delicacy in Edinburgh. The roe is remarkably large. When boiled it forms an extremely fat and oily food. The name of sea snail is sometimes given to it, from the soft and unctuous texture of it, resembling that of the land snail. It is almost transparent and soon dissolves and melts away. On the shores of Greenland and Kamschatka these fish often attain a foot to eighteen inches in length. The flesh of the fish, which is soft and oily, is devoured with avidity by the inhabitants of Greenland, who esteem it as highly nutritive and delicious.

New Zealand Fish.—There occurs in the fresh water lakes of New Zealand a little fish very nearly resembling, both in appearance and flavour, our English whitebait.

The natives cook them by rolling them up in bundles in the leaves of the *Phormium tenax*, or New Zealand flax, and bake them in ovens in the ground, precisely as do the Fijians. When thus cooked they form a delicious repast.

The New Zealand seas and coasts abound in wholesome fish, suitable both for immediate use in a fresh state, and for preserving as an article of commerce. There are about 150 kinds of indigenous fish and many Europeans ones have been introduced.

The first on the list of marketable fish is the hapuka (*Oligorus gigas*), a fish having a close affinity to the famous Murray cod of Australia. The head and shoulder of this fish is most dainty food, but the flesh of the remainder is somewhat coarse and stringy. It is, however, well adapted for pickling, and may yet become a valuable article of commerce.

The kahawai, sometimes called the native salmon (*Arripis salar*), is excellent eating and weighs from two to seven pounds.

The commonest fish is the snapper (*Pagrus unicolor*), which has a brilliant metallic lustre, and is of an average weight of five pounds. Large numbers are taken by the natives. Further south it is represented by an allied species, the tarakihi (*Chilodactylus macropteros*), a very common fish in the market.

The trumpeter (*Latris hectori*), called kohikohi by the natives, is considered the best flavoured of the New Zealand fishes. The frost-fish or para of the natives (*Lepidopus caudatus*) is one of the most delicious fish in the southern seas.

Many of the lakes and ponds in New Zealand abound with carp, of the species known as Prussian carp (*Carassius vulgaris*). These were first introduced into Tasmania from Europe. In Lake Taupo, North Island, especially, they are in very large quantities. The temperature of this lake only varies from 54° in winter to 63° in summer, so that it is peculiarly suitable for this fish.

z

The trevally (*Caranx georgianus*) is a highly esteemed fish and very common. The flesh is delicate, but gets coarser in the large-sized fish.

The warchou (*Neptonemus brama*) is a very valuable fish, and forms one of the chief articles of diet among the natives in Cook's Straits. It sometimes weighs twenty to thirty pounds, but usually is much smaller. The flesh is rich, with a delicate flavour.

The rock cod or coal fish (*Percis colias*) is the most commonly caught fish along the coast, and averages about five pounds. They are largely consumed by the natives; the quality of the flesh is improved by slightly salting it for twenty-four hours.

The flesh of the king-fish (*Seriola lalandii*) is rich and well-flavoured; it sometimes weighs forty pounds. The Maories prize them very highly, and the coast tribes send them inland as gifts.

The butter-fish (*Coredodax pullus*), known as marare among the natives, is a stock fish in the markets during the winter months. It is good eating, being exceedingly short in the grain and well flavoured, without being rich; every part of the fish is singularly deficient in oil. It weighs from four to five pounds. It is a singular fact that the bones of this fish are of a bright green colour, and this is so persistent that it resists prolonged maceration, bleaching and even boiling.

The patiki or flat fish (*Rhombo-solea monopus*) is a staple fish in the market, and the flavour is very good.

The gar-fish (*Scomberox Forsterii*) is a small fish but much esteemed by the colonists for the table.

Tasmanian Fish.—With a population of only 120,000 persons it cannot be expected that the fishing industry of Tasmania can be very extensive; nevertheless it is estimated that there are about 1,050 persons directly dependent upon the capture and sale of fish, and Hobart Town is the chief centre of the industry. *

---

* R. M. Johnston, F.L.S., in the " Proceedings of the Royal Society of Tasmania, 1882."

Out of the 188 known species of fish of the Tasmanian waters, there are about a third good edible fish. The most important fresh-water fishes, so far as the market is concerned, are

Lates colonorum.—Brackish-water perch.
Gadopsis marmoratus.—Blackfish.
Anguilla australis.—The common eel.
Retropinna Richardsoni.—The smelt or whitebait.
Prototrocles maranœna.—The fresh-water herring.

Various species of *Galaxias.* The first-named three are the only fish attaining any size; the remainder are small, valued for their quality as food, and in most cases for their wonderful abundance throughout nearly all the rivers and streamlets of Tasmania.

Lates colonorum is a well-known fish in Australian waters, although limited in Tasmania. The Chinamen cut a slit down the back of the fish, and put them into a composition which they keep secret; they then hang and dry them, without removing the intestines.

The black-fish somewhat resembles a small ling in markings and general appearance. It is much esteemed as food, and is welcome fare to the bushmen and settlers who are far removed from the centres of population. Their average weight is three to four pounds, although they do attain to ten pounds. The common eel is very abundant, some have been taken over 30 lbs. in weight, and over twenty inches in girth.

The fresh-water herring or cucumber fish, although rarely exceeding ¾ lbs. weight, and twelve inches long, is perhaps the finest of the native fresh-water fishes.

The fish passing as whitebait, in Tasmania, are *Retropinna Richardsoni*, Gill., *Galaxias attenatus*, and a species of *Atherina.* They are much esteemed as food for the breakfast table.

The lamprey, though abundant in some rivers, seems not to be in favour in the markets, as they are rarely seen there.

Passing now to the marine fishes; of the perch family as far as the fish market is concerned, the most impor-

tant members are *Anthias rasor*, the Tasmanian barber
or red perch; *Arripis salar*, the native salmon, and *A.
truttaceus*, the native salmon trout. The first of these
from its quality is highly esteemed. The second enter
rivers and wharves in myriads at certain seasons. The
trout is but the immature form of *A. salar*. They
sometimes reach 7 lbs. weight, but are most esteemed
as food when they are under 1 lb. weight.

The snapper (*Pagrus unicolor*) is seldom seen in the
southern waters of Tasmania. This splendid fish seems
to favour the warmer latitudes, for it abounds and
forms the chief market supply, along the coasts of
Australia.

The perch and trumpeter family is by far the largest
and most important, so far as the edible fishes of Tasmania are concerned.

The real or Hobart Trumpeter (*Latris hecatei*, Rich.)
is deservedly held in high repute as the finest of the
Australian edible fishes. It commands a ready sale
in the neighbouring colonies, whether fresh, smoke-
dried, or salted. Many, indeed, consider the smoked
trumpeter equal, if not superior, to the Findon haddock
of Scotland (*Gadus æglefinus*).

The bastard trumpeter (*Latris Forsteri*, Cast.),
rarely exceeds 6 to 7 lbs. weight; it is most prized
for food in the silver bastard or mature well-condi-
tioned form.

The carp of the fishermen (*Chilodactylus spectabilis*,
Hutton), although a somewhat coarse-looking fish,
appears to be highly esteemed. The rock gurnet
(*Sebastes percoides*) is held in great esteem for the table.

The flatheads (*Platycephalus bassensis*, Cuv. and Val.)
are the most important members of the Triglia family
on the Tasmanian coasts. They are good edible fish,
and would be much more highly prized for the table
were it not that they are repulsive-looking and very
common.

The Tasmanian whiting (*Sillago ciliata*) is a most
valuable market fish. It fetches a higher price, for its

size, than any other fish. They are a delicious little fish, averaging a quarter of a pound in weight.

The frost-fish (*Lepidopus caudatus*) is esteemed the most of all the edible fishes in New Zealand, where it appears to be more frequently caught than in Tasmania.

The barracouta (*Thyrsites atun*) is caught all round the coast in the greatest abundance. They are much esteemed and command a ready sale. The fish usually measure about three feet long and average 8 lbs. in weight. Fishermen say that it would pay them if 3s. a dozen could always be got for them, *i.e.*, under $\frac{1}{2}$d. a pound. Another species (*T. Solandri*) averages from 12 to 14 lbs. weight, and sometimes reaches 20 lbs. They appear at times in immense numbers; three fishermen have frequently been known to capture over forty dozen of these fish in a single night. The usual price in the market is 5s. per dozen. When abundant they are largely exported.

The snotgall trevally (*Neptonemus brama*, Gunth.), although inferior in quality to the white or silver (*Caranx georgianus*, Cuv. and Val.), and mackerel trevally (*Neptonemus dobula*, Gunth.), from its abundance and size, is of much greater importance as regards the general market supply. They are exported in considerable quantities to Victoria.

The rock cod (*Pseudophycis barbatus*, Gunth.), exist in such wonderful abundance that they are captured during a portion of the year in quantities far exceeding the local demand. The rock cod rarely exceeds $2\frac{1}{2}$ lbs. weight. The flesh is rather soft, but it is held in fair estimation as food. When smoked with cedar sawdust they are highly prized.

There are four members of the flat-fish family stated to exist in Tasmanian waters, but only two are found abundantly. These are the sole of the fishermen (*Amnotretis rostratus*, Gunth.), and the flounder (*Rhombosolea monopus*, Gunth.). They are among the most highly prized fishes for the table, and are taken in considerable quantities all the year round.

Fish to the value of £60,000 annually are taken at the lake of Tonli-sap, Cambogia, and sold, salted; also the fish-maws or swimming bladders; the Chinese use this fish-glue or gelatine largely in cooking and in the arts and industry. There are about twenty principal varieties of fish taken, but we have only the native names, which are useless for identification. *

Ceylon imports many tons of dried fish annually from India and the Maldive Islands. The singularly weird-looking red fire-fish (*Pterois volitans*) is much prized as food by the Singhalese, the flesh being firm, white, and nutritious.

That the water can be made to yield a larger percentage of nutriment, acre for acre, than the land, is well known. China, with its enormous population, greater to the square mile than that of any other part of the world, derives the largest portion of its animal food from the interior waters of the empire, the methods of fish cultivation there being conducted in a very efficient manner, and every cubic yard of pond and stream thoroughly utilised.

The samlai or shad of China (*Alosa Reevesii*, Rich.), according to Mr. Salter, extend their migrations up the Yang-tse-Kiang for over a thousand miles, and, according to Dr. Macgowan, to a distance of three thousand miles from its mouth.

The ordinary esculent fish of the seas of the Indian and Philippine islands are numerous. In the markets of Celebes it is said that not fewer than 300 different species are at one time or another offered for sale. A few of them are of excellent quality, equalling if not surpassing in delicacy and flavour those of the European seas. The curing of ordinary fish and the pickling of prawns forms a considerable branch of trade between the coast and interior.†

---

* A long descriptive article on this fishery is given in the French " Revue Maritime et Coloniale," vol. lxi., p. 534.

† Crawfurd's "Indian Islands," p. 16.

Fish constitutes the chief animal aliment of all the inhabitants, and everywhere of those of the sea coast, who are by profession fishermen.

In Japan fish are very abundant and varied, and reputed excellent; fish enters largely into the food of the people. Everything produced by the sea is considered edible—whale's flesh, fish of all kinds, mollusca, and octopi, marine animals of every description, sea plants and weeds, are all made to contribute to their support, as they have few edible land animals. Among both rich and poor the red flesh of the whale, which looks like beef, is considered very wholesome and nutritious, and is largely consumed when obtainable.

The markets are always well supplied, and the stranger is struck by the abundance and variety of species, amongst which are found the principal food fishes of Europe. The tunny is often seen in the markets of Yeddo and Yokohama. The Japanese often eat it raw, cut in thin slices, which they dip in mustard. The mackerel is also common, and the sardine, at the time of its passage, is very abundant on all the coasts, but the consumption cannot absorb the catch. The people on the coast preserve large quantities of fish by simply drying in the sun, and they keep very well by this simple mode of preparation, with only the inconvenience of an unpleasant smell. The cod, sole, flounder, and other flat-fish are taken. The shark is for the Japanese an edible fish, as with the Chinese. There is always a large quantity to be seen in the markets, but they are mostly small ones, and belong to the common species; the hammer-headed shark, met with on the southern coasts of China, is not seen. The rays attain a large size. The Tai (*Serranus marginalis*) is considered, with just reason, to be one of the most esteemed of the sea fish. It is as abundant on the Japanese coasts as on those of China. They eat it raw, seasoned with soy. The herring, like the sardine, is carried to the interior either in its sun-dried state or slightly salted. The salmon, carp, and other fresh-water fish are also abundant. The salmon forms a considerable article of commerce, and is sent salted all through the interior. This fish also abounds in Hakodadi, and great quantities are caught in all the rivers of the province of Niagata and those to the north-east.

So far as the bounty of Nature goes, fish in Victoria should be as plentiful as it is in Kamschatka, where the law forbids any dog having the roes of more than six salmon given to it in a day. Yet there is scarcely any part of the civilised world where fish is at such a price. In London fish and poverty go together. As the experienced navigator recognises his approximation to the coast by the successive specimens of gravel, sand, and mud brought up by the lead, so the wanderer in the giant metropolis may pretty accurately estimate his distance from the opulent West End by the increasing number of stalls covered with ancient flounders and offal fish.

From 1,500 to 2,000 tons of fish are taken annually by the fishermen of San Francisco, and as there are about ninety different kinds of fish brought to market, the population would seem to be well supplied.

Brazil, with its long coast line and bays, and immense rivers and lakes, is abundantly supplied with fish, crustaceans, and mollusks. The spawn, salted, of many fish forms an article of commerce. The Bay of Rio Janeiro abounds occasionally with sardines, which are equal to those of Nantes. The river Amazon alone and its tributaries furnish more than eighty species of fish. Notwithstanding this abundance of fresh fish, there is a large import of salt fish for the supply of the negroes, averaging in value about £400,000 a year.

The whole valley of the Amazon abounds in streams that help to make up the entire volume of waters. These spread out into lakes, lagoons, and swamps, that extend over large regions of country. This is especially so in the rainy seasons or flood times.

The channels and lakes are abundantly supplied with fishes. Even large ones are often left in the swamp lakes and streams when the water is low. A hundred different kinds of fish can be bought in the markets of Rio, many of which come from the Amazon.

Those most valued are piranhas and pirarucus (*Vastris cuverii*). They are the largest, but there are numerous smaller varieties. The Indians catch the latter with hooks and lines, or shoot them with arrows. But the larger fish are speared with a kind of trident.

In the summer months the people come by hundreds to the lakes and channels to fish for the great *pirarucu*, or red fish, and to prepare it much as codfish is prepared by the northern fishermen. Some of these fish are seven or eight feet in length. They are first dressed and cut into wide thin slices. These are well rubbed with salt and hung on poles to dry in the sun. The slices are taken under cover every night and carried out again in the morning. The stranger does not at once relish this dried fish, yet it is the standard flesh food of all the poorer classes throughout a large part of Brazil, especially the provinces of Para and Amazonas.

The piranhas are much prized and are easily caught, for they are greedy to bite at almost anything, from a bit of salt meat to a bather's toe.

The Tupi word *piranha* is a contraction of *pira sainha*, meaning "toothed fish." The same word is used by the Indians to describe a pair of scissors. There are several species of these savage piranhas, some being more than two feet long. They make nothing of biting an ounce or so of flesh from a man's leg.

Fish are abundant in the rivers of the Argentine Confederation, and of a large size, such as the dorado (*Coryphæna suereii*, Cuv. and Val.), surubi (*Tetraodon lineatus*), and pacou. The catch is plentiful, especially in the Parana and Vermejo, but the fish of the Uruguay river are the most delicate.

No fishing is carried on on the shores of the ocean, notwithstanding that excellent fish are to be found, as also oysters, lobsters, and other crustacea. About 550 tons of salted fish are imported into Buenos Ayres annually, besides the fish locally caught.

In Paraguay, besides the *Silurus* and the pacou (*Tetra-odon lineatus*), which reach a weight of 40 lbs., there are a great many edible fishes. There is one called a trout, of a handsome yellow colour, and hence named dorado, the flesh of which is excellent ; it often attains the weight of 20 to 30 lbs. When the rivers fall, large quantities of fish are caught in baskets, and simply boiled down for the oil, which is skimmed from the top.

The pompano (*Trachynotus sp.*), caught only at Chorillos on the Chilian coast, is not always to be obtained, but is so highly esteemed at Callao, that one weighing eight or ten pounds readily commands five or six dollars.

As already mentioned (p. 333), this fish is also highly prized in the North American markets.

CHAPTER X.

Various Insects Eaten as Food.

Cockchafers or Vers Blanc Eaten—Modes of Cooking—Bees and
Ants Eaten—Cossus of the Ancients—Gru-grus or Palm-
worms—Caterpillars—Tobacco Worms—Locusts—Extensive
Use of Locusts in Africa, Asia, and America—Various Modes
of Cooking—Termites Eaten in India and Africa—Silkworm
Chrysalids—Red Ants—Honey—Statistics of Production—
Lerp and Trehalose.

DESCENDING low in the scale of animal life we find on
investigation that insects furnish more food delicacies
than is generally supposed.

In warm countries omnivorous man wages war in turn
upon the petty insect tribes as upon the larger animals
of creation, and converts them into food dainties. There
are many insects looked upon with disgust, which, in
reality, are more clean, more wholesome, and feed on
better food than those other animals with which we
constantly load our tables. The old poet, Herrick,
seemed well acquainted with this fact, for some two
hundred years ago he thus described a feast given by
Oberon to the fairy elves :—

> " Gladding his palate with some store
> Of emmet's eggs : what would he more ?
> But beards of mice, a newt's stew'd thigh,
> A bloated earwig, and a fly.
> With the red-capp'd worm that's shut
> Within the concave of a nut,
> Brown as his tooth ; a little moth,
> Late fattened in a piece of cloth."

The common rain-worm is carefully gathered in China,
and raw or roasted considered most palatable food. Still
it is the poor mainly that appreciate, by the side of

pleasant taste, the cheapness of such provisions. But what shall we say to the *gourmet* who praises the luscious wood snipe, and still more the black mass from the inside that he carefully places on his toast and eats with a feeling akin to veneration? He is eating the worms that live in the snipe's intestines. How many, too, eat ripe or decayed cheese with the cheese mites and maggots crawling over it.

A few years ago at the Café Custoza, in Paris, a grand banquet was given for the special purpose of testing the *vers blanc*, or cockchafer worm. This insect, it appears, was first steeped in vinegar, which had the effect of making it disgorge the earth, etc., it had swallowed while yet free; then it was carefully rolled up in a paste composed of flour, milk, and eggs, placed in a pan, and fried to a bright golden colour. The guests were able to take this crisp and dry worm in their fingers. It cracked between their teeth. There were some fifty persons present, and the majority had a second helping. The larvæ, or grubs, generally, not only of the cockchafer, but those of the ordinary beetles, may, according to some naturalists, be eaten safely. Cats, turkeys, and different birds devour them eagerly.

We find in a Continental journal, the *Gazette des Campagnes*, the following receipt for cooking these insects, which is adopted in certain parts of France:—

" Roll the *vers blancs*, which are short and fat, in flour and bread crumbs, with a little salt and pepper, and wrap them in a stout piece of paper, well buttered inside. Place it in the hot embers and leave it to cook for twenty minutes, more or less, according to the degree of heat. On opening the envelope a very appetising odour exhales, which disposes one favourably to taste the delicacy, which will be more appreciated than snails, and will be declared one of the finest delicacies ever tasted." *

* " Les Insectes Utiles," par Henri Miot, p. 89. Paris, 1870.

The Goliath beetles are roasted and eaten by the natives of South America and Western Africa, and the Roman epicures were very partial to certain breeds of European larvæ.

The famous palm-worm of the West Indies, roasted on tiny spits and richly spiced, forms one of the best dishes of luxurious dinners. Its near relation, the grugru worm of Java, is said to be richer still and more delicate. Nor do the costly chrysalids of the silk-worm escape the fate of all that is eatable; freed from their cocoons, and daintily dressed, they are highly honoured and largely swallowed by the people of China and the noblemen of Madagascar. The discarded chrysalids after reeling silk from the cocoons are hawked about the streets of China and sold to the lower classes as an article of diet. The price is about 5d. per pound.

At Chinkiang they are sold at thirty-four dollars per picul of 133⅓ lbs. The Chinese, with their incredible power of overcoming all natural instincts, go here also farther; they raise the larvæ of blue-bottle flies in heaps of putrid fish near the sea-coast, and value the produce more highly than the facility of obtaining it would lead us to believe. They place themselves thus, with all their boasted superiority, on a level with the poor Indians of the Orinoco, whom the traveller Schomburgk saw eagerly dig in the ground for grubs and worms. It is true they ate them raw, while the children of the Flowery Kingdom dress their worms with spices and sauces. Huge centipedes are eagerly devoured by the Indians of South America, and leeches adorn the tables of the very princes of Japan.

If the palate has, like the eye, its laws of beauty, which would lead it to prefer nobler forms, insects ought to be eaten as little as molluscs. They are rarely blessed with a beauty that is intended for other senses but the sight; their long, dry bodies, their restless, countless feet and quaintly-shaped heads are interesting in their ugliness, but far from attractive to the hungry. What natural taste could lead us to carry to the mouth a larva that changes its shape from day to day—now looks dry and dark, and to-morrow bursts and pours forth a yellow, dismal fluid ? Like a true Proteus it defies all knowledge of its next shape, and, in all stages, inspires disgust rather than desire. Still, insects are eaten, but their lowest kinds only by the lowest races of mankind. Tschudi saw the natives of Peru hunt assiduously in the forests of hair on the heads of their children and eagerly devour the minute game—a taste which they share with the Hottentots and other African tribes. New Caledonians prefer spiders to all common food; and the amiable inhabitants of New South Wales catch even moths (*Euplaca hamata*), remove the gray powder on their tiny bodies, and roast them in masses. Bees—which civilised nations deprive of the fruit of their labour—are eaten in Ceylon as spice, and on account of the fragrant odour they give to the breath. The pleasant acid taste of ants tempts many races of Brazil and the East Indies; and even in other more fastidious countries the old and the feeble consume them under an impression that they strengthen the spinal marrow ! The acid they contain bears a striking resemblance to that of the lemon ; and many a European has learned, in Java and Eastern countries, to thrust his arm into a hill of white ants and to eat the quaint food without cooking and dressing. The huge termites, however, those skilful artists of Africa, require, even at the hands of the natives, a more careful treatment. They are caught, as they fall into the water, in calabashes, and roasted like coffee-beans in huge iron-pots ; then they are flung, by the handful, into their mouths. The Hottentots also are fond of them, and admire their fattening power. In the East Indies they are caught by thousands and baked in pies, which are brought to the public markets —a custom which prevails in South America also, where they are sold after having been roasted.

Mr. Max Buchner's " Contributions to the Ethnography of the Bantus " contains the following interesting notes,

which show that insects are by no means despised as
food by this tribe of negroes, which inhabit a large portion of South-eastern Africa. Toward the end of the
rainy season, in April, when the white ants are swarming, the conical buildings of these insects are covered
with a dense matting of banana leaves, while, within
this cover, vessels are placed with funnel-shaped en-
trances. In these vessels a large number of white ants,
males and females, are caught and roasted on the spot.
They are considered a great delicacy, even Mr. Buchner
finding them very palatable. A large, fat, subterranean
cricket, as well as a large coleopterous larva, living in
hollow trees, are equally sought for and roasted over fire.
But it is especially a large caterpillar called "ugoungoo,"
which is harvested by the natives like a field crop. It
is about five centimetres long, black, with yellow rings,
occurs on the savannas, and "belongs perhaps to the
butterfly Crenis." Whenever it appears in large numbers,
the negroes march out in full force from their villages,
camping out for weeks in the wilderness to gather and
cure the crop. After the intestines have been pressed
out, the caterpillars are dried before the fire and rolled
up in packages of fresh leaves. To a civilised taste they
are most disgusting, the smell reminding one of that of
our cabbage worms. In view of this custom it seems to
to be strange that the Bantus refuse to eat snakes and
amphibia of all sorts, even frogs and lizards not being
touched by them in times of starvation.

Locusts furnish the favourite food of many numerous
races of Africa; some nations live exclusively on them ;
but, it is said, they rarely grow older than forty years,
and mostly die a miserable death, produced by fearful
diseases. Alfred Cole tells us, in his graphic manner,
how a whole kraal of Caffres once died after having
consumed an unusual quantity of locusts. We read, not
without wonder, that even in classic Greece this repulsive food was not rejected. The same Athenians that,
later, wore golden crickets in their hair as proof that
they were natives on their own soil, like the insects

themselves, ate the smaller varieties skilfully dressed
But we must remember that antiquity also was not
always faithful to the first laws of beauty and humanity. Were not their costliest fishes fattened upon
the bodies of slaves thrown into the ponds for that
horrible purpose ? In our day the locusts are rarely
seen, but at long intervals, and permanently only in the
Orient. There the Arabs resort to them in years of
famine ; they dry and grind them to powder, and bake
them with flour into cakes, or roast them in butter.
Legs and wings are always rejected, the bodies are often
preserved in vinegar, and are considered a rare delicacy.
In Germany, where, in 1748, they committed incredible
ravages, the eggs at least were eaten and highly
prized.*

That the old Romans were partial to a certain large
wood-boring larva as an article of food, is certain ; we
know, too, that it bore the name of Cossus ; but beyond
that we are left in darkness, except that the animal is said
by Pliny to live on trees, to change into an insect with
long antennæ, and to have the power of emitting a
rather shrill sound—" Sonum edunt parvuli stridoris "
(" Hist. Nat.," book xvii. chap. 24). The larva, whatever
it was, was held in the highest estimation by the *gourmets*
of Rome as a singular delicacy, and was fattened for the
table on meal.

Naturalists are much divided on the knotty question
of the true Cossus of the ancients. Some are inclined
to give the distinction to the stag-beetle, whose larva is
sufficiently large to make a juicy mouthful ; others con-
tend for some species of rhinoceros beetle (*Oryctes*) ;
while some are in favour of the exotic *Rhynchophorus*.
Kirby and Spence are in favour of some large species of
the " Capricorn tribe "; and of these the French entomologist Mulsant has fixed upon the larva of the handsome beetle called *Cerambyx* (or *Hammatochœrus*) *heros*.
In many parts of Europe " *heros* " is counted among the

pests of the forest, the female depositing her eggs on the oak.

Les vers palmiste, as the French term them (*Calandra palmarum,* Oliv.), are eaten broiled, with poor man's sauce, that is water, salt, lemon, and chillies.

Even the gigantic centipedes of Brazil, many of them a foot and a half long and half an inch broad were seen by Humboldt to be dragged out of their holes and crunched alive by the children. Darwin assures us that the caterpillar of the hawk-moth is delicious. Kirby and Spence think the ant good eating, distinguishing between the flavour of the abdomen and the thorax; and Reaumur recommends the caterpillar of the *Plusia gamma* as a delicate dish.*

A certain large grub (probably the larva of a species of *Buprestis*), found abundantly in Western Australia, at the roots of the Acacia, is much in request with the natives, who eat it.

The larvæ of all the wood-boring beetles are eagerly sought after by the aborigines of Australia, especially *Bardistes cibarius*, which, though exhaling an odour at least as pungent as that of the goat moth, is much relished by the natives of King George's Sound. The negro of the West Indies and Tropical America searches diligently for the gru-gru worm (*Rhyncophorus palmarum*). The grub is an inch and a half long, of a white colour.

In the Moluccas, Wallace tells us that the grubs of the palm beetles are regularly brought to market in bamboos and sold for food. The natives of Mexico make the larva of *Trichoderes pini* a part of their fare.

An old writer—Brookes, " On the Properties and Uses of Insects," 1772—says, " The larvæ are eaten by the French, in the West Indies, after they have been roasted before the fire, when a small wooden spit has been thrust through them. When they begin to be hot, they powder them with a crust of rasped bread, mixed with salt, and a little pepper and nutmeg. This powder keeps in the

---

* " History of Insects."

A A

fat, or at least sucks it up; and when they are done enough, they are served up with orange juice. They are highly esteemed by the French, as excellent eating."

The large caterpillars of a beetle (*Cerambyx cervicornis?*) commonly called "Macaccas," are eagerly sought for in the decayed timber of trees in the West Indies, and considered a great delicacy. They are nearly three and a half inches long, and about the thickness of a man's little finger. The body is of a white colour, and sustains a small brown head, which is generally cut off when they are used. They are always gutted, opened, and washed before they are dressed; and when well fried are thought by many people to be one of the greatest delicacies in America.*

The Malagasy eat, fried in oil, various kinds of white fat caterpillars without hair.

The larva of the *Calandra palmarum* is considered a great delicacy by the inhabitants of South America, so is that of the *Curculio palmarum*, found principally in the South of India, where it feeds on the pith of the sago palm. The gum grub, or gru-gru, is by some Australian gastronomists considered a great dainty, and similar to fine marrow, when fried with bread crumbs; the natives, however, prefer it raw. The insect is about six inches long and half an inch in diameter. When in season the natives grow fat by feeding on them.†

Two insects, the Bugong moth, a kind of butterfly, and a thick, white grub, found chiefly in dead timber, are much esteemed by the aborigines of Australia as articles of food. The former is eaten at certain seasons by whole tribes of natives in the northern districts. Their practice is to follow up the flight of the insects and to light fires at nightfall beneath the trees on which they have settled. The smoke brings the butterflies down, and their bodies are pounded together into a sort

---

* Browne's "Natural History of Jamaica."
† Ogle's "Western Australia," p. 256. See also Bennett's "New South Wales," p. 270; and Buckton, p. 97.

of fleshy loaf. Upon this delicacy the natives not only feed, but fatten. The white grub is swallowed whole in his living state, and is much sought for by sable epicures. It is scarcely necessary to say that neither of these dainties have found favour with the white settlers.

The larva of *Mallodon costatus* are eaten by the natives of New Caledonia.

The large and fat caterpillars of *Strigops grandis* of Australia are eaten by the aborigines. The fat larva of the (*Phytophagi?*) coleopteras, which lived in the oaks, figured on the tables of the Romans under the name of *Cossus*, and the ladies, it is said, esteemed their delicate cream under the impression that it gave them an *embonpoint*, which prolonged their beauty.

In Africa and other parts, locusts are eaten salted and roasted. The chrysalids of a wild silk worm (*Borocera cajani*) are esteemed in Madagascar. In an interview which the French Ambassador had with the ill-fated Radami II., his son, a boy of ten years, had his pockets filled with roasted chrysalids, with which he regaled himself during the interview. As we already eat many crustaceans, who can tell whether we may not yet arrive at insects as an *hors-d'œuvre*.

Among the Pinos Indians, as among the savages of Africa, tobacco worms, which are the caterpillars of *Macrosila Carolina*, are gathered and made into soup, or fried until crisp and brown. Vegetables, meal, or seeds are usually added to the composition when made into pottage. A writer in the official agricultural reports of the United States records having seen this tribe gather bushels of the worms for immediate consumption, or to be dried and pounded for winter use. A whitish larva, " koōcha-bee " of the Indians, occurring in immense quantities, is much esteemed by them as an article of food. At certain seasons it is carried in by the waves and deposited on the shores of Owen's Lake, California, in layers of several inches in thickness. This was formerly collected in large quantities by the Indians, and after being dried in the sun, rubbed between the hands, and roughly winnowed, was crushed in a stone mortar and made into cakes, which furnished an important article of food.

This insect, which has been described as a white grub, is also found abundantly in the waters of Great Salt Lake, Utah, and those of other saline and alkaline lakes of the West, and appears to be the larva of a two-winged fly which is described by the late Prof. Torrey under the name of *Ephydra Californica*, and by A. S. Packard as *Ephydra gracilis*.*

Some of these larva are eaten raw by the Indians of Western Nevada, and are of a rank and oleaginous taste; others are made into soup.

Of the various insects, locusts are those most generally consumed. The law of Moses, as declared in Leviticus, chap. xi., verses 21 and 22, states:—"Yet these may ye eat, of every flying creeping thing that goeth upon all four, which have legs above their feet, to leap withal upon the earth; Even these of them ye may eat; the locust after his kind, and the bald locust after his kind, and the beetle after his kind, and the grasshopper after his kind." The locust has six feet, but Moses did not regard as legs proper the long hinder ones which enable it to spring or leap. The beetle was the *Bruchus*, or grasshopper without wings (St. Jerome, lxx.), the Attachus, a variety of the last-named, and the *Ophiomachus*, a sort of grasshopper, so called because it was said to fight the serpent (Pliny, book ii., ch. 29).

The authorities describing locusts as food in various countries are very numerous. Pliny (book xli., chaps. 32 and 35) says the Eastern nations and the Parthians considered locusts and grasshoppers as a choice food. The gourmands preferred the males, and the females after casting their eggs; while the Greeks preferred them with the eggs. St. Jerome says that to feed on these insects was to those nations as great a luxury as to the

* See Hayden's "Geol. Survey of Montana, Idaho, etc., 1872," p. 744.

Western nations the beccafico and other food delicacies.

Locusts or grasshoppers can be prepared in more ways
even than oysters; they may be eaten raw, stewed, and
fried in oil, broiled on a gridiron, smoked, or ground up
in a handmill and baked into cakes; first boiled in water
and then fried in butter they make an excellent dish.
Many savage and some civilised nations eat them with
delight.

Father Ovalle, writing in 1649, informs us that the
Indians of Chili, in the absence of grain, convert this
insect into bread. They watch where the locusts alight
to rest at night, then setting fire to the bushes, reduce
all to ashes, which are gathered and baked into cakes.
Mr. Gordon Cumming also has a word to say in their
favour. To him they proved palatable food, and he calls
them "fattening and wholesome for bird, beast, and
man." If further testimony were required, we have it
in the declaration of Dr. Livingstone that locusts are a
real blessing to the country. This eminent traveller
adds, besides, " that when reduced to meal and mingled
with a little salt, they afford palatable food, which keeps
uninjured for months." Boiled, he found locusts disagreeable, but roasted they had a vegetable flavour, and on
the whole he preferred them to shrimps.

On the other hand, we must not forget that Diodorus
Siculus says that the Acridophagi, or locust-eaters of
Ethiopia, fell victims to their diet at the early age of
forty years, innumerable insects being generated in their
bodies. Nevertheless, however unlikely it may be that
any European nation would voluntarily select such food,
it is abundantly clear that locusts are relished by millions of both Asiatics and Africans. It must be obvious,
also, that the judicious and economic storing of this insect, which at certain seasons pours over two continents
so abundantly as to become a plague and a scourge, is a
fit subject to engage the attention of our philanthropists
abroad.

Grasshoppers were eaten by some of the soldiers of

the American Revolution. In Frederick Freeman's "History of Cape Cod" (vol. i., p. 524), the author mentions that Col. Nathaniel Freeman, of Sandwich, Mass. and Major Samuel Osgood, of Andover, Mass., were appointed Commissioners, in 1777, to attend to some business in the American camp at West Point. He then adds, in a footnote :—

"One of the Commissioners above named related to the writer that when on this service at West Point, the attention of the Commissioners was arrested by certain inexplicable movements among the French troops encamped at some distance from the Americans. Perceiving that they had kindled numerous fires in the adjoining fields, and were running about in strange disorder, Major Osgood and himself, accompanied by General Washington and other officers, mounted horses and rode to the encampment. It was found that the Frenchmen were enjoying rare sport in a campaign against grasshoppers, which were unusually numerous at that time. These insects, as soon as captured, were impaled upon a sharpened stick on posts, and held for a moment over the fire, and then eaten with great *gusto*. The fires were furnished with fuel of deposits from cattle in the fields, made by the excessive heat and drought of the autumn sufficiently dry and combustible."

From a digested paper by Mr. W. F. Kirby, naturalist, Dublin, and papers by Mr. Riley, I condense the following details on the use of this insect as food :—With the exception of locusts, most other insects that have been used as food for man are obtained in small quantities, and their use is more a matter of curiosity than of interest. They have been employed either by exceptional individuals with perverted tastes, or else as dainty tit-bits to tickle some abnormal and epicurean palate. Not so with locusts, which have, from time immemorial, formed a staple article of diet with many peoples, and are used to-day in large quantities in many parts of the globe.

Any one at all familiar with the treasures on exhibition at the British Museum, must have noticed among its Nineveh sculptures one in which are represented men carrying different kinds of meat to some festival, and among them some who carry long sticks, to which are tied locusts, thus indicating that, in those early days represented by the sculpture, locusts were sufficiently esteemed to make part of a public feast. They are in Scripture counted among the "clean meats," and are frequently referred to in the Bible as food for man.

In most parts of Europe, Asia, and Africa, subject to locust ravages, these insects have been, and are yet, extensively used as food. Herodotus mentions a tribe of Æthiopians "which fed on locusts that came in swarms from the southern and unknown districts"; and Livingstone has made us familiar with the fact that the custom yet prevails among many African tribes. We have it from Pliny that locusts were in high esteem among the Parthians, and the records of their use in ancient times, as food, in Southern Europe and Asia, are abundant. This use continues in those parts of the world to the present day. In Morocco, where, as I am informed by one Mr. Trovey Blackmore, of London, who has spent some time in that country, they do more or less damage every year, they are used extensively for food whenever they abound, so as to diminish the ordinary food supply, while they are habitually roasted for eating, and brought into Tangier and other towns by the country people, and sold in the market-places and on the streets. The Jews, who form a large proportion of the population, collect the females only for this purpose, having an idea that the male is unclean, but that under the body of the females there are some Hebrew characters which make them lawful food. In reality there are, under the thorax, certain dark markings—the species used, and which is so injurious to crops, being the *Acridium perigrinum.*

Radoszkowski, president of the Russian Entomological Society, tells us that they are also, to this day, extensively used as food in Southern Russia; while many of the North American Indian tribes, and notably the Snake and Digger Indians of California, are known to feed upon them. No further evidence need be cited to prove the present extensive use of these insects as articles of food.

Let us, then, briefly consider the nature of this locust food and the different methods of prepáring it. The records show us that in ancient times these insects were cooked in a variety of ways. *Œdipoda migratoria* and *Acridium perigrinum*, which are the more common devastating locusts of the " Old World," are both of large size, and they are generally prepared by first detaching the legs and wings. The bodies are then either boiled, roasted, stewed, fried, or broiled. The Romans are said to have used them by carefully roasting them to a bright golden yellow. At the present day, in most parts of Africa and especially in Russia, they are either salted or smoked like red herrings.

Chanier, in his account of the Empire· of Morocco (London, 1788), says that thus cured they are brought into the market in prodigious quantities, but that they have "an oily and rancid taste, which habit only can render agreeable." The Moors use them to the present day in the manner described by Jackson in his " Travels in Morocco," viz., by first boiling and then frying them. But the Jews in that country—more provident than the Moors—salt them and keep them for using with the dish called *Dafina*, which forms the Saturday's dinner of the Jewish population. The dish is made by placing meat, fish, eggs, tomatoes—in fact, almost anything edible—in a jar which is put in the oven on Friday night, and taken out hot on the Sabbath, so that the people get a hot meal without the sin of lighting a fire on that day. In the Abbé Godard's " Description et Histoire de Maroc" (Paris, 1860), he tells us that "they are placed in bags, salted, and either baked or boiled. They are then dried on the terraced roofs of the houses. Fried in oil they are not. bad."

The Hill Damaras collect locusts by lighting fires in the direct path of the devouring swarms. In roasting the wings and legs crisp up and are separated; the bodies are then eaten fresh or dried in hot ashes, and put away for future use. The American Digger Indians roast them, and grind or crush them to a kind of flour; which they mix with pounded acorns, or with different kinds of berries, make into cakes and dry in the sun for future use. The species employed by the ancients were doubtless the same as those employed at the present day, viz., the two already mentioned, and, to a less degree, the smaller *Calopterus Italiacus*.

We have no records of any extended use of the Rocky Mountain species (*Calopterus spretus*), unless, which is not improbable, the species employed by the Indians on the Pacific coast should prove to be the same, or a geographical race of the same. "It had long been a desire with me," says Mr. Riley, "to test the value of this species (the Rocky Mountain locust) as food, and I did not lose the opportunity to gratify that desire which the recent locust invasion into some of the Mississippi Valley States offered. I knew well enough that the attempt would provoke to ridicule and mirth, and even disgust, the vast majority of our people, unaccustomed to any thing of the sort, and associating with the word insect, or 'bug,' everything horrid and repulsive. Yet I was governed by weightier reasons than mere curiosity, for many a family in Kansas and Nebraska was brought to the brink of the grave by sheer lack of food, while the St. Louis papers reported cases of actual death from starvation in some sections of Missouri, where the insects abounded and ate up every green thing the past spring. Whenever the occasion presented I partook of locusts prepared in different ways, and one day ate of no other kind of food, and must have consumed, in one form and another, the substance of several thousand half-grown locusts. Commencing the experiments with some misgivings, and fully expecting to have to overcome disagreeable flavour, I was soon most agreeably surprised to find that the insects were quite palatable in whatever way prepared."

The flavour of the raw locust is most strong and disagreeable, but that of the cooked insects is agreeable, and sufficiently mild. to be easily neutralised by anything with which they may be mixed, and to admit of easy disguise, according to taste or fancy. But the great point I would make in their favour is, that they need no elaborate preparation or seasoning. They require no disguise; and herein lies their value in exceptional emergencies, for when people are driven to the point of starvation by these ravenous pests, it follows. that all other food is either very scarce or unattainable.

A broth, made by boiling the unfledged *Calopteri* for two hours in the proper quantity of water, and seasoned with nothing in the world but pepper and salt, is quite palatable, and can scarcely be distinguished from beef broth, though it has a slight flavour peculiar to it, and not easily described. The addition of a little butter improves it, and the flavour can of course be modified with mint, sage and spices, *ad libitum.* Fried or roasted in nothing but their own oil, with the addition of a little salt, they are by no means unpleasant eating, and have quite a nutty flavour. In fact, it is a flavour, like most peculiar and not unpleasant flavours, that one can soon learn to get fond of. Prepared in this manner, ground and compressed, they would doubtless keep for a long time. Yet their consumption in large quantities in this form would not, I think, prove as wholesome as when made into soup or broth; for I found the chitonous covering and the corneous parts, especially the spines on the tibiæ, dry, and chippy, and somewhat irritating to the throat. This objection would not apply with the same force to the mature individuals, especially of larger species, where the heads, legs, and wings are carefully separated before cooking; and, in fact, some of the mature insects prepared in this way, then boiled, and afterwards stewed with a few vegetables, and a little butter, pepper, salt, and vinegar, make an excellent fricassee.

Lest it be presumed that these opinions result from an unnatural palate, or from mere individual taste, let me add that I took pains to get the opinions of many other persons. Indeed, I shall not soon forget the experience of my first culinary effort in this line—so fraught with fear, and so forcibly illustrating the power of example in overcoming prejudice. This attempt was made at an hotel. At first it was impossible to get any assistance from the followers of the *ars coquinaria.* They could not more flatly have refused to touch, taste, or handle, had it been a question of cooking vipers. Nor love nor money could induce them to do either, and in this respect the folks of the kitchen were all alike, without distinction of colour. There was no other resource than to turn cook myself, and operations once commenced, the interest and aid of a brother naturalist and two intelligent ladies were soon enlisted. It was most amusing to note how, as the rather savoury and pleasant odour went up from the cooking dishes, the expression of horror and disgust gradually vanished from the faces of the curious lookers-on, and how at last the head cook—a stout and jolly negress—took part in the operations; how, when the different dishes were neatly served upon the table and were freely partaken of with evident relish and many expressions of surprise and satisfaction by the ladies and gentlemen interested, this same cook was actually induced to try them, and soon grew eloquent in their favour; how, finally, a prominent banker, as also one of the editors of the town joined in the meal. The soup soon vanished, and banished silly prejudice; the cakes, with batter enough to hold the locusts together, disappeared, and were pronounced good; then baked locusts without condiments; and when the meal was completed with dessert of baked locusts and honey *à la* John the Baptist, the opinion was unanimous that that distinguished prophet no longer deserved our sympathy, and that he had not fared badly on his diet in the wilderness.

"Professor H. H. Straight, of the Warrensburg (Mo.) Normal School, who made some experiments for me in this line, wrote : ' We boiled them rather slowly for three or four hours, seasoned the fluid with a little butter, salt, and pepper, and it made an excellent soup, actually ; we would like to have it even in prosperous times. Mrs. Johonnot, who is sick, and Professor Johonnot pronounced it excellent.' I sent a bushel of the scalded insects to Mr. John Bennet, one of the oldest and best known caterers of St. Louis. Master of the mysteries of the *cuisine*, he made a soup which was really delicious, and was so pronounced by dozens of prominent St. Louisans who tried it."

Shaw, in his " Travels in Barbary " (Oxford, England, 1738), in which two pages are devoted to a description of the ravages of locusts, mentions that when sprinkled with salt and fried, they taste like crayfish ; and Mr. Bennet declares that this locust soup reminded him of nothing so much as crayfish *bisque*, which is so highly esteemed by connoisseurs. He also declared that he would gladly have it on his bill of fare every day if he could get the insects. His method of preparation was to boil on a brisk fire, having previously seasoned them with salt, pepper, and grated nutmeg, the whole being occasionally stirred. When cooked they are pounded in a mortar with bread fried brown, or a purée of rice. They are then replaced in the saucepan and thickened to a broth by placing on a warm part of the stove, but not allowed to boil. For use, the broth is passed through a strainer and a few *croutons* are added. Fried locusts have been tasted by numerous persons, including the members of the London Entomological Society and of the Société Entomologique de France. Without exception, they have been pronounced far better than was expected, and those fried in their own oil with a little salt are yet good and fresh ; others fried in butter have become slightly rancid—a fault of the butter.

When dense flights of locusts visited India, the natives fried and ate them. Mr. C. Horne, F.Z.S., writing to *Science Gossip* about swarms of locusts which visited parts of India in 1863, says : " In the evening I had asked two gentlemen to dinner, and gave them a curry and croquet of locusts. They passed for Cabul shrimps, which in flavour they much resembled, but the cook having inadvertently left a hind leg in a croquet, they were found out, to the infinite disgust of one of the party and amusement of the other."

These testimonies as to the past and present use of locusts as human food might be multiplied almost indefinitely, but I have said enough to prove that the nature of this food is by no means disagreeable. In short, not to waste time in further details, I can safely assert, from my own personal experience, that the Rocky Mountain locust is more palatable when cooked than many animals that we habitually use on our tables. I mention this species more particularly because the flavour will doubtless differ according to the species, or even according to the nature of the vegetation the insects were nourished on. I have made no chemical analysis of this locust food, but that it is highly nourishing may be gathered from the fact that all animals fed upon the insects thrive when they are abundant; and the further fact that the locust-eating Indians, and all other locust-eating people, grow fat upon them. Locusts will hardly come into general use for food except where- they are annually abundant, and the Western farmers of America who occasionally suffer from them will not easily be brought to a due appreciation of them for this purpose. Prejudiced against them, fighting to overcome them, killing them in large quantities, until the stench from their decomposing bodies becomes at times most offensive —they find little that is attractive in the pests. For these reasons, as long as other food is attainable, the locust will be apt to be rejected by most persons. Yet the fact remains that they do make very good food. When freshly caught in large quantities, the mangled mass presents a not very appetising appearance, and emits a rather strong and not over pleasant odour; but rinsed and scalded, they turn a brownish red, look more inviting, and give no disagreeable smell.

It is well known that locusts have been eaten from time immemorial in the East, and hence there was nothing extraordinary in their forming one of the staple resources of John the Baptist in the desert, where there was little else to be got. It is reported that they devoured everything in Utah in 1855 to such an extent that the inhabitants had nothing else to eat but the locusts themselves, and hence it is not surprising that the Americans again tried to utilize them as an article of diet. Another visitation, in 1874-75, also was more serious than had been known for many years.

Mr. Riley, the State Entomologist of Missouri, to whose writings I am indebted for most of my information, stated at a late meeting of the Entomological Society of London that a very good and nourishing soup was made of the locusts. He had some baked locusts with him, which he distributed to the members present, but he did not recommend them when cooked in that manner. They were not much relished in London, being compared by those who tasted them to burnt mutton fat and other unsavoury aliments. The common migratory locust is said to taste like stale shrimps. But although they are not likely to form a favourite article of food in civilised countries, yet I think that American ingenuity may find some other means of utilising these pests, and I would suggest that cockchafers are sometimes used in Germany to make an oil which can be applied to various common purposes.

By the Indian tribes of California grasshoppers are caught in great numbers. When the insect attains its best condition, the Indians select some favourable locality and dig several little pits, in shape somewhat like inverted funnels, the aperture being narrower at the surface than at the base, the object being to prevent the insect which chances to tumble in from hopping out again. The pits being ready, an immense circle is formed, the surrounding grass is set on fire, and the Indians, men, women, and children, station themselves at proper intervals around the fiery belt, keeping up a continual ring of flame, until the luckless grasshoppers are caught in the pits or roasted at the brink. Mixed with pounded acorns, they constitute one of the national dishes.

The Editor of the *Empire County Argus* (California) describes a great dish among the Digger Indians, in the districts where the grasshoppers are very numerous, and gives the following account of their mode of preparing the delicacy:—"A piece of ground is sought where they most abound, in the centre of which an excavation is made, large and deep enough to prevent the insect from hopping out when once in. The entire party of Diggers, old and young, male and female, then surround as much of the adjoining ground as they can, and with each a green bough in hand, whipping and thrashing on every side, gradually approach the centre, driving the insects before them in countless multitudes, till at last all, or nearly all, are secured in the pit. In the meantime smaller excavations are made, answering the purpose of ovens, in which fires are kindled and kept up till the surrounding earth, for a short distance, becomes sufficiently heated, together with a flat stone large enough to cover the oven. The grasshoppers are now taken in coarse bags, and after being thoroughly soaked in salt water for a few moments, are emptied into the ovens and closed in. Ten or fifteen minutes suffice to roast them, when they are taken out and eaten without further preparation, and with much apparent relish, or, as is sometimes the case, reduced to powder and made into soup. And having from curiosity tasted, not of the soup, but of the roast, really if one could but divest himself of the idea of eating an insect as we do an oyster or shrimp, without other preparation than simple roasting, they would not be considered very bad eating even by more refined epicures than the Digger Indians." Grasshoppers are also pounded up with service, hawthorn or other berries. The mixture is made into small cakes, pressed hard and dried in the sun for future use.*

---

* Report of Com. of Agriculture, 1870, p. 426. Washington.

It is a well ascertained fact that locusts are in Arabia and Northern Africa used as food now, as well as in former times. They also form an article of commerce. The inhabitants usually tear off their wings and wing coverts and then bake them. *Gryllus lineola*, Fabr., seems to be the species which is eaten and prepared in the manner above detailed in Barbary. The natives of Senegal dry another species, of which the body is yellow, spotted with black, and which Shaw and Denon have figured in the account of their Voyage in Africa; they then reduce them to powder which they use as flour. Capt. Burton tells us that the black leather-like variety of locust called by the Arabs " Satan's ass," is eaten by the Africans, as are many other edibles upon which strangers look with disgust.

There is some compensation in the circumstance that if the locusts devour the food of man they are themselves a source of food. In Morocco they are collected in sacks by night, and first boiled in salt and water, and then fried. Only the softer part of the body is eaten, much as we eat prawns, which they resemble in taste. They are considered to be wholesome food, and in perfection as soon as the insects can fly.

The inhabitants of Madagascar are ill fed for half the year; they prefer fried grasshoppers and silkworms, esteeming the latter a great delicacy. The author of " A Mission to Ava " also speaks of them as a Burmese dainty.

" The most notable viand produced consisted of fried locusts. These were brought in, hot and hot, in successive saucers, and I was not sorry to have the opportunity of tasting a dish so famous. They were by no means bad, much like what we might suppose fried shrimps to be. The inside is removed, and the cavity stuffed with a little spiced meat."

The locusts seem to be one of the greatest plagues of the Philippines, and sometimes destroy the harvests of entire provinces. It is the *Œdipoda subfasciata*, Haan; *Acridium Manilense*, Meyer; but the species does not belong

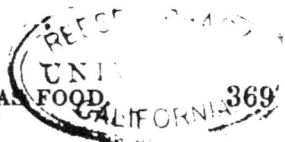

to the genus *Acridium* in the modern sense. It occurs also in Luzon and Timor, and is closely allied to our European migratory locust (*Œdipoda migratoria*).

The natives endeavour to reduce them by devouring the locusts themselves, for Mr. Jagor tells us, that when a swarm, which was more than five hundred feet in width, and about fifty feet in depth, arrived, whose extremity was lost in the forest, old and young eagerly endeavoured to catch as many of the delicate creatures as they could, with cloths, nets, and flags, in order, as Dampier relates, " to roast them in an earthen pan over a fire until their legs and wings drop off, and their heads and backs assume the colour of boiled crabs, after which process," he says, "they had a pleasant taste." In Burmah, at the present day, they are considered as delicacies. In papers, published June, 1869, on Colonel Fytches' mission to the Mandalay Parliament, we are told—"After the king had withdrawn, sweetmeats were brought, and also roasted locusts, which were pressed upon the guests as great delicacies."

In Mexico a species of ant (*Myrmecocystus melligerus*) has the translucid abdomen filled with a species of syrupy fluid which is eagerly sucked by children, and commonly employed in cases of earache. These ants are sold by dozens simply fastened in square pieces of paper, from which they cannot escape, if they are suspended.

The larvæ of ants are considered a great dainty in China, resembling flesh in taste. A certain species of red ant which makes its nests on tree tops are also eaten with ginger and salt, used as a condiment. It is very pungent. Termites, or white ants, as they are called, are also used as food, acccording to Dr. Macgowan.

Cameron, in his " Across Africa," mentions that dried white ants are eaten by the natives with porridge as a relish, on account of the scarcity of animal food.

" The ants are caught in rather an ingenious manner. A light framework of canes or twigs is built over a large ant hill and covered with leaves cleverly fastened together by sticking the mid-rib of each into the one above it. A very small entrance is left open at the bottom, and under this is dug a round hole a foot in diameter, and two feet deep. When the winged ants come out of the hill ready to migrate, they all make for this entrance and hustle each other into the hole, where they lose their wings, and are unable to get out. In the morning they are collected by the natives, who smoke them over slow fires to preserve them."

The small white bodies which ants are sometimes seen to carry are commonly but erroneously called ant eggs. They are in fact the larvæ (small worms or maggots) and the chrysalis, the young of the ants in various stages of growth.

The Digger tribe of Indians of California and the Plains feed upon ants, catching them by spreading a damped skin or fresh peeled bark over their hills, which immediately attracts the inhabitants to its surface. When filled, the cover is carefully removed and the adhering insects shaken into a tight sack, where they are confined until dead, and are then thoroughly sun-dried and laid away. Bushels are thus gathered annually, and are not more offensive than snakes, lizards, and crickets, which the tribe also eat. *

The Marquis de Compiegne, in his work on "Equatorial Africa," states that there is a small red ant called ntchongou which the Pahouins eat boiled.

When roasted the termites are said to be palatable as food, and as such to be highly esteemed by the natives in Central Africa. A Bayeye chief who paid a ceremonial visit to Dr. Livingstone's camp, was offered some bread and apricot jam. "Did you ever eat anything so good?" inquired the doctor. "Ah," responded the chief, "you should try roast white ants."

Capt. Carmichael thus speaks of them in a published work :—" One evening, it was I think about the middle of May, as we sat enjoying ourselves at dinner, we observed

---

* " Report of Com. of Agriculture, 1870," p. 426. Washington.

a number of flies of an uncommon aspect, flitting past the tent. We started up and endeavoured to catch one of them, but without effect. Some Hottentot children, who were standing on an opposite bank, remarking our anxiety, came and offered us whole handfuls of them, and directing us to the spot where they had caught them; our astonishment is not to be expressed when we beheld millions of winged insects issuing into daylight from fissures in the earth, and through the pores as it were of the ground where no opening was perceptible. Near these outlets the children had posted themselves, and collecting the insects as they emerged, greedily devoured them. Such of them as escaped the Hottentots were snapped up as they flew along by the small birds and by the *Libellulæ* and other predatory flies. The body of these tiny insects is so small and the wings are so large and unwieldy, that they could hardly support themselves in the air, as they floated along at the humour of the breeze. They were the males of the *Termes capensis*, commonly known as the white ant."

I have discoursed with several gentlemen (says Smeathman) upon the taste of the white ants, and on comparing notes we have always agreed that they are most delicious and delicate eating. One gentleman compared them to sugared marrow, another to sugared cream and a paste of sweet almonds.

In some parts of the East Indies the natives catch the winged insects just before their period of emigration, in the following manner. They make two holes, the one to the windward, the other to the leeward; at the leeward opening they place the mouth of a pot, the inside of which has been previously rubbed with an aromatic herb, called Bergera; on the windward side they make a fire of stinking materials, which not only drives these insects but frequently the hooded snakes also into the pots, on which account they are obliged to be cautious in removing them. By this method they catch great quantities, of which they make with flour a variety of pastry that they can afford to sell very cheap to the poorer ranks of people. When this sort of food is used too abundantly it produces cholera, which kills in two or three hours.

It also seems that in some form or other these insects are greedily eaten in other countries. Thus, when after swarming, shoals of them fall into the rivers, the Africans skim them off the surface with calabashes and bringing them to their habitations parch them in iron pots over a gentle fire, stirring them about as is usually done in roasting coffee; in that state without sauce or any other addition they consider them delicious food, putting them by handfuls into their mouths, as we do comfits. " I have," says Smeathman, "eaten them dressed in this way several times, and think them delicate, nourishing, and wholesome; they are somewhat sweeter, though not so fat and cloying, as the caterpillar or maggot of the palm tree snout beetle (*Curculio palmarum*), which is served up at all the luxuriant tables of the West Indian epicures, particularly of the French, as the greatest dainty of the Western world."*

The large saubas (red ants) and white ants are an occasional luxury to the Indians of the Rio Negro; and when nothing else is to be had in the wet season, they eat large earth-worms, which, when the lands in which they live are flooded, ascend trees, and take up their abode in the hollow leaves of a species of *Tillandsia*, where they are often found accumulated by thousands. Nor is it only hunger that makes them eat these worms, for they sometimes boil them with their fish to give it an extra relish. †

To sum up we may remark that all nations do not participate with us in the neglect of insects as food. It is not only savage nations we find indulging in these gastronomic dainties, but the more civilised races; those which have indeed been the cradle of refined civilisation have not scrupled to indulge in various insects as food.

---

* " Natural History of Insects."
† Wallace's " Travels on the Rio Negro."

Honey.—There is another insect product which forms a species of subsidiary food product, and that is honey. It is very largely used by many people and therefore deserves a few words of notice in this volume.

In 1869 we imported 15,000 cwts. besides a home production of about 2,000 tons. As honey is not enumerated now in the Board of Trade returns it is not possible to ascertain what our imports at present are.

At the present day all the civilised countries of the globe produce honey and give more or less attention to apiculture, according as the climate and vegetation are suited to the bees. The best honey is, however, the product of the milder parts of the temperate zone.

The principal European countries for honey are Russia, France, Austria, Germany, Spain and Portugal. A good deal of wild honey is, however, obtained by the native tribes in Australia, India, Africa and South America.

In no other country is the consumption of honey so large as in Russia, viz., some 13,000 tons. The reasons for this are the following: The fast days in the course of the year are numerous among the people attached to the orthodox church. Tea is in general use and honey is preferred to sweeten it, because as bullock's blood is employed in refining the beet-root sugar, it would be considered an infringement of the fasting rules to use it. But this is not the only reason, as a vast number of wax tapers and candles are burned in the churches, hence the demand for beeswax renders apiculture a very profitable branch of industry.

The annual production of honey in France in 1873 was estimated at 186,224 cwt., but it is now said to have reached 12,000 tons. The departments which possess the greatest quantity of hives are Morbihan, Ille-et-Vilaine, les Cotes du Nord, and La Manche, forming parts of the ancient province of Brittany. Those of which the honey is most esteemed and fetches the highest price are Aude, Herault and Savoy.

Italy, Greece, and in fact all the countries on the

Mediterranean, appear to have been famous lands for honey.

Among the delectables with which Arsinoë nourishes Adonis are "honey cakes" and other titbits made of "sweet honey." In the country of Theocritus this custom is said still to prevail. When a couple are married the attendants place honey in their mouths, by which they would symbolize the hope that their love may be as sweet to their souls as honey is to the palate. Every Eastern traveller can tell how the Arab dips his fresh flour-cake into the mingled cup of honey and butter, and needs no better sustenance in crossing the desert. St. John lived on locusts and wild honey in the desert.

According to the census returns the production of honey in North America was in—

						lbs.
1850	...	...	...	...	...	14,853,790
1860	...	...	...	...	...	23,366,357
1870	...	...	...	...	...	14,702,815

About thirty-five million pounds of honey are sold annually in the United States at the present time, and before long it is expected that it will sell at nearly the price of raw sugar and be able to be substituted for glucose or starch sugar in cooking, in confectionery, and in brewing. It is stated, I know not with what truth, that honey, which is used instead of sugar in the Cyclades, causes scrofula.

Like Galicia, Croatia and Slavonia are great honey countries and send to market 1,680 tons annually. At Segne there is a large honey refinery from which 28 tons are sent out in the year.*

There are a few other insect saccharine products eaten, but they are not of sufficient importance to require detailed description. Such are Lerp, a sweet

---

* Those more especially interested in the subject of honey, I may refer to a long article of mine in the "Journal of Applied Science," vol. 2, p. 84.

insect product of Australia formed on the Eucalypti, relished by the natives; trehalose, a peculiar sugar to the amount of nearly 29 per cent. contained in the small cocoons of *Larinus maculatus*, eaten in Persia; mopane on Bauhinia leaves, with the edible secretion of an insect *Psylla*, and some products of gall insects.

CHAPTER XI.

ANIMAL FOOD FURNISHED BY THE CRUSTACEANS AND MOLLUSCA.

Lobsters — Chemical Composition of the Lobster — Trade in, from Norway and Sweden — American Lobster Trade — Canned Lobsters—Cape Lobsters—Lobster Fisheries on the American Shores—Shrimps, varieties of—Prawns—Dried Shrimps — Feasting on Live Shrimps — Crayfish — Crabs, varieties of—Land Crabs—Mollusca—Edible Snails—Limpets—Whelks—Periwinkles—Haliotids, or Ear-shells.

THE extensive order of Crustaceans at present furnishes but a small number of species which are usually eaten, but there are no doubt many others that might probably be utilised. The common crustaceans are very generally used as food and greatly relished where they can be cheaply obtained. The lobster is most esteemed, but the French prefer the crayfish. Crabs and lobsters are in best condition in warm weather. Shrimps and prawns are other food delicacies furnished by this order.

Some years ago it was stated in the *Illustrated News* * that the number of crabs and lobsters annually consumed in the metropolis exceeded two millions and a half. Assuming that the populous cities of Liverpool, Manchester, Edinburgh, and Dublin together consume about the same quantity, we have a total of five millions of these large crustacea, to say nothing of the millions of shrimps and prawns consumed.

In Brazil, India, and China, dried shrimps form an extensive article of consumption. They are pounded into a powder with salt and spices. From the port of

---

* December 6th, 1862.

Newchang, 2,000 cwt. of dried shrimps are sent to other parts of China.

Of the crustaceans, the lobster is that which is principally in demand, although the more common crab is, of the two, most digestible and nourishing.   But the lobster has always been held in estimation as a food delicacy, and from being so sought for, leads to a very extensive commerce.

Lobsters.—About 3 million lobsters are annually taken in Norway and Sweden, and of these over 1 million are sent to England, sometimes $1\frac{1}{2}$ million have been shipped.   They are sold at from 3d. to 6d., according to size.   Those which are not 21 centimetres, or which have cast a claw, are only worth one-half.   They are kept in reservoirs and sent off in sailing vessels which take 15,000 to 20,000 at a time.

The shell of the Norwegian lobster (*Nephrops norvegicus*) is thin and of a bright red colour ; that of the Scotch lobster (*Homarus gammarus, Astacus marinus,* Fab.) is thick, and when boiled of a dark colour and covered with white specks.

Besides our home supplies—of which we have no very reliable returns—the bulk of our imports come from Norway and Sweden, and it may be interesting to glance at the statistics of the trade.   Lobsters are brought to Greenock in large numbers from the western islands, chiefly from Skye, in boxes containing from four to five dozen, and are there transferred for facility and economy of carriage by rail, to tea chests, into each of which from fifty to a hundred, according to size, are carefully packed, and forwarded regularly and in large quantities, in this way, to Liverpool, Manchester, Birmingham, and London, in each of which towns is located a branch of a great firm—originally of Aberdeen—to whom are continually consigned enormous quantities of fish from all parts of the coast.   Much might be done on the coasts of the British islands in the matter of lobsters, especially in Ireland.   In a report on the Irish Fisheries, it was stated that:—"Lobsters may be taken in any quantity; 20,000 or 30,000 a-week might be easily captured on about twenty miles of the coast of Clifden, Buffen Island, and Bunown, but the people have no means of taking them. They only fish close to the shore, and large lobsters cannot go into the pots used; those of five or six pounds', or eight or nine pounds' weight, are only taken by clinging to the sides of the pots; and if the fishermen had boats sufficient to go out to the rocks seven or eight miles off, they, with proper gear, would take the finest fish in the world, and in the greatest quantities. They may be had in season every day in the year that men could venture out to set the pots, but they never do so in the winter." The size and age to which they sometimes attain was evidenced by one caught a few years ago in Plymouth Sound in a trawl net, which was reported in the *Field*. Its length was, from the tip of the claws to end of tail, 3 ft. 2 in.; weight, 15 lbs. 2¼ oz. Several small oysters, mussels, and barnacles were adhering to the shell, and it was supposed to be one hundred years old, although what grounds there were for the assumption were not stated.

M. Payen gives the following as the percentage composition of the edible parts of the lobster:—

	Flesh.	Soft Internal Substance.	Spawn.
Nitrogenous Matter	19·170	12·140	21·892
Fatty Matter	1·170	1·144	8·234
Mineral Matter...	1·823	1·749	1·998
Non-Nitrogenous and Loss ...	1·219	0·354	4·893
Water	76·618	84·313	62·983
	100·	100·	100·

There is no substance which conveys phosphorus so readily into the human system, and which the system so readily and quickly assimilates, as the flesh of oysters, crabs, and lobsters. For this reason they should form the diet of those engaged in business or literary pursuits, where much wear and tear of the nerve powers takes place from day to day. Care must, of course, be taken that the organs of digestion are not disturbed by too large a quantity of this kind of diet. According to careful observations made at the Marine Laboratory, Concarneau, France, it appears that the first year the lobster sheds his shell six times, the second year six times, the third year four times, the fourth year three times. The following shows the rate of growth of the lobster after each casting of its shell:—

	Length in Inches.	Weight. Oz. Drms.
8th Shedding	2	0 1¾
9th ,, ...	2¼	0 2¼
10th ,, ...	2½	0 3¼
11th ,, ...	3	0 5¾
12th ,, ...	3½	0 9½
13th ,, ...	4	0 10¾
14th ,, ...	4½	1 4½

After a time, lobsters and crabs cease to shed their shells at all. From a lobster weighing from three to three and a half pounds, six ounces of berries may be obtained in the month of May; but in the month of August not six ounces of eggs could probably be obtained from a hundred lobsters. Mr. Scott, who boils lobsters for Scott's, at the top of the Haymarket, states that he has collected in April and May for the cooks from fourteen to eighteen pounds of lobster spawn. Mr. Buckland informs us that there are 6,720 eggs in an ounce of lobster spawn; here, then, we have destroyed eggs which might have represented, say in sixteen pounds of eggs, no less than 1,720,320 lobsters.

The Norway lobster is the *Nephrops norvegicus*. This crustacean is caught in the fiords from the southern extremity up to the Loffoden Islands, but it has been noticed for some years that there is a tendency in the lobster to keep more towards the north, where they are found of larger size. They are often taken by means of a common cask, the bottom of which is replaced by boughs, and a hole is left for the lobster to enter, attracted by the bait of the fresh herring suspended, but it cannot get out again. Osier pots are also used, but of a more oblong shape than those employed with us. The lobster fishery is prohibited between the 15th of July and the 15th of September, and they are not allowed to be taken under nine inches long. The trade is pretty much centralised at Christiansund. The lobsters are there placed in large reservoirs made in the centre of the fiord, where they are kept alive until dispatched to Belgium or England. A part are sent off in wooden boxes, and others in quick-sailing vessels, with holds having reservoirs capable of containing many thousand lobsters, the sea water passing freely through holes pierced in the ship's side.

The commerce in lobsters in Belgium is not in a very good state. In 1871, several cargoes were imported from Brittany; these lobsters are larger than those of Norway, but the flesh is not so good, and yet they sell at a somewhat higher price.

The whole of the fishery in Norway is monopolised by English speculators, so that it is difficult to buy a lobster, excepting of a diminutive size, without breach of contract, or paying comparatively an exorbitant price. The number exported annually ranged in the early part of the century from 600,000 to 800,000; from 1825 to 1829 it was higher, reaching an average of 1,280,000; in 1848 607,282 were sent away. The annual export from 1853 to 1859 was about 800,000. In the ten years ending with 1870 the average number shipped was 1,500,000. The shipments were in 1878, 1,081,000; 1879, 1,019,000; in 1880, 991,000.

From Sweden lobsters are almost exclusively exported from the port of Stromstad, on the western coast. The following shows the shipments for some few years :—

1853	...	...	60,200	1857	58.260
1854	...	...	72,440	1858	64,380
1855	...	...	39,540	1859	98,260
1856	...	...	49,246		

In 1871 56,509 were exported, of which 49,500 were sent to England.

Lobster fishing has been followed at Marshfield and Plymouth, Massachusetts, for thirty years and more. From 50,000 to 100,000 lobsters are taken annually, and sold to the smacks for the Boston market, and to pedlars for inland sale.

On the North American coasts a large trade is done in putting up lobsters in tins. For some years past the packing houses of Portland, Maine, have shipped lobsters in tins to England in ever-increasing quantities. The taste thus acquired has created a demand for the article in a fresh and more palatable state. To supply this demand the Portland firm of Marston and Sons, extensive dealers, have conceived the idea of shipping live lobsters by means of the British steamers which ply between Liverpool and that port. Lately a trial was made of a first consignment of this novel mer-chandise across the Atlantic from Portland. A tank was built on the main deck of the steamer "Sardinian," twenty feet long, eight feet wide, and three feet high, with a cover working on hinges. Through this tank a stream of salt water, pumped from the ocean by a donkey engine, and supplied by six faucets, constantly flowed. 200 live lobsters were placed in it, but only 25 arrived at Liverpool alive. This was merely an ex-periment, and future trials are expected to be more successful. Lobsters can be purchased at Portland for fourpence each.

Lobsters prepared in tin cases are exported from Nova Scotia to the United States and West Indies. There is an extensive establishment in Sambro Settlement, Halifax. The proprietors employ coasters to visit the fishing stations along the shore. These collect lobsters in immense quantities to supply their extensive fishing establishment, which puts up and exports 150,000 tins annually. Lobsters are found in various parts of the Annapolis basin. In Nova Scotia, in 1869, 52,400 cans or tins of lobsters, of one pound each, were recorded as being put up. In 1870 the quantity was more than ten times as great, viz., 553,000 cans, valued at 7½d. per can, or 82,950 dollars. In 1871 the quantity preserved in the province had increased to 905,500 tins, and in 1872 the trade had actually grown so wonderfully that no less than 2,422,508 tins, valued at 1s. each, were accounted for in the returns. Even this enormous yield became vastly increased in 1873, when 3,462,298 tins, of the gross value of 865,574 dollars, were preserved.

At Quebec the first record of the new business was in 1872, when 88,320 tins, of one pound each, were preserved, the value of which, estimated at 7½d. per tin, was 13,248 dollars. Here we find the industry falling off in the following year to 15,000 tins, worth 2,250 dollars. In the North American provinces generally, in 1873, 4,864,998 tins of lobsters were actually put up and sent to the markets of the world; and besides this, no account is taken of the quantity sold alive, or in a fresh state untinned. The exports in recent years have been as follows from the Dominion of Canada:—

	Lbs.		Lbs.
1873 ...	... 1,564,793	1879 ...	... 10,980,374
1876 ...	... 4,575,285	1880 ...	... 9,211,527

The American standard size at which lobsters may be taken varies in different States from 10 inches to 11½ inches clear in the body. The minimum size allowed in the British American provinces of 9 inches is considered too small. The lobsters caught annually in the Dominion are valued at £400,000.

The quantity taken in the last two years were :—

		1882.	1883.
Preserved in pound cans	...	16,803,736	13,364,020
Lobsters in weight	tons	1,812	964
,, alive	thousands	258,000	1,195,120

chiefly in Nova Scotia, New Brunswick, and Prince
Edward Island. New Brunswick preserved in tins in
1883, 4,042,954 cans, and 925 tons of live lobsters were
shipped in the year, and Prince Edward Island 3,844,573
cans at 8d. per can. The average quantity canned in
Nova Scotia is 5,000,000 cans. An extensive trade has
sprung up in shipping live lobsters to the United States,
about 1,000,000, a large number are also consumed
locally. In Nova Scotia there was a short catch in 1883,
although 17,000,000 lobsters were trapped, about four
to five lobsters were required for one pound can;
5,198,720 cans, equal to 108,307 cases of forty-eight
cans, were put up in 1882, and 4,870,339 cans in 1883.
The prices in 1883 were 5½ dollars a case, against 4½
dollars in 1882. About £2,000 worth of lobsters were
sold to American smacks.

In Newfoundland the average annual value of the
lobsters exported is about £21,700.

From 20,000 to 30,000 lobsters are collected annually
on the rocks of Heligoland; the close season being from
the 13th June to the 13th of September. These are
stored in lobster boxes containing often as many as 200
each, the lobsters being either for local use or sent to the
Continent, where Heligoland lobsters are greatly prized.

Lobsters are taken in wicker baskets called lobster
pots. These are about three feet long and two feet wide,
semi-cylindrical in form, that is, the bottom is flat and the
sides and top are in the form of an arch. At each end
is an opening for the ingress of the lobster; around this
opening are placed short, flexible pieces of wood, project-
ing into the basket, so arranged that they will easily
separate and allow the lobster to enter; but their points
close together after him and prevent his egress. They
have a door upon the top, through which the lobster is
taken out. A long line is attached to these pots; a

heavy stone, sufficient to sink it, is placed inside. They are baited with the heads or offal of fresh fish, and sunk to the bottom at about low water mark; the other end of the line is made fast to a block of light wood, called a buoy. The fishermen go out with their wherries freighted with these pots, and drop them at short intervals along the shore. During the season of lobster fishing, which lasts from March to July in America, hundreds of these buoys may be seen bobbing up and down like so many seals' heads. The fishermen visit them every morning, draw them up alongside of their boats, take out the lobsters, replenish the bait, and drop them again into the water. The lobsters, when first taken, are very fierce, and seize with their strong pincers upon whatever may be within their reach. When thrown together in the boat they will grapple and tear off each other's feelers and legs. Without much care in handling them the fingers of the fishermen get many a hard bite. To prevent them from injuring each other, the fishermen provide sharp-pointed wooden pegs, which they insert into the joint or hinge of their pincers; this prevents them from closing. When they have visited all their pots they row to the landing-place. If they now wish to preserve them for several days, they put them into a long box or kennel, made of plank, and bored full of holes, which is moored in the water at a little distance from the shore. If they wish to prepare them immediately for market, they are taken ashore in handbarrows and carried to a sort of shed, in which is fixed a large cauldron in which they are boiled. In some parts of the Gulf of St. Lawrence lobsters are so plentiful that, notwithstanding their increased commercial value since the foundation of this new industry, good, marketable lobsters are used to manure the fields.

"The heavy gales of August, 1873," writes the proprietor of a large establishment at Shippegan, "drove more lobsters ashore within five miles of my packing-houses, than I could make use of during the whole summer. They formed a row from one to five feet deep, and

I should estimate them at an average of one thousand to every two rods of shore."

And yet notwithstanding the wonderful abundance of this crustacean, there are signs that the yields are falling off, in all probability in consequence of the immense drain upon the supplies. The whole of the edible part of the lobster is not utilised by the curers, who say that the trouble of picking out the flesh from the claws is too great, and that lobsters are too cheap to make it worth while to go to the expense of this slight additional labour. These wasteful habits will, we fear, bring their own inevitable consequences in their train, unless some check be placed upon the destructiveness of those engaged in the trade.

Lobsters large or small, breeding or not, are, or were, at one time treated alike, and the immense destruction which the foregoing figures indicate, naturally had its effect upon the supply. If the breeding stock and the growing supply of any kind of produce be systematically killed down, the result will be a gradually decreasing and ultimately exhausted field, and this was the threatened fate of the lobster treasure. Fortunately, the Government of the Dominion of Canada interfered. The Inspector of Fisheries at New Brunswick in a recent report on the fisheries of that province, made the following remarks:—" In view of this rapidly increasing business done in preserved lobsters, and the large number of those shell-fish which are now yearly caught in both provinces, I respectfully recommend that the lesson to be learnt from our oyster-beds be pondered in time, and means taken to prevent a like result in the case of the lobster. Heretofore this shell-fish has been plentiful on some of our coasts. There are many other countries probably where the business of preserving lobsters in tins could be profitably carried on, and whenever this is the case, I trust the above figures and facts will lead in the first place to the foundation of such an industry, and in the second place to the adoption of proper precautions to prevent the exhaustion of the beds."

C C

In a curious old bill rendered in the reign of Charles II. to Mr. Walter Tucker, Mayor of Lyme, Dorset, when entertaining the Judges on their assize visit, occur the following items :—Thirty lobsters, £1 10s., six crabs, 6s. ; 100 scallops, 5s. ; 400 oysters, 4s. That the judges were partial to shell-fish seems evident, and the comparison of prices then and now is remarkable.

The Cape lobster (*Palinurus Lalandii*, Lam.) is used as food by the Cape colonists. This cray fish, peculiar to the west coast and common in Table Bay, is easily caught in vast numbers all the year round, and attains a length of thirteen inches and a breadth of nearly five inches. The flesh of the half-grown individual is tender and delicate, while that of the adult is coarse and difficult of digestion. To the poorer classes this cray-fish is a regular God-send, and it is dried occasionally for preservation.

Crayfish and lobsters are very abundant on the west coast of South America. At Juan Fernandez they are found in such quantities that the fishermen have no greater trouble to take them than to strew a little meat or other bait upon the shore, and when they come to devour it, as they do in immense numbers, to turn them on their backs with a stick. By this simple method many thousands are taken annually, and the tails, which are in high estimation, are dried and sent to Chili.

According to an article in *Scribner's Monthly*, the coast of Maine, with its deep indentations and its numberless shoals and shallows, is, perhaps, the finest lobster fishery in the world. In spring the lobster migrates from the deeper, and consequently warmer waters, and takes up his summer residence amongst the shallows inshore. The period of this migration marks the commencement of the principal lobster-harvest. Lobsters may be caught at any season, but a State law forbids their being "canned" at other times than between the 1st of March and the 1st of August. Lobsters of from 25 to 43 lbs. in weight are found exceptionally, but they are likely to be still rarer in the future, since the average size is being diminished by a rapacity similar to that which has ruined several of our English fisheries. Placed within a floating "lobster car," the finer specimens are selected for consumption in Boston, New York, and other centres of population, and the smaller ones are consigned to the smacks of the various lobster factories. In the factory—not altogether a savoury place—they are boiled wholesale in large coppers, and are then taken out with "scoop-nets" and thrown over the shoulders of the operators. A rapid dissection follows, and the meat is forced out by various appliances. The "cracker," by two dexterous blows with a cleaver, breaks the claws, and their contents are picked out with forks by a troop of young-lady "helps." Other female functionaries place an assortment of meat in each tin and complete the weighing operations. The cover is put in place, and the tin comes under the hands of the solderer, a workman who commands a high price for his exertions. The solderer closes the "can," with the exception of a minute hole, through which the enclosed air is expelled during a subsequent boiling in a "bath-caldron." The tins are then taken out, completely sealed, and are subjected to a second boiling lasting several hours. The remaining processes are connected with ornamentation and the affixing of labels. Nine-tenths of the lobsters "packed" in this way are sold in foreign markets.

As much as 30,000 tons of lobsters are said to be caught every season in the Lower Provinces, and more than 14,000,000 1lb. tins of lobster are sent annually into the markets of the world from British America alone, besides those packed in the United States. In 1879 there were preserved in tins in Prince Edward Island, 2,272,825 1 lb. tins of lobsters. The Bay of Chaleur and the Madelaine Islands are the great seats of the lobster fishery. This species is *Homarus Americanus.*

Of lobsters and crayfish 1,367,045 in number, and of

shrimps and prawns 1,537,107 kilos (of 2 lbs.) were caught in France in 1876. Of the larger crustaceans the supply to France in 1878 was 1,466,249, and of shrimps and prawns 1,369,741 kilos. in weight. The number of crustaceans brought into the French markets by their own fishermen in 1879, was 1,790,463.

From an establishment at Roscoff, Paris receives annually not less than 30,000 lobsters, and Russia, Belgium, and Germany also make large demands upon it, 1,500 being often sent off at a time. They are fed in these enclosures or tanks, with sharks, conger eels, and other waste fish, as they are very voracious.

Mr. Richard Scovell has, at Hamble near Southampton, a large reservoir in which 50,000 lobsters can be kept alive for at least six weeks. Vessels are employed in visiting the fishing grounds and bringing in from 5,000 to 10,000 lobsters each.

The largest crustacean is the spiny lobster (*Palinurus vulgaris*) which often weighs as much as twelve or fifteen pounds. It was in great esteem amongst the ancients, who denominated it *Locusta*.

Crayfish.—In Victoria there are no true lobsters and no crabs fit for the table, except a spiny crayfish, of about the same size and shape as the English species, which is supplied abundantly to the market. It is nearly, or quite identical, with the *A. annulicornis*. The gigantic Murray river crayfish (*Astacoides serratus*) is sent down alive in great numbers to the markets for the table; the smaller river crayfish (*Astacoides quinque-carinatus*) is also often eaten in the country.

In France the government has granted an appropriation by which more than 300 rivers and brooks can be stocked with German crayfish. Even these are not sufficient for the great demand, and large numbers are still imported from Germany. From Styria fattened crayfish have been sent to Paris by Baron de Washington.

Our river crayfish (*Potamobius astacus*) is largely caught, and when fresh boiled is a dish not to be despised.

It is largely imported into London for the purpose of garnishing dishes.*

The small river crayfish "ecrevisses" are in great demand in France, for making the celebrated *bisque* soup, and for serving up as a garnish to other dishes. From Berlin they are sent weekly to the Paris market to the value of £160 during the season of summer.

In the San Francisco market crayfish are sold at 6d. to 7½d. the pound.

The large crayfish of Tasmania (*Palinurus Edwardsii*) forms an article of export to New South Wales. This species attains a length of from 1 foot to 18 inches, and finds a ready sale at from 1s. 6d. to 2s. 6d. each. The fresh-water species (*Astacopsis Franklinii*) exceeds that of its representative on the main land.

There is brought in annually to the Vienna markets from Upper Austria about 123½ million pounds of crayfish (*Astacus fluviatilis*). It is considered a great table delicacy in Europe and sells at high prices.

The river crayfish in the lakes on the borders of the Danube, attain extraordinary dimensions, equalling in size small lobsters. Those of the ponds and rivers, though not so large, are equally savoury. They are caught in great quantities and largely consumed, especially in the fast days of spring.

Shrimps and Prawns.—Although at first sight shrimps might be thought to be of small value, yet for food purposes the shrimping industry is of very great importance in many countries.

In the great Thames estuary, between the North Foreland on the south and Harwich on the north, are thousands of acres of sand plateaus, favourable to shrimps. From this great shrimp farm are netted up hourly, daily, from April to October, thousands and ten thousands of shrimps; yet in spite of the number caught there does not appear, except at times, to be any falling off of these "sea flies," as they are sometimes called.

---

* Cassell's "Natural History."

The principal shrimping grounds near Margate are the " Queen's Channel," the " Gore," and the grounds below the Nore Light.

The art of shrimping was first discovered at Margate by Mr. J. Shrubsall, fish merchant, of that town. When he first began, half a century ago, he could take from 30 to 100 gallons at one haul. In the neighbourhood of Pegwell Bay and Ramsgate most of the shrimps are caught by " pushing "—i.e., by a hand-net worked by a man wading. Morecambe Bay may be said to be placed next in importance as regards shrimps to the Thames estuary. We learn from the report of the Commissioners for Sea Fisheries that the Morecambe Bay shrimp fisheries alone are worth about £4,000 a year. Shrimps from this part of Lancashire are sent mostly to the vast manufacturing populations of the iron districts and the midland counties.

A very large number of shrimps are used in London for food. Sometimes the red shrimps are sold mixed with the brown, but generally they are sent to market separately. The most abundant of the two kinds is the bunting, the " chevrette " of the French. It is of a grayish brown colour, dotted all over with brown spots, and does not become red by heat. It is also called the " grey shrimp " and the " sand shrimp." Connoisseurs in shrimps consider the red or beaked shrimp much better than the brown or flat-nosed species.

The costermongers of London sell annually about 770,000 pints of shrimps at 2d. per pint, which is rather below the market price. The value of this quantity will be £6,400 a year. To this we must add the enormous quantities sold in shops, and those consumed in Birmingham, Manchester, and Liverpool ; in fact, all over England. Shrimps are boiled before being carried to market, and there is an art even in the apparently simple process of boiling shrimps. They are placed in nets, and plunged alive in water that is fiercely on the boil. The putting in of the shrimps lowers the temperature of the water for a moment. The experienced shrimp boiler, therefore heats the poker and stirs up the water in which the shrimps are placed, in order that the temperature of the water shall be kept up to the boiling point while the shrimps are being cooked. Shrimps are in season during the whole year, though the chief demand is in spring. A preparation of potted shrimps is sold.

In North America shrimps are pickled and spiced. By the Chinese in California they are sold plain, peeled, and also strung on matting. The meat after being dried is pulverised and put through a fanning mill. Shrimps of a very large size, crabs, and other crustacea are abundant on the coasts of Peru.

A species of *Palæmon* is brought dried in sacks from the Pacific coast to Mexico to be eaten in Lent. They are pounded, and the powder is mixed with rice and chillies to flavour the little cakes or croquettes, which are fried in oil. The flavour is something like old dried codfish.

The large dried prawns ("Camarones") of Brazil, so delicious when eaten fresh, may please the lovers of highly-spiced food. The fish of the Amazon, salted, dried, and reduced to powder, may be useful to those who voyage on that river, and the numerous Indians who coast it, but would not suffice for the basis of nourishment of the Europeans or North Americans.

Enormous quantities of shrimps are obtained on the coasts of Belgium and Holland; in the latter country they were formerly used to manure land. They are often salted to be sent to tropical countries. In 1867 there were exported from Holland to England 350,000 kilos., and to Belgium 104,000 kilos.; in 1882 we received 1,178,000 kilos. from Holland. There are now 2,000 to 3,000 men employed in Holland and Belgium catching shrimps.

Shrimps are now three times as valuable as they were, they sell at 3d. to 6d. a quart.

The Boston fishermen believe there are three kinds of shrimps, the sea shrimps (*Pandanus annulicornis*), which come in June; the land shrimps (*Crangon vulgaris*), which are always there; and the prawns (*Palemon serratus*). The common brown shrimps or buntings (*C. vulgaris*), are caught from the 1st September to 1st of April, the red shrimps from 1st of April to 30th of September. The brown shrimps are taken in the mud, the red shrimps are not. The Leigh fishermen catch shrimps all the year round from Gravesend to Margate.

Shrimp canning has recently been added to the industries of New Orleans. One establishment there employs 150 boys and girls and from twenty to thirty skilled workmen. Already the output is 10,000 cans a day, and it is expected that the product will soon be doubled. The shrimps are cooked and canned by a new process. It is intended to undertake also the canning of oysters, which are abundant along the Gulf coast.

Tunis, the ancient Carthage, was always celebrated for prawns, and the Roman emperors used to send for them for their banquets. They are of great size, six to seven inches long. Dried shrimps are eaten in Persia.

The prawn is caught in great abundance in Norway, especially in the east. The Svelvig prawn (*Pandanus borealis*), which is distinguished by its red colour, and is two or three times as large as the ordinary prawn, is caught exclusively at Svelvig, and sold at Drammen where it is much sought after.

At Mergui, Burmah, there are over 550 men employed in fishing for shrimps and prawns, by boats with submerged nets. The prawns when brought in are spread on mats and exposed to the sun for several days until quite hard and dry; they are then put into wooden mortars and pounded with wooden mallets, which knock off all the skin or husky shell. They are then sold for £8 or £10 per hundred viss (the viss is 3 lbs. 2 ozs.), and the husk is sold as a manure at £3 per 100 baskets.

The Rev. M. Stewart, a chaplain in the United States navy, in his work " A Visit to the South Seas," describing a dinner given by the native monarch of Owhyhee, says :—" We greatly relished a repast so well prepared and so neatly served. After the meats were removed,

Madame Boke (the governor's wife) drew the casters and salad bowl near her, as I at first supposed, to give us a specimen of her tact in salad-dressing; but on seeing a servant approach with a parcel handsomely done up in green leaves, dripping with water, and observing a smile of archness playing on the features of her ladyship as she received it from him, I began to suspect it was only in preparation for some *bonne bouche,* peculiarly epicurean in its character. Such it proved to be, for on carefully untying it, while her eye brightened more and more with pleasantry, she suddenly scattered the contents, a quantity of live shrimps, as pure and transparent as could be, and as sprightly as crickets, over the cresses, and dashing the cruet of vinegar upon the whole, caught up a half dozen of the delicate creatures in the leaves of the salad and tossed them with a laugh into her mouth, by way of encouragement to us to join in the course. The captain is too courteous a gentleman to stop short of any civility due to the lady of the house, and considering this a kind of challenge, went through the movement of taking a similar quantity in his fingers, and in raising it to his mouth, whether with the intention of following the example farther on or not, I cannot say; but *ruse* or not, I saw one at least of the nimble fry hop fairly down his throat."

From the small port of St. Gilles-sur-Vie, in the depart- of Vendée, there are sent annually to Paris during the season (which lasts from April to October) 26,000 lbs. of shrimps worth 1s. 3d. per pound. The species are *Palæmon serratus* and *P. squilla,* called locally " crevettes " and " chevrettes." The whole quantity taken in France in 1879 was stated at 1,647,588 kilogrammes (3,600,000 lbs.)

The small pea crab (*Pinnotheres pisum*), which lives within the shell of the common American oyster, is much valued by oyster-eaters in the United States. In opening a large quantity of oysters these little crabs are collected apart, and serve to gratify the palate of gourmands. They are only seven-twentieths of an inch long, by two-fifths wide.

In Japan, among the crustaceans used for food, figure first the crabs, which are called kagni. They are common and belong to different species, some of which attain a large size. The lobster is also caught, but does not attain so large a size as in Europe, indeed it may probably be another species. There are a great quantity of shrimps and prawns of various kinds, some of which attain a large size.

Crabs are caught like lobsters in great quantities on the coast of Norway, in traps or casks prepared for the purpose. Although large and fine they are little esteemed, being never eaten on the coasts, and fetch but low prices in the inland towns. They are chiefly chopped up for bait. Lately the Norwegians have commenced to preserve the crab in hermetically sealed tins. Specimens of this new product were shown at the Paris Exhibition in 1878, and there is ground for the hope that, thanks to this preparation, the crab will in time find a foreign market. Two to three million crabs are sent yearly from Finland to Russia and Sweden.

In the London market crabs boiled sell at from 1s. 6d. to 4s. each, according to size. In the San Francisco market they fetch about 1s. each; and at Victoria, British Columbia, they retail at 2s. to 3s. the dozen. The excellence of the crab is mainly due to the enormous development of the liver, which occupies the two anterior sides of the carapace, and is deemed by most the "tit-bit."

The chief time for the sale of the great crab (*Cancer pagurus*, Lin.) is May to August. The demand falls off in October and is not resumed till March, as in the winter they are watery. Crabs are brought to market both in a boiled and in a raw state. The male is of greater value than the female, and has larger claws. Before boiling, a good crab is known by the roughness of its shell, particularly on the claws. When boiled, its quality is tested by holding the claws tight and shaking the body, which will rattle, or seem as if water were in the inside, if it be not in perfection.

The spiny spider crab (*Maia squinado*) frequents nearly all parts of our coasts and is by far the largest of the family. It is eaten by the poorer classes, though it is but indifferent food.

The common or shore crab (*Carcinus mœnas*) is very abundant on the coasts of France. Although its flesh is not delicate, large quantities are consumed, and during the months of June and July a great many are sent both to the Paris markets and those of the large towns in the interior.

(*Cancer fluviatilis*, Belon.), is eaten in Italy, in seasons of abstinence, and wonderful properties are ascribed to its flesh for the cure of throat affections.

In Central and Southern Italy a freshwater crab (*Telphusa fluviatilis*) is pretty common, and sought for; near Florence they are kept for some time in the dark, isolated in earthen jars, so that they may shed their carapace, and becoming soft are more easily eaten.

In Chili, under the name of "Centollas," *Herbstia condyliata* is eaten by the natives. The edible or blue crab of New Jersey, America, is *Callinectes hastatus*, Ordway.

Land Crabs.—A tropical food dainty, which we never see in this country, is the land crab (*Gecarcina ruricola*). These literally swarm in the Bahamas and afford food for the inhabitants the greatest part of the year; even the hogs are fed with them. It is the grey or white kind of crab, common to Cuba and the Bahamas. In the autumn they are very fat, and equal in flavour to the black species of Jamaica. They are found in myriads in all parts and thought a great delicacy.

The *Cardisoma carnifer*, Latr., of the mangrove swamps is regarded as a luxurious article of food by the West Indians. They are caught in box rat traps, baited with a piece of the Anona fruit, of which they are very fond. After their capture they are usually kept some time and fattened with broken victuals.

The robber crab (*Birgus latro*) common to the Islands of the Pacific and the East, is considered a table delicacy;

moreover under the tail of the larger ones there is a great mass of fat, which when melted, sometimes yields as much as a quart of limpid oil.

The island of Taboga, near Panama, has always been celebrated for its land crabs. Towards the end of Lent, but more particularly after the first heavy showers of the rainy season, they leave their holes in the mountains and descend in great numbers to the seaside, marching during the night, being steadily bent on reaching the sandy beaches of the island. The females are loaded with ova, and the males are as ill-tempered as a Londoner who has to take his family to the seaside whether he will or not. Men, women and children, start out after dark with lanterns, and hunt the crabs in their descent. Large kettles are left at home ready with boiling water into which the bag full of doomed land crabs is emptied when the hunt is over.

This wonderful animal migration is looked on as a sort of Godsend to make up for the rigour of Lent.

It is found in this locality only on the group of islands of which Taboga is the largest.

The land crabs are considered a great luxury both in Panama and in Jamaica. It is reported of a governor of the latter island, that in his opinion the two best things in Jamaica were the land crabs and the Sambo girls. In Jamaica and some other West India islands millions on millions, at certain periods, may be seen progressing from the hills to the sea, and from the sea back to the hills, uniting at certain periods in vast numbers, and moving in the most direct course to the sea, marching in squadrons and lines, just like bands of soldiers proceeding to a battle point of concentration, but halting twice a day for feeding and repose.

When the black or violet mountain crab is fat and in a perfect state, it surpasses everything of the sort in flavour and delicacy ; and frequently joins a little of the bitter with its native richness, which renders it not only the more agreeable in general, but makes it sit extremely easy upon the stomach. They are frequently boiled and served up whole, but are commonly stewed when served up at the more sumptuous tables.

MOLLUSCA.

We pass now to the Mollusca, a large number of which afford food for man and other animals. Upwards of 15,000 species have been described, but the number which deserves notice here is but limited.

Snails.—Many land and marine mollusca are eaten as food. Among the land ones various snails are considered dainty morsels. The species principally eaten in Europe is the apple snail (*Helix pomatia*, Lin.) but several other kinds are also used, such as the garden snail (*H. aspersa*, Lin.), the wood snail (*H. nemoralis*, Lin.), the banded snail (*H. pisana*, Lin.), *H. aperta*, *H. rhodostoma*, *H. vermiculata* and *H. lactea.*

Besides the ancient Romans the noble Danes ate snails in the eighteenth century.

The taste for eating snails prevails in Austria, France, Switzerland, Spain, and Italy, and has even extended to the United States. At Cape Coast and beyond Ashantee, as well as on several parts of the West Coast, the African *Achatina* are much esteemed as food; they are, with the species of *Bulimus*, the largest of land shells, many being eight inches long. Three or four hundred of these dried molluscs strung together will sell for a dollar.

Not very attractive to the stranger is the favourite dish of many a European nation—roasted or pickled snails. The slimy, slippery form of these animals makes them to most persons peculiarly repulsive, but their extraordinary nutritive power and excellent taste has long since served to defeat all prejudice. While the Ashantees, and other African natives of low grade, smoke them and eat them as daily food all the year round, more civilised races employ them only as relish, or for special occasions.

The large land snails, *Achatina* and *Bulimus* of Africa

and America, are highly relished. The Romans already valued the cochleana and fattened them until they reached truly gigantic dimensions. Horace informs us they were served up broiled upon silver gridirons to give a relish to wine

Many are familiar with the passage in Pliny (*Hist.* lib. ix., c. 56), who, on the authority of Varro, relates the incredible size to which the art of fattening had brought the snails. Even assuming the snails were African *Achatina* or *Bulimi*, there must, one should think, be some mistake in the text, which says, " Cujus artis gloria in eam magnitudinem perducta sit, ut octoginta quadrantes caperent singularem calices." Pennant, referring to this and to Varro (*De Re Rustica*) says, " If we should credit Varro, they grew so large that the shells of some would hold ten quarts ! "

But this is a misapprehension, the quadrans referred to being a small copper coin $\frac{3}{4}$ of an inch in diameter about the size of a sixpence and $\frac{1}{16}$ of an inch thick.

Shortly before the outbreak of the civil war with Pompey, Fluvius Hirpinus was the first in the Tarquinian district to establish snail ponds. He arranged them in separate divisions; one for the white snails from Reatine, one for the Illyrian snails, distinguished by their great size, one for the African snails, which are very fruitful, and another for the Solitanian snails, which are the finest of all. He even invented a special kind of food for them, prepared of thick must, flour, and other ingredients, and by means of this artificial diet, they grew to an enormous size. The ancients knew how to prepare even sea urchins and star fish as dainty dishes.

The Capucins of Lorraine also carried on this industry of fattening snails.

The large Roman or edible snail is renowned both as a delicacy and on account of its reputed virtues as a remedy in cases of consumption, which it is said has in several instances been entirely cured by a regimen of the mucilage from these snails. On the Continent the Roman snail is considered a great delicacy; but the garden and yellow banded snails are the kinds more commonly eaten. A snail feast is held annually in the South of France, on Ash Wednesday, when large numbers of them are consumed. An analogous custom is said to prevail in our own country amongst the operatives of Lancashire and at Newcastle.*

In our day also they are prescribed as eminently useful to sufferers in consumption, and all Southern Europe affects them during the times of animal fasting. In Switzerland and Italy the traveller finds large establishments where they are carefully raised, and either disposed of at home or potted and sent by millions to foreign counties. *Helix hortensis* makes a capital broth for weak persons, and *H. pomatia* may be found in many countries. In Venice all snails are eaten, at least by the poor, in France they are consumed in incredible numbers, and in Germany and America they are also eaten. In summer great quantities of snails are consumed in Roumania.

Snail eating has been prevalent in Italy for many centuries. In Pliny's time Barbary snails stood first in repute, those of Sicily ranking next; and it was the custom to fatten the creatures for the table by dieting them upon meal and new wine.

In modern Rome fresh gathered snails are hawked by women from door to door for the benefit of housewives, who boil them in their shells, and stew or fry them in oil. It is a common sight to see in an Italian city the people gathered around a number of baskets filled with snails, waiting to be thrown into a large iron pot standing over a fire made between four stones, and boiled with herbs and tomatoes for retailing to the expectant crowd.

Chambers's Journal informs us that an Englishman at dinner with a Sicilian gentleman, was invited to partake of some snails treated in this way, and for politeness sake, forced himself to swallow two of them, although he found it impossible to feign the delight with which

---

* B. B. Woodward, in " Science for All," p. 246.

the host and his daughter sucked the mollusks out of their shells.

A century ago, some 4,000,000 snails were annually exported from Ulm in "kegs" of 10,000, fetching from 25 to 40 florins a keg. In Tyrol youngsters of both sexes are employed during the summer months collecting snails as stock for the snail gardens—small plots of land cleared of trees, and covered with heaps of moss and pine twigs, and separated from each other by moats, having gratings at their outlets, to prevent any truants that may get into the water from being carried beyond bounds. The prisoners are supplied daily with fresh grass and cabbage-leaves, until their appetites fail, and they retire into the moss heaps for their winter's sleep, the last one they will enjoy; for when spring comes, they are routed out of their beds, packed into straw-lined boxes and sent to market. In a favourable season, one of these gardens will turn out 40,000 snails. The consumption of them in the South Tyrol is great; the Italians and Tyrolese are not the only people who appreciate the merits of these clean-feeding mollusks; in Paris, Burgundian snails are worth one halfpenny apiece, and £500 worth of snails are disposed of in the markets in the course of a year. Indeed a special portion of the market has been allotted for the sale of snails.

In the canton of Appenzel, Switzerland, they raise and fatten snails, of which large consignments are made to Vienna to be consumed in Lent. The provinces of Burgundy and Provence are also places of its cultivation. Throngs of women and children scour the country, collecting the snails in immense numbers, and depositing them in little tracts of land, enclosed with simply a trail of sawdust. This last the snail hates; he cannot cross it, and avoids its vicinity as a matter of preference. Therefore, for his confinement it is as good as a stone wall. After incarceration for two or three days, he is permitted to starve, and then the plot is laid out in patches of turf intersected by paths of sand. Above, boards are hung to serve as shelter for the snails, which instinctively gather in large groups. The food provided consists of aromatic plants, such as mint, or lettuce and fragments of vegetables. This is given to them three times a day in enormous quantities. At the end of eight days, the snails become quite obese, and besides have attained a very succulent flavour. Then comes another period of starvation for several days, after which transmission to market follows.

Gourmands, it is said, prefer the snail when taken wild, so long as the capture is made at a particular period. After the eggs are laid in May, the mollusks conceal themselves under stones to avoid the autumn frosts. There they become perfectly free from excretions, and, drawing themselves into their shells, close up for the winter. It is when they are collected in this state that their flavour is said to be best.

Rossmassler (" Reise-Erinerungen aus Spanier ") mentions having seen fourteen different species of *Helicidæ* brought to the markets in Mexico and Valencia and sold to be eaten. He adds that snails are not food for the poor alone in Spain, for many kinds are too costly for them. One species, called *Serranos*, is sold for a penny each of our English money; but they are not half that price bought by the dozen. They cook them by stewing, shells and all, in a richly-spiced sauce, and then they put the shell to the mouth, and draw out the animal by sipping or sucking it. *H. lactea* is brought in great numbers to the markets in Andalusia, as well as *H. aspersa*, but the former is the best tasted and most delicate.

A large snail, probably *Plectrocheilus undulatus*, is found in immense quantities in the forests about the Gold Coast and other parts of West Africa, and contributes greatly to the food of the natives.

Something like 90,000 lbs. of snails are sent up daily to the Paris markets from the gardens of Poitou, Burgundy, Champagne, and Provence, where they are specially reared for this purpose, the natural delicate flavour of their flesh being improved by feeding them on beds of aromatic herbs. It is not only as a delicacy that snails are so generally appreciated in France. They also take high rank as a most nutritive food, and from the time of the Romans downward have been regarded as an excellent medicine in consumption and weakness of the chest. According to Payen they contain 70 per cent. of water, 16 per cent. of nitrogen, 1 per cent. of fat, 2 per cent. of salts, and 5 per cent. of undetermined matter.

M. Charles Mene gives the following analysis of the edible snail, which is even more favourable: —

Water	...	...	...	...	...	72·747
Nitrogenous matter		...	...	...	...	17,652
Fatty substance	...	...	...	...	...	1,125
Non-nitrogenous	...	...	...	...	...	6,300
Salts	...	...	...	...	...	2·176

Nitrogen 2·823.

Doctor Ebrard,* who has made it the object of his peculiar attention, declares that the weight of meat represented by the snails sold amounts to that found on cutting up a whole flock of calves and young heifers. The doctor in his report enters largely into the mode of preparation for the table. He is aware that he is treading on tender ground,—very tender ground indeed,— and wishes, while the gourmand is enjoying the nutrition which the snail affords, to make him forget as much as possible, whence that nutrition proceeds. He recommends that they should be boiled in the shell, baked in the oven, and then chopped up with parsley and butter. But, alas! the first thing provided by the municipality of Paris alarms us, and makes us pause before we precipitate ourselves upon this new gastronomic delight. It is a superintending officer whose business it is to see that the creatures are in a fit state to be served as food, and to ascertain whether their digestive tubes are in

---

* " Les Escargots, au point de vue de l'Alimentation," etc.

proper order, because if they have been feeding in places where hemlock and belladonna grow, the most horrible convulsions, delirium, and death will follow on indulgence in a feast of snails. Some people are delighted to behold this new element of food introduced into the market, for snails have been the object of the most especial grudge ever since they destroyed the vines, and forced the people who devoured them to do so without the sour sauce which renders them so delicious; and already have the exhortations of the municipality met with some success, as the report sent in concerning the ratio of their consumption shows that ever since their registration at the Halle this has gone on steadily increasing.

In preparing snails for the table in France they are first well washed and then thrown shell and all into boiling water, where they are allowed to remain till well cooked. The liquor is then strained off, the contents of the shells extracted with a suitable instrument, and chopped up into a fine hash with sardines and bread crumbs. The shells are then crammed with this forcemeat, boiled lightly in butter, garnished with parsley, and served up with a sauce prepared from the broth obtained in the boiling stages of the process. It is not generally known that the French first acquired their appreciation of these mollusks from the Germans, who introduced the custom of eating them into the Eastern provinces, whence it spread rapidly through the whole country. In Germany it has fallen into complete disuse, except in some few parts of Bohemia.

Snails, as we have seen, were highly esteemed by the Romans, our masters in gastronomy, and are now raised in many of the departments of France with success. In the sixteenth century the Capuchins of Fribourg recovered the art of breeding and fattening snails, an art which is not lost in our day, for in Franche-Comte, Lorraine, and Burgundy they raise excellent snails, which find a sure demand in the Paris market.

There are now fifty restaurants and more than twelve

hundred private tables in Paris where snails are accepted as a delicacy by from eight thousand to ten thousand consumers. The monthly consumption of this mollusk is estimated at half a million. The market price of the great vineyard snails is from two francs fifty cents to three francs fifty cents per hundred, while those of the hedges, woods, and forests, bring only from two francs to two francs fifty cents. The proprietor of one snailery in the vicinity of Dijon is said to net over 7,000 francs annually.

That our ancestors in Britain ate snails and considered them delicacies is certain. In Ben Jonson's "Every Man in his own Humour" old Henswell, when excusing himself for having taught extraordinary and luxurious habits to his son, says—

> " Neither have I
> Drest snails and mushrooms curiously before him,
> Perfumed my sauces, taught him how to make them."

Robert May, who had been cook to Sir Kenelm Digby, and published his "Accomplished Cook," the best of the old English cookery books, the fruit of fifty years' experience in the best and most hospitable English families, in 1660, gives no less than nine different recipes for cooking snails; one to dress snails, three to stew snails, two to fry snails, one to hash snails, one to dress snails in pottage—"very nourishing and excellent food against consumption,"—and one to bake snails. Here is the last recipe, and really it reads very well:—

"*To bake Snails.*—Being boiled and scoured, season them with nutmeg, pepper and salt, put them in a pie with some marrow, large mace, a raw chicken cut in pieces, some little bits of lard and bacon, the bones cut out, sweet herbs chopped, sliced lemon or orange, and butter; being full, close it up and bake it, and liquor with butter and white wine."

Lister, in his "Tres Tractatus Historiæ Animalium Angliæ," published in 1678, says, "Snails are boiled in river water, and when seasoned with oil, salt and pepper, make a dainty dish."

Indeed snails were a favourite dish in the London restaurants when the last century was well advanced. In the reign of George the Second "a ragout of fatted snails" and "chickens not two hours from the shell" were considered the *chef d'œuvres* at Pontacte's famous guinea ordinary. Hogarth let no folly of his era escape him. In his remarkable picture, "Taste in High Life," painted in 1742, the monkey, who represents the fashionable dandy of the time, reads a bill of fare on which we can read "a fricasey of snails," and from my own experience in snail eating, I must say that the *Helix pomatia* as an edible snail has no advantage save in its superior size, *H. nemoralis* and *H. aspersa*, the common brown and grey garden snails are equally as tender and well-flavoured.

"The late Grant Thorburn, of New York, with whom I was once intimate, and who is better known as Galt's 'Lawrie Todd,' bears witness in his autobiography to the great benefit derived from snails by a weak sickly child. Thorburn's mother died when he was barely three years old, leaving the unfortunate infant to the neglect and rough usage of a Scottish cottager. When ten years old he could not walk, and was even then no larger than an ordinary child of five years. That he might get strength he was sent to one of the hills in Midlothian, nine miles south of Edinburgh. 'This hill,' he says, 'abounded with a small snail that carried a beautiful shell on its back, striped, and painted. My employment in the afternoon was to collect half a pint of these snails. In the morning they were boiled in new milk; the milk when nearly cold was given me with oatmeal for breakfast. It was very palatable. I soon regained my health and spirits, but not my growth. I believe that the means used to restore my health gave me an entirely new constitution; for from my twelfth year I have been free from any of the hereditary complaints with which my father, mother, sister, and brother were afflicted." *

* Sir W. Pinkerton in *The Field*.

In Algeria large heaps of snails are sold by the bushel and the hundred, in the markets, as an article of food. They are also carried about for sale in the streets of Cairo, and are occasionally eaten in Syria. The Greeks feed principally upon them during Lent.

The snail (*Helix pomatia*) is used as food by some of the European residents in Chili. Within thirty years past it has become so acclimatised and is so prolific that in some vineyards it causes such damage that means are taken to destroy it utterly.

For various recipes and modes of cooking and serving up snails, I may refer the reader to Dr. Ebrard's work on "Les Escargots," or to the popular work of Mr. S. Lovell, "On the Edible Mollusks of Great Britain and Ireland" (London : Reeve and Co., 1867).

Marine Mollusks.—The marine edible mollusks have been popularly treated of in the pleasantly written work just named, published some fourteen years ago, at least as far as relates to the British species; and a former work of mine, on "The Curiosities of Food," has been largely drawn on by the author. However, there is much still to be said on this subject, especially the more extensive use made of mollusks for food in foreign countries. We may range them under the two heads of univalves and bivalves, and will take the former first, although they are the least important.

Among the marine *Univalves*, the animals of which are eaten as food, we find whelks, limpets, periwinkles, and the ormer, or ear-shell (*Haliotis sp.*)

Limpets (*Patella vulgata*), and species of *Acmæa*, are rather leathery and not of an agreeable appearance, but it is said they can be rendered palatable by boiling, then salting, adding spices, and after removing the salt, placing them in olive oil, and thus we are agreeably surprised to find a delicious *hors d'œuvre* which has lost much of its toughness.

Although used by the ancients as an article of food, the limpet is seldom brought to market in this country. Among the villages along the coasts of Scotland this shell-fish is frequently used, and its juice obtained by boiling, mixed with oatmeal, is held in high estimation. It is considered in season about the end of May. At Naples they are made into soup.

Periwinkles and whelks and all the species of sea snails are comparatively tough and indigestible.

Whelks (*Buccinum undatum*, Lin., and *Fusus antiquus*), though not much used by the higher classes, are of the greatest public importance; first as a favourite food dainty for the poor people, and secondly, as bait for the deep-sea lines of the fishermen.

On many a street-vendor's stall in London, Liverpool, etc., saucers of whelks in vinegar may be seen. A quarter of a century ago Mr. Poole stated that 24,300 bushels of whelks (about 600 tons), worth £2,500, were sold yearly in Billingsgate. The quantity now must be larger. The whelks are sent in bags and sold by the " wash," or three-quarters of a bushel, for 4s. About £8,000 a year is paid to the fishermen in the estuary of the Thames for whelks for bait for the cod fisheries.

The common periwinkle (*Litorina litorea*, Lin.), is in this country more extensively used as food than any other of the testaceous univalves. They are in general eaten after being simply boiled, and are consumed in large quantities by the poor inhabitants on the coasts and in London. About 3,000 tons, valued at £15,000 or £16,000, are consumed in the metropolis. Large quantities are received from Scotland and Ireland.

Strombus Lichuanus is eaten by the fishermen in India.

Hyria corrugata, Sow., *H. avicularis*, Lam., and *Castalia ambigua* are eaten in different quarters. *Neritina zebra* is often seen in the markets of Para, being eaten by the negroes. *Modiola lithophaga*, vulgarly called the " Deltao deallá," is introduced at most tables at Nice, and esteemed. The ovaries of the Brunnion, a snail without a shell, are also eaten in Nice. The *Pyrula melongena*, and *P. patula*, inhabiting respectively the Atlantic and Pacific shores of tropical America, are eaten by the natives. The *Cymbas* are also eaten for food under the name of Yet in Western Africa. The high winds sometimes drive shoals of them on shore.

Several other univalves will be subsequently noticed incidentally.

Haliotids.—The mollusks of the very beautiful group of sea ear-shells or ormers (*Haliotidæ*) are often cooked. The shells, which present a very brilliant nacre, golden green, orange, pink, etc., according to the species, form a regular article of trade for ornaments, when polished and for inlaid work. In Jersey, the common British species is sold at 6d. per dozen. It has been praised by old authors as a most delicate morsel. One writer speaks of the ormer as a lump of white pulp, very sweet and luscious. In that island they are boiled slowly for two or three hours, when they may be scalloped as an oyster, or browned in a pan with butter. If they are to be fried, they require to be well beaten first to make them tender. They are also pickled in vinegar.

The Indians of California, the Chinese, and others are very fond of *H. gigantea.*

As an article of food the Haliotids are by no means to be despised. We have eaten *H. tuberculata*, Lin., and when served by a good cook it is tender and sapid. The large fleshy foot, if not properly managed, is apt to be tough.

The mutton fish as it is termed (*Haliotis iris*), is prized by the inhabitants of New Zealand, although tough eating. The Chinese, settled in Victoria and Tasmania, capture them largely.

The habitat of these fish is on stones below the surface of the water, to which they adhere, with a tenacity truly wonderful, by what is called the foot. Armed with a long, iron-pointed spear, the fisher thrusts it through the shell, whereupon the mollusk relaxes its hold, and is brought to the surface. The mode of preparing these fish for exportation is to parboil them, when the mollusk comes away freely from the shell. They are then dried, and in that state have the appearance and consistence of leather. The estimation in which such pabulum is held by the disciples of Confucius, I regard as being solely due to a taste acquired by long cultivation. This opinion is founded upon the fact of having partaken of one of these mollusks after its having been cooked according to true Celestial fashion.

The economical value of the *Haliotis tuberculata* and its foreign congeners is very great. They are collected by the fishermen, who go out in boats at spring tides, and after collecting them from the rocks take their haul to market. Before, however, being fit for food, they have to be repeatedly washed in water; that which has been used for this purpose being almost as black as ink when thrown away. After this washing they are beaten with wooden mallets for some time, and are then ready for cooking. When cooked (usually fried) they are excellent food, eating somewhat like veal cutlets; they are also like veal in another respect, namely, their solidity. Three of them form a very good meal.

The species of haliotids eaten as food on the Californian coast are *H. corrugata, H. rufescens,* called abalone, *H. cracherodii,* the white abalone; *H. splendens* and *H. Kamschatkiana* in Alaska.

The various places whence this article are brought to Hakodati, Japan, for shipment are—the west coast of Yesso, Shendai, Tsugani, and Nambu. The fishing season commences in March, and after being dried, this commodity is brought to Hakodati until November, after which there is a great scarcity. The prices paid in 1864 varied from 17 to 18 dollars the picul (133 lbs.), but in 1865 rose to 22 dollars, owing to the high prices the exports were smaller.

Hokadikaimi, a species of oyster, comes from Nambu, and varies in price from 8 to 10 dollars the picul. From Japan there was exhibited at the Paris Exhibition in 1878, oysters preserved in *shotsion,* a kind of spirit made from rice.

Irico (dried shrimps), also an article of food for the Chinese, is brought from the west coast of the island of

Yesso. The fishing season is the same as that of Awabi, and the prices paid are from 21 to 23 dollars per picul.

Prices at Kanagawa in August, 1864, were for cuttle fish, 13½ dollars; shrimps, 13 dollars; sharks' fins, 16 dollars per picul.

The flesh of the ear-shell (*Haliotis sp.*), called Awabi, is cut into slices or strings, which are extended on a board and dried. As this mollusk was the common food of their necessitous ancestors, when the Japanese entertain company at dinner, they always provide a dish of it. Kaempfer states that it has hence become a custom among all classes, when they forward one another presents of any kind, to send along with it a string or piece of this dried flesh, as a good omen, and as a reminder of the indigence of their forefathers; Awabi having been in days of yore the first sustenance and support of the Japanese, as acorns were formerly the primitive diet of the inhabitants of Europe.

Amongst the mollusca none are more eagerly caught and none have such a deserved reputation in South Africa as the sea-ear, *Haliotis Midæ*, Linn., and a species of *Stomatia* called by the Dutch Paarl-moer. In Cape Town these oceanic productions, which, by the bye, require a great deal of preparation, seasoning and ingredients, before they reach the dinner table, are pronounced to be the most exquisite dainty—the very pitch of delicacy. The ordinary *Mytilus edulis*, Linn., and *Donax denticulata*, Linn., called "white mussels," are also eaten. The latter are innocuous at some seasons, but venomous at others. Several large species of limpets (*Patella*) and a kind of *Nerita* are also made use of as a palatable and nutritious dish.

CHAPTER XII.

Animal Food Furnished by the Mollusca and Radiata.

Oysters—Classification and varieties of—Statistics of French Production—Magnitude of American Oyster Trade—Green Oysters—Shipments of Oysters in Barrels and Cans—Statistics of American Production—Canadian Oysters—Scallops—Razor-fish—Clams, varieties of—Clam Bake Feasts in the United States—Other Species of Mollusks, Tapes, Venus, Pholas, &c.—Mussels—French Trade in—British Consumption—Zoophytes, Actinia—Modes of Cooking—Curious Fish Dinner—Cephalopods, Sepia, Octopi, Squids, Sea-Urchins—Trepang or Beche-de-Mer—Varieties of—Large Consumption of in China—Indian Exports—Leeches and Worms Eaten.

Bivalves.—Among the bivalves there is a much larger variety which are esteemed food delicacies in various quarters than of the univalves; thus we have cockles, oysters, scallops, clams, mussels, &c.

The poor Malays and Chinese use most kinds of shell-fish as food, and they search the shores and coasts of the islands and peninsula most diligently for species of *Spondylus* and *Chama,* &c.

Cockles (*Cardium edule*) are deservedly esteemed a delicious and wholesome food in this country, although in France they are little regarded. They are in season during March, April and May, after which they become milky and insipid. They are considered by the people very nutritious, especially when boiled with milk.

"The natives of the seignory of Gower cook cockles in various ways; sometimes they fry them with ham. They also make excellent pies of cockles with chopped chives, a layer of bacon being placed at the bottom of the dish; or they fry the cockles with oatmeal and chives, or oatmeal alone; they also make of them an excellent and nutritious soup."*

Since oysters have become so scarce and dear, cockles have assumed a much greater importance than heretofore, and they not unfrequently do duty for oysters both in patties and sauce. A quart of cockles costing 2d. will contain about 84 cockles, weighing one pound fourteen ounces. The meat of them will weigh six ounces, therefore the price of cockle meat is about 5½d. per pound.

There are at least 100 carts (with six or seven people to a cart) employed collecting cockles in Morecambe Bay. The cockles are sold at 5s. or 6s. a box. There are about 70 quarts in a box of cockles. They are retailed there at about 1d. a quart, there being 25 to 30 cockles in a quart. The total quantity of cockles sent away by railway from Furness and some other stations in 1877 was 2,254 tons, more than one-half from Cark station. Cockles are worth about £5 a ton. Hence the above quantity may be valued at £11,000. This does not include local consumption. Thirty-three per cent. may probably be added to this estimate for local consumption, which would make the entire value about £14,000 a year from about fifty miles of coast, and the produce of the south side of the bay is 3,000 tons now. A sack of cockles weighing 1½ cwt. is worth about 2s. There is a great cockle fishery in the bays near Carmarthen. There are 500 or 600 families dependent on it, and at only 10s. per week per family it must be worth at least £15,000 a year.

The Italian markets are well supplied all the year round with cockles, especially the following species: *C. rusticum, C. tuberculatum, C. edule,* Linn., and *C. codiense,* Ren. They are preferred in the winter; in some localities they become large and well flavoured.

Oysters.—One of the most appreciated of the mollusks has always been the common oyster. From very ancient

* " The Edible Mollusks," p. 36.

times the oyster has been esteemed a luxurious food delicacy, and those of Lake Lucerne were renowned among the Romans.

Oysters are met with more or less plentifully in most seas, but according to Dr. Senoner, those which have the most pleasant flavour are only found in seas where the proportion of salt is about 37 per cent.

Almost all the species are edible, and they are numerous. The oyster of Great Britain, however, has always been held to be superior to those of other European countries.

Among the various "unclean" animals enumerated in the Levitical law those creatures of the water "that have neither fins nor scales," are specifically mentioned, and it may be argued that oysters do not come within this category, but do we not speak of green-finned oysters, and are not the shells virtually "scales"? On the other hand snails are specifically forbidden, and it is claimed that oysters are really snails, but then snails might be said to be covered by the prohibition of "creeping things," and those that "go upon the belly," so that the mention of snails ought not to be taken as including more than those particular creatures. Altogether the problem is as delicate as it is curious and interesting. It ought to be met fairly and settled authoritatively.

Oysters in England may be generally divided into "Natives," "Commons," and "Deep Sea" oysters. These again are sub-divided into many kinds; which it is not necessary here to describe or enumerate. The great deep sea oyster banks are situated on patches in the North Sea, especially off the Dutch coast, where they catch enormous quantities and the quality is very good. They fetch from 5s. to 7s. 6d. a box and there are sixty to seventy oysters in a box. They are of two kinds: 1st, handsome white-shelled oysters; and 2nd, heavy brown-shelled specimens, with black ink-like spots on the shells. They are sold retail at one penny each.

It is commonly supposed that these delicious esculents are rich in iodine, and Dr. Champouillon, of Paris, in a report on oysters in 1876, especially praised the Portuguese oysters, which are obtained from about thirty miles of coast extending from Lisbon to Cacillias Point.

Dr. Fonssagrives, the learned author of "A Treatise on Healthy Food," and Marine Surgeon-in-Chief at Brest, thus speaks of the oyster, and his remarks within certain limits may probably be applied to other mollusca:—

" May we not suppose that these mollusks, living in localities rich in iodine, collect this product and communicate it to those organisms which feed upon them, as in the savoury products of Ostend and Concale. I am in the practice myself of recommending oysters for weak and lymphatic children with soft flesh, and making them drink a sufficient quantity of the liquid given forth when the oyster is opened, and I have found this exercise a very favourable action."

But there are other mollusca which may be said to possess beneficial alimentary properties besides the oyster.

The oyster is almost the only animal substance which we eat habitually, and by preference, in the raw or uncooked state ; and it is interesting to know that there is a sound physiological reason at the bottom of this preference. Dr. Roberts, from whom we quote,* explains this. The fawn-coloured mass which constitutes the dainty of the oyster is its liver, and this is little else than a heap of glycogen. Associated with the glycogen, but withheld from actual contact with it during life, is its appropriate digestive ferment—the hepatic diastase. The mere crushing of the dainty between the teeth brings these two bodies together, and the glycogen is at once digested without other help by its own diastase.

The oyster in the uncooked state or merely warmed, is in fact self-digestive. But the advantage of this provision is wholly lost by cooking ; for the heat employed

---

* Lumleian Lectures before the Royal College of Physicians.

immediately destroys the associated ferment, and a cooked oyster has to be digested like any other food by the eater's own digestive powers.

The coasts of Brittany were formerly rich in natural beds of oysters; they were not worth more than 1½d. per hundred, and a man on payment of a penny might enter an oyster boat and eat as many as he chose. But the abuse of the dredging and the fishing, and the increased demand ruined the natural beds, and it has only been by artificial means and care that any recovery has taken place. As an oyster produces from one to two millions of young, by proper care and attention this propagation and increase is easily carried on.

The average annual consumption of oysters in Paris in the four years ending 1861 was 54,000,000, and the average price 3s. 6d. per 100.

In 1876 the parks at the Isle of Oleron yielded to commerce 70 millions of oysters and Marennes 80 millions.

We have some recent official data to guide us as to the consumption of oysters in France.

The fishing boats brought in from dredging as follows:—

1875	...	...	...	...	...	97,226,592
1876	...	...	...	...	...	160,267,396
1878	...	...	...	...	...	169,397,046
1879	...	...	...	...	...	157,579,968
1880	...	...	...	...	...	144,552,625

Those taken from the artificial parks or preserved oyster-beds have to be added, which were in—

1874-5	...	...	...	...	...	227.640,212
1875-6	...	...	...	...	...	335 774,070
1878	...	...	...	...	...	471,487,628

The total number of oysters sold in France in 1876 were therefore 640,884,674, of the declared value of £888,486. The number sold in 1880 was 563,943,358, valued at £674,280, and in 1883 but 157,500,000 were brought in by the dredgers. The consumption of oysters in Paris in 1883 was reckoned at 5,270 tons, and it is worthy of note that the price of them is nearly 50 per cent. dearer than it was ten years ago.

The oyster will breed best in salt water, but it will become fatter and of better flavour in moderately brackish water. The " natives " of the Thames—those that are fattened in the mouth of the Thames, the Crouch, the Roach, and other rivers on the Kent, Essex and Suffolk coasts—are most prized for the reason that they find there the conditions best suited to their growth. The Roach oysters are green-bearded. These have for years been sent to Ostend, and from thence to Paris, Berlin, etc., as Ostend oysters.

It is somewhat curious to notice that while over one million bushels of oysters, valued at 311,515 dollars, were received in the districts of the United States in 1870, the value had gradually declined year by year to 31,600 bushels, valued at 24,845 dollars in 1878. This must arise evidently from the home production in the river beds and parks being now amply sufficient for the home demand.

There is now a large export trade in oysters from the United States across the Atlantic; commencing with 42,839 barrels in 1876 it has increased to 90,663 barrels, valued at 453,306 dollars. They are shipped in barrels by the steamers, and generally arrive in good condition, being packed with seaweed and corn meal. The great bulk come to England, and those for the Continent go almost exclusively to Amsterdam. Dried oysters are imported into the States to the value of 13,447 dollars. The imports of other mollusks or shell-fish into America range in value from 300,000 to 600,000 dollars.

The American species of oyster are *Ostrea virginica*, Gmelin, *O. borealis*, Linn., and *O. lurida*, Cpr., of the west coast.

Some idea of the magnitude of the American oyster business may be gained from the reports of the Oyster Commission in 1868. They stated the aggregate collected in Chesapeake Bay at about twenty-five million bushels, exclusive of those taken from private beds, cultivated by residents for their own use.

In the City of Baltimore seventy houses were engaged in the oyster business, mostly canning for exportation, while at various points in the bay are establishments that employ from fifty to 400 hands each during the season, in opening and canning. By the official reports there were 15,000 persons engaged in the business of oyster fishing, and a fleet of 1,700 vessels, of fifty tons burthen, and over 3,000 smaller craft, duly licensed to the trade. There was also a population of 20,000 persons on the islands and mainland with whom oysters form an article of general consumption throughout the season. It was estimated that thousands of bushels of this bivalve were taken annually on the coast from Massachusetts to Virginia.

The Americans hold oysters in esteem, and they have a very great variety of choice ones, such as the small Blue Points, the Rockaways, the Morris Cove from New Jersey, the Saddle Rocks (a particularly fat variety), the Norwalls from Connecticut, and others. Many of these now arrive in London. Besides the quantities of fresh oysters eaten in the United States, a large trade is done in canning or tinning them. They are pickled, spiced, and hermetically sealed for export.

The Chinese boil them and then dry them in the sun.

The green colour of oysters has been noticed in several localities, at Marennes, the Isle of Oleron, Cornseulles, &c., and the cause of this has long occupied the attention both of breeders and scientific men. In Lovell's "Edible Mollusks," it is stated to arise from a submarine kind of moss. Gaillon ("Journal de Physique," Sept. 1820, tome XCI.) attributes it to an animalcule, which he named *Vibrio ostrearius*. Later investigations assign it to a variety of the diatom, *Navicula fusiforma*.*

---

* See a paper by Mr. G. Puysegur on this subject, with an illustration, in the "Revue Maritime et Coloniale," Paris, vol. lxiv., p. 248.

The "green" oyster, so much prized in France, will not sell in the American markets. The "greening" of oysters is extensively carried on at Marennes, on the banks of the river Seudre; and this particular branch of oyster industry extends for leagues along the river, and is also sanctioned by free grants from the State. The peculiar colour and taste are believed by the French to be imparted by the vegetable substances which grow in the beds where the oysters are cultivated.

A resident of London claims that that city spends over £5,000,000 sterling a year in oysters, and that more than twice the number of these bivalves would be used if they could be obtained at as reasonable prices as in America. The genuine Whitstable oyster fetches about 3s. a dozen. Oyster culture in England is yet in its infancy. The most popular size for eating are those with a shell about as large as a crown piece. They are packed in barrels very closely and kept right side up during the voyage. Quite a trade is now springing up in carrying "seed" oysters from America to Europe.

Car loads of oysters are shipped to California from New York every few days. The "native" oyster of the western coast is obtained in the Gulf of California, and is small and of coppery taste. A moderate supply is being obtained on the Oregon or Washington territory coast. These are better than the more southern.

About 40,000 barrels were shipped from the Columbia river in 1882, valued at 3 dollars per barrel.

The seaboards of Georgia, South Carolina, and Texas abound in oysters. In some places they have grown up into reefs extending for twenty miles along the coast. Much of this oyster wealth may yet become available for Northern markets. Various river mouths and estuaries along the Connecticut and New York shores would be most excellent oyster grounds, if some means could be provided to keep the deposits of mud from covering and smothering the young oysters. The time may be near when enterprising men will seek to clear off these ruinous deposits as they now drain marshes and fill up swamps and pools. The recent law of Connecticut creating a State Commission to sell the deep water ground of the Sound, has served to inspire great activity in securing farms in the sea. Many thousands of dollars have already been realized for grounds appropriated.

The production of oysters has more than doubled in quantity in and about New York Harbour, Staten Island, and Perth Amboy during the past five years. It is believed if the mud could be kept out of New York Harbour it would make one of the finest oyster beds in the world. The natural oyster beds on the east side of Staten Island are the places whence much of the "seed" for all the various famous kinds of oysters about New York is obtained.

In Fulton market on the East River, New York, there are several kinds of rude restaurants, which are interesting to visit about noon, when merchants and workmen come from all quarters for their dinners. They are popular establishments in every sense of the word, and oysters, cooked in various ways, constitute almost the entire repast. Americans have a special predilection for roasted oysters   The mollusks used for this purpose are of large size, and generally come from New Jersey on the East River. They are placed upon a gridiron, the deeper valve below, and when sufficiently cooked in their own juice they are withdrawn from the fire and served to the customers. Large oysters prepared in this way are excellent, especially when seasoned with a little pepper and a few drops of lemon juice.

The river Quinnipiac, which is the eastern boundary of the city of New Haven, had long since been a famous place for oysters. These bivalves were also abundant along the shores east and west of New Haven. The Indians had depended much upon them for food. The new settlers did the same also. The banks along the shore are lined several feet deep with shells left by many generations of oyster-eaters.

For nearly two hundred years the dependence of the people seeking the shore of Long Island Sound with its

E E 2

bays and estuaries for oysters, was upon the natural supplies. These seemed inexhaustible, as the habits of use then were. The Indians who came from the interior at certain seasons and remained for weeks, living mainly upon shell and other fish, carried none away with them. The whites only visited the shores for an occasional "salting."

One of the results of an increasing love of oysters was the growth of a class who sought a livelihood by selling as well as catching these shell-fish. Hence a business began to be developed. But there were no private grounds. The various natural beds were open to all persons in the State who wished to take oysters therefrom. The only restriction put upon the people was the reserving of several months as "close" months each year, during which no oysters could be caught. These were the summer months, when the bivalves were known to be giving off their spawn.

The "law was off," as the expression was, about November 1st. In anticipation of that time great preparations were made in the towns along the shore, and even for twenty miles back from the seaside. Boats and rakes and baskets and bags were put in order. The day before large numbers of waggons came toward the shore from the back country, bringing hundreds of men with their utensils. The more thickly covered beds were quickly cleared of their bivalves. The boats were full, the waggons were full, and many had secured what they called their "winter's stock" before the day was done. Those living on the shore usually secured the cream of the year's crop. They knew just where to go, they were better practised in handling boats, rakes, &c.; they formed combinations to help one another.

That first day was the great day. It presented an exciting scene. Often crowds of spectators came to look on, as at a fair or Fourth of July parade. The oysters were very poor then compared with those now obtained. Such indiscriminating raking caught them before they were half grown. Nor were there many to be procured after that first day.   In a week or two later a bushel of oysters could not be bought for less than four dollars.

The Quinnipiac River, New Haven Harbour, and the waters adjacent have for some years been all assigned to private parties.   The first use made of such grounds was to lay down oysters brought from other waters, especially Southern bays.   A very large trade grew up in Virginia and Maryland oysters brought to Fair Haven, to be opened and sold in the New England and other Northern States.   In some late years as many as one million bushels have been brought annually to this place from the South.   Such oysters are greatly improved by even a few weeks' feeding in the waters of the bays and river mouths.

A large business is done with opened oysters as well as with those in the shell.   Some Providence firms employ forty openers at a time.   These are paid for their work at the rate of twelve cents a gallon of solid meats.   They can earn good wages at it, one man being known to open nineteen gallons in four hours.   The city, though containing over one hundred thousand people, does not use one hundredth part of the oysters raised and handled there.   They are sent out through all the New England States and as far West as Toledo, O.

The first arrivals made large returns.   The eager retailers would pay almost any price to secure the earliest supplies.   From the first oysters have been sold by Staten Island dealers "by the count;" that is, so much a hundred or thousand.   The enormous tide of travel through New York city creates a constant demand for this food whatever may be the price.   Some will have oysters if they have to pay, like the American in Copenhagen, one shilling a piece for them.   Hotels and first-class saloons always expect to have them on hand however costly they may be.

The opened bivalves were at first put up in small wooden kegs, holding from one to two gallons each. The most common receptacle now is a strongly made tub, with a lid securely fastened. Each, containing a number of gallons, is furnished with handles, with which it can be easily lifted. In warm weather ice is put in with the oysters. Tin cans are used to a considerable extent. These are filled and soldered, then packed in wooden boxes with ice between. Thus, as with the tubs, oysters are carried long distances in good condition even in summer.

All shell-fish are improved by an infusion of fresh water. This explains the superiority of the shell-fish of the northern coast of Long Island Sound to those on the southern coast of the same water. Many fresh-water streams flow in from the north. One reason of the fine flavour of Fair Haven oysters is the flow of fresh water from the Quinnipiac, Mill, and West Rivers.

Cultivation has greatly increased the supply of good oysters. In New Haven, ten years ago, it was difficult to secure ten bushels at short notice. Now five hundred bushels can be obtained in a few hours.

One peculiarity is found in Staten Island oysters, making them superior to most others for several purposes. Their shells are unusually hard and firm, and preserve their meats better than other kinds. Therefore they can be shipped farther in good condition than almost any other. They are in considerable demand for the foreign and other distant markets, being sent in large quantities north, south, and west. One firm forwarded three thousand barrels to California a year ago. They have been sent as far east as Constantinople.

Some patrons are so attached to these oysters they continue to send for single gallons of them, even when they go to reside in distant country places.

The demand for them increases in every direction from year to year. They are sold in three grades. The "box" is the finest grade, commanding the highest price. They must be good size, good colour, good shape, hard shells, and even size. The next are "barrel" oysters, running a little smaller and a little less even. The third are "culls." The second grade are also called "counts."

The " culls " sell from thirty to forty-five cents a hundred, when the "box" grade cost from sixty to ninety cents per hundred.

Those that are sold out of the shell are opened on the boats at New York. A single firm on the North River sometimes opens one hundred and fifty thousand counts in a single day. Men who open oysters there are able to earn about three dollars a day.

Ernest Ingersoll's census report on the oyster business shows that the total wholesale value of the oysters annually sold in Boston is 705,000 dollars; the annual value of the oysters produced in Narragansett Bay is 680,000 dollars; the value of those sold in New Haven Harbour is 480,000 dollars; in the East River and Peconic Bay, 708,000 dollars; on the south shore of Long Island, 400,000 dollars; in New York Bay, excluding New York city, 375,000 dollars; in New York city, 2,758,000 dollars; on the ocean shore of New Jersey, 370,000 dollars; in Delaware Bay, 2,425,000 dollars; in Philadelphia 2,750,000 dollars; and in Virginia nearly 2,000,000 dollars; and about 125,000 dollars will cover the value for the remainder of the Southern coast line, not including the Gulf line, where the value slightly exceeds 300,000 dollars. The total of these figures is nearly 14,000,000 dollars, or £2,800,000. Some set the value of the American oyster fishery at £5,000,000.

Oysters salted are brought into Mexico from the Pacific coast. Before they are eaten they are soaked in water, or in oil, for a night, and they retain some of their flavour, but naturally are nothing like fresh oysters.

Large quantities of oysters are sent to San Francisco by rail from New York, and are kept for a year in the beds of the bay to fatten. The imports are about 12 million oysters annually. About 40 million oysters are also obtained from local banks and deposited in parks in the bay to fatten. Clams are also obtained in the bay.

The waters of half of Prince Edward Island were once stocked with natural beds. So lately as 1832 live oysters were so plenty that legislation had to forbid their being burned for lime. In many places the dead shells of once productive beds, remain many feet in thickness. The great drawback of the oyster fishery of this Province is the digging of oyster shells for manure under the name of " mussel mud." The oyster fishery is but a mere scrap and vestige of what it once was, and might again be made, nevertheless the oyster fishery of this Island nets £23,000 per annum by way of export, over and above supplying a large quantity for local consumption. They have long maintained a good fame and are shipped to all the neighbouring cities of the Dominion of Canada. Two forms are found indiscriminately in the beds, namely circular and long. It may be curious to ascertain scientifically whether these are two distinct species—the *Ostrea Canadensis* and the *O. borealis*—or merely difference of form. At all events the variation is established in their earliest growth. Both are equally valued for food.

The value of the Canadian oyster fisheries for 1883 was officially returned at £30,324, which was £8,000 less than the previous year. The quantity obtained was about 51,000 barrels. New Brunswick produced 10,317 barrels, Prince Edward Island, 38,880 barrels, against 57,042 barrels in the previous year. Nova Scotia 1,343 barrels. The demand for oysters and the good prices obtained have stimulated production everywhere, and the depleted beds are now raked more industriously than ever. Over-fishing and indiscriminate raking have done their work very effectually.

The oysters of Trieste and Venetia are still considered the best in the Adriatic Sea. They are fat and savoury after they have reached three years. They are sent from thence to many quarters, and to prevent their opening, they are tied round with string, for the loss of the water or liquor causes the death of the mollusk.

The two species of oysters most eaten as food, *O. edulis* and *O. hypopus*, are being cultivated in the Mediterranean, but they produce very large shells there, the waters being more calcareous than that of the ocean ;

and there are difficulties found in the way of rearing them.

Scallops.—The common lid scallop (*Pecten opercularis,* Linn.) is much smaller than the great scallop (*P. maximus*). Scallops are found pretty generally distributed in all seas and are much sought after for food.   There are large scallop beds off the Isle of Man, and at Weymouth the trawlers dredge up about five bushels per week.

Pecten varius is sent in quantities to the market of Bordeaux.   At Vigo *P. maximus* is the constant food of all classes from Christmas to Easter.

The scallop as seen in the fishmongers' shops, when shelled, consists of a small creamy white cylinder, and it is a great mystery to many how this can be a shellfish. This is the only part of the scallop that can be eaten, the "mouth," or rim, being very bitter and pungent when cooked.   It has a remarkably sweet taste, much like that of the flesh of crabs, and is highly relished by many, though not considered particularly digestible.

Scallops are not much eaten in England, although occasionally seen in the fishmongers' shops.   In America, however, they are largely consumed, and in some localities they are obtained in quantities by dredging.   Unlike the clam or the oyster, which seem incapable of progressive motion, the scallop is a rover.

When the tide is running fast and the water shallow, it will rise from the bottom with open shells to the top of the sea, squirt out the water contained between the shells, and by means of the impetus given, and the force of the tide, will swim a yard or so at every spring. The motion is a laughable one, as the shells come together with a snap that can be heard at some distance, and the motion is zigzag instead of direct.

In some seasons the mollusk is much larger and finer in America than others.   The catch is from twenty to a hundred bushels a day according to the size of the boat and the number of men engaged.   From November 1st till March, is the dredging season.   The catch varies; thus in 1879 it was a light one, and prices at the grounds were as high as one dollar for a gallon of "meats," or as the fishermen call them "eyes." The largest quantity obtained was in 1877, when it was estimated that from the ports of Riverhead, Mattiluck, New Suffolk, and Greenport, the shipment to New York ran up to the large number of 40,000 gallons, representing a catch of 80,000 bushels of scallops. The price then, however, fell as low as 50 cents per gallon, barely paying expenses. The fishermen say that the scallop lives but three years; that the spawned mollusk is two years reaching maturity; the third year it is full grown and spawns and then dies.

The scallop was held in high estimation by the ancients and still is sought after in Catholic countries. *Pecten maximus* is frequently used in England. It is pickled and barrelled for sale, and esteemed a great delicacy. Another species, the quin, *P. opercularis*, is employed for culinary purposes in Cornwall, where it is known by the name of "Frills" or "Queens."

The *Anomia ephippium* is used as food at Languedoc and is there considered as preferable to the oyster.

Shellfish are largely used by the natives of India when available on the Madras coast, purely marine species are not common, or easily procured, but in lagoons, bivalves are abundant and often collected as food. The land snails, *Paludina melanostoma*, Benson, and *Ampullaria globosa*, Swainson, are eaten.

The pearl-wombs, as the mantles or flesh of the mother of pearl oyster (*Meleagrina margaritifera*) is called, are strung together and dried, and when cooked with cassia buds, are eaten with rice.

All the razor fish (species of *Solen*) are good for food, *S. siliqua*, the largest British species, is that generally collected for the purpose. *S. marginatus* is greatly prized by the Neapolitans, a dishful selling for about two shillings. They are eaten boiled and fried, but are best of all when roasted on the coals till their shells open. In Japan the *Solens* are said to be so highly prized that, by the express order of the prince of that country, it is forbidden to fish them until a sufficient quantity has been provided for the emperor's table.

There is a large species of bivalve with a thin shell, sought for by the negroes of Senegal, the flesh of which is exceedingly good, when boiled and dressed properly, and is even esteemed by Europeans.

Clams.—Some species of razor fish (*Solen ensis*) as well as *Machæra patula*, *M. costata*, &c., pass in the United States under the name of razor clams, and the term is commonly applied there to many edible bivalves.

The *Mactra solida*, and *M. stultorum*, are used as food by the common people about Dartmouth, and *Venus pullastra* by the inhabitants of Devonshire. In North America the various species of *Mactra* are called " hen clams."

The people of the United States use clams in a variety of culinary preparations, the most popular of which is undoubtedly a kind of soup especially esteemed in Boston. In Rhode Island and Massachusetts, clams serve as a pretext for fêtes of a very peculiar kind called *clam bakes.* These, which take place every year near Bristol, as well as in several other localities of Rhode Island and Massachusetts, have their origin in an old Indian custom. The aborigines of these States were accustomed to assemble in great numbers every year for a feast, consisting of clams and green corn (maize), cooked together with seaweeds. The modern clam bake is an improvement on the old one. A circular hearth or bed is first made in the sand, with large flat stones, upon which a fire is kept up until they are red hot. A layer of seaweed is then placed upon them, and on the seaweed a layer of clams about three inches thick covered by more seaweed; then follows a layer of green corn in the husk, intermixed with potatoes and other vegetables ; then a layer of poultry cooked and seasoned; then more seaweed; then fish and lobsters again covered by seaweed. This arrangement is continued according to the number of persons to take part in the feast, and when the pile is complete it is covered with a linen cloth to prevent the steam from escaping. When the whole is cooked each one helps himself without ceremony. These feasts are delicious beyond description, and it is said no one is ever made ill by them. In former times the most renowned warriors came from afar to take part in them ; and now they are attended by persons of the highest social standing, sometimes to the number of several hundreds.

Here is another more detailed description :—The clambakes are a Rhode Island institution ; and although " society " at Newport turns up its nose at them, gentlemen go often to enjoy them at the various resorts along the shores of Narragansett Bay. To get up a " bake," large clean stones are laid closely together in a circle, and a hot wood-fire is kept up on them until the stones are thoroughly heated. The ashes and coals are then swept from the stones, which are covered with damp fresh seaweed. On this are placed several bushels of clam, green corn, and sweet potatoes, which are covered with a layer of damp seaweed, and over all is thrown a covering of sail-cloth, to keep in the steam generated by the wet seaweed and the hot stones. Meanwhile accomplished cooks are busy at a neighbouring stove making chowder, baking fish, and frying onions. On a round table beneath the shade of a grove, or in a shed the sides of which are removed, are plates heaped with brown bread and crackers, bottles of pepper-sauce, and other bottles not containing pepper-sauce. The veteran epicures watch the progress of the " bake " with a critical eye, and when the man in charge says that it is "about done," they repair to the tables, where they first enjoy plates of clam or bluefish chowder. A little brandy-and-water is then taken medicinally, and then come the clams brought in baskets from the smoking " bake," and emptied on the table. Each person is also supplied with a cupful of melted butter, which is seasoned with pepper-sauce. The clams, the shells of which have been opened by the heat, are then taken by the fingers of the left hand, the upper shell is torn off by the fingers of the right hand—the black neck is seized by the thumb and fore-finger of that hand, the other part is dipped into melted butter and then tossed into the mouth, when the teeth close, leaving the neck of the clam between the thumb and forefinger. This neck and the shells are thrown into a basket, while the luscious clam is swallowed. Between each half-dozen clams or so a few mouthfuls of green corn or brown bread are taken, and perhaps fried onions also, in which case brandy-and-water has to be taken medicinally. It is a primitive way of eating, yet to a Rhode Islander a "bake" is an epicurean treat, throwing the most elaborate Parisian *menus* into the shade.

Clams the size of small native oysters, or even less, served on a plate filled with pounded ice, are, particularly in summer, a most refreshing and appetite-reviving dish. In 1882, 2,400 lbs., and in 1883, 8,640 lbs. of clams were preserved or canned in British Columbia.

Soft clams (*Mya arenaria* and *M. truncata*) form upon the coast of New England immense banks, upon which constant demands are made by the poorer classes as a means of sustenance, without any apparent diminution of the products. · The consumption of these mollusks is considerable during every season, but especially in summer, along the entire coast of the Northern States, from New York to Maine ; but nowhere is it so great as at Boston. In most places the regular fishermen sell the clams in their natural condition ; but in some localities, like New York, they are generally taken from the shell and sent to market in packages of twenty-five, which are sold on an average at three shillings the hundred.

Clams make a palatable breakfast dish, stewed, or made into fritters. They possess tonic properties, and are esteemed by invalids. They may be eaten raw like oysters. To stew, wash the shells clean with a scrubbing brush. Add water enough to prevent their burning, and boil until the shells open ; then take out and remove the shells. Cook the clams in the same water, adding pepper and butter. Stir in rolled crackers. Long clams are nice broiled or roasted in the shell.

Several species of *Mya* are used as food both in Britain and on the Continent, as *M. arenaria*, known to the fishermen about Southampton by the whimsical name of "old maids." In some parts of England and Ireland they are much used. Another species (*M. truncata*), known to the inhabitants of the northern islands as "smurslin," is eaten boiled as a supper dish. It is not so delicate as some other shell-fish, but is by no means unpalatable. In the San Francisco market clams are sold at two shillings the hundred.

The round hard shell clams or quahogs (*Venus mercenaria, Mercenaria violacea,* and *M. kennicottii*) are almost as abundant on the American coast as the soft clam, and rival that mollusk as an article of food. They are also known as "little necks." In summer the consumption of these in the cities of New York and Philadelphia is very considerable, much greater than that of the *Mya arenaria*. Like the latter, sold in their natural condition or out of the shell, they furnish many excellent dishes, the most esteemed of which is clam chowder. Many persons eat the smaller specimens raw, and when flavoured with a few drops of lemon juice, they are as palatable as the clovisses (*Tapes sp.*), and the "paires doubles" (*Venus verrucosa*), which are the especial favourites of the people of Marseilles.

Large quantities of shell-fish, especially clams and mussels, are eaten, both raw with vinegar and pepper, and boiled in milk, in America, France, and also in Spain and Portugal, and are a cheap and healthy food.

Several species of *Tapes* are eaten in different countries as *T. pullastra, T. decussata, T. virginea, T. staminea* and *T. aurea*. In England they pass under the name of "pullet" or "cullyock," in France as "clovisse" and "palourde." By some they are considered richer and better than cockles. It is a favourite dish at Continental seaports. They sell at Bordeaux for threepence the hundred. At Vigo thousands are gathered at every tide.

Some species of *Tellina* are used as food abroad. In Iceland *Psammobia resputina* is eaten, and *P. gari* in India.

Donax trunculus is esteemed a delicacy in Italy, Spain, and on the French coasts.

Several of the borers, as species of *Pholas*, *Lithodomus*, and *Platyodon cancellatus*, are edible, and known in the United States under the name of " date fish."

All the *Pholades* are edible, a large West Indian species (*P. costata*) is much prized, and is regularly sold in the markets of Cuba. In Jersey they are sold boiled ready for eating. They are also met with in the markets of Dieppe, La Rochelle, and other French towns. *Pholas dactylus* is not often eaten in England, but in Spain they are esteemed next to oysters, and are sometimes eaten raw.

Mussels.—Black mussels, *Mytilus edulis*, *M. Californica*, and other species, serve for food in many quarters, and so do the brown mussels, species of *Modiola*, in China where they are sold dried for food. The mussel is held in high estimation by our lower classes, especially in the country districts.

The common mussel (*Mytilus edulis*) is equally widely distributed as the oyster, and is found upon our coasts in the greatest. abundance. In this country they are conveyed direct to the market; but in some parts of France they are kept for a time in salt ponds, to fatten like the oyster, into which they admit small quanties of fresh water. The flesh of the mussel is of a yellowish colour, and considered very rich, especially in autumn. It is eaten here either boiled or pickled, seldom in soup. To the generality of stomachs it is difficult of digestion, and to many constitutions it is deleterious. This is attributed to the food of the mussel, which at certain seasons consists chiefly of the noxious fry of the star-fish. In the San Francisco market mussels sell at one shilling the hundred.

The mussel, formerly disdained, has now risen in esti-mation in France, and is also becoming a food luxury; it therefore behoves the food providers to turn their attention to some of the more neglected mollusks, which might under proper cooking and preparation be far more generally utilised. Many might also be preserved cooked in butter or oil and inclosed in tins. Mussels and others of this kind thus prepared were shown in tins at Arcachon and other fishery exhibitions.

On the French coasts the fishermen gather enormous quantities of fresh mussels every day, and take them in carts, or on the backs of horses to La Rochelle and other places, from whence they are sent as far as Tours, Limoges, and Bordeaux.

The number of mussels taken in France and used for food was in 1876, 396,344 hectolitres (of 2¾ bushels), and in 1878, 506,648 hectolitres; in 1879, 503,170; and 1880 514,814. In 1883 the quantity of mussels brought into France was 578,000,000 hectolitres, or little more than half the take of the previous year. Of other mollusks, 151,628 hectolitres in 1876; 145,536 hectolitres in 1878; 128,677 in 1879; and 191,183 in 1880.

The Billingsgate market is chiefly supplied with mussels from Holland, the east coast of England, Cornwall, and Devonshire. About ten or twenty tons' weight arrive at a time, though of course the quantity varies according to the season, and they are sold at one shilling a measure. Mussels are fit to be eaten at two years old, they are then two inches long, and there is a regulation that they must not be sold under that size. The growth, however, partly depends on the nature of the beds. There are two trades in mussels, one in those used for food, and the other those sold as bait for fishermen. In 1871 the sales at Boston amounted to £5,000 in value, but I have not later statistics.

The greater part of the mussels taken at Morecambe are sold for food in Lancashire and Yorkshire. They fetch from two shillings the cwt. upwards. In the three years ending 1878 the Midland Railway brought from Morecambe on an average about 1,700 tons of mussels a year. From Listowel about 20,000 tons are sent to London yearly by the London and South Western Railway from September to February, when they cease to be fit for food.

Mussels and whelks are sold in large quantities at Birmingham, but no cockles.

The quantity of mussels consumed in Edinburgh and Leith is about ten bushels per week, " say for forty weeks each in the year," in all 400 bushels annually. Each bushel of mussels, when freed from all refuse and shelled, will probably contain from three to four pints of the animals, or about 900 to 1,000, according to their size. Taking the latter number, there will be consumed in Edinburgh and Leith about 400,000 mussels. This is a mere trifle, however, compared to the enormous number used as bait for all sorts of fish."* At least 50,000,000 or 60,000,000 must be so used on various districts of the British coast.

From Lynn, in Norfolk, in the winter of 1873-4, 2,480 tons were sent to market; in 1874-5, 445 tons; and in 1875-6 about the same quantity. There are sixteen bags or thirty-two bushels in a ton, and each ton is worth about £1. The average value, therefore, of the mussels of Lynn Deeps is about £3,400 a year.

During the year 1884, there were delivered at Billingsgate Market 16,531 tons of shell-fish, exclusive of shrimps, &c.

Shell-fish are present in enormous quantities in Iceland, especially the mussel (*Mytilus edulis*), which is so abundant that its shell might supply the whole island with lime; at present they are only used as bait.

Some of the fresh-water mussels (*Unios*) are eaten in the south of Europe, either roasted in their shells and drenched with oil, or covered with bread crumbs and scalloped.

Other Mollusca.—On the coasts of France the people eat as food *Cardium edulis, Donax anatinum, Lutraria compressa, Mya arenaria, Pholas dactylus, Solen vagina, Venus decussata, Pecten varians, Turbo littoreus, Patella vulgata, Petunculus sp.,* and *Echini.* These varieties may be kept alive for from two to four days. The only

* Forbes and Hanley, " British Mollusca," vol. ii., p. 174.

F F

mollusks that are much known or eaten in the interior of France are the oyster and the mussel. Formerly the oyster was within the reach of the most humble, but now it is only available for the rich, or for extraordinary repasts.

Several species of *Pinna* or wing-shell are eaten, more especially in the Mediterranean. As an article of food the animal is said to be nearly as good as the scallops, and it is mentioned as forming one of the dishes at an Attic banquet—

> And Pinnas sweet and cockles fat were there,
> Which the wave breeds beneath its weedy bed.

It seems to have been a favourite article of food among the ancients, and was as highly prized by them as it is at Naples in these days, where it is considered a *recherché* morsel and too expensive for the poor people to indulge in. The Pinnas are cooked at Naples with pepper, oil, and lemon juice, and served with baked prunes. They are also fried like cutlets, and made into soup.

In the Adriatic a great many more species of mollusks are eaten as food than in this country, both by poor and rich. Among the gasteropods may be mentioned *Murex brandaris* and *M. trunculus*, known as " bulos," and also under the name of " garusola," which are met with all the year round in the markets, and form a large portion of the food of the poor. The white colour of the flesh turns green after being kept for some time, and when exposed to the light it gives a fine red purple, from which the ancients obtained their celebrated Tyrian purple.

Chenopus pes-pelicani is also much appreciated as food by the poor. It is known under the common name of " zumarugola." *Cerithium vulgatum* is also frequently met with in the markets, as well as *Turbo rugosus, Trochus fragarioides*, Lin., *Trochus albidus, Trochus cinerarius*, Lam., *Fissurella costaria*, Desh., and *Bulla hydatis*. The flesh of the last is delicate, although not often eaten.

Among the acephalopods which furnish food may be named *Pholas dactylus*, already alluded to, which is very good eating; the ship-worm (*Teredo navalis*), well tasted, but not generally appreciated; the razor fish (*Solen vagina* and *S. siliqua*), which are broiled or made into a sort of soup. The first-named Solen is excellent, but the second has rather a disagreeable taste. Then follow *Mactrea lactea*, Poli, and *M. stultorum*, Lin., *Tellina fragilis*, Lin., a very savoury food, *Psammobia vespertina*, Lam., *Scrobicularia piperata*, Gm. This last is abundant in the markets, and is made into a kind of soup. Many species of *Venus* are eaten, as *V. lactea*, Poli, *V. verrucosa*, *V. decussata*, and *V. aurea*, Lin., *V. virginea*, Gm., *V. longone*, Ol., and *V. gallina*. *Cytherea chione* is also much esteemed for its agreeable taste.

The mussels most prized in Italy are those obtained about the arsenal of Venice; *Modiola barbata*, Lin., is frequently met with in the markets. *Lithodomus lithophagus* is less frequently seen, but is a very agreeable food. *Pinna nobilis* and *Arca noae* are also eaten, as well as many species of scallops, as *Pecten polymorphus*, Bronn, *P. varius*, *P. glaber*, Lin., and *P. jacobæus*, Lam. All these, either boiled or seasoned with oil and pepper, are considered excellent food. Some other kinds of edible mollusca may be named, viz.; *Lima inflata*, Lam., and one or two species of *Spondylus*.

There are scarcely any molluscous animals of much economic importance in Australia. Two species of oysters are commonly used for food in Sydney, and are shipped to Melbourne. The *Venus strigosa* is sold in the fish-shops under the erroneous name of "cockle," and the *Limetta undulata* is eaten by persons near the coast under the equally incorrect name of "winkles."

Among the preparations of mollusks used are the dried abalones (*Haliotis sp.*), already mentioned, used by the Chinese and Japanese, dried siphons of *Schizothænus*, prepared by the Indians of the north-west coast of America, and dried slugs (*Limax*, etc.), used by other Indians.

There are doubtless many other kinds of edible mollusca besides those already mentioned, which are or might be made available as food for man, native and civilised.

FF 2

*Zoophytes.—Actinia.—*We have thus found that the higher orders such as oysters and many other mollusca are commonly eaten by nearly all nations. But leaving the more familiar kinds aside, it would seem that scarcely a single inhabitant of the sea, from the mere shadow of a jelly to the roughest and toughest of shell-fish, is spared by the insatiable hunger of man.

The shapeless red sea-nettles, that hang without shell on the sides of submarine rocks or float about at the mercy of waves, were a favourite dish as early as the time of Aristotle, who praises their hard, firm flesh in the wintry season, while the more fastidious Apicius recommends them as best in September. Now they are mainly eaten in Italy and the south of France, where they divide the attention of seafaring men with the countless medusæ that sail in crowds through the ocean. Roasted in oil, after flour has been strewn on them, they are as palatable as they are nutritious. The tough and indigestible Sepia, which in Venice the poor only venture to cook, is a favourite dish of the Greeks, especially during their fasts. They cut them lengthwise and cook them fresh in saltpetre, which gives their meat a bright red colour, or they dry them and eat them at leisure, cooked with herbs and dressed with lemon-juice, oil, and pepper. The smaller varieties, which are rarer, are said to be better and more delicate.

The deep crimson sea anemone (*Actinia Jordiaca*), which is found in the Mediterranean, is esteemed a great delicacy by the Italians.

Mr. P. H. Gosse ("Naturalist's Rambles on the Devonshire Coast") says: "Dicquemare's testimony to the excellence of *Actinia crassicornis* for the table, tempted me to taste it, and I determined to take an early opportunity of cooking some. In a few minutes I collected about half a dozen of different sizes at low water near Wildersmouth, and having rubbed them with my fingers in a tide pool till the coating of gravel was pretty well got rid of, brought them home. I put them into a pan of sea-water for the night to cleanse them, and most beautiful and gorgeous was the appearance they presented when expanded ; no two alike in colours, and yet all so lovely that it was difficult to say which excelled. Perhaps one with the tentacles partly cream colour and partly white was as beautiful as any.

" The next morning I began operations. As it was an experiment, I did not choose to commit my pet morsels to the servants, but took the saucepan into my own hand. As I had no information as to how long they required boiling, I had to find it out for myself. Some I put into the water (*sea* water) *cold*, and allowed to boil gradually. As soon as the water boiled, I tried one : it was tough and evidently undone. The next I took out after three minutes' boiling : this was better, and one at five minutes was better still; but not so good as one which had boiled ten. I then put the remaining ones into the *boiling* water and let them remain over the fire boiling fast for ten minutes, and these were the best of all, being more tender, as well as of a more inviting appearance. I must confess that the first bit I essayed caused a sort of lumpy feeling in my throat, as if a sentinel there guarded the way and said ' It shan't come here.' This sensation, however, I felt to be unworthy of a philosopher, for there was nothing really repugnant in the taste. As soon as I had got one that seemed well cooked I invited Mrs. G. to share the feast; she courageously attacked the morsel, but I am compelled to confess it could not pass the vestibule ; the sentinel was too many for her. My little boy, however, voted that ' tinny was good,' and that he liked 'tinny' and loudly demanded more, like another Oliver Twist. As for me, I proved the truth of the adage *Ce n'est que le premier pas qui coute;* for my sentinel was cowed after the first defeat. I left little in the dish.

" In truth the flavour and taste are agreeable, some-what like those of the soft parts of the crab ; I ate them hot, with the usual crab-condiments of salt, pepper, mustard and vinegar, mixed into a sauce. The internal parts, including the ovaries and the tentacles, though from their mottled appearance rather repelling to the eye, were the most agreeable in taste; the integuments somewhat reminded me of the jelly-like skin of a calf's head. I wonder they are not commonly brought to table, for they are easily procured, and are certainly far superior to cockles, periwinkles, and mussels. After a very little use, I am persuaded any one would get very fond of boiled actinias.

"Some I had left with a little of the gravel still adhering, in order to see whether this would be thrown off when life departed; but it was not so. They should be cleansed before cooking, which can be easily and quickly done with the fingers under water; the base also should be scraped, so as to remove any bits of slate, or rock, or dirt, that adhere to it. Attention to these particulars greatly improves the appearance when cooked. They are of a pellucid rosy hue; of a firm consistence, at least sufficiently firm to be readily cut with a knife.

"The next that I tried were prepared in a different manner, and truth to say the experiment was far more successful; this time I cleansed them more perfectly, carefully scraping the bases, until they were freed from every particle of extraneous matter and from slime. These I had fried in egg and bread crumbs, and they were very far superior to even the best on the former occasion. All prejudice yielded to their inviting odour and appearance, and the whole table joined in the repast with indubitable gusto. I know not if my readers are familiar with a dish, which in Newfoundland during the cod fishing season we used to consider worthy of an epicure—the tongues of the cod taken out as soon as the fish are brought on shore, and fried immediately. The Actiniæ fried as above described I should be scarcely able to distinguish, either by the eye or by the taste, from fresh cods' tongues, except that perhaps my protégés are slightly firmer in consistence.

"*Anthea cereus* I subsequently tried, prepared in the

manner last mentioned. They too were savoury, but the sliminess of the tentacles was somewhat disagreeable. They are far less substantial, in proportion to their apparent size, than the actiniæ, little indeed remaining but a mass of tentacles. When Dr. Johnston speaks of the hot and peppery *Anthea*, I presume he glances at its urticating properties, for there is no pungency in its taste."

Puiris, a species of *Actinia*, with hard membranous cover, is eaten, the inner body being only used. It is allowed to soak twelve hours before being eaten.

Sea ears, barnacles (*Balanus*), *Lithodomus*, sea urchins, and *Actinia*, are eaten in Chili.

During the Centennial Exhibition at Philadelphia in 1876, the American Fish Culturists' Association gave a fish dinner, at which the choicest international delicacies and rarities of fish preparations were served to a meeting of connoisseurs.

The second annual dinner of the Ichthyophagous Club, held on the 28th May, 1881, was a complete success, not only as a social gathering, but for the more important and practical object of developing hitherto neglected varieties of fish for human consumption.

Among the company, which numbered nearly one hundred guests, were men distinguished in the world of arts, of letters, and of science, and not a few who are deeply versed in the mysteries of the ocean. It is thus described by Mr. A. W. Roberts in the *Scientific American:* " The tables were ornamented with flowering plants, and designs composed of materials collected from the sea, the most noteworthy being a pyramid, twenty feet high, consisting of the empty shells of the horseshoe crabs, between which were introduced sharks' fins and sea robins' heads (*Prionotus sp.*).

" While the gathering was naturally social in its character, the practical result accomplished was the utilizing for food of certain fishes which have been considered the very refuse of the ocean. Strange and repulsive-looking creatures were served up during the evening as the choicest of viands. These various dishes of strange fish were partaken of with a relish, which, until the experiments of last year and this were made and proved successful, were considered valuable only for fertilizers or curiosities for aquaria.

"The consommé of moss-bunker (*Brevoortia tyrannus*) was very palatable, and entirely free from all oleaginousness.

"The 'Bisque of razor clams' was as delicate in flavour as oyster soup. 'Gray snapper à la Blackford' was another equally palatable dish. Although the gray snapper is not equal in flavour to the red snapper, there is no reason why it should be neglected by our fishermen, as it generally is, as a marketable fish.

"'Horseshoe crabs à la diable' were served from dishes composed of the empty shells of the horseshoe or king crab (*Limulus moluccanus*). The flesh of this crab was found to be coarser and more stringy than that of the ordinary crab, and the flavour more pungent, but not sufficiently so to make it unpalatable.

"'Drumfish à la Cope' was very suggestive of sheepshead. The drumfish (*Pogonias chromis*, Lacep.) is never to be found in the markets, and in the severest sense is looked upon as an 'evil' fish by the fishermen, it being one of the greatest enemies to the oyster.

"'Sauté of shark, Chinese style,' was not very successful, as the portion that I partook of left a disagreeable taste in the mouth, though others declared it equal to halibut steak; perhaps I got the evil part of the beast.

"'Squid à la Starin.' Without exception the squid is one of the most repulsive-looking animals of our coast, and yet from it was produced a black-coloured and gelatinous soup, which, if you could forget the disgusting form of the creature, was very pleasant to the taste. Next on the menu came hell-benders, sea robins, 'Lophius à la Beard' (*L. piscatorius*) and blow fish, with sea-lettuce salad, from which were produced fries, broils, and salads, all more or less enjoyable."

Cephalopods.—"Cuttle fishes are very common in the Mediterranean, and are highly prized by the Neapolitans. The modern Greeks also make use of them, and especially the *Octopodia*, as a principal article of food; they dry them in great quantities and store them away for use, to be boiled or fried. Several kinds of *Cephalopods* are eaten abroad. The *Octopus vulgaris* is eaten when young and small at Nice, where it is more plentiful in the market than at Genoa, and if it weighs less than a pound and is still tender it is much esteemed. The flesh is said to have a peculiar taste, consequently that of the cuttle fish and calmar *(Loligo)* are preferred. At Naples they are sold ready cooked. They are also found regularly exposed for sale in the markets of Smyrna and the bazaars of India, and the North American Indians are also partial to them."* It is also one of the great treats of the natives of Madrid; they are either broiled on a gridiron or stewed in red wine in an earthen jar. The Italians fry them in oil and they taste like skate.

The most largely distributed of the class of cephalopods is the *Sepia officinalis* (Lin.). It is seen in numerous shoals in spring and summer, frequenting all the coasts of Algeria. In October they seek deep water, from which they do not emerge until the month of May to seek favourable situations, with water of a density and temperature suitable for depositing their myriads of eggs among the algæ. It is an esteemed food much sought after by many, the flesh being considered savoury and delicate.

Other species esteemed for the delicacy of their flesh are *Loligo vulgaris*, Lamarck, also very common in the Mediterranean, and *Loligo parva*, Rondelet, a smaller species, well known to the Italian fishermen by the name of "Calamaretto," and to the French sailors as "Casseron."

The fishery for octopus or devil fish in Eastern Asia is of great importance. In 1873, 9,000 boats were

* Lovell's "Edible British Mollusks."

engaged in capturing them, each boat being manned by six men. The annual yield was over 14,520,000 pounds, valued at £75,000. Eighty thousand persons were also engaged in preparing and packing the dried flesh.

In Japan squids are regularly collected as food. Near Hakodadi there is a small fishing village exclusively devoted to the catching and curing of the squid, and many hundreds of thousands may be seen daily drying in the open air, all nicely cleaned, each kept flat by means of little bamboo stretchers, and suspended in rows on lines, which are raised on poles about six feet from the ground. The open spaces and all the houses in the village are filled with these squid-laden lines.

Ika, Surami and Tako are Japanese names for species of *Sepia* which are esteemed delicate eating in China and Japan. They form a common soccano or side dish, and are eaten either fresh, boiled or pickled. One mode of preparing them is as follows: They are first macerated in a solution of alum for three days, and then rubbed, washed and cleaned till transparent, when they are pickled and preserved for use. When pickled and brought to table, they are in substance, colour and taste like the edible birds' nests.

Mrs. Brassey, in her " Voyage of the Sunbeam," tells us the fish markets of Japan are well supplied with octopi. A real octopus in a basket, with its hideous body in the centre, and its eight arms, covered with suckers, arranged in the form of a star, is worth from a dollar to a dollar and a-half, according to its size.

The pulps and the sèches are much sought after on some of the coasts of France, although their flesh is rather hard. They are eaten both raw and cooked. But the most esteemed of the cephalopods is *Loligo sagitta*, vulgarly known as the cornet, or "encornet," the flavour of which is stated to be exquisitely fine and delicate, and far preferable to the common calmar and sèche.

At Banyuls-sur-Mer there is an enormous consumption of an Ascidian (*Cynthia microcosmus*) known under the name of bitoig (pronounced bitotche) or violet, of which considerable quantities are taken daily. It is believed to have special properties against affections of the chest, and marvellous cures are attributed to it. It can be kept fresh out of the water several days. Many of the ascidians, or sea squirts, are esteemed as articles of food in Brazil, China, and the Mediterranean.

M. Charles Bretagne, in a report on Edible Mollusca to the Paris Society of Acclimatation, observes, "The sepia is a cephalopod which is eaten in many localities, and on our coasts from the ocean to the Mediterranean. Although very abundant in our seaports, it is to be regretted that it is not brought to Paris. Its repulsive aspect in its raw state has hitherto kept it from our tables, which yet encourage frogs. It only requires to be disguised to become an agreeable and wholesome food, according to the manner in which it is prepared. I have made successful efforts in this direction, and have marinaded some, after bleaching them in boiling water, and my guests were satisfied with them as hors-d'œuvre."

The polypus or octopus is fished for at Tunis, and is exported to the Levant and the Greek market during Lent, there being no prohibition against them in the orthodox Church. In a good year about 6,200 cwt. are obtained, and they fetch from 6d. to 1s. 3d. a pair. Prepared octopi are higher in price, as they have to be macerated by beating them on a slab, then salted and dried. *Octopus brevipes*, Orb., is eaten in Norway.

Octopus vulgaris is dried, and under the name of Tako, is exported from Japan. *Eledonne octopodia* smaller, and a *Sepia,* known as Ika, *Loligo sagitatta*, and *Echinus esculentus*, under the name of "Uni," are all eaten in Japan and China. The Sepia is very abundant on the coasts of Cochin China and Tonkin. It is much esteemed by the rich there, who eat it with their tea. It sells at one shilling and sixpence the pound.

Of the Radiata or Echinodermata there are only two requiring prominent mention here, the common sea-egg or sea-urchin and the *Holothuridida*. Of the former several species are eaten, among others *Echinus esculentus,* *E. sphæra,* Muller, and *E. granulosus.*

Sea-urchins crowd in vast numbers all around the shores of Europe, Africa, and the East Indies; they feed upon crabs and sea-nettles, and are, in return, eaten by millions. Their bright saffron-yellow bodies may be seen in every market from the Ganges to the Loire, and from Benares to Marseilles. They furnish an ample proportion of the daily bread of the lower classes.

In Naples they are especially valued just before they deposit the roe, as the aggregate egg-masses are termed, being larger and in as much repute as the soft roe of the herring. They are highly esteemed by the inhabitants of Chili, the Faro Islands and other districts, and are usually eaten raw like oysters, being cut into four quarters, and the flesh eaten with a spoon. When cooked this becomes red like crab, and is said to resemble it in flavour. In the Italian markets, near the rocky coasts of Italy, may often be seen baskets of sea-urchins (Echini), of which the following species are commonly eaten, *Echinus melo, E. lividus, E. brevispinosus, E. saxatilis,* and *E. coelenterata.*

Two species of anemone used as food in Italy are commonly known under the name of "Ogliole," they are *Actinia viridis* and *A. equina.*

Trepang or Beche-de-Mer.—In all that pertains to a due appreciation of sea-worms—if that term is admissible—the Chinese must be acknowledged as feast-masters. They ascribe to mollusks peculiar virtues, and pay most extravagant sums for their favourite kinds. Among these the trepang holds probably the first rank —an ugly, shapeless, fearfully-smelling Holothuria of Eastern seas. Thousands of Malay, English, and American vessels are annually busy in those waters catching the disgusting, worm-shaped animal. Its principal homes are the coral-banks of the South Sea and Australian waters, but Chinese fishermen go as far as New Guinea, and American ships to the Caroline Islands, in pursuit of this favourite of the Chinese taste. The greatest market for the trepang is Macassar, where not less than thirty-six varieties are exposed for sale, the choicest of which bring incredible prices. The worm is caught either by long pointed sticks, that are thrust down at random, or is brought up from the deep by skilful and well-paid divers. In Sumatra they are thrown alive on heaps of coral lime, which induces them to disgorge their whole contents; at other places they are cooked for two whole days, when they begin to resemble calf's-foot jelly, and, by the aid of powerful spices, become fit for the table.

This food-article, which is of large consumption in China, gives rise to considerable fisheries and an extensive commerce. It is known as Trepang or Beche-de-Mer, or edible Holothuria.

The best-known species of the family are *Holothuria edulis* and *H. nigra*, but there are more than thirty species, varying greatly in size and general aspect. These animals do not present much elegance of form when living; and when cured, the trepang is an unseemly-looking substance of a dirty light or dark-brown colour, hard, rigid and repulsive, with a strong fishy odour. The largest kinds, when alive, sometimes attain the length of two feet; but when dried they shrivel up to half that size. The length of those brought to market averages from four to eight or nine inches. Fashion and custom have caused each variety to have a different market; while the gourmand of the south smacks his lips on the juicy brown and black kinds, the less cultivated taste of the people of the north is satisfied with the red and white inferior kinds.

In the process of curing, the animal is split down one side, the viscera removed, boiled, and pressed with a weight of stones, then stretched open with strips of bamboo, dried in the sun, and afterwards in the smoke for four days, when it is fit to be packed away in bags, but requires to be examined at intervals and exposed to the sun, as it soon imbibes moisture and mildew.

For fuller details of the fishery, commerce, and preparation of Trepang, I must refer the reader to another volume of mine.*

Some species of Holothuria called "Namako" are eaten raw in Japan, and when steamed and dried are largely shipped to China.

The mode of cooking trepang is as follows:—Soak it in cold water for an hour, then clean it and scrape it carefully. Boil it for eight hours in water with a little salt added, wash, scrape and clean it anew; and soak it in cold water for two hours. Then cover it with meat gravy, season and cook it for half-an-hour more, and serve it hot.

The export of trepang from the French island of New Caledonia amounts in value to £4,000. The specimens shown at the Paris Exhibition in 1878, from New Caledonia, were thus classed and priced:—

1st quality, black, 1.90 to 2 francs. the kilo.
2nd quality, small black, 1.25 to 1.30 francs. the kilo.
3rd quality, red fish, 1 franc. the kilo.
Large white, 70 cents. the kilo.

9,131 kilos of trepang, value 7,255 francs, were shipped from Tahiti, in 1875, they are taken principally at the Pomotous.

From a careful investigation of the returns of imports at the Chinese trade ports, the receipts of trepang in 1871 were about 10,000 piculs, or 12,500 cwt. In 1875 it was 21,360 cwt.

The average annual imports into China of marine food products, were in the five years ending respectively as follows:—

	1870.	1875.
Beche-de-mer	16.674 Piculs.	19,487 Piculs.
Fish, dried and salted	38,437 ,,	36,439 ,,
Isinglass	2,953 ,,	3,943 ,,
Shell fish and crustacea, Awaba (*Haliotids*), dried shrimps, &c.	10,060 ,,	17,439 ,,

The picul is a little over 133 lbs. avoirdupois.

* "The Commercial Products of the Sea," Griffith and Farran.

The following quantities of Beche-de-mer were caught on the Indian coasts and shipped from India, chiefly to Singapore :—

				Lbs.		Value, £.
1875-6	...	...	...	9,255	......	96
1876-7	...	...	...	70,220	......	1,032
1877-8	...	...	...	26,596	......	469
1878-9	...	...	...	15,056	......	264
1879-80	...	...	...	10,072	......	141
1880-1	...	...	...	21,104	......	347
1881-2	...	...	...	28,957	......	359
1882-3	...	...	...	23,630	......	379
1883-4	...	...	...	52,117	......	937

In 1884, 10,430 lbs. were imported into India from Ceylon and the Straits Settlements. 807,032 lbs. of foreign catch was shipped to Hong Kong.

Much of this is imported and then re-exported.

The trepang abounds on the reefs that fringe, for so many hundred miles, the northern coast of Queensland, and many stations have been established for curing the different edible species. Of late some of the hordes of Chinese who have poured into the colony, have taken up this fishery, and a regular junk, manned by Mongolian sailors, trades between the fishing stations and collects the dried slug for export. There are probably 600 tons annually exported from the northern coast of Australia.

There formerly existed on the coasts of the peninsula of Giens in the Mediterranean, a species of Ascidian, popularly termed " Violet " or " Vichet," which was much esteemed by the gourmands of Marseilles and Toulon. In consequence of excessive dredging it has almost disappeared. They used to sell in the Marseilles market at 1d. and 1½d. each, and owing to the seaweed beds among which they were found, they had an exceptionally pleasant flavour.

About the Bahamas and other parts of the West Indies, the edible Beche-de-mer abounds, but there is no demand for them. It is quite possible, however, that an enterprising individual, or firm, might reap such a harvest as would make it worth while to participate in the Eastern trade. The improved means of preserving such products in a commercial form in tins or bottles, as well as the old-fashioned method of sun-drying, however, suggest the possibility of opening up quite a new market in America and in Europe. A soup made of Beche-de-mer is extremely nutritious and very palatable, and if introduced in an attractive form, and under a taking name, might prove a formidable rival to the time-honoured turtle. Even if England should prove sceptical, France would in all probability welcome this addition to her list of food delicacies.

Worms.—There is a minute American variety of leech which attaches itself to the native mollusks; they are eaten alive in large numbers by the hard-clam lovers. Mr. A. W. Roberts says he had a mess of these leeches collected and cooked, and found them very palatable, and of the flavour of the highly prized little neck clams, from which brand they had been taken. The Chinese regularly eat both marine and fresh-water leeches. * The leech was one of the forbidden meats of the Jews.

The *Pall Mall Gazette* gravely reports that a group of French gourmets have tested the edible qualities of the common earth-worm, whose agricultural services have been recently demonstrated. .

" Fifty guests were present at the experiment. The worms, apparently lob-worms, were first put into vinegar, by which process they were made to disgorge the vegetable mould. They were then rolled in batter and put into an oven, where they acquired a delightful golden tint, and, we are assured, a most appetising smell. After the first plateful the fifty guests rose like one man and asked for more. Could anything be more convincing? Those who love snails, they add, will abandon them for ever in favour of worms."

* " Scientific American."

INDEX.

G G

www.ingramcontent.com/pod-product-compliance
Lightning Source LLC
Chambersburg PA
CBHW031817270326
41932CB00008B/450